INTERNATIONAL RELATIONS IN SOUTHEAST ASIA

ASIA IN WORLD POLITICS
Series Editor: Samuel S. Kim

INTERNATIONAL RELATIONS IN SOUTHEAST ASIA

The Struggle for Autonomy

Second Edition

Donald E. Weatherbee

ROWMAN & LITTLEFIELD PUBLISHERS, INC.

Lanham • Boulder • New York • Toronto • Plymouth, UK

ROWMAN & LITTLEFIELD PUBLISHERS, INC.

Published in the United States of America
by Rowman & Littlefield Publishers, Inc.
A wholly owned subsidary of The Rowman & Littlefield Publishing Group, Inc.
4501 Forbes Boulevard, Suite 200, Lanham, Maryland 20706
www.rowmanlittlefield.com

Estover Road, Plymouth PL6 7PY, United Kingdom

British Library Cataloguing in Publication Information Available

Library of Congress Cataloging-in-Publication Data

Weatherbee, Donald E.
  International relations in Southeast Asia : the struggle for autonomy
  / Donald E. Weatherbee. — Rev. 2nd ed.
    p. cm. — (Asia in world politics)
  Includes bibliographical references and index.
  ISBN-13: 978-0-7425-5681-2 (cloth : alk. paper)
  ISBN-10: 0-7425-5681-6 (cloth : alk. paper)
  ISBN-13: 978-0-7425-5682-9 (pbk. : alk. paper)
  ISBN-10: 0-7425-5682-4 (pbk. : alk. paper)
  [etc.]
  1. Southeast Asia—Foreign relations. 2. Southeast Asia—Politics and government—
1945- 3. ASEAN. I. Title.
  DS526.7.W44 2008
  327.59—dc22   2008030596

Printed in the United States of America

∞™ The paper used in this publication meets the minimum requirements of American
National Standard for Information Sciences—Permanence of Paper for Printed Library
Materials, ANSI/NISO Z39.48-1992.

Contents

Tables and Boxes

Tables

Boxes

Abbreviations

ABAC	APEC Business Advisory Council
ACCORD	ASEAN and China Cooperative Operations in Response to Dangerous Drugs
ACD	Asian Cooperation Dialogue
ACFTA	ASEAN–China Free Trade Area
ACMECS	Ayeawady–Chao Phraya–Mekong Economic Cooperation Strategy
ACP	ASEAN Cooperation Plan (U.S.)
ADB	Asian Development Bank
AEC	ASEAN Economic Community
AEMM	ASEAN economic ministers' meeting
AEMM	ASEAN–EU ministerial meeting
AFAS	ASEAN Framework Agreement on Services
AFMM	ASEAN Finance Ministers' Meeting
AFP	Australian Federal Police
AFTA	ASEAN Free Trade Area
AIA	ASEAN Investment Area
AIC	ASEAN Industrial Complementation
AICO	ASEAN Industrial Cooperation
AIJV	ASEAN Industrial Joint Venture
AIP	ASEAN Industrial Project
AMAF	ASEAN Ministers of Agriculture and Forestry
AMBDC	ASEAN–Mekong Basin Development Corporation
AMDA	Anglo-Malay Defence Agreement

AMF	Asian Monetary Fund (proposed)
AMM	ASEAN Ministerial Meeting
AMME	ASEAN Ministerial Meeting on the Environment
AMMTC	ASEAN Ministerial Meeting on Transnational Crime
APEC	Asia-Pacific Economic Cooperation
APT	ASEAN plus 3
ARCPPT	Asia Regional Cooperation to Prevent People Trafficking
ARF	ASEAN Regional Forum
ARMM	Autonomous Region in Muslim Mindanao (Philippines)
ARTIP	Asia Regional Trafficking in Persons Project
ASA	Association of Southeast Asia
ASC	ASEAN Security Community
ASC	ASEAN Standing Committee
ASCC	ASEAN Socio-Cultural Community
ASEAN	Association of Southeast Asian Nations
ASEANAPOL	ASEAN Chiefs of Police
ASEM	Asia–Europe Meeting
ASEP	ASEAN Subregional Environment Program
ASG	Abu Sayyaf Group (Philippines)
ASOD	ASEAN Senior Officials on Drug Matters
ASOEN	ASEAN Senior Officials on the Environment
ASPC	ARF Security Policy Conference
ATS	methamphetamine-type stimulants
AusAID	Australian Agency for International Development
BIMP-EAGA	Brunei, Indonesia, Malaysia, Philippines, East ASEAN Growth Area
BIMSTEC	Bay of Bengal Initiative for Multi-Sectoral Technical and Economic Cooperation
BNPP	Barisan Nasional Pembebasan Pattani (National Front for the Liberation of Pattani)
BSA	bilateral swap agreements
CAVR	Commission for Reception, Truth, and Reconciliation (Timor-Leste) [Portuguese language abbreviation]
CCDAC	Central Committee for Drug Abuse Control (Myanmar)
CCI	Chamber of Commerce and Industry
CDCF	Cambodia Development Cooperation Forum
CEPEA	Comprehensive Economic Partnership in East Asia
CEPT	common effective preferential tariff
CER	closer economic relations (Australia-New Zealand)
CGC	Consultative Group for Cambodia
CGI	Consultative Group on Indonesia
CGDK	Coalition Government of Democratic Kampuchea

CGV	Consultative Group for Vietnam
CLMV	Cambodia, Laos, Myanmar, Vietnam
CMI	Chiang Mai Initiative
CMI	[Finnish] Crisis Management Initiative
CNOOC	China National Offshore Oil Corporation
COBSEA	Coordinating Body for the East Asian Seas
COMMIT	Coordinated Mekong Ministerial Initiative against Trafficking
COST	[ASEAN] Committee on Science and Technology
CPC	countries of particular concern
CPI	Corruption Perception Index
CPP	Cambodia People's Party
CPP	Communist Party of the Philippines
CRT	Country Report on Terrorism
CSCAP	Councils for Security Cooperation in the Asia-Pacific
CTF	Commission on Truth and Friendship (Indonesia–Timor-Leste)
DEA	[U.S.] Drug Enforcement Agency
DI	Darul Islam
DRET	Democratic Republic of East Timor
DRL	[U.S. Department of State's] Bureau of Democracy, Rights, and Labor
DRV	Democratic Republic of Vietnam
EAEC	East Asia Economic Caucus
EAEG	East Asia Economic Group
EAFTA	East Asia Free Trade Area (proposed)
EAP	[U.S. Dept. of State Bureau of] East Asian and Pacific Affairs
EAS	East Asia Summit
EASG	East Asia Study Group
EAVG	East Asian Vision Group
ECCC	Extraordinary Chambers in the Courts of Cambodia
ECOSOC	[United Nations] Economic and Social Council
EEP	Expert and Eminent Persons group
EEZ	Exclusive Economic Zone
EGAT	Electrical Generating Authority of Thailand
EIA	Environmental Investigation Agency
EPA	economic partnership agreement
EPG	eminent persons group
ESCAP	[United Nations] Economic and Social Commission for Asia and the Pacific
FAO	[United Nations] Food and Agriculture Organization

FDI	foreign direct investment
FLEG	Forest Law Enforcement and Governance
FOC	friends of the chair
FPDA	Five Power Defence Arrangement (Australia, Great Britain, Malaysia, New Zealand, Singapore)
FRETILIN	Frente Revolutionária do Timor Leste Independente (Revolutionary Front for an Independent East Timor)
FTA	free trade agreement
FTAAP	Free Trade Area of the Asia Pacific (proposed)
FTO	foreign terrorist organization
FULRO	Front Unifié pour la Libération des Races Opprimées (United Front for the Liberation of Oppressed Races)
FUNCINPEC	Front Uni National pour un Cambodge Indépendent, Neutre, Pacifique, et Coopératif (United National Front for an Independent, Neutral, Pacific, and Cooperative Cambodia)
GAM	Free Aceh Movement (Indonesia)
GDP	gross domestic product
GMS	Greater Mekong Subregion
HDI	Human Development Index
HPAI	highly pathogenic avian influenza
IAI	Initiative for ASEAN Integration
IBRD	International Bank for Reconstruction and Development
ICJ	International Court of Justice
ICK	[United Nations] International Conference on Kampuchea
IDA	International Development Association
IFC	International Finance Corporation
IFI	international financial institutions
IGGI	Inter-Governmental Group on Indonesia
IISS	International Institute for Strategic Studies
ILO	International Labor Organization
IMB	International Maritime Board
IMF	International Monetary Fund
IMS-GT	Indonesia, Malaysia, Singapore Growth Triangle (= SIJORI)
IMT	international monitoring team
IMT-GT	Indonesia, Malaysia, Thailand Growth Triangle
INGO	international nongovernmental organization
IOM	International Organization for Migrants
IOR-ARC	Indian Ocean Rim Association for Regional Cooperation
INTERFET	International Force for East Timor

IRN	International Rivers Network
ISA	Internal Security Act
ISC	information sharing center
ISF	International Stabilization Force
ISG	Inter-sessional Support Group
ISM	Inter-sessional Meeting
ISM-CTTC	inter-sessional meeting on counterterrorism and crime
ITLOS	International Tribunal for the Law of the Sea
ITTA	International Tropical Timber Agreement
ITTO	International Tropical Timber Organization
JCLEC	Jakarta Center for Law Enforcement Cooperation
JDA	joint development area
JI	Jema'ah Islamiyah
JIM	Jakarta Informal Meetings
JMSU	Joint Marine Seismic Undertaking
JSOTF-P	Joint Special Operations Task Force—Philippines
KMM	Kumpulan Mujahideen Malaysia (Malaysia Mujahideen Group)
KPNLF	Khmer People's National Liberation Front
KR	Khmer Rouge
LDC	least developed countries
LPDR	Lao People's Democratic Republic
LPRP	Lao People's Revolutionary Party
MAPHILINDO	Malaysia, Philippines, Indonesia
MBA	military bases agreement
MDG	Millennium Development Goals
MDT	Mutual Defense Treaty
MGC	Mekong-Ganga Cooperation group
MIA	missing in action
MIGA	Multilateral International Guarantee Agency
MILF	Moro Islamic Liberation Front (Philippines)
MMI	Majelis Mujahideen Indonesia (Indonesian Mujahideen Council)
MNC	multinational corporations
MNLF	Moro National Liberation Front (Philippines)
MOU	memorandum of understanding
MRA	mutual recognition agreements
MRC	Mekong River Commission
MSSI	Malacca Strait Security Initiative
MTJA	Malaysia–Thailand Joint Authority
NAFTA	North American Free Trade Agreement

NAM	Nonaligned Movement
NFLSV	National Front for the Liberation of South Vietnam
NGO	nongovernmental organization
NLD	National League for Democracy (Myanmar)
NPA	New People's Army (Philippines)
ODA	official development assistance
OIC	Organization of the Islamic Conference
OPM	Organisasi Papuan Merdeka (Free Papua Organization)
PAF	Philippine Armed Forces
PAS	Parti Islam se-Malaysia
PAVN	People's Army of Vietnam
PECC	Pacific Economic Cooperation Council
PICC	Paris International Conference on Cambodia
PKI	Indonesian Communist Party
PMC	post-ministerial conferences
PNG	Papua New Guinea
PNOC	Philippines National Oil Corporation
PNTR	permanent normal trade relations
PPP	People's Power Party (Thailand)
PPP	purchasing power parity
PRC	People's Republic of China
PRK	People's Republic of Kampuchea
PTA	preferential trade agreement
PTA	[ASEAN] Preferential Tariff Agreement
PULO	Pattani United Liberation Organization (Thailand)
ReCAAP	Regional Cooperation Agreement on Combating Piracy and Armed Robbery against Ships in Asia
REDD	Reduced Emissions from Deforestation and Degradation
RELA	Ikatan Relawan Rakyat (Peoples' Volunteer Corps, Malaysia)
RMSI	Regional Maritime Security Initiative
RTA	regional free trade agreement
RWESEA	Rivers Watch East and Southeast Asia
SAARC	South Asia Association for Regional Cooperation
SARS	Severe Acute Respiratory Syndrome
SCO	Shanghai Cooperation Organization
SEAC	South-East Asia Command
SEANWFZ	Southeast Asian Nuclear Weapons-Free Zone
SEARCCT	Southeast Asia Regional Center for Counter-Terrorism
SEATO	Southeast Asia Treaty Organization
SEOM	Senior Economic Officials' Meeting

SLORC	State Law and Order Restoration Council (Myanmar)
SOM	Senior Officials' Meeting
SOMTC	Senior Officials' Meeting on Transnational Crime
SPAE	Strategic Plan of Action on the Environment
SPDC	State Peace and Development Council (Myanmar)
SPNFZ	South Pacific Nuclear Free Zone
SRP	Sam Rainsey Party
TAC	Treaty of Amity and Cooperation in Southeast Asia
TIFA	trade and investment framework agreement
TIP	trafficking in persons
TLDPM	Timor-Leste and Development Partners Meeting
TOC	transnational organized crime
TP-SEP	Trans-Pacific Strategic Economic Partnership
TPA	trade promotion authority
TRT	Thai Rak Thai
TVPA	Trafficking in Victims Protection Act of 2000
UMNO	United Malays National Organization
UNAMET	United Nations Assistance Mission in East Timor
UNCHR	United Nations Commission on Human Rights
UNCLOS	United Nations Convention on the Law of the Sea
UNDP	United Nations Development Program
UNEP	United Nations Environment Program
UNGA	United Nations General Assembly
UNHCHR	United Nations High Commissioner for Human Rights
UNHCR	United Nations High Commissioner for Refugees
UNHRC	United Nations Human Rights Council
UNIAP	United Nations Inter-Agency Project on Human Trafficking in the Greater Mekong Sub-Region
UNMISET	United Nations Mission in Support of East Timor
UNMIT	United Nations Integrated Mission in Timor-Leste
UNODC	United Nations Office on Drugs and Crime
UNOTIL	United Nations Office in Timor-Leste
UNSC	United Nations Security Council
UNTAC	United Nations Transitional Authority for Cambodia
UNTAET	United Nations Transitional Administration in East Timor
USIP	United States Institute of Peace
UWSA	United Wa State Army
VAP	Vientiane Action Programme
VFA	Visiting Forces Agreement (U.S.–Philippines)
WCD	World Commission on Dams
WHO	World Health Organization

WSSD	World Summit on Sustainable Development
WTO	World Trade Organization
WWF	World Wildlife Fund
ZOPFAN	Zone of Peace, Freedom, and Neutrality
ZOPGIN	Zone of Peace, Genuine Independence, and Neutrality

Preface to the Second Edition

IN PREPARING THIS REVISED SECOND EDITION of *International Relations in Southeast Asia: The Struggle for Autonomy,* I have had the benefit of critical commentary on the first edition as well as feedback from instructors who have used it as a text. Those familiar with the first edition will find a number of changes and in many respects it is a new book. This edition is single authored. I would again thank Ralf Emmers, Mari Pangestu, and Leonard Sebastian for their contribution to the first edition. Chapters 6 and 7 contain entirely new material. In this edition, there is less emphasis on the war on terror. There is a more structured discussion of human security as an issue area in international relations in Southeast Asia. The new ASEAN Charter and the ASEAN community building process are highlighted. There is a more extended consideration over the course of the text of the China–ASEAN–United States triangle. And, of course, all of the topics and issues have been updated. On the basis of suggestions from users, I have added more footnotes to primary sources and secondary sources available on the Internet.

To my scholarly debts acknowledged in the preface to the first edition, I would add my thanks to Dr. Thitinan Pongsudhirak, Director of ISIS Thailand, and Dr. Susuma Snitwongse, Chairperson of the Advisory Board, ISIS Thailand, for inviting me to participate in the ISIS October 2006 conference on Democracy and Human Security in Southeast Asia. I would also like to acknowledge the stimulation provided by the Columbia University Southeast Asia Seminar.

The stylistic skills of Dr. Epsey Cooke Farrell of Seton Hall University's Whitehead School of Diplomacy again improved the text chapter by chapter. I also appreciate the encouragement and patience of Susan McEachern and the assistance of Alden Perkins at Rowman & Littlefield.

Donald E. Weatherbee
Morristown, N.J., and Jamestown, R.I.

Preface to the First Edition

THIS BOOK IS DESIGNED AS AN INTRODUCTION to the issues and dynamics of international relations in contemporary Southeast Asia. Its goal is modest. Planned as a textbook, it does not pretend to present new research findings or theoretical insights. Footnotes have been held to a minimum with an emphasis on directing the reader to documentary sources available on the Internet. The hope is to stimulate deeper investigation by interested students into the topics covered, perhaps recruiting members of a younger academic generation to consider further study of Southeast Asian politics and international relations.

When initially approached to do the book, I hesitated, uncertain as to whether I wanted to devote the time and discipline required for a textbook. What convinced me to do it were the expressions of interest from faculty currently involved in basic Southeast Asia–related courses who felt that it would fill a gap in available text resources. Rather than country-by-country case study chapters, the book is thematically organized around some of the central policy questions facing Southeast Asia's decision makers. The scope extends beyond the problem of security that has historically dominated the academic study of international relations in Southeast Asia to include nontraditional issue areas in international relations. I have also tried to bring the state as the primary actor in international relations in Southeast Asia back into focus to balance the great academic attention that has been given to ASEAN—the Association of Southeast Asian Nations—the collective framework for intraregional and international interaction.

The intellectual genesis of the work is four decades of teaching courses on Southeast Asian international relations to upper-division undergraduate and graduate students with an interest in Southeast Asia. The scholarly debts I have accumulated in a career devoted to studying, teaching, and writing about politics and international relations in Southeast Asia are profound and many. I acknowledge my gratitude to the late Richard Louis Walker who created at the University of South Carolina's Institute of International Studies, now bearing his name, a collegial and supportive base for many years. I also give due to generations of my students whose own interests and enthusiasms helped keep mine alive. Over the years, I have enjoyed the company, wisdom, and expertise of hosts of academic counterparts and government officials in the United States, Europe, and Southeast Asia. They are too numerous to even begin to think of singling out. I am particularly grateful for my long-standing associations with the Institute of Southeast Asian Studies in Singapore, the Center for Strategic and International Studies in Jakarta, and the Institute of Strategic and International Studies in Bangkok.

In preparing the manuscript for the book, I am indebted to Dr. Ralf Emmers and Dr. Leonard Sebastian in Singapore and Dr. Mari Pangestu in Jakarta for their generous willingness to provide what are chapters 6 and 7. In addition to the helpful comments and criticisms of the anonymous reviewers of the draft manuscript, I would also mention Dr. Epsey Cooke Farrell, who teaches the kind of course at which this book is aimed. Both her classroom feedback and stylistic skills improved the text chapter by chapter. I also appreciate the encouragement and patience of Susan McEachern and Jessica Gribble at Rowman & Littlefield.

Donald E. Weatherbee
Columbia, S.C.
Jamestown, R.I.

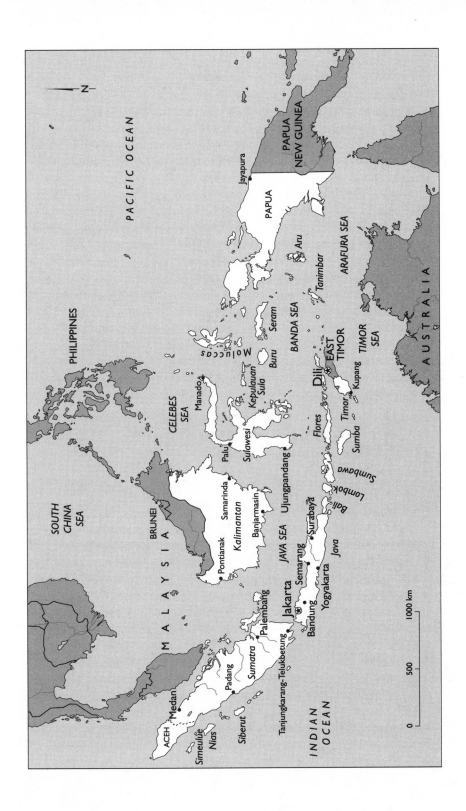

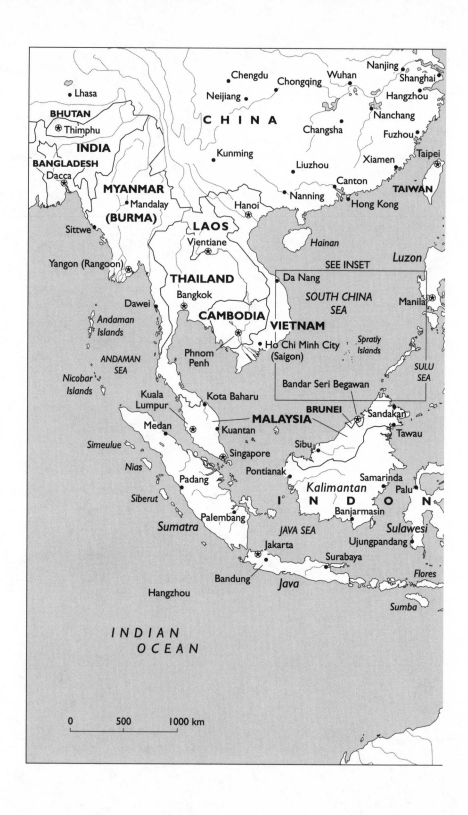

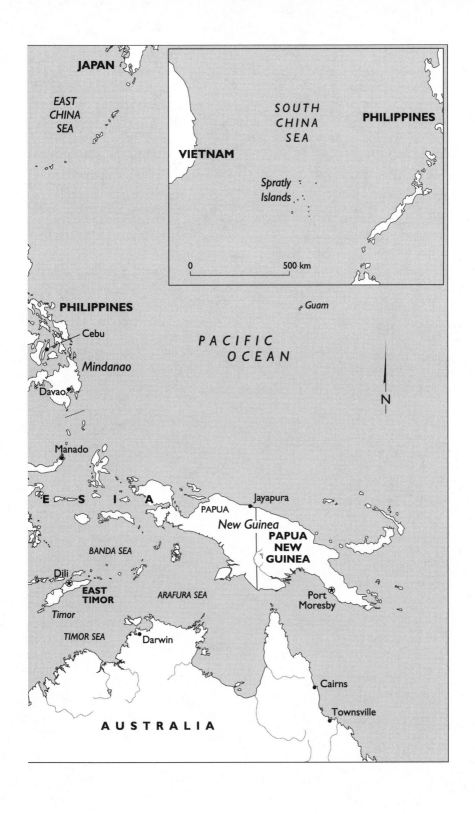

1

Introduction: The What and Why of Southeast Asia

O N 20 NOVEMBER 2007, the heads of government of the ten Southeast Asian states belonging to the Association of Southeast Asian Nations (ASEAN) signed a charter providing a new legal and institutional base for the organization.[1] Although the charter's preamble begins with the invocation of "We, the Peoples of the Member States," the "peoples"—totaling nearly six hundred million—had little input into its drafting. It is a treaty instrument subject to ratification according to the constitutional requirements of the signatory states. As such, it is the outcome of a political and diplomatic process that framed at high levels of generalization the compromises necessary to win the signatures of ten sovereign leaders, each with a view of his/her own country's national interests and role in the region and the international system.

The reinvention of ASEAN in the 2007 charter came forty years after the foreign ministers of Indonesia, the Philippines, Singapore, and Thailand and the deputy prime minister of Malaysia issued the "Bangkok Declaration" establishing ASEAN on 8 August 1967.[2] In the interval, much had happened that is part of the history of international relations in Southeast Asia. Significant and transforming events in that history will be noted where relevant in the chapters to follow. The most important difference for the way in which Southeast Asian states related to each other and the region in 1967 compared to 2007 has to do with the changed great power relations to Southeast Asia and to each other.

It was the height of the Cold War in Southeast Asia in 1967, when the United States, the predominant regional political and strategic presence, looked across the battlefield divide of Vietnam to its Cold War antagonists, the USSR and the

TABLE 1.1
The Southeast Asian States

Country	Capital City	Area (sq mi/sq km)	Population (millions)
Brunei	Bandar Seri Begawan	2,227/5,765	0.4
Cambodia	Phnom Penh	69,900/181,040	14.0
Indonesia	Jakarta	736,000/2,000,000	245.5
Laos	Vientiane	91,430/236,800	6.5
Malaysia	Kuala Lumpur	127,316/329,749	26.9
Myanmar (Burma)	Nay Pyi Daw	261,969/678,500	57.6
Philippines	Manila	117,187/300,000	88.7
Singapore	Singapore	271/704	4.4
Thailand	Bangkok	198,270/514,000	65.1
Timor-Leste	Dili	5,794/15,007	1.1
Vietnam	Hanoi	127,243/331,114	85.2

Sources: U.S. Department of State "Country Background Notes"; U.S. Central Intelligence Agency, *World Factbook*, as of November 2007.

People's Republic of China. The dominant economic presence was Japan, which through trade, investment, and official development assistance (ODA) was seemingly turning Southeast Asia into an economic dependency. Today, the great power equation has fundamentally changed. The USSR has ceased to exist and Russia has not replaced it as a great power actor in Southeast Asia. Almost as dramatic has been the rise of China as a regional great power economic and political actor, peacefully challenging the relative power positions of both the United States and Japan. Not to be overlooked as a possible future regional great power actor, India too is rising, with its eye not so much on the United States and Japan, as on China.

What has not changed historically for the states of Southeast Asia is the policy problem of how to pursue their national interests within the constraints of the dynamics of the great powers' presence in the region. The original invention of ASEAN was a response to the regional uncertainties of the Cold War. The contemporary reinvention of ASEAN is a response to the uncertainties of the rise of China and the American and Japanese responses. In both cases, for the Southeast Asian states, the goal has been to create a platform for greater maneuverability among the great powers. To augment—but certainly not re-place—traditional bilateral diplomacy, the Southeast Asian states built a mul-tilateral institutional structure to engage the external powers in a regional for-mat as well as the bilateral. In the quasi-ideological language of ASEAN's proponents, the pooling of the member states' national resilience (for re-silience, read capabilities) creates regional resilience, which through a feed-back loop should enhance national resilience in a bilateral context. This is now explicit in the ASEAN Charter, which states as one of its purposes: "To maintain the *centrality* and *proactive* role of ASEAN as the *primary driving force* in its relations and cooperation with its external partners in a regional architecture that is open, transparent and inclusive" [italics added].

Since ASEAN's creation, international relations in Southeast Asia have played out at two levels: the state-to-state bilateral level and the ASEAN multilateral level. At each level there are two sets of relationships. At the bilateral level, there are the relationships among the Southeast Asian states themselves and the relationships of the Southeast Asian states to external actors, in particular the great powers. At the ASEAN level, there are the relationships of the member states to ASEAN and ASEAN's relationship to the external world, again particularly the great powers. An analysis of Southeast Asia's international relations has to address the question of how the two levels with the four categories of transactions mutually interact in terms of behavior at one level influencing behavior at a different level. For example, at the policy level this question is apposite to discussions of Myanmar's and Indonesia's regional roles and impacts.

A second question is, if, as noted, ASEAN claims to be the central driving force of the region's relations with its external partners, what is the basis of its "centrality"? The cumulation of national resiliences into an empirically unverifiable regional resilience has not altered the real power asymmetries between ASEAN and the great powers. Two hypotheses can be advanced. First, ASEAN is emerging as a hub of its own global network with spokes of different sizes running to all of the great and not-so-great power actors and is becoming the fulcrum of a regional balance of power. A second hypothesis suggests that because of their own competitive rivalries, the great powers have implicitly granted to ASEAN by default the right to define the terms of an amorphous regionalism in which real commitment is limited and poses no threat to great power interests.

Both hypotheses assume that the state actors are seeking to promote national interests. At one level, there are interests originating in a dominant international system driven by the great powers and potent stateless transnational forces that are summed up in the term *globalization*. Southeast Asia, particularly with the evolution of ASEAN, might be considered a subordinate subsystem of the dominant system.[3] In the Southeast Asian subsystem, there are local national interests derived not just from the economic, social, and political requirements of a modern state, but also from each state's unique matrix of history, culture, and religion. One of the dynamics of international relations in Southeast Asia is how global and local interests complement or conflict with one another at both the bilateral and ASEAN level.

Southeast Asia as an Interest Area

The Southeast Asian subsystem is becoming an increasingly important unit of the international system. This is the result of three interrelated developments. It is derived in part from key regional states' increasing capabilities and national ambitions. It also reflects the interdependencies being established as the ASEAN region is integrated into the global economy. Finally, Southeast Asia has become a stage where great power rivalries and competition for influence are being played out. The details of the script are constantly changing and past interactions of the external actors with the countries of the region will be different in the future. The historical constant for both the regional and extraregional actors is interests. As Rupert Emerson, a pioneer in the political study of newly independent postcolonial states, put it, once the nation has been taken as the measure of the state, "the goal of policy inevitably becomes the promotion of national interest, however that uncertain concept may come to be defined."[4]

Security Interests

The traditional security concerns involving the threat and use of force by one state against another state in Southeast Asia have waned. The regional perils presented by the Cold War conflicts that pitted the great powers and their local surrogates against one another are no longer present (chapter 3). A fundamental interest that underpinned those conflicts was strategic access to Southeast Asia and that is still an interest. It is most obviously at work in shaping policies for maritime security in the South China Sea (chapter 5) and the Strait of Malacca (chapter 6). Within ASEAN itself, it has been argued that a durable security community has been constructed on the basis of the collective acceptance of the norms of peaceful change and nonuse of force in international relations. This remains to be demonstrated, since the potential for intra-ASEAN armed clashes exists (chapter 5). From the ASEAN vantage, all countries with interests in Southeast Asia have a common interest in a peaceful, politically stable, and open strategic regional environment. The ASEAN states have also joined their security interests to the wider East Asia and Pacific security environment in the ASEAN Regional Forum (ARF). The ARF provides an intergovernmental venue to address security concerns from Northeast Asia to South Asia (chapter 5).

The greatest challenge to the vital security interests of individual ASEAN states comes from nonstate actors using force to attack both the basis of the state and its territorial integrity. One group of nonstate actors is those using terror tactics to further radical Islamist agendas (chapter 6). For the United

States, Southeast Asia is a second front in a global war on terror. While Southeast Asian states have a common interest with the United States in combating terrorism, the Islamist terror threat in Southeast Asia is to pluralist societies, unconnected to U.S. interests in Iraq or Afghanistan. The Islamist terrorist threat has been in some cases connected to, but historically independent of, Muslim separatist movements in the region (chapter 5). Ethnic conflict in the region is not confined to Muslim separatists. The plight of ethnic minorities in Burma in particular has become a matter of international concern (chapter 8).

Economic Interests

As the twentieth century ended and the new millennium began, the historic geostrategic significance of Southeast Asia was matched by its growing geoeconomic importance. The rapidly growing economies of developing Southeast Asia have become an integral part of the East Asian regional and global markets (chapter 7). Even the states left behind, like Myanmar and Laos, have rich potential for energy resources exploitation to fuel the growth industries of their neighbors (chapter 9). By the end of the Cold War, the five newly industrializing economies of Southeast Asia—Indonesia, Malaysia, the Philippines, Singapore, and Thailand—had achieved sustained levels of high economic performance based on strategies of export-led growth. The local economic Crash of '97 followed by a wider global economic downturn gave them a reality check, but firm platforms for recovery for future growth were quickly put in place. The laggard socialist states have largely abandoned the command model of development, hoping to emulate the successes of their regional partners. Vietnam now outpaces Thailand in economic growth.

In pursuit of their national interests in economic growth, the countries of ASEAN have sought to maximize access to markets and investment through regionalist initiatives (chapter 7). Since 1977, ASEAN has tried to expand intraregional trade through a variety of initiatives. The earlier, hesitant efforts at regional integration have evolved to the current goal of an ASEAN Economic Community by the year 2015. In theory, this would create a single market and production base, strengthening the region's capabilities to deal with the international economy. The more economically advanced ASEAN countries have forged numerous bilateral free trade agreements (FTA) with external trading partners and in their collective format have negotiated ASEAN + 1 regional trade agreements (RTA) and other framework agreements for enhanced economic cooperation. In terms of regionalist frameworks, a future problem for ASEAN will be whether its members' interests will be best served in inclusive open regionalism such as the Asia-Pacific Economic Cooperation (APEC) forum or the exclusive regionalism of an East Asian bloc.

Political Interests

As the new millennium began, it was thought that important Southeast Asian countries had been lapped by the "third wave of democratization."[5] This can be doubted. Little if any democratizing change has taken place in Southeast Asia's recognized undemocratic and authoritarian states. The formal democratic fabrics of Cambodia, Malaysia, Singapore, and Timor-Leste are badly torn and frayed. The once praised democracies of the Philippines and Thailand have been severely eroded by coups and leadership failings. Only Indonesia stands out as the exception (chapter 2).

Even though resisted by conservative forces, a democratic political culture is gradually spreading among the people in Southeast Asia. Civil societies are emerging in the most economically dynamic states from new modern social classes. The frequent use of harsh repressive measures by ASEAN governments defending against democracy activists clashes with Western liberal interests in promoting democracy and defending human rights. Efforts to apply Western-defined standards of civil and political rights as a benchmark for the quality of political relations have become the most visibly contentious part of the political agenda (chapter 8). In the chapters that follow, this clash is highlighted by the West's campaign against the ruthless Myanmar military junta and ASEAN's solidarity with the junta. China has no problem with democracy and human rights issues. It joins with ASEAN in asserting noninterference in the internal affairs of a sovereign country.

Nontraditional Interests

Even as the states of the region grapple with the traditional transactions of international relations involving security, high politics, and economic advantage, they are confronted by a nontraditional contemporary agenda. International relations have been redefined in the context of globalism. The successes of their economic development strategies have enmeshed Southeast Asian governments in a transnational nexus of economic, social, and cultural interests and norms articulated by the industrialized West. Issues having to do with narcotics trafficking, gender discrimination, environment, minority rights, refugees, migrant labor, and child labor have become part of international relations in Southeast Asia. The concept of security has been broadened to include human security as a goal of the international community (chapter 8). The politics of this agenda challenges the adaptive capabilities of the regional states' policymakers. The issues of human security challenge the immutability of the fact of "sovereignty," the founding principle of the modern state, and the concomitant claim to noninterference in matters of domestic jurisdiction.

In many international policy conflicts arising out of the new agenda, Southeast Asia often finds China, a strong advocate of sovereign boundary maintenance, an ally, while the United States and the EU can be adversaries.

Before examining the working out in Southeast Asia of the traditional and nontraditional international relations agendas, it is first necessary to test two underlying assumptions informing both the preceding paragraphs and the book. The premise is that the eleven countries of Southeast Asia can be treated as part of a definable international political/economic region, and that the Southeast Asian region itself objectively exists for extraregional international actors.

The Origins of the Southeast Asian "Region"

The concept of Southeast Asia as a geopolitical region is a product of World War II in the Pacific. In the Allies' war against Japan, a South-East Asia Command (SEAC) was created in 1943. Headquartered at Kandy in Ceylon (now Sri Lanka), SEAC did not fully geographically correspond to today's Southeast Asia. It did, however, give a political context to the notion of a region with political and strategic coherence that was barely hinted at in the travelogues and anthropological use of the term Southeast Asia before the war.[6]

At the outset of World War II, Thailand was the only independent Southeast Asian state. Its independence was qualified by unequal treaties and imperialist pressures. There was no sense of a politically or economically coherent Southeast Asian region. It was a geographic area where European states and America had carved out sovereign domains, connected not to each other but to the metropolitan capitals. Foreign empire did not disrupt any existing Southeast Asian regional political order. There was no overarching Southeast Asian unifying geopolitical structure. Before the Europeans there were indigenous claimants to empire whose historical memories are evoked in modern nationalisms: Cambodia's Angkor; Indonesia's Majapahit; Thailand's Ayudhya; and Myanmar's Pagan.

After the defeat of Japan in 1945, the returning European colonial powers faced nationalist resistance to the reimposition of alien rule. The imperial responses to the local waves of nationalism differed. The United States had committed itself before the war to Philippine independence. This was accomplished in 1946. A war-weakened Great Britain, once shorn of India in 1947, did not resist independence for Burma in 1948. Malaya's independence from Britain was delayed until 1957, while Malay and British Commonwealth forces fought a communist insurgency, known as the "Emergency." The British decolonized Singapore, Sarawak, and British North Borneo (Sabah) in 1963 by

---

BOX 1.1
United States' Early Contacts in Southeast Asia

After American merchant ships began showing the American flag in Southeast Asian waters in the early nineteenth century, the first official contact was the signing in 1833 of a Treaty of Amity and Commerce between the United States and the Kingdom of Siam, eleven years before the first U.S. treaty with China and twenty-four years before a treaty with Japan. In 1845, during the U.S. naval frigate *Constitution*'s ("Old Ironsides") circumnavigation, the ship's captain, in an attempt to free imprisoned French priests in Annam, confronted a local population and shots were fired by the Americans. This has been identified as the first use of armed force against Vietnam by Western military forces. Five years later, President Zachary Taylor apologized to the Annamese emperor. His letter was delivered by Taylor's special diplomatic agent Joseph Balestier, who was credentialed as his presidential envoy and minister to "South Eastern Asia." This may be the earliest American geopolitical designation of the region as such. Balestier also negotiated a Treaty of Friendship, Commerce, and Navigation with the Sultan of Brunei in 1850.

---

incorporating them with Malaya into a new federal Malaysia. After only two years, Singapore and Malaysia parted ways, and Singapore became independent in 1965.

The road to independence was not that smooth for the Netherlands Indies and French Indochina, comprised of Vietnam, Cambodia, and Laos. In August 1945, Indonesia proclaimed its independence. The Dutch used military force to try to restore their authority. After two Dutch "police actions," stout Indonesian resistance, and strong international pressure, the Netherlands was forced to cede sovereignty in 1949. France fought a costly war in Vietnam for nearly a decade against a nationalist–communist coalition led by Ho Chi Minh. This was the First Indochina War. During the course of that war, Cambodia and Laos were able to throw off French protection. France gave up in Vietnam in 1954, and the United States picked up the struggle in a partitioned Vietnam, with extensions into Laos and Cambodia, until 1973. This was the Second Indochina War. After three decades of war and tens of thousands of casualties, it was only in 1975 that a unified independent Vietnamese state emerged.

Little oil-rich Brunei, a British protectorate, reluctantly became independent in 1984. Fearful of designs on it by its Malaysian and Indonesian neighbors, it was reassured by a residual British defense commitment. Finally, in the wake of the overthrow of dictatorship in Portugal, after four centuries of Portuguese rule, East Timor declared independence in November 1975, only to be invaded one month later by Indonesia. Independence was restored to the state of Timor-Leste (East Timor) in 2002, under the aegis of the United Nations.

At independence, the leaders of the new states of Southeast Asia faced similar tasks. First, rule had to be consolidated in states that were weak and vulnerable. Revolutionary violence and separatist urges threatened the territorial and political integrity of the states themselves. The old nationalism had been built on opposition to imperialism. A new nationalism had to be founded on real achievement in nation-building. Second, working relationships had to be established with former colonial rulers on the basis of sovereign equality rather than colonial dependence. Third, they had to obtain access to international sources of capital and markets in order to deliver on the promise to their populations of economic development and social welfare. Trade, aid, and foreign direct investment were the mantras of the economic planners. Finally, their peoples having been long separated by history and imperialism, the new states of Southeast Asia had to establish relations with each other. This was no easy task given historical antagonisms and contested borders.

Defining the Southeast Asian Region

It was only with the post–World War II emergence of the newly independent nation states of Southeast Asia that foreign policymakers and students of international relations began to think of this group of countries as an international region. The external awareness of a Southeast Asian region at this early point was primarily a product of its geostrategic position in the Cold War (chapter 3). In today's very different global international political context, a first question to be asked in examining international relations in the Southeast Asian region is, what kind of region is it?

The Geographic Region

Geographic proximity is a basic criterion of a region. On a map, Southeast Asia lies within the space roughly bounded in the north by China, the east by the Pacific Ocean, the southeast by Australia, the south by the Indian Ocean, and the southwest by the Bay of Bengal and India. Nearly half of the space in this cartographic box is water: the archipelagic seas and straits of Indonesia, Malaysia, Singapore, and the Philippines, and the South China Sea. These waters are the maritime commercial and military links between Northeast Asia and South Asia, the Middle East and on to Europe. Their geostrategic significance is one of the reasons why Southeast Asia has been a region of great power competition.

Southeast Asia is a physical region. Its climate is humid and tropical. It experiences the annual alternation of the wind patterns from continental Asia, the northeast or wet monsoon, and from the Australian continent and Indian Ocean, the southwest or dry monsoon. The monsoon pattern dominates Southeast Asia's agricultural calendar based on the cultivation of irrigated rice. Even though agriculture as a percentage of gross domestic product (GDP) is diminishing, it is still the source of livelihood for tens of millions of Southeast Asians, and irrigated rice the main staple food of the populations.

The geographic region is resource rich. Its rapidly depleting forests are the world's principal source of tropical hardwoods. Deforestation has become a major issue in the dialogues on climate change (chapter 9). Southeast Asia is a major producer of oil and natural gas. A factor in the competition for jurisdiction in the South China Sea is the prospect of oil and gas fields under the seabed (chapter 5). Mineral deposits include commercially valuable tin, nickel, copper, and gold. Southeast Asian fisheries, both natural and farmed, provide the major source of protein in the people's diet as well as export earnings. Aggressive exploitation of fisheries has become a source of political irritation as countries seek to defend their Law of the Sea–defined maritime exclusive economic zones (EEZ).

Nesting inside the Southeast Asian geographic box are two smaller boxes: continental or mainland Southeast Asia and maritime or island Southeast Asia. This division is bureaucratically replicated in the U.S. State Department's Bureau of East Asian and Pacific Affairs' Office of Mainland Southeast Asia (EAP/MLS) and Office of Maritime Southeast Asia (EAP/MTS).

Continental Southeast Asia

Continental Southeast Asia has been the historical seat of civilizations, empires, and states centered on the valleys, plains, and deltas of north–south running great rivers: from west to east, the Irrawaddy and Salween in Myanmar, the Chaophraya in Thailand, the Mekong, and Vietnam's Red River. The Mekong River is the central artery of mainland Southeast Asia, giving it whatever natural unity it might possess. Rising in Tibet, the mighty Mekong runs more than three thousand miles from China, touching Laos, Myanmar, Thailand, and Cambodia before emptying into the South China Sea at delta Vietnam. It is the twelfth longest river in the world, and in volume of flow it is the tenth greatest world river. The Mekong drainage basin is the focus of overlapping ambitious developmental planning frameworks that envision it as a liquid engine of economic activity (chapter 4 and chapter 9). North of the Mekong Delta, Vietnam is cut off from its continental neighbors by a chain of hills and mountains. It shares, however, a key strategic feature with them. Bordering and politically looming above continental Southeast Asia is the Chinese land and population mass.

Maritime Southeast Asia

Maritime Southeast Asia has margins on the South China Sea as a common natural feature. Depending on the controlling political perspective, the states of this subregion are joined or separated from each other by water: the two great archipelagoes of the Philippines and Indonesia; East and West Malaysia divided by the southern reach of the South China Sea; island Singapore off the tip of peninsular Malaysia; Brunei wedged between the East Malaysian Sabah and Sarawak states; and Timor-Leste, trapped in the Indonesian archipelago. Maritime Southeast Asia's political patterns historically evolved from networks of coastal trading points that from the end of the first millennium B.C. were engaged in commercial exchange with India and China. Maritime Southeast Asia's strategic outlook is fastened on the South China Sea, most of which is also claimed by China (chapter 5).

The Human Geography of Southeast Asia

Bounded geography, climactic similarities, common ecological features, and other observable shared natural characteristics of the states of Southeast Asia are not enough to define a political region. There must be other commonalities that relate to how the states behave toward each other and the extraregional international environment. In fact, beyond the macrogeographic unity of the latitude–longitude box, there are few qualities that we usually associate with a world region to be found in Southeast Asia. There is no region-wide identity such as race, ethnicity, language, religion, culture, and history such as we find in the Arab world, Western Europe, or, with the exception of Brazil, Latin America.

Ethnic Diversity

Complementing and partially overlapping the fragmented geography of Southeast Asia are its ethnic and cultural maps. In continental Southeast Asia, there are three major ethnic-linguistic groups with many languages and dialects reflecting its prehistoric population. The Austro-Asiatic language family includes Mon, Khmer (Cambodian), and Vietnamese. The Tibeto-Burman group has Burmese as its major language. Tai speaking tribal groups from Southwest China were the latecomers, beginning to move from Southwest China into Southeast Asia at the beginning of the last millennium in a migration that continued into the last century. The largest number of Tai speakers is in Thailand, followed by Laos, and the Shan who straddle the Thailand-Myanmar border. The ethnic-linguistic roots of maritime Southeast Asia are found in the Austronesian migrations southward from a coastal China-Taiwan homeland that by 1500 B.C. had spread its Malayo-Polynesian languages and culture through the archipelagoes to the South Pacific. The complexity of the ethnic-linguistic map is demonstrated by the fact that in Indonesia, alone, up to three hundred distinct ethnic-linguistic groups have been identified.

We must add to the indigenous ethnic mix the generations of Chinese immigrants. They number about twenty-five million or less than 5 percent of the total Southeast Asian population. Chinese trading settlements existed in precolonial Southeast Asia, but it was during the European imperialist period that the foundations for the contemporary Chinese communities in Southeast Asia were laid. The largest minority Chinese population by percentage of national population is the 24 percent in Malaysia. Singapore is a 77 percent majority Chinese state. Concentrated in urban areas and engaged in critical businesses and trade, the Chinese minority's economic influence is far out of proportion to its numbers. This has been a source of indigenous nationalist resentment since independence. There has also been a question of the loyalties of local Chinese. The issue was first raised in suspicions about a Chinese Trojan horse for communism. It has been reframed in terms of concerns about local Chinese investment capital flowing to China rather than national development in Southeast Asian host states.

Religious Diversity

Differences in religious belief and practice in Southeast Asia roughly correspond to the continental–maritime geographic divide. On the mainland, Theravada Buddhism dominates in Myanmar, Thailand, Cambodia, and Laos. The Indic cultural background of most of continental Southeast Asia, excluding Vietnam, earned it the earlier soubriquet of "Farther India" or "India beyond the Ganges." It is a Western myth that Buddhists are inherently fatalistic, passive, and nonaggressive. As centuries of warfare have demonstrated, Buddhists can be just as savage as anyone else.

Islam is the predominant religion of maritime Southeast Asia. More than 40 percent of Southeast Asia's population makes the profession of faith: "There is no God but Allah, and Mohammad is his prophet." Arab and Indian traders brought Islam to the region as early as the thirteenth century. By the end of the sixteenth century, Islam had swept in a great arc from the Malay Peninsula through the archipelagoes. The vision of Indonesia-based Jema'ah Islamiyah (JI), one of the most radical Islamist networks with links to terrorism operating in the region, is the unification of all Southeast Asian Muslims in a new caliphate transcending secular state boundaries.

At both the western and eastern ends of the Islamic arc, the Muslim populations have become national minorities. The Muslim majority in the four southern provinces of Thailand are cut off from their co-religionists in Malaysia by a border set on European colonial terms. In the Philippines, after four centuries of Spanish colonialism and half a century of American rule, the Muslim population is confined to the extreme south of the archipelago. In both cases, separatist and irredentist sentiments and violence have had international relations consequences (chapter 5).

Southeast Asia's Muslim population is not homogeneous. The political subsets are usually termed "moderate" and "fundamentalist" or "radical" to indicate their orientation toward the secular state and non-Muslims. All Muslims in Southeast Asia have a transnational identity. They are part of the *ummat*, the universal community of believers. They feel for, and support, the struggles of Muslims anywhere in the world, be it Bosnia, Kosovo, Afghanistan, or particularly Palestine. With the declaration of the war on terror, this became a critical factor in shaping Islamic Southeast Asia's response to the call to join the campaign. In many Muslim minds, the war on terrorism is translated as a war on Islam. This became even more marked after the invasion of Iraq (chapter 6).

Vietnam and the Philippines are outliers from the two large cultural groupings in the region. The traditional Vietnamese royal courts had been a southern extension of the Chinese cultural sphere. Among the population are Theravada Buddhists, Mahayana Buddhists, Christians, and Confucians. The different religions and sects in Vietnam have in common submission to the demands of a secular Leninist regime. The Philippines' population is more than 90 percent Christian. The Roman Catholic Church still plays an important political role. Underneath the "great religions" of Southeast Asia there remain numbers of minority ethnic groups classified as animists, that is, propitiators of localized deities and spirits.

Historical Antagonisms

Even though the independent states of Southeast Asia are relatively new to the modern state system, they bring with them the baggage of a history of war. Burmese and Thai armies laid waste to each other's territories for centuries. The Thais have not forgotten that Burma sacked and destroyed their capital Ayudhya in 1767. Nor have the Laotians erased from their national memory the fact that an invading Thai army laid waste to Vientiane in 1827, carrying away the Jade Buddha, the national palladium. It still rests in the National

Palace in Bangkok. In the nineteenth century, Thai and Vietnamese dynasties wrestled for control of Cambodia. The blood-soaked traditional Cambodian–Vietnamese relationship, represented in thirteenth-century sculpture at Angkor Wat, was continued in modern Cambodia by the wholesale murder of Vietnamese nationals in the aftermath of the 1970 military coup that installed a pro-American Cambodian government. At the primordial level of analysis, the Vietnamese invasion and occupation of Cambodia and ensuing Third Indochina War was a continuation of the conflict-filled traditional relationship (chapter 3). During World War II, Thailand grabbed back Cambodian, Laotian, Burmese, and Malayan territories wrested from it by France and Britain. They were returned as part of the postwar settlement. Thailand's irredentist past still fuels suspicions among its neighbors about its subregional ambitions. The 2003 attack on the Thai embassy in Phnom Penh is a reminder (chapter 5).

In maritime Southeast Asia, the pan-Indonesia elements in the Sukarno era's radical nationalism raised fears among its neighbors that Indonesia sought to restore the supposed fourteenth-century "golden age" boundaries of Java's Majapahit empire. These suspicions seemed confirmed when Indonesia used military force in the early 1960s to try to prevent the formation of Malaysia (chapter 3) and were rekindled by Indonesia's invasion and occupation of the former Portuguese territory of East Timor in 1975 (chapter 2).

Diversities in Modern State Development

The ethnic, cultural, and historical diversities in Southeast Asia are the background of relations among the contemporary states of the region. Since independence, the states have pursued different political and economic paths.

Political Diversity

There is no common Southeast Asian political culture. Until the 1990s, the internationally relevant macropolitical division of the region was between communist and noncommunist Southeast Asia. High politics was conducted along that divide with little reference to the internal political differences among the states on each side of the divide. The formal political institutions in Southeast Asia vary greatly: an absolute monarchy (Brunei), three constitutional monarchies (Malaysia, Thailand, Cambodia), four representative republics (Indonesia, Philippines, Singapore, Timor-Leste), two socialist states (Laos and Vietnam), and a military junta (Myanmar). In terms of governmental structure, Indonesia and the Philippines are presidential; Cambodia, Timor-Leste, Malaysia, Singapore, and Thailand are parliamentary. Laos and Vietnam are Leninist command states. Myanmar is a military dictatorship and Brunei, as already noted, an absolute monarchy.

More important than the constitutional basis or institutional form given to authority in a state is the quality of the relationship of state authority to its population. The most significant distinguishing political factor for contemporary international relations is the degree to which governments are representative of and accountable to their citizens. Certainly for the liberal democratic countries of the West, attitudes about and policies toward the individual countries of Southeast Asia are influenced by the "democratic" content of their domestic politics. An important component of this is human rights (chapter 8). It also can impact the way Southeast Asian countries relate to one another.

Clark Neher and Ross Marley devised a scale for democracy in Southeast Asia that ranks the countries in four categories of democracy, semi-democracy, semi-authoritarian, and authoritarian based on citizen participation, electoral competition, and civil liberties.[7] Utilizing their methodology, in 2007, there was only one democracy in Southeast Asia—Indonesia. The semi-democracies are Malaysia, the Philippines, Thailand, and Timor-Leste. The semi-authoritarian bracket contains Cambodia and Singapore. On the Neher-Marley spectrum, Brunei, Laos, Myanmar, and Vietnam are authoritarian. This, of course, is a snapshot in time. Political change is a dynamic process in which countries can move along a spectrum from authoritarian to democratic or back. For example, Thailand, democratic at the beginning of the millennium but after the 2006 military coup authoritarian, become semi-democratic in 2008, after elections allowed a civilian government to rule, but with the military still in the background. The Philippines seems to be slipping from semi-democratic toward semi-authoritarian and Cambodia toward authoritarian. Indonesia has transited from Suharto's military-oligarchic rule to a fragile representative democracy. Laos and Vietnam are determined Leninist, single-party command states. Like China, they seek to open their economies while keeping politics closed. Myanmar is in the grip of coercive military rule, a political generation behind the rest of the region. The discussion in chapter 2 of the individual national actors will give greater substance to these placements.

Another measure of political diversity is Freedom House's annual Freedom Index, which measures freedom on two dimensions, political rights and civil liberties, and scores from 1 to 7—with 7 being the lowest score—to determine whether a country is free, partly free, or not free (NF). Table 1.2 shows the scores for Southeast Asia.

TABLE 1.2
2007 Freedom Index for Southeast Asia

Country	PR Score	CL Score	Status
Indonesia	2	3	F
Philippines	3	3	PF
Timor-Leste	3	4	PF
Malaysia	4	4	PF
Singapore	5	4	PF
Cambodia	6	5	NF
Brunei	6	5	NF
Thailand	7	4	NF
Vietnam	7	5	NF
Laos	7	6	NF
Myanmar	7	7	NF

Note: PR=political rights, CL=civil liberties, F=free, PF=partly free, NF=not free.
Source: Freedom House, *Freedom in the World*, subcategory scores, www.freedomhouse.org/template.cfm?
page=372.

Economic Inequalities

At independence, the Southeast Asian states, with the exception of Brunei and Singapore, had similar economic problems. Like the largest part of the immediate postcolonial African-Asian world, they were classified as underdeveloped, later to be called less developed, and then developing. This status was characterized by low per capita GDP, poor living standards, inadequate human resources, primary product exploitation, few value-added industries, and other measures of low economic performance.

A priority of the Southeast Asian states has been economic development. Initially, divergent routes for development were chosen that can be roughly categorized as socialist and mixed-capitalist. Even though socialist Vietnam and Laos have now turned to the market strategies that propelled the economies of their capitalist neighbors, they continue to lag behind. Four Southeast Asian nations—Cambodia, Laos, Myanmar, and Timor-Leste—are still on the fifty-country United Nations list of Least Developed Countries (LDC) where human security is most at risk (chapter 8). LDC status is based on the combination of extreme poverty, structural weakness of the economy, and lack of development capacity.[8]

The World Bank's classification of country economies by income has four income categories: low, low middle, upper middle, and high.[9] In Southeast Asia the low income countries are Cambodia, Timor-Leste, Laos, Myanmar, and Vietnam. Indonesia, the Philippines, and Thailand are in the low middle income bracket and Malaysia is found in the upper middle income ranks. Brunei and Singapore are high income countries. Table 1.3 illustrated some of the development differences in Southeast Asia.

TABLE 1.3
Selected Basic ASEAN Economic Indicators

Countries	2006 GDP Current Prices U.S. $ Millions	Per Capita GDP (PPP)† U.S. $*	GDP % Growth 2007 Est.*	2006 Trade U.S. $ Millions	2006 FDI U.S. $ Millions
Brunei	11,571.8	25,600	0.4	9,108.3	433.5
Cambodia	7,256.3	2,899	8.5	6,437.4	483.2
Indonesia	364,258.8	3,900	6.1	161,864.1	5,556.2
Laos	3,521.8	2,200	7.0	190.2	184.7
Malaysia	159,924.2	12,800	5.7	285,543.0	6,059.7
Myanmar	11,951.0	1,800	3.5	5,630.3	143.0
Philippines	117,457.1	5,000	6.3	99,183.8	2,345.0
Singapore	134,273.4	31,400	7.4	510,089.9	24,055.4
Thailand	208,645.1	9,200	4.3	248,688.3	10,756.1
Vietnam	60,965.2	3,100	8.2	77,270.5	2,360.0

* Per CIA *World Factbook*, November 2007.
† Per capita GDP is given in purchasing power parity, a measure of relative purchasing power made by converting a currency's market exchange rate to a standardized weighted dollar rate.
Source: ASEAN Secretariat, www.aseansec.org/stat/Table1.pdf.

The Southeast Asian states' economic strengths and weaknesses contribute to their foreign policy capabilities and activities in the regional and international systems. The wealthier and poorer countries of the region have been built into an economically tiered ASEAN system. The latecomers Cambodia, Laos, Myanmar, and Cambodia—collectively called the CLMV countries—have been granted a longer period of time to meet the ASEAN regional integration targets.

Region and Regionalism

It is clear from the above discussion that diversity rather than homogeneity is the compelling characteristic of Southeast Asia. In order to study Southeast Asia as a region, it will be necessary to identify unifying transactional or institutional patterns. One scholar paradoxically finds in the diversity itself the unifying theme making Southeast Asia a region.[10] Another argues that "the notion of 'Southeast Asia' is more a result of American and European professors looking for a convenient way to study a geographic region than it is a meaningful term for an area that systematically shares commonalities."[11] A premise of this book is that the foundations of international relations in Southeast Asia rest on national diversities not regional unity. Southeast Asia can be conceived of as an aggregation of overlapping geographic, ethnic, cultural, political, and economic subregions. Potent divisive, not unifying, forces originate in these diversities. The idea of "unity out of diversity" is an elite conceit, not a natural political phenomenon.

Yet, despite the fact that Southeast Asia has few of the characteristics commonly utilized to define a political region, we continue to treat it as such. This is because of the existence of the Association of Southeast Asian Nations. ASEAN gives institutional expression to an essentially declaratory regionalism that originates not from natural circumstances, but in the political will of Southeast Asian policy elites. Very importantly, this proclaimed Southeast Asian regional identity has been nominally accepted by members of the global international system. What we might call the Southeast Asian "virtual" or "imagined" region is a product of a process of regionalism that is as much ideational as structural on both sides of the regional boundary. In fact, the term ASEAN itself is often used as a synonym for geographic Southeast Asia, even though Timor-Leste is excluded. What Donald Emmerson describes with respect to Timor-Leste as a "slippage between a spatial Southeast Asia and a political ASEAN"[12] would be even more stark if Myanmar left—or was forced out—of the ASEAN fold. ASEAN's insistence on the permanency of Myanmar's membership is in part an almost reflexive devotion to its founders' vision of a congruency of ASEAN with Southeast Asia.

In many respects, the idea of regionalism is more powerful than the loose, poorly articulated, voluntary institutions and multilateral structures that give it an institutional form. Nearly every Southeast Asian multilateral grouping, from chambers of commerce to educators, has been "ASEAN-ized"; that is notionally assimilated to a sense of regionalism that has its political expression in ASEAN. Annex 2 of the new ASEAN charter lists more than seventy "entities" officially associated with ASEAN. Since its creation in 1967, and particularly since the ending of the Third Indochina War followed by communist–noncommunist state reconciliation in its organizational framework, ASEAN embodies the analytical existence of a Southeast Asian region. Because of the demonstrable lack of substantial real regionalized policy achievements, ASEAN's critics have trumpeted its failures. It has been called, for example, an "uncertain collocation of fragile states that connote the failed delusional entity of Southeast Asia."[13] Certainly, movement has been slow for regionalism as a process, in part because ASEAN is inner-conflicted. Still, a Southeast Asian region exists because leaders have a minimum, lowest-common-denominator consensus on what regional interests are and some degree of collective expectations of how they should act in pursuit of those interests. Rather than considering ASEAN an example of failed regionalism, it is perhaps more accurate to view ASEAN in terms of aspirational regionalism.

The Study of International Relations in Southeast Asia

International relations theories and analyses seek to explain how change occurs in relations among states to provide a basis for making probabilistic statements about state behavior.[14] A central concern is the mode of change in the quality of relations between national units, often reduced to a dichotomy of conflict or cooperation. The fact that the "virtual" region of ASEAN and the real geographic region of eleven very disparate sovereign states have policy coexistence complicates the study of international relations *in* Southeast Asia. Note the emphasis on the preposition "in" in the preceding sentence. This is because there are no international relations *of* Southeast Asia. Because ASEAN is the voluntary creation of its still fully sovereign state members, we are presented with a level of analysis question that influences the theoretical paradigm to be applied. Do we start with the states or the region?

The Realist Approach

The dominant paradigm for interpreting international relations in Southeast Asia has been realism. The pillars of realism are the sovereign state, national self-interest, and power. National elites acquire and mobilize national capabilities to pursue national interests in a competitive international environment in which there is no central governing order. For a state's relations with other states, national interest is defined by the elites that have authority in the state. National interests are not based simply on temporally situated pragmatic political or material goals. They are determined in a social and psychological context of history, culture, and religion that makes the definition of interest an exercise unique to each set of national policymakers.

At the heart of realist theory is security interest, usually narrowly defined as state independence, territorial integrity, and maintenance of the political system. In Southeast Asia, the latter is often implicitly qualified to mean continuity of the incumbent elite. The greatest part by far of the literature on Southeast Asian international relations is focused on security as traditionally defined. The most influential body of work on Southeast Asian international relations from a realist foundation is that of Michael Leifer.[15] As interests clash and threats to security mount, nations resort to self-help, seeking through alliances and alignment a balance of power, or shelter under hegemonic protection. There are more comprehensive definitions of security relating not just to the state but also to the political, economic, and social human conditions of the state's population. The "needs of the common man" as contained in the concept of human security is newly in vogue (chapter 8). Even if we adopt a people-centered approach as opposed to the traditional statecentric, it remains the fact that it is principally the state that negotiates the "people's interests" in the international system.

The unrelieved realist's Hobbesian view of international relations as an anarchic jungle is qualified by an approach that emphasizes cooperation among states as well as conflict as a way to pursue national interest. This involves a calculation of relative gains. International relations, rather than being a zero-sum game, can be win-win, although some win more than others. In this approach, ASEAN is a mode of international cooperation through which member states pursue national interest. With security still the realist heart of interest and the balance of power its mechanism, ASEAN as a regime for cooperative security can be placed in a realist balance of power perspective (chapter 5).[16] ASEAN's policy output cannot be explained without locating and understanding the national interests being expressed through it. Whatever is understood as an ASEAN regional interest is based on the consensual harmonizing of national interests in order to present a formal united front. As the chapters to follow will show, the cooperative face of ASEAN is best seen in its dealings with extraregional actors, not its intramural dealings where conflict is often present.

Liberalism

With the advent of ASEAN, attention shifted from state actors to the assumed regional institutional actor.[17] Initially, ASEAN was viewed through the lens of international integration studies, relying too much on analogy from the Western European experience. Functionalist theory was employed to suggest that through ASEAN specific transnational structures in the economic, technical, and social fields would evolve, to which ASEAN-wide decision-making authority would be transferred. This would build community from the bottom up as institution building in the nonpolitical issues areas would spill over into more politically sensitive areas of states' interactions. However, after nearly four decades, not one such structure can be located. For the liberal integrationists, for whom ASEAN has proved a theoretical disappointment, ASEAN's failure is the failure of the political will of leadership. For the realists, what integrationists call failure is in fact the political will of leaders at the state level who make conscious decisions based on national interest about which issues and at what level cooperation in ASEAN will be offered.

A different approach to ASEAN draws from regime theory, which looks at habit-forming experiences of cooperation over time. These create international regimes that are sets of implicit or explicit principles, norms, rules, and decision-making procedures around which participating actors' expectations converge in a given issue area.[18] Regime theory accepts the fact that states act on the basis of interest but are disciplined to the reciprocally understood obligations of the "regime." The sense of regime is unconsciously captured in the notion of an "ASEAN way" of addressing issue-specific problems through informal consultation and consensus. The most productive, but still unsatisfactory, effort to apply regime theory to Southeast Asia is in ASEAN as a security regime (chapter 5).[19]

Constructivism

It is only a theoretical step from regime to community, but in practical policy terms, a perhaps insurmountable gulf. A regime is founded on learned expectations about behavior in functionally specific state interactions. A community, on the other hand, is defined not so much by interests, as shared values. An attempt to bridge that gulf intellectually is the separation of "interest" from "identity" found in constructivist theory.[20] For constructivists, a community is socially constructed through knowledge, norms, culture, and other cooperative associations that over time cognitively promote a collective identity.[21] For ASEAN, then, the lack of legal or institutional progress is not important. What is important is mutual recognition of an ASEAN identity. The decoupling of identity from institutions, however, leaves open the question of what is the link from identity to state action.

Critics also point out that any ASEAN "identity" is only one among multiple identities that leaderships in Southeast Asia have—national, ethnic, religious, class—and that this special ASEAN identity is not shared with their own populations, some of whom have less than fully solidified national identities.[22] The expansion of ASEAN to include a military junta, Leninist command states, and Islamic absolutism makes the constructivist approach problematic. Paradigms based on "collective identity" are insufficient for understanding international relations in Southeast Asia. ASEAN identity is not superior to national interest when it comes to actual policy choices.

The Link between State and Region

ASEAN is only one aspect, albeit an important one, of international relations in Southeast Asia. The academic concentration on ASEAN tends to obscure the fact that for Southeast Asian policymakers, critical areas of conflict and cooperation exist bilaterally and subregionally in both traditional interest areas and the new global agenda. ASEAN has proved itself singularly unsuccessful in dealing with issues internal to the region since ASEAN's overriding organizational principle is the inviolability of member-state sovereignty. National leaders in Southeast Asia rhetorically affirm the regional identity and cooperate where interests are served, but the state is still the primary actor. Former ASEAN Secretary-General Ong Keng Yong, a Singaporean, realistically recognized this fact in pointing out that membership in ASEAN was in addition to the national policies of each member government: "Each of the members has every right to formulate its own national position based on its circumstances *that will best serve its own national interests*" [emphasis added].[23]

This was the case in March 2003 when ASEAN was deeply split over the Iraq war issue. The division was both political and cultural. The Philippines, Thailand, and Singapore refused to accept the Malaysian and Indonesian denunciation of the war. The traditional allies of the United States found themselves pitted against the Muslim states' sympathies with their Iraqi co-religionists. As a result, the ASEAN foreign ministers placed no blame.[24]

Leaders in Southeast Asia consciously and rationally understand that there are national interests that can be promoted in concert with other Southeast Asian states that have similar interests. The relationships in ASEAN are intergovernmental, which, as Leifer pointed out two decades ago, "means that while interests may be shared they are rarely held truly in common."[25] This is especially true with respect to bargaining with powers that have greater political, economic, and even military capabilities. The member states can amplify their international voice through ASEAN as a kind of diplomatic caucus. Similar or complementing national interests can be translated to a regional interest even though the outcomes are received at the state level. The way that national interests are cooperatively associated through ASEAN represents the link between the levels of state-region analysis. The management of this depends on decision making at the state level.

The Argument and Structure of the Book

The chapters to follow will detail the major actors, interests, issues, key relationships, structures, and institutions involved in an understanding of international relations in Southeast Asia. The material is presented in the context of a thematic argument that gives a pattern to Southeast Asian international relations that includes "regionalism" as a variable but also accounts for the behavior of the state units as well as nonstate actors.

The thematic proposition can be put simply. From independence, the states of Southeast Asia, individually and collectively, have struggled in their international environments for policy autonomy. By autonomy is meant the ability to pursue self-defined national interests within the limits of national capabilities, free from externally imposed political, economic, or military constraints. The limits on policy independence can originate in dependencies located in the external environment, such as foreign assistance or conflict with the interests of regional or extraregional actors with greater capabilities. It can be asked whether and how ASEAN itself might constrain the policy options of its member states.

Initially, limits on autonomy were set in the context of the global Cold War and American security primacy in Southeast Asia. As U.S. political hegemony is diminished in the post–Cold War era, Southeast Asia now sees on the policy horizon a prospective Chinese hegemony. The irony in the struggle for autonomy is that while Southeast Asian states enhance their capabilities through globalization, they meet new categories of nontraditional policy-limiting demands aggressively promoted not only by states, but also by international nongovernmental organizations that, unlike states, can penetrate sovereignty with direct links to domestic NGO counterparts.

Chapter 2 introduces the state and nonstate actors whose actions shape foreign policy outcomes in Southeast Asia. Chapter 3 briefly reviews international relations in Southeast Asia during the Cold War. This background is necessary to comprehend the major discontinuities and reorientations in the post–Cold War era as well as the loss of ASEAN's political cement. Chapter 4 examines the institutional structures of regionalism in Southeast Asia. Chapter 5 addresses conflict and modes of conflict resolution in traditional areas of security interests. With security still in mind, Chapter 6 turns to nontraditional security issues. Terrorism, narcotics trafficking, piracy, and smuggling are some of the concerns. Southeast Asia's regional structures for international economic cooperation are the topic of chapter 7. Chapter 8 examines human security in Southeast Asia on both the freedom from want and the freedom from fear conditions of human security. The case of Myanmar is given special attention in this chapter. Chapter 9 looks at environmental issues in Southeast Asian international relations as a nontraditional issue area, bringing the region into collision not only with the West, but causing antagonisms within ASEAN itself. Chapter 10, the concluding chapter, returns to issues raised in the introduction. It asks three questions, the answers to which will shape the future of international relations in Southeast Asia. Will democratic regimes transform international relations in Southeast Asia? Will national leaders succeed in reinventing ASEAN as a more effective collaborative mechanism? Finally it will ask how the evolving Chinese great power position, balancing and perhaps displacing the United States, will affect Southeast Asia's struggle for autonomy.

Notes

1. The text of the Charter and its annexes can be accessed at www.aseansec.org/21069.pdf.

2. The text of the "Bangkok Declaration" can be accessed at www.aseansec.org/1212.htm.

3. The concept of a subordinate Southeast Asian subsystem of the international system was introduced by Michael Brecher, *The New States of Asia: A Political Analysis* (Oxford: Oxford University Press, 1963).

4. Rupert Emerson, *From Empire to Nation: The Rise to Self-Assertion of Asian and African Peoples* (Cambridge, Mass.: Harvard University Press, 1960), 97.

5. Samuel P. Huntington, *The Third Wave: Democratization in the Late Twentieth Century* (Norman: University of Oklahoma Press, 1991).

6. Donald K. Emmerson, "'Southeast Asia': What's in a Name?" *Journal of Southeast Asian Studies* 15, no. 1 (1984): 1–21.

7. Clark D. Neher and Ross Marley, *Democracy and Development in Southeast Asia: The Winds of Change* (Boulder, Colo.: Westview, 1995), 193–95.

8. The full list and criteria for the LDC can be found at the website of the United Nations Office of the High Representative to the Least Developed Countries, Landlocked Developing Countries, and Small Island Developing Countries, www.un.org/ohrlls.

9. The World Bank's classifications can be accessed at www.worldbank.org using the data and research link.

10. Amitav Acharya, *The Quest for Identity: International Relations of Southeast Asia* (Singapore: Oxford University Press, 2000), 3.

11. Clark Neher, "Review of Acharya, *Quest for Identity*," *Journal of Asian Studies* 61, no. 3 (2002): 1101.

12. Donald K. Emmerson, "Challenging ASEAN: A Topological View," *Contemporary Southeast Asia* 29, no. 3 (2007): 427.

13. David Martin Jones and M. L. R. Smith, *ASEAN and East Asian International Relations: Regional Delusion* (Cheltenham, United Kingdom: Edward Elgar, 2006), 73.

14. The theoretical pluralism that informs international relations theory in Southeast Asia is illustrated in a special issue of *The Pacific Review* 19, no. 2 (2006). The editors, Amitav Acharya and Richard Stubbs, survey the field in their introduction "Theorizing Southeast Asia Relations: An Introduction," *The Pacific Review* 19, no. 2 (June 2006): 125–34.

15. A major collection of Leifer's writings is in Chin Kin Wah and Leo Suryadinata, eds., *Michael Leifer: Selected Works on Southeast Asia* (Singapore: Institute of Southeast Asian Studies, 2005). Leifer's influence is surveyed in Joseph Chinyong Liow and Ralf Emmers, eds., *Order and Security in Southeast Asia: Essays in Memory of Michael Leifer* (London: Routledge, 2005).

16. Ralf Emmers, *Cooperative Security and the Balance of Power in ASEAN and the ARF* (New York: RoutledgeCurzon, 2003).

17. Sheldon W. Simon, "Realism and Neoliberalism: International Relations Theory and Southeast Asian Security," *The Pacific Review* 8, no. 1 (1995): 5–24.

18. Stephen Krasner, "Structural Causes and Regime Consequences: Regimes as Intervening Variables," *International Organization* 36, no. 2 (Spring 1982): 186.

19. This literature is surveyed in Nicholas Khoo, "Constructing Southeast Asian Security: The Pitfalls of Imagining a Security Community and the Temptations of Orthodoxy," *Cambridge Review of International Affairs* 17, no. 1 (2004): 137–53; see also, Donald K. Emmerson, "Security, Community, and Democracy in Southeast Asia: Analyzing ASEAN," *Japanese Journal of Political Science* 6, no. 2 (2005): 165–85.

20. Alexander Wendt, "Constructing International Politics," *International Security* 20, no. 1 (Summer 1995): 71–81; Jeffrey T. Checkel, "The Constructivist Turn in International Relations Theory," *World Politics* 50 (1998): 324–48.

21. Constructivism as an approach to Southeast Asian international relations is represented by the work of Amitav Acharya; see his *The Quest for Identity: International Relations of Southeast Asia* (Singapore: Oxford University Press, 2000) and *Constructing a Security Community in Southeast Asia: ASEAN and the Problem of Regional Order* (New York: Routledge, 2001).

22. Donald E. Weatherbee, "ASEAN's Identity Crisis," in Ann Marie Murphy and Bridget Welsh, eds., *Legacies of Engagement* (Singapore: Institute of Southeast Asian Studies, 2008).

23. As quoted in "ASEAN split over Iraq 'to be expected,'" *The Straits Times Interactive*, 23 March 2003.

24. "Statement by the Chairman of the ASEAN Standing Committee on the Looming War in Iraq," 19 March 2003, accessed at www.aseansec.org/14532.htm.

25. Michael Leifer, *ASEAN and the Security of South-East Asia* (London: Routledge, 1989), 148.

Suggestions for Further Reading

For a comprehensive regional geography, refer to Thomas R. Leinbach and Richard Ulak, eds., *Southeast Asia: Diversity and Development* (Upper Saddle River, N.J.: Prentice Hall, 2000). Another geography is Chia Lin Sien, ed., *Southeast Asia Transformed: A Geography of Change* (Singapore: Institute of Southeast Asian Studies, 2003). A concise history is Milton Osborne, *Southeast Asia: An Introductory History*, 9th ed. (Sydney, Australia: Allen & Unwin, 2005). Another introductory history is D. R. Sar Desai, *Southeast Asia: Past and Present*, 5th ed. (Boulder, Colo.: Westview, 2003). A history with country-specific chapters is Norman G. Owen, David Chandler, and William Roff, eds., *The Emergence of Modern Southeast Asia: A New History* (Honolulu: University of Hawaii Press, 2004). Clark D. Neher, *Southeast Asia: Crossroads of the World*, 2nd ed. (DeKalb: Center for Southeast Asian Studies, Northern Illinois

University, 2000) is an overview of society, culture, and politics in Southeast Asia. Another general introduction to the region is Mark Beeson, ed., *Contemporary Southeast Asia: Regional Dynamics, National Differences* (New York: Palgrave Macmillan, 2004). Donald G. McCloud, *Southeast Asia: Tradition and Modernity in the Contemporary World* (Boulder, Colo.: Westview, 1995) focuses on continuities in the historical evolution of the Southeast Asian region. Clark D. Neher, *Southeast Asia in the New International Era* (Boulder, Colo.: Westview, 2002) presents country case studies of the politics of foreign policy in the region.

There are a number of serial publications that contain current scholarship on problems and policies in Southeast Asian international relations. Singapore's Institute of Southeast Asian Studies publishes the quarterly journal *Contemporary Southeast Asia*, which features analyses by Southeast Asian scholars. It also produces the annual volume *Southeast Asian Affairs* covering the important political and foreign policy events of the previous year on a country basis. A leading American journal with current Southeast Asian politics and international relations articles is the bimonthly *Asian Survey* from the University of California Press. Its annual January/February number, "A Survey of Asia" is a country-by-country retrospective of the previous year's events. Georgetown University's Walsh School of Foreign Service Asian Studies Program publishes an annual *Georgetown Southeast Asia Survey*. The annual volume of *Strategic Asia* published by the National Bureau of Asian Research in Seattle includes a thematic chapter on Southeast Asia. The quarterly *Pacific Affairs*, published at the University of British Columbia, also covers Southeast Asian contemporary politics, economics, and international relations. *The Pacific Review*, published in London, focuses on security and strategic issues in the region. *The Far Eastern Economic Review* is published in Hong Kong ten times a year with articles on current issues in Southeast Asia.

There is a large array of Internet resources for the study of Southeast Asian international relations. *Comparative Connections* is a quarterly e-journal published in Honolulu by the Pacific Forum CSIS, which provides overviews and chronologies of U.S.–Southeast Asian relations and China–Southeast Asian relations. It can be accessed at www.csis.org/pacfor/ccejournal.htm. Most of Southeast Asia's leading English language newspapers have Internet editions— *The Strait Times* (Singapore), *Jakarta Post*, *Bangkok Post*, *New Straits Times* (Kuala Lumpur) to mention only a few. In addition, there are Internet news services with Asian content such as CNN, Reuters, BBC, ABC (Australia), and Voice of America, Bernama (Malaysia), and Antara (Indonesia). The ASEAN website, www.aseansec.org, has links to the official sites of member governments. The Department of State website, www.state.gov, is the major source for official information on U.S. policy and relations in Southeast Asia.

2

The International Actors in Southeast Asia

INTERNATIONAL ACTORS IN SOUTHEAST ASIA, as elsewhere, can be grouped in two broad categories: state actors and nonstate actors. There are eleven state actors in Southeast Asia. Ten of them are joined in the Association of Southeast Asian Nations (ASEAN). The eleventh, Timor-Leste, became independent only in 2002. The three primary extraregional actors with significant national interests in Southeast Asia are the United States, China, and Japan. Their policies set the basic economic and political parameters for the autonomy of the Southeast Asian states. Other extraregional state actors with important interests in Southeast Asia include Australia, India, Russia, and, in relation to Indonesia, Papua New Guinea (PNG). Increasingly, the European Union (EU), collectively acting for its members, looms large, not only economically but also politically.

Nonstate actors include intergovernmental international organizations, the majority of which operate under the umbrella of the United Nations system, and a wide variety of international nongovernmental organizations (INGO) that are independent of government mandates. Multinational corporations (MNC) are not included as a separate category in this IR-focused book since, despite their local political impact, their ultimate objectives are private economic interests. International terrorist groups, such as al-Qaeda with its Southeast Asian links to the local Jema'ah Islamiyah (JI) terrorist network, are included, as well as criminal enterprises (chapter 6).

Finally, there is the question of what kind of international actor the regional organization ASEAN is. As noted in chapter 1, some analyses would treat ASEAN as a separate actor with an identity independent of its member states. In a state-centered analysis, however, ASEAN is a multilateral structure through which the collective policy will of its member states is expressed in areas of multilateral consensus. Unlike the EU, ASEAN has no legal or political capacity to act on behalf of its members in a binding fashion. Whether or not the new ASEAN charter adopted in 2007 will change the organization's fundamental relationship to its member states is problematic (chapter 4). While the charter confers an international personality on ASEAN, its preamble and operational principles continue to enshrine sovereignty, noninterference, and the other principles of the "old" ASEAN, guaranteeing the supremacy of the state in the conduct of international relations in Southeast Asia. Only if and until ASEAN develops an organic unity in which elements of member-states' sovereignty have been delegated can it be considered as an actor separately from the states. In the chapters to follow, references to ASEAN's activities are interpreted as the collective consensual voluntary product of the real actors, the member states.

Regional State Actors

Southeast Asia's state subsystem is incorporated in an international state system in which the basic principle governing state interaction is sovereign equality. Even though Southeast Asian states may challenge the Western bias in the workings of the international system, they fully embrace sovereign equality in their relations with each other and with extraregional state actors. It is obvious that despite the underpinning legal fiction of sovereign equality, all states in the Southeast Asian international system are not equal in terms of capabilities to promote their national interests, including defending their sovereignty. The aggregate of economic, political, military, cultural, and psychological factors that enable a state to defend and further its interests internationally is usually termed power. Some states have more power than others, and power is relative in both bilateral and multilateral settings. For this chapter introducing the Southeast Asian state actors, it is necessary to choose an order of appearance. Adhering to the principle of sovereign equality, the states are ordered alphabetically, since to use power for ranking purposes would seem to ignore the fact of the relativity of power. The reality of power in international relations in Southeast Asia is demonstrated in the chapters that follow.

Brunei (Negara Brunei Darussalam [Abode of Peace])

Brunei is a very rich microstate. Its tiny population sits atop large oil and natural gas reserves. It is Southeast Asia's fourth largest oil producer and the world's ninth largest exporter of liquid natural gas. The actual size of its re-

BOX 2.1
Southeast Asian Heads of Government and State (January 2008)

Country	Head of Government	Head of State
Brunei	Sultan Hassanal Bolkiah	same
Cambodia	PM Hun Sen	King Norodom Sihamoni
Indonesia	Pres. Susilo Bambang Yudhoyono	same
Lao PDR	PM Bouasone Bouphavanh	Pres. Choummaly Sayasone
Malaysia	PM Abdullah Badawi	King Syed Sirajuddin
Myanmar	PM Gen. Thein Sein	Chair, SPDC, Senior Gen. Than Shwe
Philippines	Pres. Gloria Macapagal-Arroyo	same
Singapore	PM Lee Hsien Loong	Pres. S. R. Nathan
Thailand	PM Samak Sundarajev	King Bhumibol Adulyadej
Timor-Leste	PM Xanana Gusmão	Pres. José Ramos-Horta
Vietnam	PM Nguyen Tan Dung	Pres. Nguyen Minh Triet

serves is the state's greatest secret, although it is thought oil reserves are sufficient to maintain current export levels until 2030 and gas to mid-century. Brunei is ruled as an absolute Islamic sultanate. Sultan Hassanal Bolkiah, who came to the throne in 1967, is the twenty-ninth ruler in a dynasty that goes back to the fifteenth century. Brunei was once a great maritime empire that reached to Manila. A history of political intrigue, succession struggles, and especially the depredations of colonialism left modern Brunei surrounded by the East Malaysian Sarawak state.

Brunei became independent from Britain on 1 January 1984 and, a week later, ASEAN's sixth member. Brunei participates fully in ASEAN despite its limited human resource pool. ASEAN is important to Brunei in providing a multilateral framework within which to deal with Malaysia and Indonesia, the other occupants of the island of Borneo. In the years leading up to independence, the self-governing British protectorate had contentious relations with both neighbors. In addition to the ASEAN security blanket, a 1,500-man British Gurkha battalion is stationed (at Brunei's expense) at the oil center of Seria. Although outside of the Five Power Defence Arrangement (FPDA) linking Great Britain, Australia, New Zealand, Singapore, and Malaysia, Brunei has cooperative defense relationships with its British Commonwealth partners. In 1994, Brunei signed a memorandum of understanding (MOU) with the United States on defense relations and regularly engages with the United States in exercises and training programs. Brunei's strategic vulnerability was demonstrated in 2003, when the Malaysian navy ran off an exploration team from an offshore oil concession block that had been tendered by Brunei to the French oil company Total. The disputed Sarawak–Brunei maritime jurisdictions are one part of the broader conflict zone in the South China Sea (chapter 5).

Cambodia

Cambodia has still to overcome fully the human cost of the primitive communism of the savage rule of the Khmer Rouge ("Red Khmer"). The KR seized power in Phnom Penh in April 1975 and proceeded to root out Cambodia's social and cultural infrastructure while cruelly eliminating its middle class. In December 1978, Vietnam invaded Cambodia, sparking the Third Indochina War, expelling the KR government, and installing in its place a government of the People's Republic of Kampuchea (PRK) led by ex-KR dissidents who had taken refuge in Vietnam (chapter 3). Among them was Hun Sen, at first PRK foreign minister and then prime minister, who remains prime minister of Cambodia and is the longest serving head of government in Southeast Asia.

The contemporary Cambodian state was born in 1993; its midwife, the United Nations Transitional Authority for Cambodia (UNTAC). UNTAC was the international mechanism to manage in a democratic framework the reconciliation of the Hun Sen government and ASEAN-sponsored Cambodian nationalist opposition, while at the same time marginalizing and eventually eliminating the internationally detested KR. In UNTAC-organized elections, Hun Sen's Cambodian People's Party (CPP) came in second to the royalist United National Front for an Independent, Neutral, Pacific, and Cooperative Cambodia (FUNCINPEC, Front Uni National pour un Cambodge Indépendent, Neutre, Pacifique, et Coopératif). Under threat of renewed violence, the international community forced FUNCINPEC to share power with the CPP. Hun Sen became co-prime minister with Norodom Ranariddh, FUNCINPEC's leader. Ranariddh is a son of Norodom Sihanouk, who had led Cambodia from independence from France, first as king and then as prime minister, until he was deposed by a military coup in 1970. In the new Cambodian government, Sihanouk was a relatively powerless constitutional monarch, symbol of a renewed Khmer nationalism. In old age and illness, he abdicated in favor of his son Norodom Sihamoni in 2004.

In 1997, Hun Sen challenged the UN and ASEAN by a coup against Ranariddh (chapter 4). Threatened by international economic sanctions and denial of ASEAN membership, Hun Sen was forced to accept new elections in 1998. A new government was brokered with Hun Sen as sole prime minister and Ranariddh as leader of the CPP-dominated parliament. Cambodia became

ASEAN's delayed tenth member in 1999. Elections held in July 2003 exposed the fragility of Cambodian political stability. After five years of ruthlessly consolidating power, Hun Sen's CPP could not manage to win the two-thirds majority of parliamentary seats needed to form a government. The deadlock threatened to plunge the country again into political turmoil. Finally, under international pressure, a new coalition government was formed at the end of 2004 with Hun Sen as prime minister and FUNCINPEC and the Sam Rainsey Party (SRP) as junior members. Cooperation in the coalition soon collapsed over the division of the spoils. By 2006, Hun Sen's relentless political attacks forced FUNCINPEC to dump Ranariddh, who went into exile to avoid imprisonment. The antidemocratic quality of the Hun Sen regime has been denounced by the United Nations human rights officials, the United States, and the European Union. In their reports, the UN's human rights envoys to Cambodia have charged the Hun Sen government with the systematic violation of political and human rights as an iron-fisted tool of oppression to maintain power.[1]

Hun Sen's political excesses may have been somewhat constrained by Cambodia's need for international economic assistance. The legacy of wars, political instability, and corruption has left Cambodia one of Southeast Asia's poorest states. Since 1996, the state has been dependent for more than 60 percent of its budget on the largesse of an international donor community organized in the Consultative Group for Cambodia (CGC), which in 2007 became the Cambodian Development Cooperation Forum (CDCF). Historically, Japan and the United States have been the pledge leaders in the consortium, but in 2007, when the consortium pledged $689 million, China, joining the consortium for the first time, made the second largest aid pledge of $91 million behind Japan's $115 million and ahead of the United States' $48 million. Even though the CDCF urges reform and accountability, little reform has taken place in governance. Corruption is endemic as the country is plundered in a culture of impunity (chapter 8).

Domestic political frustrations tend to be vented in xenophobic demonstrations. The ethnic Vietnamese presence in Cambodia became a major election issue in 2003. In 2007, Cambodian Buddhist monks demonstrated against Vietnamese treatment of Vietnamese monks. Thailand suspended diplomatic relations with Cambodia for several weeks in 2003 after physical attacks on Thai interests in Phnom Penh (chapter 5). The discovery in 2005 of potentially large oil deposits off Cambodia's southern coast may be a mixed blessing. It is projected that the new revenue source will begin to come on stream in 2010. It is doubtful, however, that Cambodia will have the institutional infrastructure or political will that would guarantee that it will not be just another honey pot for the ruling military-political elite. The potentially oil-bearing Cambodia–Thailand overlapping claims area in the Gulf of Thailand is a possible new bilateral flash point. Cambodia has already decided to triple its naval strength to defend its off-shore oil. This adds a new dimension to the resource conflicts in maritime Southeast Asia (chapter 5).

Indonesia

Shortly before the toppling of the authoritarian government of General Suharto in May 1998, Indonesia had been characterized as a "pivotal state," one whose future was poised at a critical turning point and whose fate would strongly affect regional and even global international relations.[2] Indonesia had become the dominant regional power in Southeast Asia, a major player in the East Asian and Pacific region, and a leader among the nations of the South. After a long struggle back from the political and economic disaster of the Sukarno years (chapter 3), in the Suharto era Indonesia finally felt itself accorded a position consonant with its geographic location, resource endow-ment, population, and political stability. What one long-time Indonesia watcher described as Jakarta's "sense of regional entitlement" was being real-ized in and beyond Southeast Asia.[3] All of this changed in the economic wreckage of the Crash of '97, which laid waste to Indonesia's financial sectors, and the ensuing political turmoil of the end of Suharto's presidency.

Through 2004, there were three successive governments of post-Suharto presidents: B. J. Habibie, Abdurrahman Wahid, and Megawati Sukarnoputri. Caught up in the upheaval of the transition from Suharto to the volatile poli-tics of democratization, their governments were characterized by leadership failure embedded in a pervasive culture of corruption, impunity, and the seek-ing of short-term advantage. Rather than a pivot of Southeast Asia, Indonesia became a problem—no longer a core for regional stability providing leadership in ASEAN. Its capability to act internationally to promote national interests was at its lowest point since the mid-1960s, and this as it faced critical eco-nomic, political, and religious challenges. The domestic political order was characterized by political drift and state decay. For economic rescue Indonesia turned to its international donor consortium, the World Bank–led Consulta-tive Group on Indonesia (CGI) and the International Monetary Fund (IMF).

Despite a slow and grudging compliance with the strictures put in place by the international financial community, aid continued to be pledged and dis-bursed even in the absence of meaningful reform. This suggests that, perhaps like Russia after the collapse of the communist regime, Indonesia was believed to be too big and important to be allowed to fail. As the post-Suharto govern-ments wrestled with the economy, they were also preoccupied with maintaining the integrity of the unitary republic. The lifting of the authoritarian controls of the Suharto years allowed ethnic and religious conflict to resurface politically. The emancipation of East Timor was seized upon as a model by separatist movements at both the western—Aceh—and eastern—Papua—extremities of the archipelago. The international context of these conflicts will be dealt with in greater detail in chapter 5.

Indonesia has the world's largest Muslim population with 88 percent of its 245 million people professing Islam. They are part of the *ummat*, the universal Muslim community, and are subject to the same political and emotional forces touching Muslims everywhere. Islamic fundamentalists, suppressed by the Suharto regime, rose to challenge the secular basis of the Indonesian state. Jema'ah Islamiyah (JI), a shadowy militant Islamic terrorist organization, emerged to carry out a violent struggle for the creation of an Islamic state in Indonesia. The JI is held responsible for the horrific October 2002 Bali blast and other attacks on Western soft targets. The JI shares with radical Islamists elsewhere in Southeast Asia a vision of a pan-Southeast Asian Islamic state. Like some other Islamist terrorist groups in Southeast Asia, the JI has been linked to Osama bin Laden's al-Qaeda group (chapter 6).

Since the Indonesian national elections in 2004, the bleak picture of Indonesia's future has been relieved. These elections gave a strong popular mandate to President Susilo Bambang Yudhoyono. He is Indonesia's first directly elected president. Under Yudhoyono, Indonesia now stands out as a Southeast Asian success story. The state is politically stable in a consolidating democracy.[4] The war in Aceh has been ended. Despite walking a fine political line with the Muslim community, the government has aggressively pursued counterterrorism, cooperating with, but without relying on, the United States, Australia, and other allies in the war on terror (chapter 6). As Yudhoyono approaches the end of his first term in 2009, he can also claim a degree of economic success with macroeconomic reforms leading to growing investor confidence and with a real GDP growth projection for 2007–2008 of more than 6 percent. Indonesia seems poised to rise from the political ashes of the Suharto regime and the false starts of the early post-Suharto governments to reassume its leading role in the region. After election to the UN Security Council in 2006, it has raised its voice again as an important and large Third World Muslim country. Its political stability, internal security, and improved economic performance, together with its inherent power factors of geostrategic position and population, provide a platform for Indonesia to claim again to be *primus inter pares* in ASEAN, thus regaining its "strategic centrality" in Southeast Asia.[5]

Laos (Lao People's Democratic Republic, LPDR)

Laos is Southeast Asia's only landlocked country. China, Vietnam, and Thailand compete for economic and political influence in Laos. At the cultural level, it is an unequal competition since the Thai and Lao share the same ethnic/linguistic and Buddhist background. With a long common Mekong River border, Thailand is Laos's dominant trade partner and source of private investment. After 1975, Laos was heavily dependent on Vietnam, but it now seeks to diversify its external ties. China has the second largest investment stake in the LPDR, ahead of Vietnam. The LPDR's relations with Vietnam and China are based less on ideology than the desire to keep the country from becoming a Thai dependency. Membership in ASEAN also helps to balance its relations within the region. A political irritant in LPDR–United States relations is low-level insurgent activity by elements of the Hmong ethnic minority, once allied with America in the Second Indochina War. The Laos government accuses Hmong refugees in the United States of supporting and financing the dissidents. In June 2007, U.S. federal agents arrested the former Hmong leader General Vang Pao and some followers for conspiring to forcefully topple the Vientiane government.

The LPDR is a diehard communist state. The Lao People's Revolutionary Party (LPRP) maintains an absolute monopoly of political power. There is barely the beginning of a rudimentary civil society. Laos began experimenting with free market reforms in 1986, but the pace of change is slow and grudging. The economy has been growing at a 6.5 percent rate since 2001, largely through the exploitation of national resources and tourism, but there is still a heavy dependence on foreign official development assistance (ODA). Laos is the hub of Mekong Basin development schemes focused on building infrastructure linking southwestern China to mainland Southeast Asia as well as exploiting hydroelectric generating potential for export to Thailand and Vietnam (chapters 4 and 9). The risk in the competition for Laotian resources is that Laos will become simply a platform for projects benefiting its neighbors with little developmental payoff for Laos itself. At the global level, Laos hopes to join the World Trade Organization (WTO) by 2010.

Malaysia

On 31 October 2003, Malaysia's long-serving prime minister, Dr. Mahathir bin Mohamad, handed over leadership to his deputy, Abdullah Ahmad Badawi. For more than two decades Malaysia's international role had been defined by Mahathir. For most of his career as Malaysia's prime minister, Mahathir operated in the international shadow of Indonesia's Suharto. Challenging Suharto's accommodation to the globalization agenda, Mahathir presented an alternative view for Southeast Asia. Rather than the inclusive loose trans-Pacific regionalism represented by the Asia-Pacific Economic Cooperation (APEC) forum, Mahathir championed an exclusively Asian economic grouping, the East Asia Economic Group (EAEG), which would have excluded the United States, Australia, and New Zealand (chapter 7). During the 1997–1998 Asian financial crisis, Mahathir defied international financial orthodoxy by refusing recourse to the IMF. His speeches were laced with the rhetoric of economic nationalism. Before Mahathir came to power, Malaysia was closely tied to Great Britain and Australia. Mahathir wrenched the country around with his "Look East" policy, which took as its economic model Japan and South Korea. Prime Minister Mahathir's verbal attacks on American policy were tempered by a pragmatic view of Malaysian national interest. There is no question but that Malaysia is a relative economic success story.

With Abdullah, what changed is not Malaysian national interests or even the policies that support interests, but a tone and style that is no longer outspokenly and deliberately confrontational with the West, particularly the United States. Unlike his predecessor, Abdullah is not vying for an international spotlight. Malaysia still looks east, particularly to China as a natural partner in Southeast Asia. Abdullah has promoted a vision of an East Asian Community that is more expansive than Mahathir's EAEG. Even though the United States is often the whipping boy for Malaysian nationalism, the bilateral relationship, while not filled with warmth, is reasonably good at the functional working levels. The United States is Malaysia's largest single trading partner and investor. Malaysia continues to try to project an international image of a modern Islamic state. Abdullah has picked up from Mahathir a prominent position in the Organization of the Islamic Conference (OIC). In addition to Malaysia's standard anti-Zionist positions and support for the Palestinians, Abdullah's government has cultivated close relations with Iran. Malaysia's foreign minister has said that Malaysia and Iran held "identical views" on a range of global issues including Iran's nuclear program.[6]

In part, the government's international Islamic activism is to burnish its credentials with a Malay electorate that has a clear choice between the "moderate" government party, the United Malays National Organization (UMNO), committed to a pluralist parliamentary democracy, and the fundamentalist Parti Islam se-Malaysia (PAS) whose goal is an Islamic state. Malaysia is a multiethnic state in which Malay Muslims make up 60 percent of the population; Chinese, 26 percent; Indians, 8 percent; and the balance, other minorities. The state is organized on the basis of Malay supremacy, in which the Malays are privileged by laws and policies that non-Malays view as politically, economically, socially, and culturally discriminatory. UMNO rules in a parliamentary coalition with smaller non-Malay ethnic parties. Sharpening ethnic divisions threaten the stability of the coalition as opposition minority parties charge that their ethnic interests are being sold out. Abdullah, like Mahathir before him, has shown that he is quite willing to use the draconian Internal Security Act (ISA) to suppress dissidents (chapter 8). Kuala Lumpur also has to accept the criticism of its human rights practices by Western democracies.

The contest between UMNO and PAS for the allegiance of Malay Muslims has also complicated relations with Malaysia's neighbors. There is sympathy among Muslim Malays for the causes of Islamic separatism in South Thailand, the southern Philippines, and earlier, Indonesia's Aceh province (chapter 5). At the state-to-state level, the government has acted properly, denying any official interference in the affairs of its ASEAN partners. At the same time, it cannot deny the aspirations of co-religionists at the peril of losing votes to its fundamentalist domestic opposition.

Elsewhere within ASEAN, Malaysia has a long list of bilateral issue areas. The more than four-decade dispute with the Philippines over sovereignty in Sabah is still unresolved. Malaysia's expulsion and treatment of thousands of illegal Indonesian and Filipino migrant workers has angered Manila and Jakarta. Malaysia is a contestant in the South China Sea jurisdictional struggle. For ASEAN's future, Malaysia's most important bilateral problem is the ongoing, bitterly vituperative, multi-issue economic, social, and political conflict with Singapore that tests the fundamental underpinnings of the "ASEAN way." These issues will be treated in detail in subsequent chapters. The sharpening ethnic divisions were reflected in March 2008 parliamentary elections. Disaffected Chinese and Indian voters joined Anwar's democratic activists to give the ruling coalitions their worst electoral setback since 1969. The opposition won more than a third of the parliamentary seats and took control of five Malaysian states, seriously weakening Abdullah's government.

Myanmar

Myanmar is Southeast Asia's only remaining military dictatorship. The army, known as the *tatmadaw*, has ruled since crushing democracy in 1990. The junta has exercised power first through the State Law and Order Council (SLORC) and, since 1997, the State Peace and Development Council (SPDC). It was the junta that changed the state's name from Burma to Myanmar and its capital Rangoon to Yangon. In 2005, the administrative capital was suddenly moved from Yangon to Nay Pyi Daw, deep in the central plain between Yangon and Mandalay. For the democratic world, the SPDC government is illegitimate, the product of a violent nullification of the 1990 election won by an 80 percent margin by the National League for Democracy (NLD) led by Aung San Suu Kyi, daughter of the martyred national hero Aung San. Since then, NLD partisans have been arrested, harried, and forced into exile. Aung San Suu Kyi remained under arrest until 1995. She was rearrested in 2000, released in May 2002, and rearrested again in June 2003. While a prisoner, she was awarded the 1991 Nobel Peace Prize.

Since 1993, the junta has sought a constitutional basis for its rule through a convention process that excludes the NLD and other opposition groups. Adjourned from 1996 to 2004, the convention was reinvigorated in 2006. In February 2008, the government announced a constitutional referendum to precede parliamentary elections in 2010, forestalling UN efforts to promote a dialogue between the SPDC and Aung San Suu Kyi's NLD (chapter 8). The junta's goal is to transfer nominal power to a proxy civilian government in which the military's dominant role will be institutionalized, its interests protected, and it would still retain an ultimate policy veto. Finally, there would be no accountability for the egregious and systematic violations of human rights by the military during its years of oppressing democratic and ethnic minority opposition. In the years since seven successive UN human rights special envoys began reporting on the junta's abuses in 1990, no progress toward democracy has been found. A violent assault by government forces in September 2007 on demonstrating Buddhist monks only reinforced to a shocked international audience the reality of the unchanging quality of a harsh and bloody regime (chapter 8).[7]

Myanmar's international relations have become inextricably intertwined with the struggle for democracy in Myanmar. Myanmar's relations with the West and the UN are discussed in detail in chapters 4 and 8. Here we note only that Myanmar has become a pariah state, ostracized by the liberal democratic West and serving as an embarrassment to its ASEAN partners. Cut off by sanctions from major Western sources of desperately needed foreign investment, assistance, and markets, Myanmar's economy has been badly managed as a corrupt and inefficient *tatmadaw* fiefdom. Except for the military and subservient civilian bureaucratic and business elite, the people are impoverished. Only a lifeline from China and revenue from the exploitation of Myanmar's natural resources keeps the economy afloat. Whatever benefits there are from the infusion of external capital in the competition for Myanmar's energy resources only helps the *tatmadaw* and its elite accomplices maintain their hold on the state. There is no trickle-down to the society at large.

The Philippines

For the first forty-five years of its existence as an independent republic, the Philippines enjoyed a "special relationship" with its former colonial ruler, the United States. For the United States, what was special was extensive military basing rights that made the Philippines a key element in the American strategy of forward deployment in Asia during the Cold War (chapter 3). That tie was severed in 1991, with the termination by the Philippines of the base agreements. New life was injected into the security relationship in 1999, when the Philippine Senate ratified a Visiting Forces Agreement (VFA) allowing the U.S. military again to exercise in the Philippines with the Philippine Armed Forces (PAF). In 2002, the United States deployed Special Forces to support the PAF in its campaign against the al-Qaeda-linked terrorist Abu Sayyaf Group (ASG) (chapter 6).

The twin Islamic separatist threats posed in the archipelago's south by the insurgent warriors of the Moro Islamic Liberation Front (MILF) and the Moro National Liberation Front (MNLF) are more threatening to the integrity of the Philippine state than the ASG. For almost four decades Manila has sought to defend the state's territorial unity from Muslim separatists while being sensitive to the concerns of Muslim ASEAN neighbors Indonesia and Malaysia. (The international dimension of Muslim separatism is dealt with in chapter 5.) The continuing struggle of the Communist Party of the Philippines (CPP) New People's Army (NPA) adds to the Philippines' insecurity. The CPP/NPA is the only remaining communist revolutionary insurgency in Southeast Asia. Although the government is determined to wipe the NPA out by 2010, the senior military leadership admits that this is unlikely given the commitment to the counterterrorist struggle in the south.

More than two decades after the democratic revolution that overthrew the Marcos dictatorship, the political stability and legitimacy of the Philippine government is again under siege. President Gloria Macapagal-Arroyo came to office in 2001 under the cloud of a quasi-coup and was elected president in 2004 in a fraudulent and corrupt process. Through 2007, there had been three efforts to impeach her. She has used Marcos-like maneuvers to ward off domestic opponents (chapter 8). To maintain power, Arroyo has forged an alliance with the military, which she has deemed the foundation of stability, but the military itself is not cohesive. During Arroyo's administration there have been three coup attempts.

For a beleaguered Arroyo government, the strategic link to the United States is vital both in terms of security assistance in its ongoing internal wars and as a mark of political support to President Arroyo herself. At the same time, she has undertaken high-profile efforts to hedge against U.S. disengagement by closer relations with China. The government has retreated from confrontation over China's forceful challenge to Philippine claims of sovereignty in the South China Sea (chapter 5). A host of Philippines–China economic agreements have been signed as trade delegations have gone back and forth during what has been called a "golden age" of bilateral economic ties. Some of the gold turned to dross in 2007, however, as the endemic corruption among the Filipino elite—including the president's husband and members of her administration—forced Manila to cancel four bribery-tainted Chinese investment and project deals. To ease the strain with China, President Arroyo met Chinese President Hu Jintao in Shanghai to explain the corruption scandal. At home, President Arroyo called on the military to stand behind her as new waves of protest against government corruption broke out in early 2008 calling for her resignation or impeachment.

Singapore

Security concerns animate Singapore's approach to international relations. It is, in the words of a Singapore analyst, "a very small island state perpetually haunted by its sense of vulnerability."[8] The ethnic dimension exaggerates its geostrategic vulnerability. It is a Chinese nut in the jaws of an Indonesian-Malaysian nutcracker. The independent state of Singapore was born in the political trauma of forced separation from Malaysia in 1965. The festering wounds of a messy divorce still impede normal relations between Malaysia and Singapore and continue to be a source of worrisome bilateral disputes (chapter 5).

Led at independence by Prime Minister Lee Kuan Yew, now minister-mentor to his son Prime Minister Lee Hsien Loong, Singapore's strategy for international survival is four-pronged. It has adhered to the principle that domestic political stability is the sine qua non of security and economic growth. To that end, the government has unrelentingly stifled political opposition through one-party electoral domination and application of its internal security act. There is a determination to use its human and technical resources to build an economy that would be a major regional player. Singapore strives to be the financial services, communications and information technology, and trading eye of Southeast Asia. In the metaphor of the "poison shrimp," Singapore has built a credible armed force with technical skills and weapons platforms second to none in ASEAN.

Singapore consciously practices balance-of-power politics so it is not isolated with bigger, and often unfriendly, neighbors. The island-state has been accused of using its economic and financial clout to disadvantage its ASEAN partners. Its highly visible relations with China, the United States, and India are part of that balance. Even though there is no formal United States–Singapore military alliance analogous to those that the United States has with Thailand and the Philippines, Singapore has been named a Major Security Cooperation Partner and, with a 2005 Strategic Framework Agreement, is perhaps the closest U.S. ally in Southeast Asia.[9] At the same time, Singapore has vigorously promoted itself to China as an exemplary model of the "administrative state" that can aid China's development.

Thailand

Historically, Thailand's foreign policy has been likened to the bending of bamboo in the wind, keeping its options open and siding with the stronger in its dealings with the great powers. During the imperialist period, the Thais tried to play off the French and the British. In World War II, the Thais used an alliance with initially victorious Japan to seize "lost" territory in Cambodia,

Laos, Burma, and Malaya. Although forced to retrocede the territories after the war, an exile Free Thai movement, however, mitigated postwar accountability to the allies. During the Cold War, Thailand, under a series of military dictatorships, opted to ally with the United States, rather than balance through nonalignment. Communist victories in the Indochina wars made Thailand ASEAN's frontline state with the American alliance for insurance. In the post–Cold War era, the alliance endured. It is demonstrated in the annual Cobra Gold Thai–American joint/combined military exercise, the largest in the region. In recognition of the depth and scope of the bilateral security relationship, President George W. Bush designated Thailand a major non-NATO ally in December 2003.

The American–Thai connection was shaken in September 2006, when Prime Minister Thaksin Shinawatra's democratically elected government was toppled by a military coup. Martial law was proclaimed and the most democratic constitution in Southeast Asia abolished. Thaksin had become prime minister of a coalition government in 2001. After elections in 2005, when his party, the Thai Rak Thai (TRT) won 376 of the 500 seats, he formed the first single-party majority government in Thailand's parliamentary history. A populist with strong rural backing, Thaksin challenged the entrenched Bangkok elites, including the military and royalists, who viewed their right to rule as an entitlement rather than a democratic reward. As Thaksin concentrated power in his hands, the army finally shut down the political system. The United States distanced itself from the Thai junta. The immediate bilateral consequence was the invocation of U.S. law prohibiting security assistance to a country whose elected government is deposed by a military coup. China quickly stepped in by offering a military assistance package to compensate for loss of U.S. funding. The junta welcomed China's support and understanding. The appointed prime minister, retired General Surayud Chulanont, traveled to China in May 2007, where he signed a five-year Joint Strategic Plan of Action covering a variety of programs of functional cooperation.

From the end of the Third Indochina War in 1991 (chapter 3), Thailand had viewed itself as the focal point of a stable Southeast Asian continental bloc. Thaksin's policy of "forward engagement," sometimes called "Thailand plus," was designed to make Thailand the energizing hub for subregional economic growth and development (chapter 4). Thaksin's self-assurance about Thailand's regional and international role was based on an appreciation of Thailand's political stability and economic growth as compared to the political and economic stagnation of its neighbors. In the months following the coup, however, such assurance quickly evaporated. The junta, through its appointed military and civilian managers, proved to be singularly unsuccessful and incompetent. Once the leader of Southeast Asia's "little tiger" economies,

Thailand's growth rate at 4.3 percent in 2007 trailed the region and was less than half that of major competitor Vietnam. Poorly conceived measures for a "sufficiency economy," as opposed to Thaksin's embrace of globalism, were disastrous for the economy. The World Bank's lead economist in Thailand minced no words, ascribing the poor performance to a "lack of policy clarity and policy direction."[10] Political uncertainty also roiled the economy as the junta tried to find a way to disengage from direct politics and move to behind-the-scenes control. During 2007, a junta-picked drafting commission wrote a new constitution. It was designed to prevent the reemergence of a strong popular leader, returning the Thai parliamentary system to a pattern of weak factionalized coalition governments of the past, and leaving real power in the hands of the traditional bureaucratic-military-royalist elite. The military also rammed through the junta's appointed National Legislative Assembly a new internal security law that gave sweeping domestic power to the military even in a postjunta elected parliamentary regime.

The first elections under the new constitution for the 480-seat parliament were held on 23 December 2007. Despite junta-supervised Electoral Commission obstacles and local intimidation, including martial law in thirty-three provinces, the TRT's populist successor, the People's Power Party (PPP), won a strong plurality, garnering 233 seats, just short of a majority. One of the platform planks was bringing Thaksin back. The outcome was interpreted as a popular repudiation of the junta. In January 2008, the PPP formed a coalition government dominated by Thaksin allies headed by Prime Minister Samak Sundaravej. The leader of the outgoing junta warned the new civilian leaders to be sensitive to military concerns. Former Prime Minister Thaksin returned from exile in February 2007, but fled again into exile in mid-2008 to avoid prosecution.

The new government was faced with the enormous internal security problem and foreign policy irritant of a Muslim separatist insurgency in Thailand's southern provinces (chapter 5). From January 2004 to the beginning of 2008, almost daily violence had taken over three thousand lives. One of the major indictments leveled by the military against Thaksin was that he had not brought peace to the south. In the year and a half of overt military rule, the war in the south widened and the violence intensified. The junta's insistence that the war against the insurgents could be won without concessions seemed self-defeating. The political instability and economic deterioration resulting from the coup mean that Thailand's role as a contender for regional leadership will not soon be recovered. This was acknowledged in January 2008 by incoming ASEAN Secretary-General Surin Pitsuwan, a former Thai foreign minister, who bemoaned the fact that because of its internal conflicts Thailand had lost its capability to contribute to regional development.[11]

Timor-Leste (East Timor)

Timor-Leste joined the Southeast Asian region as a fully independent actor on 20 May 2002 and shortly thereafter became the UN's 191st member. Its independence is noteworthy, husbanded as it was by a successful UN peacekeeping and political reconstruction mission. Ruled until 1974 by Portugal, it shares the island of Timor with Indonesia's West Timor, deep inside the Indonesian archipelago. After Portuguese authority collapsed in 1974, an East Timor nationalist declaration of independence was nullified by an Indonesian invasion and absorption of the territory as Indonesia's twenty-sixth province (chapter 3). Neither the East Timorese nor the international community recognized the legality of the act, although countries with major interests in Indonesia accepted the fact of the integration of East Timor into Indonesia. For a quarter of a century the UN General Assembly called for an internationally supervised act of self-determination. The Revolutionary Front for an Independent East Timor (FRETILIN, Frente Revolutionária do Timor Leste Independente) mounted an armed resistance challenging Indonesian military control. This was paralleled by an international advocacy campaign for East Timor's independence. Indonesian rule was harshly repressive. In 1999, after the fall of Indonesia's President Suharto, his successor, President B. J. Habibie, agreed to an internationally supervised referendum on the province's future.

On 30 August 1999, the East Timorese people overwhelmingly chose separation from Indonesia in a "popular consultation" supervised by the United Nations Mission in East Timor (UNAMET). A terrifying rampage by army-backed pro-Indonesian militias followed the referendum, killing hundreds of East Timorese, destroying infrastructure, and uprooting a quarter of the population. A UN-sanctioned intervention by the Australian-led International Force for East Timor (INTERFET) restored order and prepared the way for UN peacekeepers and the United Nations Transitional Administration in East Timor (UNTAET). For three years UNTAET worked to reconstruct economic and administrative structures and prepare the country for independence. UNTAET was succeeded by the United Nations Mission in Support of East Timor (UNMISET). The UNMISET mandate ended in May 2005 and it was succeeded by the United Nations Political Office in Timor-Leste (UNOTIL). Renewed political violence and civil strife in 2006 led to a second Australian-led peacekeeping intervention called the International Stabilization Force (ISF) and the UN Security Council's authorization of a fifth UN mission, the United Nations Integrated Mission in Timor-Leste (UNMIT) with an international police presence.

New elections in 2007 replaced the FRETILIN government with one led by former FRETILIN independence heroes José Ramos-Horta as president and Xanana Gusmão as prime minister. The government was shaken in February 2008 by a failed coup attempt that left President Ramos-Horta critically wounded. Australian military reinforcements for the ISF rushed to the country, and the government appealed to the UN Security Council for a continued and sustained UN presence in the country. The Security Council responded by unanimously extending UNMIT's mandate to February 2009.

Timor-Leste is Southeast Asia's poorest country, depending on ODA from donor nations organized in the World Bank–led Timor-Leste and Development Partners Meeting (TLDPM). Timor-Leste's long-term economic hopes are based on prospective oil and gas revenues from the Timor–Australia Timor Sea overlap (see discussion on Australia below). Timor-Leste's most important foreign policy task is to regularize its relations with Indonesia. This was initially complicated by the continued presence of East Timorese refugees in Indonesian West Timor (chapter 8) and issues of reconciliation over the postreferendum atrocities (chapter 8). A host of legal issues such as Indonesian assets, border demarcation, and maritime overlaps also remain to be settled through an Indonesia–Timor-Leste Joint Commission that first met in October 2002. Border demarcation will be completed by 2009. Timor-Leste is considered a possible future member of ASEAN. It acceded to ASEAN's Treaty of Amity and Cooperation (TAC) in January 2007. Unlike Papua New Guinea, Timor-Leste has not been accorded "special observer" status. Its foreign minister attends the annual ASEAN Ministerial Meeting as a guest of the chair. In 2007, Timor-Leste suggested a possible five-year preparatory period for entry in 2012. Whether ASEAN will be willing to accept membership of a possibly failing state remains to be determined.

Vietnam (Socialist Republic of Vietnam, SRV)

Vietnam's 1995 admission to ASEAN was the final act of regional political reconciliation following the Third Indochina War pitting communist Vietnam against noncommunist ASEAN over the future of Cambodia (chapter 3). Despite the political and economic gulf separating Vietnam from its new ASEAN partners, accession to the grouping with Hanoi's adoption of the ASEAN norms of international peace and cooperation symbolically heralded Vietnam's entrance into the Western market-oriented global system. Vietnam's rapid economic growth, at more than 8 percent annually, has increased its capabilities to promote its national interests as one of Southeast Asia's "little tigers" and is the basis of its emergence as an increasingly important actor in the regional balance of power. A new global presence was signified by Vietnam's election as one of the fifteen nonpermanent members of the UN Security Council for 2008–2009. As the World Bank Vietnam country director put it in 2007, "there is probably no country that, over the past 15 years, has moved its development so far and so fast."[12] But Vietnam's full participation in the global economy, signified by WTO membership in 2007, had to await the normalization of relations with the United States.

It took two decades from the end of the Second Indochina War—the Vietnam War—for the United States and Vietnam to have diplomatic relations. An important issue was Vietnamese cooperation in the search for Americans killed or missing in action during the war years. Even though bilateral relations continued to be marred by human rights issues (chapter 8), normalization was capped by President Bill Clinton's official visit to Vietnam in November 2000. After lengthy negotiations on economic and human rights issues, the U.S. Congress finally accorded Vietnam Permanent Normal Trade Relations (PNTR) status in 2006, which was the key to Vietnam's accession to the WTO. President George W. Bush's visit to Vietnam in 2006 was reciprocated by Vietnam President Nguyen Minh Triet's 2007 visit to the United States.

China, Vietnam's giant neighbor to the north, looms largest in Vietnam's geostrategic perceptions. Vietnam forged its historical national identity in centuries of struggle to resist Chinese hegemony. Vietnam's consciousness of being Southeast Asian, according to one historian, is not for its own sake, "but rather for the refreshment and reinforcement it provides in the grim business of maintaining the northern border."[13] It was grim in February 1979, when China briefly pushed its military across the border during the earliest stages of the Third Indochina War. Up until the collapse of the Soviet Union, communist-ruled Vietnam had relied on Moscow as its security patron. In the post–Cold War environment, Hanoi has adopted a mix of strategies to manage its relations with China.[14] On the bilateral level it has sought friendly and cooperative relations. The friction-ridden China–Vietnam 874-mile-long (1409 km) land border was settled in a 1999 agreement, followed by a process of demarcation and erection of border markers that is expected to be completed by the end of 2008. The border agreement was criticized by Vietnamese nationalists for ceding too many of the contested areas to China, but the tight political control exercised by the Vietnam Communist Party kept protest in check.

Vietnam's maritime borders have proven more difficult. Hanoi reached an agreement with China defining territorial seas and exclusive economic zones in the Tonkin Gulf in 2000. China refuses to discuss the Paracel Islands, which it seized from South Vietnam as the Second Indochina War was winding down. Vietnam's claims in the South China Sea, along with those of other ASEAN claimants, clash with China's (chapter 5). China's navy routinely intimidates or fires on Vietnamese fishing vessels in the contested waters. Up to a point, the Vietnamese government has tolerated anti-China protests by Vietnamese nationalists. In December 2007, Beijing warned Hanoi that anti-Chinese protests over issues in the South China Sea threatened to undermine the bilateral relationship, holding Hanoi responsible for preventing future disturbances. Vietnam still has maritime jurisdictional issues with Cambodia, and it was only in 2003 after thirty-two rounds of meetings spread over twenty-five years that it reached agreement with Indonesia over continental shelf borders.

Engagement and interdependence within ASEAN and as part of ASEAN in the various ASEAN + 3 functional frameworks give Vietnam's relations with China a broader regional framework. Furthermore, Vietnam has sought to balance its China connection with vital links with other great powers. Russia, the successor to Vietnam's former patron, the USSR, still has a stake in Vietnam. President Vladimir Putin signed a "strategic partnership" pact with Vietnam during his 2001 state visit. A key item was the Russian promise to aid in the modernization of the Vietnamese armed forces. Japan is a critical economic partner to Vietnam. Although the booming U.S.–Vietnam economic connection has received great attention, very quietly the two former adversaries have been constructing a stable bilateral political relationship that adds to the regional balance of power. Both Hanoi and Washington have added a strategic dimension to the development of their comprehensive interactions. This was explicit in the United States' December 2006 authorization of defense sales to Vietnam in which it was deemed that "[the] furnishing of defense articles and defense services to Vietnam will strengthen the security of the United States and promote world peace."[15]

Extraregional State Actors

The United States

Depending on geopolitical perspective, the United States' role in Southeast Asia has been variously described as contributing to a stable international order; essential to the regional balance of power; a benign hegemony; or imperialism. Whatever the characterization, there is no disagreement with the fact that since 1945, the United States has been the dominant great power external influence on international relations in Southeast Asia. The implementation of American global political/military strategy of Cold War containment of communism was consequential to the political and economic development of all of Southeast Asia (chapter 3). The focus of that strategy was American security interests. With the ending of the Cold War, the global threat posed by a bipolar confrontation with the Soviet Union no longer is the basis for United States–Southeast Asian relations. Replacing it in the immediate post–Cold War period was a vague, loosely formulated strategic concept initially articulated by President Bill Clinton in his 1993 vision of a Pacific Community resting on three pillars: economic growth, political democracy, and security.[16]

The geoeconomic dimension of American post–Cold War strategy in Southeast Asia has been characterized by efforts to advance the American economic agenda of international trade and investment liberalization. This was to be achieved in Southeast Asia through bilateral trade agreements and the open and inclusive Pacific regionalism of the Asia-Pacific Economic Cooperation (APEC) structure. The succeeding Bush administration, prodded by the awareness of a rising China, gave increased attention to ASEAN regionalism. It promoted an enhanced U.S.–ASEAN economic relationship, the first fruit being the 2006 ASEAN–United States Trade and Investment Framework Agreement (TIFA). In 2006, the United States was ASEAN's largest export market and was tied with Japan as ASEAN's second largest import source. The United States was second only to Japan as a source of foreign direct investment (FDI) in ASEAN. The United States resists what it sees as closed and exclusionary regionalism in ASEAN + 3 (China, Japan, and South Korea) arrangements or the proposed East Asia Economic Community (EAEC). Chapter 7 discusses frameworks for Southeast Asian economic relations.

Although the Cold War has ended, U.S. security interests in the region as the preponderant power, or as the balancer in a balance of power, are considered to require continued strategic access to and through the region. This is provided by the U.S. Seventh Fleet, based in Japan but with "places not bases" in Southeast Asia, and the traditional alliances with the Philippines and Thailand and strategic partnership with Singapore. A major hole in the pattern of U.S. security relations in Southeast Asia had been the disruption in defense relations with Indonesia because of the Indonesian military's human rights record. The defense relationship was fully restored by 2006 in Indonesian President Yudhoyono's democratizing administration.

The 9/11 attack and the war on terror led to direct American involvement in and support for counterterrorism in Southeast Asia (chapter 6). The joining of the United States and vulnerable Southeast Asian states in a joint struggle against elusive terrorist enemies meant that, after more than a quarter century, U.S interests in Southeast Asia were visible to the American public. The visibility to Southeast Asian publics of the United States in the Southeast Asian front of the war on terror, particularly as it was linked to the invasion of Iraq, was strongly opposed by Muslim populations. It was also criticized by non-Muslims concerned about great power unilateralism undermining the authority and legitimacy of the United Nations, which most Southeast Asian leaderships see as a bulwark for the security of small nations.

It has been the American concentration on the war on terror and Iraq and Afghanistan that has led critics in Southeast Asia to argue that the United States has neglected its broader, and in the longer-run perhaps more important, interests, allowing China to fill a vacuum. American disengagement from

Southeast Asia's real interests, they argue, has created opportunities for Chinese "soft power," as Southeast Asian statesmen try to hedge or balance against a future with a reduced American presence. The United States, unlike ASEAN's other dialogue partners, has refused to sign the ASEAN Treaty of Amity and Cooperation (TAC). America's disengagement seemed underlined to Southeast Asia in 2007 when the secretary of state did not attend the ASEAN postministerial conference or the ASEAN Regional Forum; the president twice promised and twice cancelled an ASEAN–U.S. summit meeting to celebrate the thirtieth anniversary of the ASEAN–U.S. official dialogue partnership; and the assistant secretary of state for East Asia and the Pacific did not take part in the twentieth ASEAN–U.S. dialogue. Even though there were good reasons for the absences or cancellations, the impression left was that ASEAN's priority was not as high in fact as official rhetoric suggested.

The priority given by the United States to the war on terror has also, critics argue, negatively spilled over onto the American political agenda of democratization and human rights in Southeast Asia. In prosecuting the war on terror, the United States has condoned, and in fact praised, internal security regulations that are applied not just to suspected terrorists but also to civil society advocacy groups and opposition democratic activists. The American desire to maintain the alliances with the Philippines and Thailand despite the political and human rights records of their militaries and the erosion of what were once vibrant democracies can be contrasted with the American campaign against the Myanmar junta (chapter 8).

People's Republic of China (PRC)

Once viewed suspiciously by Southeast Asian leaders, China now is seen as a responsible major actor to which the future of Southeast Asia is crucially linked. Even so, there remains an undercurrent of concern about the PRC's ultimate political, military, and territorial ambitions. To allay these concerns, a steady stream of high-level official Chinese delegations has toured the ASEAN capitals for over a decade with a focused message of common interest in regional peace and stability. A proliferation of bilateral and multilateral engagements is reorienting Southeast Asia's patterns of relations as ASEAN states accommodate a rising and proximate China.

In the background of the Southeast Asia–China relationship is a historical memory of the traditional Confucian world order in which the countries of the Nanyang—the southern ocean —were considered by the Dragon Throne to be tribute-bearing vassals. The 1949 appearance of the PRC as a regional state actor led to fears that aggressive Chinese communism might be a Marxist-Leninist-Maoist version of the traditional order. Indigenous Maoist revolutionary warfare against Southeast Asian governments from the 1950s into the 1980s gave substance to these fears. Moreover, the Chinese minorities with divided loyalties in host Southeast Asian countries were viewed as potential Trojan horses.

Contemporary post-Marxist China—although in politics still Leninist—has demonstrated to Southeast Asia that in most respects China is a "normal" country behaving in accordance with accepted international norms. While it does not yet rival the United States in military power and political and economic reach, there is a sense in Southeast Asia that inevitably China—so large and so geographically close—will be the power to be reckoned with in the future. It is the need to adapt to that future that informs the present day Southeast Asia–China relationship. China's growing economic strength immediately engages Southeast Asia. The Chinese economy with its 8 percent real growth rate competes with Southeast Asia in global markets and sucks up foreign direct investment from Japan and the West. In the long run, unless there are structural adjustments in Southeast Asian economies, a booming, lower-cost China could hollow out Southeast Asia's export manufacturing industries. Rather than competition, China and ASEAN are, at Chinese initiative, seeking closer economic integration, which holds either the promise of benefiting both sides or the threat of Southeast Asia becoming a Chinese market and resource hinterland.

Expanding China–ASEAN economic relations are paralleled in the political sphere. China has imposed political discipline on Southeast Asia with respect to Taiwan. Taiwan has an active economic presence in the ASEAN region, but the ASEAN states unquestioningly accept that Taiwan is part of China. Efforts by Taipei to utilize its "Go South" investment and trade policy to promote a heightened political profile have been rebuffed. In his state visit to Indonesia in July 2002, Chinese Vice President, now President, Hu Jintao announced a "new security concept" for Asia. He dismissed "Cold War mentality, hegemony, and power politics" in favor of an approach that would "ensure genuine mutual respect, mutual cooperation, consensus through cooperation and peaceful settlement of disputes rather than bullying, confrontation, and imposition of one's will upon others."[17] From Hu's podium, the obvious, but unnamed, promoter of the discredited old security concept was the United States. China picked up this theme when it associated itself with the ASEAN states that opposed the American war in Iraq, denouncing American unilateralism and its assumed role of global policeman.

China's first participation in international peacekeeping was the dispatch of a small detachment of civil police officers to East Timor to serve under UNTAET. China also joins the ASEAN chorus championing the principle of noninterference in issue areas on the West's social and political rights agenda. China has ratified the TAC. The proof for ASEAN of China's intention to abide by ASEAN's rules of the peace game will be found in the South China Sea jurisdictional contest where China has already used force against ASEAN states (chapter 5). China's closest relationship in Southeast Asia is with Myanmar, which has become a kind of Chinese client. Despite urgings by ASEAN leaders, China's leadership has been reluctant to use its influence to try to modify the Myanmar junta's oppression of the Burmese people.

From the Southeast Asian vantage, the central question of the future structure of great power involvement in the region will be the evolution of the U.S.–China relationship. It is understood in ASEAN capitals that, as China's economic and military power grows, the United States cannot maintain the same level of preponderance it once enjoyed. However, American interests and capabilities will still make it a major actor. The issue for the ASEAN states is not the relativity of power, but whether the United States will accommodate to a real balance of power with China or seek to contain its rising power. The last thing that Southeast Asian leaders want is to be forced to choose between the two in the event of a U.S.–PRC conflict of interest, for example, in the Taiwan Strait.

Japan

The rise of China's power profile in Southeast Asia has led to a sense that East Asian regional leadership has been psychologically transferred from Tokyo to Beijing. Japan had once been the economic engine for Southeast Asia's growth. Its trade relations, FDI, and ODA made it the region's principal economic partner. The oft-quoted metaphor describing Japan's role was that of the "flying geese," with Japan at the head of the V and the rest of Asia following behind in the different echelons of the regional division of labor. Japan's vision of its role in Southeast Asia was encapsulated in the 1977 Fukuda Doctrine, enunciated in a speech by Prime Minister Takeo Fukuda during a visit to ASEAN states. In it, Japan foreswore a military role; defined Japan–Southeast Asian relations as an equal partnership based on mutual confidence and trust; and promised assistance to build prosperity and strengthen ASEAN to help establish a stable regional international order. In the Cold War era, under the American security umbrella, Japan maximized its regional economic power without political and military concerns.

In the post–Cold War world, however, Japan seemed more like a wounded goose rather than the leader of the flock, caught in economic stagnation, a ballooning debt, and an aging population in a demographic trajectory toward significant population decline. While Japan is still an important player in the Southeast Asian economies, its future leadership role can be questioned (chapter 7). With reference to Japan's Prime Minister Yasuo Fukuda, son of Takeo

Fukuda, ASEAN Secretary-General Surin Pitsuwan in March 2008 called for a "Fukuda II" doctrine. Japan has sought to influence noneconomic areas of international relations in Southeast Asia through targeted investments in regional peace and stability. Japan is the largest economic assistance contributor to Cambodia and Timor-Leste. Japan's special interest in the Mekong Basin region is discussed in chapter 4. Japan also had limited participation in UN peacekeeping operations in Cambodia and East Timor. Tokyo hosted the conference to pledge aid to restore Indonesia's war-torn Aceh province. It has promised grants to help bring peace to the southern Philippines.

Japan's security role in Southeast Asia is essentially limited to hosting the U.S. military forces that are the main component of American forward deployment in Asia. Although the residual emotions about Japan's role in World War II are not as close to the surface in Southeast Asia as they are in China and Korea, Japan hesitates about any projection of an assertive regional policy backed by hard power even if it should be freed from domestic constitutional and public opinion constraints. Because of its energy dependencies, Japan has a vital interest in freedom of navigation through the South China Sea although it has no real capability to influence the resolution of the jurisdictional disputes there (chapter 5). Japan has cooperated with the relevant Southeast Asian states in developing measures to combat piracy in the vital straits' choke points and in the war on terror (chapter 6).

The greatest challenge to Japan's relative power position in Southeast Asia is the rise of China. The argument can be made that Sino–Japanese rivalry in Southeast Asia may have more impact on ASEAN than United States–China competition. If the decade-long trend of Chinese growth and Japanese relative decline continues, Japan could be relegated to a secondary role in Southeast Asia. Since 2002, Japan has sought to balance and preempt China's efforts to build Southeast Asian platforms for China-centric regional integration. Japan's alternative is an East Asia Economic Community. Part of the problem, however, is that real East Asia institution building cannot take place without China and Japan putting behind them their historical, political, and territorial issues. The tension-fraught Japan–China relationship has enabled ASEAN to balance between them in its claim to be the driver in command of regionalization. In December 2007, Prime Minister Fukuda made what has been called an historic visit to China during which both sides welcomed the warming of relations. In a major policy speech at Peking University, Fukuda called for a "mutually beneficial relationship based on common strategic interests" in which they in "creative partnership" could forge a bright future for Asia.[18] If there were to be such a partnership, ASEAN would find itself on the sidelines, unable to be a balancing go-between. Japan's full commitment to an East Asian identity, however, can be questioned as it continues to tout its "values-based diplomacy," aligning it with the United States, Australia, India, and the EU.

On the Margins

Australia

Australia's role in Southeast Asia is viewed ambivalently on both sides of the relationship. On the one hand, Australia has sought to define itself economically and quasi-politically as an Asian state. On the other hand, it has explicitly identified the United States as its vital security partner. Malaysia's former Prime Minister Mahathir was the most trenchant critic of Australia's Asian pretension while at the same time claiming to act as the American deputy sheriff in the region. The November 2007 election of Australian Labor Party leader Kevin Rudd as prime minister will probably lead to greater balance in Australia's commitments to the region.

The most problematic of Australia's relations in Southeast Asia is with Indonesia. Although it is officially downplayed, there is a latent "northern threat" syndrome in Canberra inherent in the geostrategic setting of densely populated Indonesia sitting just above thinly populated northern Australia. Both sides have sought to manage the relationship in terms of stability. Australian policy is founded on the premise that Indonesia is more important to Australia than Australia is to Indonesia. This was clear in twenty-five years of Australian policy toward East Timor. Vociferous domestic critics not withstanding, Australian governments refused to link East Timor to other aspects of Australian-Indonesian relations. Australia even gave official recognition to Indonesian sovereignty in East Timor in return for a generous Timor Sea border agreement. A broader perception of Australia's interest was cemented in a 1995 bilateral agreement that placed Australia's security relationship with Indonesia on essentially the same political level as those within the FPDA.

The Indonesian connection was badly frayed by the 1999 East Timor crisis. Jakarta felt betrayed by Australia's about-face on Indonesian sovereignty in the province. Australians viewed their lead in INTERFET as a UN-mandated humanitarian rescue of the East Timorese. Indonesian nationalists portrayed it as a new colonialism. The first bilateral casualty was the 1995 security agreement. Denunciation of Australia became a staple of Indonesian political life. Tragically, some Indonesians saw the terrorist murder of scores of young Australians in the 2002 Bali terrorist bomb blast as some kind of payback. Ironically, it was in part the need for counterterrorism cooperation that led to a new warming in bilateral relations as well as Indonesia's desire for inclusive regionalism in East Asia beyond an ASEAN + 3 format. A new chapter in the bilateral relationship was opened with the signing in 2006 and ratifications in 2007 of the Lombok Pact providing for cooperation in a wide range of security and defense related activities. The key for Indonesia was the mutual pledge not to support in any manner the activities of any person or entity that constitute a threat to the stability, sovereignty, or national integrity of the other party, including those who seek to use its territory to encourage or commit separatism in the territory of the other party. The Indonesian goal was to isolate Papuan separatists from an Australian support base. In that case, Indonesia is likely to be disappointed, since it is unlikely that any Australian government would act to prohibit the free speech of advocates of West Papuan independence let alone turn over to Indonesia Papuan political asylum seekers.[19]

Substantial Australian commitments, including armed forces, will continue to be necessary for building the new nation of Timor-Leste. The February 2008 rush of reinforcements to the Australian-led International Stabilization Force underlined this. A critical bilateral issue was the division of revenues from the gas fields in the Timor Sea's jurisdictional overlaps. The negotiations between Australia and, first, UNAMET and then the Timor-Leste government were protracted and difficult. Development was stalled until the conclusion of the Timor Sea Treaty in 2006. Timor-Leste was favored in a 90–10 percent split in the Bayu Undan field in the joint development area (JDA). Over the life of the field, it is expected to yield a revenue flow to Timor-Leste of up to $3 billion. Canberra delayed ratification of the treaty until Dili gave up its claim of 50 percent of the much larger Sunrise field, most of which lies outside the JDA, accepting an 80–20 percent split in favor of Australia. Australia's hard-nosed bargaining and refusal to accept arbitration was viewed by many Timorese and Australians as a betrayal of Timor-Leste's future.[20]

India

A founding member with Burma, Cambodia, and Indonesia of the Non-aligned Movement, India later blotted its copybook in Southeast Asia by taking the wrong side on two international issues important to ASEAN. India backed the Soviet Union's invasion of Afghanistan and Vietnam's invasion and occupation of Cambodia (chapter 3). New Delhi's strategic perceptions were fastened on China's ties to Pakistan and Cambodia. As a result, until the end of the Cold War, ASEAN remained cool to Indian overtures for closer association. India, with an eye to China's heightened profile in Southeast Asia, has its own geostrategic and economic interests in the region, and New Delhi has watched warily as China has forged regional and bilateral partnerships with the ASEAN states. China's rise has stimulated India's own "Look East" policy toward Southeast Asia. India's security concerns have been demonstrated by its naval deployments to the South China Sea and Strait of Malacca, and defense cooperation agreements with Singapore, Malaysia, and Indonesia; all while denying that this was part of a strategy to counter China.

Indian arms transfers and military training for Myanmar's military have greatly concerned human rights advocates. India's infrastructure projects include linking India's Mizoram state to Myanmar's Arakan state. India's desire to win access to Myanmar's energy resources has brought it into direct competition with China. New Delhi's diplomatic wooing of the Myanmar junta and abandonment of support for democracy in Myanmar have not had the hoped-for policy payoff. China is the junta's preferred partner. In the international politics of the India–Myanmar–China triangle, the junta understands that China, with its growing power and UN Security Council veto, is a stronger patron.

In addition to cultivating enhanced bilateral ties with ASEAN states, India has become part of ASEAN's regional network. Its eventual goal is to have the same standing in ASEAN as China. Ever mindful of the balance of power, Singapore has been the strongest Southeast Asian advocate for close ASEAN–India relations. India is an official ASEAN dialogue partner with an annual ASEAN + 1 Summit. It is also a member of ASEAN Regional Forum (ARF). In 2003, New Delhi acceded to the ASEAN TAC. India was finally admitted into the Asia–Europe Meeting (ASEM) in 2006. India and ASEAN signed a framework agreement in 2003 for a regional free trade agreement (RTA), but in tough negotiations no RTA had been reached by the end of 2007 (chapter 7). India is also linked to ASEAN states in three overlapping trade- and investment-focused multilateral organizations: the Bay of Bengal Initiative for Multi-Sectoral Economic Cooperation (BIMSTEC), Mekong–Ganga Cooperation group (MGC), and the Indian Ocean Rim Association for Regional Cooperation (IOR-ARC) (chapter 4).

Papua New Guinea (PNG)

PNG's primary cultural identification is Melanesian, and its regional orientation is toward Australia, New Zealand, and the South Pacific. Its primary multilateral regional organization is the Pacific Island Forum (until 2000, the South Pacific Forum). In 1981 it was given observer status in ASEAN, and in 1987 it was the first non-ASEAN state to accede to the TAC. It considers itself a prospective member of ASEAN. The PNG concept is of Port Moresby being the bridge between ASEAN and the South Pacific. ASEAN's real value to Port Moresby is connected to PNG's more compelling bilateral relationship with Indonesia.

PNG shares a more than 509-mile-long (820 km) land border with Indonesia, dividing the island of New Guinea roughly in half. From its 1974 independence from Australian trusteeship, relations with Indonesia have been dominated by Indonesian suasion, diplomacy, and intimidation to prevent the PNG side of the border from becoming a sanctuary for Free Papua Movement (OPM) separatist insurgents (chapter 5). Border sensitivity is heightened by the West Papuan refugee camps strung out its east side (chapter 8). Successive governments in Port Moresby, while sympathetic to their Melanesian brothers' struggle, realized that a more powerful Indonesia would not hesitate to use self-help measures if PNG did not cooperate on border security. Part of PNG's deference to Indonesia's security concerns is the waning of any residual defense links between it and Australia. An Indonesia–PNG basic border agreement was reached in 1979, and revised and extended in 2003. It prohibits the border areas from being used as "sanctuaries, staging areas, bases, or for illegal activities." In 1986 the two countries negotiated a Treaty of Mutual Respect, Cooperation, and Friendship that functions as a nonaggression pact unique in Indonesia's bilateral relations. Both governments have demonstrated that they want peaceful and cooperative relations. Indonesian–PNG relations would be sorely tested if the OPM's insurgency should intensify or if the PNG, because of poor governance, becomes incapable of carrying out the responsibilities it has assumed in relation to border security.

Russia

Although Russia is not the great power actor in Southeast Asia that its predecessor the Soviet Union was, under President Vladimir Putin Russia still makes its presence known, not willing to simply leave great power visibility to China, Japan, and the United States. Russia is a dialogue partner of ASEAN and has acceded to the TAC. Moscow's determination to remain regionally relevant was given a boost in June 2003 by the signing of a "Joint Declaration" for an ASEAN–Russian Federation partnership to enhance Russia's cooperative engagements with ASEAN over the full spectrum of ASEAN's interests.[21] Russia held its first ASEAN + 1 Summit in 2005. Russia's greatest bilateral visibility in Southeast Asia has been in weapons sales. The high point of Indonesian President Megawati's state visit to Russia in April 2003 was the signing of a countertrade deal for four Russian Sukhoi combat aircraft. During Putin's official visit to Malaysia in August 2003, a deal for eighteen Sukhoi jet fighters was completed. Both the Indonesians and Malaysians (and for the Russians, hopefully other Southeast Asian nations) see Russia as an alternative, and cheaper, source for high-technology weapons platforms than the United States. In Bangkok for the 2003 APEC Summit, Putin and Thai Prime Minister Thaksin signed two agreements. One involved the repayment of a Russian debt. The other was a military logistics agreement paving the way for Thai military acquisition of Russian military equipment. Russia's special attention to Indonesia was underlined by President Yudhoyono's 2006 visit to Moscow and Putin's return visit to Jakarta in 2007 for the signing of a more than $1 billion arms deal.

Nonstate Actors

For purposes of this discussion, by nonstate actor we mean an intergovern-mental or nongovernmental (NGO) agency or organization with a program of international activity defined independently of any state actor or subgroup of state actors.

The United Nations System

The United Nations and its specialized agencies have been active in South-east Asia beginning with the decolonization process itself. Indonesian inde-pendence from the Netherlands was facilitated through the fifteen-member UN Security Council as was the transfer of sovereignty of Dutch New Guinea to Indonesia. It was the Security Council that authorized UNTAC in Cambo-dia and UNTAET in East Timor. The continuing UN missions in Timor-Leste have required Security Council action. In addition to the five permanent members of the Security Council—China, France, Great Britain, Russia, and the United States—there are ten nonpermanent members. The nonperma-nent members are elected to two-year terms by secret ballot by a two-thirds majority of the 192-member General Assembly. The candidates for the non-permanent seats are drawn from regional groups with the African-Asian group allocated five seats. Every year, five seats are contested. In 2006, In-donesia was elected for a 2007–2008 period, and in 2007 Vietnam was elected to a 2008–2009 seat. The year 2008 was the first time that two Southeast Asian states held Security Council seats at the same time. Vietnam, which had been campaigning for a seat since 1997, celebrated its election as prestige-building proof of its rising global profile.[22] From the Southeast Asian vantage, however, perhaps the most important member of the Security Council is veto-wielding China.

In the General Assembly, where sovereign equality is demonstrated by one-country one-vote, the pattern of Southeast Asia's voting is similar to that of India, China, and other Asian and African members. UNGA overall voting co-incidence with the United States in 2006 was 23.6 percent and the ASEAN na-tions 20 percent.[23] The ASEAN members' caucus tends to vote as a bloc on is-sues affecting the region or a member: supporting Indonesia in its East Timor province and Myanmar against U.S. efforts to sanction the junta.

The fifty-four-member United Nations Economic and Social Council (ECOSOC) has oversight over the organization's specialized agencies, pro-grams, and funds for development assistance and other social and eco-nomic issue areas. The members are elected for three-year overlapping terms with the Asia grouping allocated eleven seats. In 2008, the Southeast

Asian members with term expiry dates were Indonesia (2009), Malaysia (2010), and the Philippines (2009). In Southeast Asia, ECOSOC's work is carried out by the United Nations Economic and Social Commission for Asia and the Pacific (ESCAP) headquartered in Bangkok. UN specialized agencies like the Food and Agriculture Organization (FAO) and the World Health Organization (WHO) have been deeply engaged in technical assistance and regional economic development. The former has worked for food self-sufficiency in Southeast Asia; the latter is most lately known for its work in the SARS, HIV/AIDS, and avian flu epidemics. The United Nations Development Program (UNDP), working with ESCAP and the Asian Development Bank (ADB), plays an important role in progress toward human security in Southeast Asia, particularly the achievement of the Millennium Development Goals (MDG) (chapter 8).

Two other UN agencies have been active in human security matters in Southeast Asia. The UN High Commissioner for Refugees (UNHCR) plays an important role in providing for refugee relief, resettlement, and repatriation. Despite its humanitarian mission, the UNHCR often finds itself colliding with agents of host governments. The office of the United Nations High Commissioner for Human Rights (UNHCHR) has had a particularly testy relationship with Southeast nations aggrieved by its activities and reporting. Both its and the UNHCR's work are detailed in chapter 8. Finally, the secretaries-general themselves have acted as agents for political change in Southeast Asia. Both former Secretary-General Kofi Annan and his successor, Ban Ki Moon, have used their post as bully pulpits to urge recalcitrant Southeast Asian nations like Cambodia and Myanmar to abide by the commitments to the norms and goals they accepted as members of the United Nations.

International Financial Institutions (IFI)

As World War II ended, two important international financial institutions were founded: the International Bank for Reconstruction and Development (IBRD), now the core of the World Bank Group, and the International Monetary Fund (IMF). Their original purpose was to promote economic recovery from war's destruction and rebuild the international economic system. Over time, their mandates expanded to include economic development and financial stability in the newly independent countries produced by decolonization. Since the Asian economic crash of 1997–1998, both the World Bank and the IMF have had greater visibility in international relations in Southeast Asia. Domestic economic nationalists have opposed their market-oriented, liberal capitalist economic doctrine that reflects what is known as the "Washington consensus."

The World Bank Group

The World Bank Group consists of the IBRD, the International Development Association (IDA), the International Finance Corporation (IFC), the Multilateral International Guarantee Agency (MIGA), and the International Centre for the Settlement of Investment Disputes. The United States, the Bank's largest shareholder, has always provided the Bank's president. The IBRD and IDA are a major source for development assistance in Southeast Asia. Indonesia is the largest single regional client. Table 2.1 shows the World Bank's cumulative lending in Southeast Asia through fiscal year 2006. Historically the Bank has concentrated on infrastructure development, which has made it a target for environmentalist activists and NGOs. This is particularly the case in Southeast Asia, where World Bank support for large-scale dam development in Southeast Asia has been vigorously protested (chapter 9). More recently, the World Bank has invested in capacity building including governance and human capital. The Bank works in close cooperation with individual donor nations and coordinates consultative donor groups, among others, the Consultative Group for Cambodia (CGC), which in 2007 became the Cambodia Development Cooperation Forum (CDCF); the Timor-Leste and Development Partners Meetings (TLDPM); and the Consultative Group for Vietnam (CGV). Until the Indonesian government decided in January 2007 that it was ready to "graduate" from World Bank– and donor-monitored development consultation, the Consultative Group on Indonesia (CGI), the 1992 successor to the Inter-Governmental Group on Indonesia (IGGI), had been a model of World Bank-coordinated economic assistance harmonization.

TABLE 2.1
World Bank Cumulative Southeast Asia Loans through June 2006
(Value in U.S. $ Millions)

Country	IBRD	IDA	Total
Cambodia		659.2	659.2
Indonesia	29,313.9	2,110.3	1,424.2
Laos		835.9	835.9
Malaysia	4,145.6		4,145.6
Myanmar	33.4	804.0	837.4
Philippines	11,913.2	294.2	12,207.4
Singapore	181.3		181.3
Thailand	8,027.4	125.1	8,152.5
Timor-Leste		16.5	16.5
Vietnam		6,327.7	6,327.7
Total	53,614.8	11,172.9	64,787.7

Source: World Bank Annual Report 2006.

The International Monetary Fund (IMF)

The original mission of the IMF was to promote foreign exchange stability and assist in balance-of-payment difficulties. It is now a critical player in managing financial rescues of failing economies. The Fund's support comes with conditions relating to performance and structural reforms directed to underlying causes of poor economic performance. It closely monitors a client country's performance against its agreements with the Fund as set out in quarterly "letters of intent" to which both sides have to agree. Critics argue that the IMF's emphasis on fiscal discipline, free markets, and privatization ignores the social and human needs of impoverished populations to whom government austerity and laissez-faire economics mean greater pain. The IMF has been the target of antiglobalists who reject its explicit commitment to integrating Southeast Asian economies into the global market system. Conditionality on the terms of loans and disbursement are attacked as a new form of Western colonialism.

The IMF's intervention in the financial crisis of 1997–1998 led to different national reactions. Thailand, where the trouble started, was bailed out by a $17.2 billion loan. Thailand successfully emerged from the IMF's oversight regime, paying off the over $12 billion it had actually borrowed by 2003. This was two years in advance of the scheduled payment. Malaysia, on the other hand, refused IMF aid and all the strings attached. It crafted its own rescue, allowing Prime Minister Mahathir to challenge the "Washington consensus." Indonesia at first resisted the IMF's stabilization plan, but was forced to accept a program that went beyond simply financial restructuring but aimed at reform of the economy as a whole. Grudging acceptance of the IMF's demands played a role in ending Suharto's rule. Prominent politicians denounced the government's subservience to the economic discipline demanded by the foreign lenders. Between 1997 and 2003, Indonesia had received $25 billion in standby loans. As the 2004 general election date approached, voices in President Megawati's party called for independence from the IMF. The government temporized. It decided not to extend the IMF's programmatic role but to enter an IMF postprogram monitoring arrangement (PPM). The last $3 billion of Indonesia's debt obligations were paid off in 2006, in advance of the 2010 due date, allowing it to free itself from the PPM.

Asian Development Bank (ADB)

The Manila-headquartered ADB was founded in 1966 as a regional multilateral development lending institution. It has sixty-seven country members—forty-eight regional states and nineteen outside the region. The United States and Japan are the largest financial backers of the ADB, with subscrip-

TABLE 2.2
Asian Development Bank Southeast Asia Cumulative
Lending and Disbursement to End of 2006 (Value in U.S. $ Millions)

Country	Lending	Disbursement
Cambodia	912.24	619,14
Indonesia	21,513.30	16,138.83
Laos	1,218.34	990.53
Malaysia	1,987.54	1,408.98
Myanmar	530.86	411.83
Philippines	9,219,03	7,116,92
Thailand	5,388.97	4,204.65
Vietnam	1,040.56	2,139.23
Total	44,839.94	33,025.11

Source: ADB Annual Report 2006.

tions of nearly $16 million. Japan always provides the president of the ADB. In 2006, it approved $7.4 billion for loans for sixty-seven projects, of which $1.8 billion went to Southeast Asia. Its largest loan grant ever of $1.1 billion was made in 2007 for a four-lane highway linking Hanoi with Kunming in China's Yunnan province. Table 2.2 shows the cumulative ADB lending to Southeast Asia through 2006.

International Non-Governmental Organizations (INGO)

INGOs can be roughly divided into three groups. First, there are the international philanthropic institutions and foundations devoted to broad programming for economic, social, and political development. Both the Ford Foundation and the Asia Foundation have operated from field offices in Southeast Asia for decades. More recently, the Soros Foundation's Open Society Institute has been making grants targeting eight Southeast Asian states. Another set of INGOs is functionally specific and provides a particular service, often humanitarian, to a country or region. In many cases these kinds of INGOs become agencies for the delivery of government-provided financial and material humanitarian relief and reconstruction, working with or under national state or UN organizations. Examples of this are the International Red Cross, International Catholic Charities, Doctors Without Borders, Oxfam, World Vision, and others too numerous to name.

A third set of INGOs is thematic interest groups that seek to influence policy in their interest area. They are advocacy organizations that, while often in consultative status with governments and UN agencies, seek to influence the policy of extraregional states toward the regional states as well as the domestic policy of the regional states themselves. Their causes in Southeast Asia can be regionally oriented or country specific, often bringing them into conflict with national governments that have wider and competing ranges of interests. For example, it was advocacy groups globally networking that kept the East Timor question alive for a quarter of a century even though governments wished it would go away. Two internationally significant issue areas in which advocacy INGOs have been intensely involved are human rights and the environment, both of which raise politically sensitive questions (chapters 8 and 9).

INGOs do not necessarily respect the political boundaries set by state sovereignty and can penetrate functionally through links to domestic NGOs with like cause. Sometimes domestic NGOs have advisory or budgetary ties to foreign governments. This means their activities can be affected by the quality of the relationship between their own government and their foreign supporters. For instance, because of Indonesian opposition to the Iraq war, the leading Indonesian NGO with environmental concerns, Walhi (Friends of the Earth Indonesia) was forced to sever its relationship to foreign donors, the U.S. Agency for International Development, the British Department of International Development, and the Australian Agency for International Development. The protest, while perhaps politically necessary, certainly degraded its functional capabilities.

Notes

1. The reports of the UN human rights envoys to Cambodia can be accessed at the Cambodia country link at www.ohchr.org.

2. John Bresnan, "Indonesia," in Robert Chase, Emily Hill, and Paul Kennedy, eds., *The Pivotal States: A New Framework for U.S. Policy in the Developing World* (New York: W.W. Norton, 1999), 15–39.

3. Michael Leifer, *Indonesia's Foreign Policy* (London: Allen and Unwin, 1983).

4. For a good overview of the democratization process in Indonesia, see Douglas E. Ramage, "Indonesia in 2006: Democracy First, Good Governance Later," in Daljit Singh and Lorraine C. Salazar, eds., *Southeast Asian Affairs 2007* (Singapore: Institute of Southeast Asian Studies, 2007), 135–57.

5. The concept of Indonesia's "strategic centrality" was developed by Anthony L. Smith, *Strategic Centrality: Indonesia's Changing Role in ASEAN* (Singapore: ISEAS, 2000).

6. As quoted in Ioannis Gatsiounis, "Malaysia's axis mysteriously shifting," in *Asia Times*, accessed at www.atimes.com, 1 September 2007.

7. This is the conclusion of veteran Burma-watcher Bertil Lintner, "The Burmese Way to Facism," *Far Eastern Economic Review* 170, no. 8 (2007): 9–13.

8. Hussain Mutalib, "The Socio-Economic Dimensions in Singapore's Quest for Security and Stability," *Pacific Affairs* 75, no. 1 (Fall 2002): 39.

9. Anthony L. Smith, "Singapore and the United States 2004–2005: Steadfast Friends," in *Special Assessment: The Asia-Pacific and the United States 2004–2005* (Honolulu: Asia-Pacific Center for Security Studies, 2005).

10. World Bank, "Thailand Economic Monitor (April 2007)," at siteresources.world bank.org/INTTHAILAND/Resources/Economic-Monitor/2007april_tem_ overview.pdf.

11. As quoted in "Surin: Thailand Lost Momentum," *The Bangkok Post*, 7 January 2008.

12. Klaus Rohland, as quoted in "New Five Year Plan for Vietnam," 7 February 2007, accessed through Vietnam country link at www.worldbank.org.

13. Keith Weller Taylor, *The Birth of Vietnam* (Berkeley: University of California Press, 1983), xxi.

14. Alexander L. Vuving, "Strategy and Evolution of Vietnam's China Policy," *Asian Survey* 46, no. 6 (2006): 805–24.

15. White House, "Memorandum for the Secretary of State," 19 December 2006, www.whitehouse.gov/news/releases/2006/12/20061229-6.html.

16. Clinton made his call for a new Pacific Community in a speech at Tokyo's Waseda University, 7 July 1993. The text can be accessed at http://findarticles.com/p/articles/mi_m1584/is_n28_v4/ai_13238867.

17. As cited by Mark Mitchell and Michael Vatikiotis, "China Steps in Where U.S. Fails," *Far Eastern Economic Review*, 23 November 2002: 22.

18. The English language transcript of the Peking University speech was accessed at www.mofa.go.jp/region/asia-paci/china/speech0712.html.

19. Hugh White, "The Lombok Pact's Empty Promise," *Far Eastern Economic Review*, 169, no. 10 (December 2006): 26–28.

20. Paul Cleary, *Shakedown: Australia's Grab for Timor Oil* (Sydney: Allen & Unwin, 2007).

21. The ASEAN–Russia joint declaration can be accessed a www.aseansec.org.

22. "Vietnam celebrates UN Security Council seat," *The Straits Times*, 17 October 2007.

23. Voting coincidence with the U.S. in the United Nations is reported annually to Congress by the State Department. The reports can be accessed at www.state.gov/p/io/conrpt.

Suggestions for Further Reading

Basic background data and statistics on each of the Southeast Asian countries can be found in the U.S. State Department's country "Background Notes" (www.state.gov/r/pa/ei/bgn); the CIA's *World Factbook* (www.cia.gov/cia/publications/factbook); and through the member-countries link on the ASEAN Secretariat's home page (www.aseansec.org).

The contemporary domestic political settings for the foreign policy of the states of the region are outlined in Damien Kingsbury, *South-East Asia: A Political Profile*, 2nd ed.(Oxford, U.K.: Oxford University Press, 2005); William Case, *Politics in Southeast Asia: Democracy of Less* (London: RoutledgeCurzon, 2002). Linkages between domestic politics and foreign policy are examined in

Jörn Dosch, *The Changing Dynamics of Southeast Asian Politics* (Boulder, Colo.: Lynne Rienner, 2007).

For the evolution over time of the international relations and foreign policies of the individual states of Southeast Asia refer to the country-chapters in the following: Charles E. Morrison and Astri Suhrke, *Struggles for Survival: Foreign Policy Dilemmas of Smaller Asian States* (New York: St. Martin's, 1978); David Wurfel and Bruce Barton, *The Political Economy of Foreign Policy in Southeast Asia* (New York: St. Martin's, 1990); Clark Neher, *Southeast Asia in the New International Era*, 4th ed. (Boulder, Colo.: Westview, 2002).

Some specific country studies are David W. Roberts, *Political Transition in Cambodia, 1977–1999* (Richmond, Surry, UK: Curzon, 2001); John Bresnan, ed., *Indonesia: The Great Transition* (Lanham, Md.: Rowman & Littlefield, 2005) especially chapter 5 on Indonesian foreign policy by Ann Marie Murphy; Grant Evans, *A Short History of Laos: The Land In-between* (Sydney, Australia: Allen & Unwin, 2003); Virginia Matthesen Hooker, *A Short History of Malaysia: Linkages East and West* (Sydney, Australia: Allen & Unwin, 2003); Donald Kirk, *Looted: The Philippines After the Bases* (New York: St. Martin's, 1998); N. Ganesan, *Realism and Interdependence in Singapore's Foreign Policy* (London: Routledge, 2005); Pasuk Phongpaichit and Chris Baker, *Thaksin: The Business of Politics in Thailand* (Bangkok: Silkworm Press, 2005); Damien Kingsbury and Michael Leach, eds., *East Timor: Beyond Independence* (Melbourne, Australia: Monash University Center of Southeast Asian Studies, 2007); Brantley Womack, *China and Vietnam: The Politics of Asymmetry* (Cambridge, U.K.: Cambridge University Press, 2006).

3

The Cold War in Southeast Asia

THE WORLDVIEW SHAPING THE FIRST FOUR AND A HALF DECADES of international relations in Southeast Asia was American. Its political and strategic
underpinning was "containment" of communism, a strategy most famously
spelled out in George Kennan's 1947 "Mr. X" article in *Foreign Affairs*.[1] Containment's central proposition was that the Soviet Union's pressure against the
West was something "that can be contained by the adroit and vigilant application of counter-force at a series of constantly shifting geographical and political points, corresponding to the shifts and maneuvers of Soviet policy."
Kennan urged the United States to enter "with reasonable confidence upon a
policy of firm containment, to confront the Russians with unalterable
counter-force at every point where they show signs of encroaching upon the
interests of the peaceful and stable world." After 1949, the People's Republic of
China was added to the communist threats that had to be contained.

The threat of communism's advance in Southeast Asia was demonstrated
early by attempted communist coups and insurgencies in Indonesia, Burma,
Malaysia, and the Philippines. At independence, Southeast Asian states were
caught up in the dynamics of great power competition. In fashioning relations
with the new states of Southeast Asia, the United States emphasized "mutual
security" against the communist threat as the basis for a wider array of economic and political ties so important for national development. The American goal was to enlist the countries of Southeast Asia into the "free world." The
pressure on Southeast Asian states to commit to that goal backfired for the
United States in Indonesia and Burma.

In Indonesia, U.S. insistence on tying economic aid to a mutual security framework created a leftist nationalist backlash that brought down a West-leaning government. The new government quickly balanced its relations by diplomatically recognizing the USSR and the PRC. Burma, with its 1,358-mile-long (2,185 km) border with China, was the first noncommunist state to recognize the PRC. Retreating Chinese Nationalist Army units carved out a sanctuary in Burma's northern Shan states and had continuing links to Taiwan. These were facilitated by Thailand and the United States. In 1953, an angry Burmese government terminated its American aid program and took the issue to the United Nations. Many of the Nationalist troops were eventually repatriated to Taiwan. Others were pushed by the Burmese army across the Thai border where they settled down. The affair confirmed Burma in the correctness of its policy of strict neutralism and nonalignment. For nearly four decades Rangoon isolated itself from the international politics of the region.

Containment in Southeast Asia

From the outset of the Cold War, the focus of containment in Southeast Asia was on Vietnam. The French were fighting the First Indochina War against the Viet Minh nationalist/communist independence movement led by Ho Chi Minh.[2] An April 1952 U.S. National Security Council memorandum outlined the American view of the strategic problem posed by communist expansion through Vietnam.[3] The document stated that "in the absence of effective and timely counteraction the loss of any single [Southeast Asian] country would probably lead to a relatively swift submission to or an alignment with communism by the remaining countries of this group." This was the core of what a few years later was called the "domino theory" of the strategic interrelatedness of the Southeast Asian states that governed American geopolitical thinking about the region for a quarter of a century.[4] If the dominoes fell, then "communist domination, by whatever means, of all Southeast Asia would seriously endanger in the short term and critically endanger in the longer term United States security interests."

The first domino was Vietnam. For Washington, all communist lines of command, including Ho Chi Minh's, ultimately ran back to Moscow. The establishment of the PRC provided the Vietnamese both material and technical assistance. China's 1950 intervention in the Korean War underlined for the United States the urgency of the task of containment of communism in Asia. Washington viewed the Korean War and the French struggle in Indochina through the same lens of communist threat. The United States did not recognize the new regime in China, blocked its entry to the United Nations, and diplomatically pressed other Southeast Asian states not to recognize the PRC.

By 1954, the French were exhausted. The United States, unwilling to intervene directly in support of the French, had provided over a billion dollars of assistance. The United States participated in the 1954 Geneva Foreign Ministers' Conference, which devised a compromise political settlement to terminate the French military role in Indochina. The United States did not associate itself with the final document but in a separate statement declared that it would refrain from the threat or use of force to disturb the agreement. Washington warned that it would view "any renewal of the aggression" with grave concern and threatening international peace and security.[5] Already in 1954, the United States was characterizing the Viet Minh's struggle for an independent unified Vietnam as "aggression."

The Geneva settlement partitioned Vietnam at the seventeenth parallel for the purposes of an armistice and regrouping of military forces. From its Hanoi capitol, Ho Chi Minh's Democratic Republic of Vietnam (DRV), with its ties to China and the Soviet Union, faced the southern government of Vietnam ensconced in Saigon and backed by the United States. The Geneva agreement called for national elections in 1956, but they were never held, with both sides blaming the other. Laos and Cambodia were theoretically neutralized.

The Southeast Asia Treaty Organization (SEATO)

In the wake of the French defeat, the United States mobilized allies to meet the threat that now seemed posed by the opening of a communist strategic window to Southeast Asia. In 1954, eight nations signed the Southeast Asia Collective Defense Treaty (the Manila Pact) and created the Southeast Asia Treaty Organization (SEATO).[6] Only two SEATO members, the Philippines and Thailand, were in fact Southeast Asian. The other signatories were the United States, Great Britain, Australia, New Zealand, France, and Pakistan. The operative heart of the Manila Pact stated that the parties to the treaty recognized that aggression by armed attack in the treaty area on a party to the treaty or any state or territory unanimously designated by the parties would endanger its own peace and safety. In that event, they would consult to meet the common danger. A separate protocol brought Laos, Cambodia, and the "free territory" of Vietnam under the SEATO cover. In an understanding to the agreement, the United States stated that the treaty obligations applied only to communist aggression.

SEATO was very different from NATO in Europe. No military units were assigned to SEATO, and there was no unified military command structure. The only obligation of the allies was to consult. SEATO's significance as an alliance was not really military; it was political. It provided a multilateral political framework for U.S. containment strategy in Southeast Asia. American forward military deployment in the Southeast Asia had been limited to the Philippines. American military base rights in the Philippines were provided for in the package of agreements in 1947 linked to Philippines independence. A bilateral United States–Philippines Mutual Defense Treaty in 1951 fixed U.S. reciprocal obligations to the Philippines. The most important of the more than twenty American military facilities in the Philippines were the naval base on Subic Bay and the Air Force's Clark Field.

SEATO's first real test came in 1961–1962, when Thailand felt threatened by a communist Pathet Lao military offensive against the theoretically neutral Royal Lao government. Because SEATO action required a unanimity that was not forthcoming, the United States and Thailand undertook a bilateral commitment. In the March 1962 Rusk-Thanat communiqué, the U.S. declared that its obligation under the Manila Pact in the event of communist aggression "was individual as well as collective" and did not depend on prior agreement of the other SEATO members. In other words, the multilateral treaty would function as a bilateral security pact between the U.S. and Thailand. This was the foundation of a U.S.–Thailand security relationship that endures to the present.[7]

Great Britain held the SEATO umbrella over Malaysia and Singapore until their independence, when they chose technical nonalignment. Both countries maintained a security relationship with British Commonwealth partners Australia and New Zealand in the 1957 Anglo-Malay Defence Agreement (AMDA). This provided the basis for Commonwealth military assistance to Malaysia during its 1963–1965 "confrontation" with Indonesia (discussed below). AMDA was succeeded by the 1971 Five Power Defence Arrangement (FPDA). The FPDA survived the end of the Cold War. It still provides a multilateral vehicle within which Malaysia and Singapore can militarily cooperate in the absence of bilateral military training links. The absence of any formal security tie to the United States allowed Malaysia and Singapore to maintain their international nonaligned stance.

By the middle of the 1950s the Cold War lines and structures were in place. The DRV and government of Vietnam faced each other across the seventeenth parallel. Through the DRV, the USSR and China faced the United States, bringing a strategic front line of the Cold War into Southeast Asia. In neutralized Laos, the revolutionary forces of the Pathet Lao menaced the status quo, and in neutral Cambodia Prince-Prime Minister Norodom Sihanouk diplomatically maneuvered to keep his country out of the fray.

The Bandung Conference and Nonalignment

Beneath the great power–inspired Southeast Asian Cold War security system, Southeast Asian states sought ways to relate to each other on an alternative basis rather than simply choosing Cold War sides. Gathering concerns over great power conflict in Asia prompted consultations among India, Pakistan, Ceylon (now Sri Lanka), Burma, and Indonesia. In two meetings in 1954, the prime ministers declared their opposition to interference in domestic affairs by external communist or anticommunist agencies. Looking to amplify their regional voice, they convened in Bandung, Indonesia an April 1955 meeting of twenty-nine African and Asian heads of government and foreign ministers. Southeast Asia was represented by communist DRV; neutralist Burma, Cambodia, Indonesia, and Laos; and American allies, the Philippines, Thailand, and South Vietnam. The Bandung Conference marked Indonesia's emergence as an important actor on the international scene. It also was the debut of communist China as a regional political actor. The conference was driven by the twin themes of anti-imperialism and peaceful coexistence. The final communiqué set forth ten principles—the Bandung Principles—by which nations could live in peace with one another and develop friendly cooperation (see box 3.1).[8] A compromise was reached with the neutralists on

---

BOX 3.1
The Bandung Principles

The normative basis for Southeast Asian international relations is the Bandung Principles adopted in April 1955 at the Bandung, Indonesia, Asian–African Conference. The principles are:

- Respect for human rights;
- Mutual respect for territorial integrity and sovereignty;
- Respect the equality of races and nations;
- Respect the right of each nation to defend itself singly or collectively;
- Abstention from intervention or interference in the internal affairs of another country;
- Abstention from use of collective defense to serve the interest of any big power;
- Refraining from aggression or use of force against any country;
- Settlement of all disputes by peaceful means;
- Promotion of mutual interest and cooperation; and
- Respect for justice and international obligations.

---

the question of security agreements. The conference recognized the right of individual and collective self-defense but with "abstention from the use of arrangements of collective defense to serve the particular interests of any of the big powers."

Although the historical record shows that the Bandung Principles have been routinely violated in Southeast Asia, they nevertheless provided the ideal foundation for structuring international relations in the region, remaining the normative reference points for Southeast Asian bilateral and multilateral relations. The Bandung Conference was the precursor to the 1961 Belgrade Conference that founded the Nonaligned Movement (NAM). Building on the Bandung foundation, the NAM theoretically adopted a position of security equidistance between the Cold War great powers. The United States viewed nonalignment with hostility, identifying it as a communist Trojan horse, since leading roles were played by states like Cuba, the PRC, and the DRV.

Over time, the NAM's agenda became increasingly more radical and anti-West. Burma, a founding member, withdrew from the NAM because it was not truly neutral. With the ending of the Cold War, the NAM sought to transform itself by shifting attention to social and economic problems in the developing world. All ASEAN states are members. Radical voices are still raised. Rather than traditional imperialism, the target of the NAM's current collective anger is the "coercive unilateralism" of the United States. The tone was set by Malaysian Prime Minister Mahathir in his opening address at the 2003 Kuala Lumpur NAM Summit when he declared that "no single nation shall be allowed to police the world."[9]

The Second Indochina War: 1961–1975

After the 1954 Geneva Conference, the United States became the principal supporter of the anticommunist government of Vietnam. American advisors and material assistance worked to build a South Vietnamese political and military capability to withstand an emerging internal war led by Viet Minh cadres left behind at partition. The revolutionary political structure was the National Front for the Liberation of South Vietnam (NFLSV). The armed insurgents were called the Viet Cong (Vietnamese Communists). Both the front and the Viet Cong were directed by the DRV. When it became obvious that promised national elections were not going to be held, the communist strategists began a classic "people's war." By 1961, it seemed clear that the government of Vietnam would not be able to defeat the insurgency from its own resources. American President John F. Kennedy decided to introduce fifteen thousand U.S military advisors. In the words of a veteran participant/observer, this was the "most fateful decision" ever made by the United States in Vietnam because it foreclosed the possibility of withdrawal and set the course for a decade of warfare.[10] The United States justified its position by reference to its SEATO obligations. Hanoi denounced the American role as imperialism.

The United States assumed major responsibility for the war after the Congress gave President Lyndon Johnson a blank check in the 1965 "Tonkin Gulf" resolution to use whatever force necessary to defeat communism in Indochina.[11] By 1967, nearly three-quarters of a million American forces were at war in South Vietnam, along with forces from Thailand, the Philippines, Australia, New Zealand, and South Korea. Regular North Vietnamese People's Army of Vietnam (PAVN) troops were operating in the south in what the United States claimed was a war of northern aggression against South Vietnam.[12] The United States carried the war north in massive bombing campaigns. The conflict spilled over into Laos and Cambodia as the United States tried to interdict North Vietnamese supply lines to the south along the so-called Ho Chi Minh trail and to strike enemy sanctuaries. In technically neutral Laos, the United States and Thailand joined forces in the fight against the North Vietnam–allied Pathet Lao. Cambodia's Sihanouk desperately tried to maintain neutrality that was routinely violated by both warring sides. He was ousted in a 1970 coup whose leaders quickly aligned with the United States. In addition to the North Vietnamese operating from bases in eastern Cambodia, indigenous Cambodian communists called the Khmer Rouge waged their own military campaign to seize power in Cambodia.

As the American war in Vietnam escalated in cost and casualties, realist critics viewed it as a strategic mistake as it degraded U.S. military capabilities to the advantage of the USSR. For the growing ranks of antiwar protesters, the war had become a moral monstrosity. American public support for the war collapsed, which in 1968 helped elect President Richard Nixon, who promised to end the war. It took four years. President Nixon and Secretary of State Henry Kissinger tried to force the DRV to the negotiating table on terms that would still preserve American credibility. Pressure was kept on the north by heavy bombing and the Sino–Soviet split was diplomatically exploited by beginning a process of normalizing United States–PRC relations. The 1973 Paris Agreement gave the United States what it described as "peace with honor."[13] The termination of American support left the government of Vietnam to face their enemy alone. Within two years, southern resistance crumbled. Saigon fell on 29 April 1975. Nine months later, Vietnam was unified. Saigon was renamed Ho Chi Minh City. As the end game played out in South Vietnam, so did the sideshows in Laos and Cambodia, with the victories of the Pathet Lao and the Khmer Rouge.

The American war in Vietnam was, until Iraq, the most controversial period in modern American political and military history. It impacted the formulation and conduct of American foreign policy for a generation. The battle cry "no more Vietnams" represented a new, limitationist view of America's role in the world. The elite consensus supporting containment seemed to have been shredded. The peculiarly American introspective and retrospective concerns that prompted the drawing of so many "lessons of Vietnam" were not shared by Southeast Asian elites. They drew different lessons. One was about the constancy of the American security presence. This was signaled in 1969 by the enunciation of the Nixon Doctrine. Providing a basis for the beginning of American troop withdrawals under the rubric "Vietnamization," the Nixon Doctrine stated that in cases of aggression other than nuclear, the United States would provide military and economic assistance in accord with treaty commitments, but that the threatened nation had the primary responsibility for its defense.[14] This prompted a Southeast Asian reassessment of the integrity of the passive American security umbrella. The perceived abandonment of South Vietnam reinforced the insecurities. Second, the domestic American political dialogue raised fears in Southeast Asia that the United States was entering a period of neoisolationism.

Southeast Asia and the Second Indochina War

The Philippines and Thailand were the only Southeast Asian countries allied with the United States in the Second Indochina War. The calculations of the leaderships in Bangkok and Manila, the former a military dictatorship, the latter, after 1972, Ferdinand Marcos's presidential dictatorship, had less to do with SEATO obligations than with obtaining a higher level of American political, military, and economic support. Malaysia's and Singapore's Commonwealth allies in the FPDA were also American allies. Burma had become a hermit nation. Indonesia under President Sukarno until 1966 actively opposed the U.S. role in Vietnam.

Indonesia under Sukarno

Between 1957 and 1965, Indonesia challenged the American-dominated international status quo in Southeast Asia. Its nonaligned position had been translated by President Sukarno into the championing of a "Jakarta–Phnom Penh–Hanoi–Beijing–Pyongyang axis" to fight Western imperialism and neocolonialism. Sukarno declared martial law in 1957, terminating parliamentary government, and by decree began to build a left-trending "guided democracy" that gave a role to the Indonesian Communist Party (PKI). When regional revolts broke out in 1958, the United States provided clandestine support to the rebel forces. The regional uprisings were forcefully suppressed, but the grievance against American subversion lingered. Sukarno also threatened the use of force to wrest Dutch New Guinea from the Netherlands. The United States offered to mediate the conflict, hoping to head off a war in the rear of its war in Vietnam. An American-sponsored face-saving political solution transferred authority in the territory to the United Nations in 1962, which in turn transferred it to an Indonesian interim administration in 1963. Nascent Papuan nationalism was suppressed. In 1969, the territory was incorporated into Indonesia as a province, laying the seeds of separatism in the province (chapter 5).

"Confrontation" with Malaysia

Sukarno's strident distancing from the noncommunist world reached its zenith in the crisis over the British plan to decolonize Singapore and its Borneo territories in a federal union with already independent Malaya. The new state was established in September 1963. Declaring Malaysia a "puppet" of British imperialism, Sukarno announced a campaign to "crush" Malaysia. In an undeclared war called by the Indonesians *konfrontasi* (confrontation), Indonesian marines were infiltrated into peninsular Malaysia and terrorist bombs were set off in Singapore. By virtue of the AMDA, British Commonwealth forces fought Indonesian incursions along the Sarawak–Indonesian border. The PKI strongly supported confrontation, hoping to become a volunteer fifth armed force with weapons from China. When Malaysia was elected a nonpermanent member of the UN Security Council in December 1964, a defiant Indonesia quit the UN, the only nation ever to do so.

Although Sukarno framed the justification for confrontation in terms of anti-imperialism, other sources for Indonesian conduct can be identified as well. A pan-Indonesia was part of an Indonesian ultranationalist vision that would include the territories that were now incorporated in Malaysia. Indonesian leaders, aware of Malaya's anticommunism and its sympathies towards Sumatran regionalists, also feared that an economically successful greater Malaysia could become a magnet for future Indonesian separatists. In terms of Jakarta's own possible regional hegemonic ambitions, a fragmented Malaya, Singapore, Sarawak, Brunei, and Sabah, even if independent, would be satellites of Indonesia. Finally, the conflict over Malaysia shifted public attention from Indonesia's failing economy and polarized political environment to a foreign target.

The Fall of Sukarno

By 1964, political competition in Indonesia had been reduced to the anti-communist army and the PKI, with Sukarno balancing in between. The PKI maintained close ties to its Chinese counterpart and had penetrated the military, particularly the air force and marines. For the United States, the specter of being outflanked in Southeast Asia was real. Against a tension-filled backdrop of undeclared war against Malaysia, economic failure, local PKI challenges to Muslim interests, and uncertainties about Sukarno's health, the army–PKI conflict bubbling below the surface erupted on 30 September 1965, when PKI-backed leftist military elements attempted a coup. The army's Strategic Reserve under General Suharto quickly regained control of the situation.

Although the full details of the coup and counter-coup are still a matter of controversy, there is no doubt about the outcome. A nationwide bloody anti-communist campaign was sponsored by the army. The PKI and its associated fronts were wiped out. The thousands of deaths have only been surpassed in Southeast Asia by the Khmer Rouge's "killing fields." Sukarno, who many thought was complicit in the coup, was politically isolated. Step by step, the new anticommunist rulers stripped Sukarno's authority and transferred it to Suharto, first as acting president in 1967 and then president in 1968.

The discontinuity in Indonesian political life had dramatic international impact as well as domestic. One of the first results was the ending of *konfrontasi*. The West, rather than being excoriated, was now tapped as a critical source of economic assistance. Diplomatic relations with the PRC were "frozen" because of the alleged PKI–Chinese Communist Party links. Cold War nonalignment remained a pillar of foreign policy, but the United States replaced the USSR as Indonesia's major defense supplier. Finally, it was the toppling of Sukarno that made ASEAN possible.

The Creation of ASEAN

Two important policy concerns impelled the noncommunist Southeast Asian states in 1967 to intensify and regularize their political contacts in a structured multilateral setting. The first was the escalation of the U.S. war in Vietnam with its uncertain regional consequences. The second was the need to integrate post-Sukarno Indonesia into a regional order in which it could collaborate but not dominate. Of the two, the Indonesian problem was the most exigent.

In addition to the shared interests derived from generalized perceptions of the regional international environment, each country had particular interests in establishing ASEAN. For the Philippines, ASEAN was a vehicle for the assertion of a regional identity rather than just being seen as a trans-Pacific appendage of the United States. Thailand's membership in ASEAN gave a Southeast Asian balance to its SEATO alliance with the United States. ASEAN gave Singapore's new sovereignty regional recognition. Malaysia hoped to find in ASEAN a political alternative to its Commonwealth ties that had been weakened by the British retreat from Asia. Indonesia's aspirations for regional leadership could play out through ASEAN in an acceptable political format that did not limit its options.

ASEAN's Antecedents

There were two earlier projects in regionalism from which the founders of ASEAN could draw. Between 1961 and 1963, Thailand, the Philippines, and Malaya joined in the Association of Southeast Asia (ASA). In the planning stage from 1959, ASA's original anticommunist inspiration was diluted in an organizationally loose grouping in which the political agenda was hidden in its public goal of the promotion of economic, social, scientific, and cultural cooperation in Southeast Asia. This did not relieve it of the Indonesian charge that ASA was a SEATO plot. Cooperation within ASA foundered on the Philippine break with Malaysia when the disputed Sabah (North Borneo) territory was incorporated into Malaysia in September 1963 (chapter 5).

A second organization, MAPHILINDO, was stillborn at a Malaya–Philippines–Indonesia summit meeting in Manila, 31 July–5 August 1963. Theoretically, it provided a loosely articulated quasi-confederal framework for relations among the three nations. Actually, MAPHILINDO was a diplomatic device through which the Philippines and Indonesia sought to frustrate or delay the creation of the Malaysian Federation. The proclamation of Malaysia one month later extinguished MAPHILINDO. The language of the Manila accords establishing MAPHILINDO had Sukarno's fingerprints all over it. With regard to the respective American and British security ties of the Philippines and Malaya, it was agreed that the bases were temporary and should not be used to subvert directly or indirectly the independence of any of the three countries. Invoking the language of the Bandung Principles, it was stated that the three countries would not use collective defense arrangements to serve the interests of any of the big powers.[15]

ASEAN's Purpose

The outlines of a regional diplomatic grouping within which Indonesia could play an active but nonthreatening role in regional affairs emerged in the diplomatic negotiations to end *konfrontasi*, crystallized in a 1966 Thai draft proposal for a Southeast Asian Association for Regional Cooperation that outlined what became ASEAN. On 8 August 1967, the foreign ministers of Indonesia, the Philippines, Singapore, and Thailand, and the deputy prime minister of Malaysia issued the Bangkok Declaration establishing the Association of Southeast Asian Nations.[16] The goal was to promote regional cooperation contributing toward peace, progress, and prosperity while being determined to ensure the members' stability free from external interference. The problem was to find an organizational framework in which the differing patterns of nonalignment and alignment could be accommodated. The solution was to borrow the MAPHILINDO formula and affirm that "foreign bases are temporary" (with no time frame fixed) and not intended to be used to subvert the independence of other states in the region.

ASEAN's stated purposes were to promote active collaboration and regional cooperation on matters of common interest in the economic, social, cultural, technical, scientific, and administrative spheres in order to strengthen the foundation for a prosperous and peaceful community of Southeast Asian nations. The organization was left open to any Southeast Asian state that accepted ASEAN's aims and purposes. No mention was made of political cooperation, let alone security. ASEAN elites expressly and repeatedly denied that ASEAN was a security organization or alliance. In cases of defense cooperation between ASEAN members, great pains were taken to point out that these were not part of ASEAN. Yet, from its outset, ASEAN functioned in terms of collective political security. A Malaysian foreign minister retrospectively underlined the fact that the creation of ASEAN was the political reaction of the noncommunist states of Southeast Asia to the perceived common threat of communism posed by the Sino–Soviet struggle, expansive Vietnam, and domestic communist insurgencies.[17] From its inception, ASEAN had two tracks. One was the program of functional cooperation stated in the Bangkok Declaration. The other was its implicit—and for twenty-five years controlling—political function as a regional diplomatic caucus. The frustration felt by proponents of functional integration at slow progress toward regional integration was because politics was in control. ASEAN was a creature of its members' foreign ministers.

Zone of Peace, Freedom, and Neutrality (ZOPFAN)

Looking to a post–Indochina War international environment, the five ASEAN states in 1971 tried to fashion a proactive regional strategy independent of the U.S. security policy that would not be threatening to the Indochinese states and would insulate the ASEAN region from great power intrusion.

In the Kuala Lumpur Declaration, the ASEAN governments agreed to exert the necessary efforts "to secure recognition of, and respect for, Southeast Asia as a Zone of Peace, Freedom and Neutrality free from any form or manner of interference by outside powers."[18]

The ZOPFAN proposal was ASEAN's first avowedly political regional initiative. As a declaratory statement of a goal of neutralization, the ZOPFAN was not self-enforcing in the sense that the ASEAN states had the capabilities to force other nations to respect the zone. Vietnam attacked the ZOPFAN as support for American imperialism that would obstruct the legitimate struggles of the peoples of Southeast Asia. The Soviet Union and China made it an issue in their own polemic. The Soviet Union argued that the ZOPFAN would be the first stage in the 1969 Brezhnev call for an Asian collective security system. China, viewing the Soviet scheme as being directed against the PRC, claimed the ZOPFAN foreclosed the Russian initiative. The ZOPFAN was essentially a rhetorical device requiring no real policy commitment by the signatories or change in their existing security arrangements. Each ASEAN state was free to construct its own meaning of the concept. Any attempt to be specific would have shattered the fragile consensus on ZOPFAN as an abstraction.

The Interwar Interval: 1975–1978

After the April 1975 communist victories in Vietnam, Laos, and Cambodia, the central problem of international politics in Southeast Asia was to devise structures to accommodate and mediate relations between the regional noncommunist states and the Indochinese states, principally Vietnam. The revolutionary triumphalism of the new rulers of Indochina intensified ASEAN Southeast Asia's concerns about Vietnam's ambitions and intentions. Vietnamese and Chinese support for domestic communist insurgents elsewhere in Southeast Asia seemed even more threatening now that a strong communist subregion had been established in continental Southeast Asia. Hope in some ASEAN quarters that victories would moderate revolutionary ardor in Indochina was dispelled by the Khmer Rouge's attack on its own Cambodian population, the Vietnamese gulags, and the flow of refugees into ASEAN Southeast Asia (chapter 8).

ASEAN states' adjustment to the new situation was immensely complicated by the great power linkages in the region. Both Laos and Vietnam were in the Soviet camp. China was the patron of the Khmer Rouge regime in Cambodia and an obstacle to Vietnamese hegemony in Indochina. Despite perceptions of American strategic distancing, ASEAN leaders privately insisted that a continued U.S. political role was an essential counterweight to the operation of the

Sino-Soviet competition for influence in Southeast Asia. This highlighted Manila's real contribution to ASEAN. The U.S. bilateral alliance tie to the Philippines was the umbilical cord of the American security commitment to the region. The code words for ASEAN support for the Philippines bases were "an active U.S. presence."

The normalization of U.S.–China relations, signaled by the 1972 Nixon–Chou En-lai "Shanghai Communiqué," gave political space for three ASEAN states to reevaluate their lack of relations with the PRC. China and some ASEAN states looked to each other through new balance-of-power lenses. For China, improved relations in ASEAN Southeast Asia would outflank the USSR and Vietnam. Malaysia led the ASEAN recognition parade on 31 May 1974. The Philippines followed suit on 9 June 1975. President Marcos saw normalization of relations with China as giving Manila some diplomatic leverage with the United States. Finally, on 1 July 1975, Thailand established diplomatic relations with China. All three bilateral joint communiqués announcing the establishment of diplomatic relations contained the "anti-hegemony" clause that was part of the Shanghai Communiqué, stating that the governments are "opposed to any attempt by any country or group of countries to establish hegemony or create spheres of influence in any part of the world."[19] This was correctly viewed by the USSR as a Chinese effort to limit Soviet influence in ASEAN Southeast Asia. One of the important security consequences for Southeast Asia of normalization of relations with the PRC was cessation of Chinese support to Maoist communist insurgencies in the region.

Indonesia and Singapore did not follow suit in the sudden rush to normalization. Beijing was unable to overcome in Jakarta the taint of its alleged complicity with the PKI. Indonesia's military leadership viewed the PRC as a politically and territorially unsatisfied revisionist power with expansionist designs. Singapore, in the shadow of its giant neighbor and with its Chinese majority population, was not going to recognize until Indonesia did. It would be another fifteen years before Jakarta defrosted its "frozen" relations with Beijing in 1999, with Singapore following suit. Only then could the PRC become organizationally associated with ASEAN.

The 1976 Bali Summit

The communist victories in Indochina in 1975 catalyzed the ASEAN states into urgent efforts for greater security cooperation. In February 1976, the ASEAN heads of government met in Bali, Indonesia, for the first ASEAN Summit. There, they laid the foundations for stronger political and economic collaboration within ASEAN without closing the door for reconciliation with the Indochinese states.

Two important political documents were endorsed in the pursuit of collective political security. The first was the Declaration of ASEAN Concord, which in its political program called for "strengthening of political solidarity by promoting the harmonization of views, coordinating positions and, where possible and desirable, taking common action."[20] Actually, that process was well underway. Beginning with an "informal" meeting of the ASEAN foreign ministers in April 1972, the ministers agreed to meet at least once a year to discuss international developments affecting the region. This became an annual ASEAN Foreign Ministers' Retreat.

The second Bali agreement was the Treaty of Amity and Cooperation in Southeast Asia (TAC).[21] The TAC promised noninterference in the internal affairs of one another; settlement of differences or disputes by peaceful means; and the renunciation of the threat or use of force. Most significantly, the TAC was left open for accession by other states in Southeast Asia. In the later expansion of ASEAN, accession to the TAC was a requirement of membership but not a guarantee of admittance. What was important in 1976 is that the TAC was an explicit gesture indicating willingness for peaceful coexistence between ASEAN Southeast Asia and communist Southeast Asia.

Indonesia and East Timor

Coincident with emerging Communist-ruled Indochina, the four-century Portuguese colonial rule in the eastern half of the island of Timor collapsed. The change in the political status quo deep in the archipelago raised red flags in Jakarta. Rival indigenous political groups, pro- and anti-Indonesian, competed for power. The Revolutionary Front for an Independent East Timor (FRETILIN) won the struggle and proclaimed the Democratic Republic of East Timor (DRET). FRETILIN's model was the radical nationalism of the former Portuguese African territories of Mozambique and Angola. Indonesia recoiled at the possibility of a communist foothold in the heart of the archipelago. This perception was reinforced by the championing of the DRET by Beijing and Hanoi. Indonesia's policy moved from clandestine support for Timorese opponents of FRETILIN to military invasion in December 1975.

The Australian and U.S. governments were not surprised by the invasion. In fact, as documents declassified only in 2001 show, President Ford who, with Secretary of State Kissinger, met President Suharto in Jakarta on 6 December 1975, promised not to interfere; this despite the fact that Kissinger had been alerted that such an invasion using American weapons would violate U.S. law.[22] Even though friendly governments acquiesced in Indonesia's de facto new sovereignty in what became its twenty-seventh province, for liberal democrats around the world the invasion was blatant aggression. From a realist perspective, one of Australia's most senior diplomats argued that it was understandable that Indonesia's leaders considered that in the national interest "they were obliged to prevent by any means the establishment within their boundaries of the small, powerless, non-viable, hence unstable, but independent country that East Timor could become."[23] The annexation of Portuguese Timor also raised again within ASEAN the question of what Indonesia's ultimate territorial ambitions might be. Indonesia's rule in East Timor was contested in the UN and its human rights record in the province remained an irritant in Jakarta's bilateral relation with Western democracies (chapter 8).

The "Peace Offensive"

ASEAN reacted to the 1973 armistice in Vietnam at a February 1973 special foreign ministers' meeting. They agreed to open the door for economic cooperation in the reconstruction and rehabilitation of Indochina. The first official ASEAN pronouncement on the new international order in Southeast Asia after the fall of Saigon came at the May 1976 ASEAN foreign ministers' meeting where they called for a "friendly and harmonious" relationship with the Indochinese states on the basis of the Bandung Principles. Vietnam initially rebuffed ASEAN overtures, considering its leaders Washington's puppets. At the 1976 NAM Summit, Hanoi denounced ASEAN's Bali Summit and opposed ASEAN's ZOPFAN, but on a state-by-state basis, Vietnam normalized relations with all ASEAN states during 1976.

Vietnam began to ease its hostility toward ASEAN in 1977. This change had a number of causes: deterioration of Vietnam's relations with China; deterioration of Vietnam's relations with Khmer Rouge–ruled Cambodia; Laos's need for normal economic relations with Thailand; Vietnam's desire for technical and economic links with the developing economies of ASEAN; and a possible desire to offset Vietnam's deepening dependence on the Soviet Union. Whatever the mix of motives might have been, the ASEAN response was positive. The negotiating climate had improved with the termination of American bases in Thailand and the dismantling of SEATO. The Manila Pact, however, remained in force.

In a peace offensive, Vietnamese officials, including Prime Minister Pham Van Dong, toured the ASEAN region in 1977 and 1978. The Vietnamese and their ASEAN counterparts entertained in their public rhetoric a vision of a future stable, peaceful, and secure Southeast Asia. There was a clear difference, however, in the proposed structures and instrumentalities to resolve the differences of interest between communist and noncommunist Southeast Asia. The ASEAN nations continued to advance their ZOPFAN concept. Vietnam surprised them by unveiling at the June 1978 UN Special Session on Disarmament its own proposal for a Zone of Peace, Genuine Independence, and Neutrality (ZOPGIN). The notion of "genuine independence" meant eliminating American forward basing in Southeast Asia and severing security ties with the United States. In his travels in the region, the Vietnamese prime minister indicated a willingness to begin a dialogue with ASEAN without preconditions. With respect to the competitive peace zones, he assured his suspicious counterparts that it was the intent that was important, not the wording, which could be mutually worked out through consultation.

The Third Indochina War

In December 1978, buttressed by a new military alliance with the USSR, Vietnam invaded Cambodia (Democratic Kampuchea), expelling Pol Pot's Khmer Rouge regime and adding to Thailand's growing Cambodian refugee burden (chapter 8). Pro-Vietnamese ex-KR members—including Hun Sen—accompanied the 180,000-man occupying army. With Vietnamese "advisors" they established the People's Republic of Kampuchea (PRK). Because of the "peace offensive" and the existence of a climate of hope for normal relations with Indochina, Vietnam's invasion and occupation of Cambodia came as a disillusioning shock to ASEAN.

BOX 3.2
The Indochina Wars

The First Indochina War, 1945–1954
The anticolonial war for independence waged by Vietnamese nationalist/communist forces against the French. It ended with the 1954 Geneva Accords that led to the partition of Vietnam.

The Second Indochina War, 1961–1975
The ground war in South Vietnam and air war against North Vietnam with extensions to Laos and Cambodia. The United States sought to prevent the unification of Vietnam under communist control as part of the American strategy of containment. The American war ended with the 1973 U.S.–DRV Paris Peace Agreement. The Indochina War ended with communist victories in South Vietnam, Laos, and Cambodia in April 1975.

The Third Indochina War, 1978–1991
The Khmer nationalists' resistance, backed by ASEAN, China, and the United States, to Vietnam's December 1978 invasion and occupation of Cambodia. It ended with the 1991 comprehensive peace agreement that created the United Nations Transitional Authority in Cambodia (UNTAC).

The Vietnamese decision to invade Pol Pot's Cambodia culminated a bitter and complex relationship between the two former erstwhile comrades-in-arms. At the primordial level of relationships, there were competitive nationalisms reinforced by centuries of ethnic antagonism. There was ideological rivalry. The KR refused to accept the political inequality inherent in its perception of Vietnamese hegemonic pretension through its promotion of a Hanoi-centered "special relationship" among the three Indochinese states. There were territorial issues along a bleeding border inflamed by KR cross-border raids and Vietnamese hot pursuit. In December 1977, Phnom Penh put an end to any "special relationship" by breaking relations with Vietnam. Finally, there was Vietnam's analysis of the strategic threat to it posed by China's ties to Cambodia. Vietnam, an ally of the USSR, feared Chinese encirclement. This brought the Sino–Soviet conflict to Southeast Asia. The Vietnamese invasion launched the Third Indochina War. What Vietnam thought would be a swift and irreversible fait accompli provoked a military and political contest that dominated international relations in Southeast Asia for more than a decade.

The ASEAN Response

No matter Vietnam's motivation, for a worried ASEAN this was the worst-case scenario. In ASEAN eyes, the first Southeast Asian domino had fallen to aggressive Vietnamese expansionism spearheaded by Southeast Asia's largest army. The Thai–Cambodian border had become ASEAN's strategic frontier. ASEAN's response was swift. On 9 January 1979, Indonesian Foreign Minister Mochtar Kusumaatmadja, chairman of the ASEAN Standing Committee, issued a statement on behalf of ASEAN, deploring the armed conflict between the two Indochinese states and calling upon the UN Security Council to take immediate steps to end the conflict. This was followed three days later by an emergency ASEAN foreign ministers' meeting that confirmed the right of the Cambodian people to self-determination and demanded the immediate withdrawal of Vietnamese forces. For ASEAN, Vietnam's fait accompli was the illegitimate and illegal consequence of Vietnamese military aggression. At the June 1979 foreign ministers' meeting the governments promised their firm support and solidarity in the preservation of Thailand's independence, sovereignty, and territorial integrity in the face of Vietnamese cross-border incursions. This position hardened in a June 1980 ASEAN "joint statement" that stated that the incursions of Vietnamese forces into Thailand "directly affects the security of the ASEAN member states."[24] At the 1980 meeting, American Secretary of State Edmund Muskie made an unqualified pledge of American support if Vietnam should invade Thailand.

ASEAN decision making in the early phase of the Cambodian crisis marked a major turning point for the grouping. Setting ASEAN on a course of resistance to Vietnam's act in Cambodia made operationally explicit the basic political nature of ASEAN cooperation. Second, it gave policy substance to the political program of the Declaration of ASEAN Concord. Third, in its stance vis-à-vis the threatening Vietnamese presence at ASEAN's front-line on the Thai–Cambodian border, ASEAN's collective political common action explicitly linked Thailand's security and territorial integrity to that of its fellow ASEAN members. This verged on collective defense. The external threat seemingly posed by Vietnam and its USSR ally had become internal political cement transforming ASEAN as a grouping into an international diplomatic/political caucus whose terms of reference were those of high politics, of traditional security interests, not the functional areas of cooperation stated in ASEAN's founding declaration.

ASEAN brought the Cambodia issue to the UN Security Council in spring 1979, where a resolution based on the ASEAN position was vetoed by the USSR. In November 1979, the UN General Assembly adopted an ASEAN draft resolution by an overwhelming vote of 91 to 21. The Vietnam-sponsored PRK government was denied Cambodia's UN seat still held by Democratic Kampuchea. In 1980, by a vote of 97 to 23 the UNGA called for a special conference on Cambodia. Over the ferocious objections and boycott by the communist bloc, the United Nations International Conference on Kampuchea (ICK) was held in July 1981. The ICK's Declaration internationally legitimized the ASEAN formula for settlement of the Cambodian crisis.[25] It called for a cease fire and withdrawal of foreign (i.e., Vietnamese) forces under the supervision of a UN peacekeeping force. A UN-arranged and supervised free election would be held allowing all Cambodians to exercise their right to self-determination. UN peacekeepers would ensure the security of these elections and the establishment of the new government resulting from the elections. The ICK declaration became the basis of later ASEAN and UN terms for a comprehensive political settlement.

On the ground, ASEAN-sponsored anti-Vietnamese Khmer resistance forces operated in western Cambodia from Thai sanctuaries. The largest and most combat effective of the three resistance factions was the Khmer Rouge, supplied and advised by China. The other two were the royalist forces of FUNCINPEC and the Khmer People's National Liberation Front (KPNLF) led by long-time political foe of Sihanouk, Son Sann. The resistance factions uneasily coexisted under the umbrella of a Coalition Government for Democratic Kampuchea (CGDK) cobbled together in 1982 by ASEAN diplomats. By bringing Sihanouk and Son Sann under the CGDK tent with Pol Pot's Khmer Rouge in the CGDK, it was easier to defend diplomatically Democratic Kampuchea's claim to Cambodia's UN seat. ASEAN was in a difficult position. It needed the KR to give combat capability to the resistance, but at the same time, it did not want the KR to return to power. This dilemma complicated the question of Vietnamese withdrawal from Cambodia. ASEAN insisted that Vietnam withdraw, but Vietnam, in defense of the PRK regime, demanded that the KR first be disarmed.

ASEAN's efforts to undo Vietnam's actions had the full political and material support of the United States and China. The PRC delivered lethal assistance to the CGDK forces through Thailand. In February 1979, China punctuated its alliance with Thailand by launching a large-scale attack on Vietnam's northern frontier. This was designed to take the pressure off Thailand's border. Its deterrence value was lessened when the Chinese army did not fare well against Vietnamese defenders. It sent counterproductive political signals to some ASEAN members who were negatively impressed by China's willingness to use force in Southeast Asia. At a special meeting, the ASEAN foreign ministers, without naming China, called on "countries outside this region to exert utmost restraint and to refrain from any action which might lead to escalation of violence and the spreading of the conflict."[26] The danger was in the possible escalation of Soviet support for Vietnam.

The United States gave full political support to ASEAN and nonlethal material assistance to the CGDK. Early in President Jimmy Carter's administration, a tentative effort to begin a normalization process with Vietnam had begun. When the American administration decided in 1978 that normalization of relations with Vietnam might jeopardize the establishment of diplomatic relations with China, it was abandoned. A key issue in the Vietnamese negotiations was gaining Hanoi's cooperation in the accounting for American servicemen missing in action (MIA). To this now was added the demand for Vietnamese withdrawal from Cambodia. For Vietnam, the American deference to China's hostility to Vietnam meant that the American economic embargo would remain in effect indefinitely.

Diverging ASEAN Perceptions

The face of ASEAN's external solidarity concealed different internal strategic perceptions. Malaysia and Indonesia, alarmed at the great power implications of confrontation with Vietnam, advanced at a March 1980 bilateral summit in Kuantan, Malaysia, the Kuantan Principle. Conceptually rooted in the ZOPFAN, it called for an end to Soviet influence in Vietnam but at the same time recognized Vietnam's security concerns with respect to China. It assumed a Vietnamese political sphere of interest in Cambodia in return for a peaceful Thai–Cambodian border. The Kuantan Principle did not become an

ASEAN position because of Thai, Singaporean, and Chinese objections. Thailand followed China's hard-line position and Singapore, sensitive to its own geostrategic vulnerability, demanded the enforcement of the UN resolutions.

The growing rift in ASEAN over approaches to a political solution that could accommodate Vietnam's interests was fully demonstrated in 1983. The foreign ministers of Malaysia and Vietnam met at the New Delhi NAM Summit and came up with a proposal for informal "bloc" to "bloc" talks between ASEAN and Vietnam and Laos outside of the ICK formula. The "5 + 2" (or with Cambodia excluded, "5 + 3 − 1") was endorsed by Indonesia and Singapore. Thailand, backed by China, objected, and ASEAN solidarity required conformity to the status quo in the absence of a new consensus.

It was the sense of missed opportunities and the implicit Chinese veto wielded through Thailand that in part inspired Indonesia to open its own bilateral channels to Vietnam in the search for a *modus vivendi*. From Jakarta's perspective, the only winners in bleeding Vietnam would be the Chinese, whose strategic window to Thailand was troubling, and the Russians, entrenching themselves in Vietnam. In return for Soviet support, Vietnam had conceded base rights to the USSR at the former U.S. military facilities at Cam Ranh Bay. Jakarta also chafed under the perceived conditions of ASEAN solidarity in which it was a follower, not a leader. Indonesia's open disaffection with the frontline state's strategy became public when Indonesia's military chief (and President Suharto's political troubleshooter) Gen. Benny Moerdani made an official visit to Hanoi in February 1984. There, he said that Indonesia did not view Vietnam as a threat to Southeast Asia. Indonesia opened a dialogue with Hanoi that supplemented the consensual ASEAN approach. In order to avoid an overt breach in ASEAN solidarity, Indonesia's ASEAN partners incorporated Indonesia's dual-track diplomacy into their political strategy by terming Indonesia ASEAN's "interlocutor" with Vietnam. Vietnam became increasingly anxious to extricate itself from Cambodia. The economic costs were great in a failing economy cut off from normal economic relations with most of the world. In 1985, Vietnam announced it would withdraw its troops from Cambodia by 1990.

The End Game

The negotiating problem was disentangling the levels of political conflict. ASEAN's formal stance was that the PRK was a creature of Vietnam and ASEAN would negotiate only with Vietnam not the PRK. From Hanoi's vantage, the PRK was the government of Cambodia and ASEAN would have to deal with Phnom Penh. The breakthrough came in a July 1987 joint statement by Indonesia's Foreign Minister Mochtar and his Vietnamese counterpart

Nguyen Co Thach proposing separating the "international" from the "internal" levels of the conflict. In "informal" settings the Cambodian factions would negotiate the ending of what was now diplomatically transformed into a civil war, to be joined by the other parties who provided external support to the combatants. In this way ASEAN did not have to recognize the PRK or Vietnam the CGDK factions as legitimate representatives of Cambodia. Indonesia's ASEAN partners reluctantly acceded to this arrangement. ASEAN's new flexibility also stemmed from Sihanouk's own overtures to the PRK that threatened to leave ASEAN alone with the dreaded Khmer Rouge.

The informal negotiating process began with the first Jakarta Informal Meeting (JIM I) in July 1988. Before JIM II met in February 1989, ASEAN's bargaining position had been transformed. Shortly after JIM I, the new Thai Prime Minister Chatichai Choonhaven opened his own extra-ASEAN bilateral channels to Phnom Penh and Hanoi, proclaiming that he wanted to turn the battlefields of Indochina into a marketplace. He shocked his ASEAN counterparts by inviting PRK President Hun Sen to Bangkok the month before JIM II. Chatichai's ASEAN detractors charged that his de facto recognition of the Hun Sen regime unilaterally undermined a decade of ASEAN diplomacy. Solidarity, however, required that ASEAN accept in negotiations the administrative reality in Cambodia of the PRK. The JIM process, however, stalled on the issues of whether Hun Sen's government should be dismantled before elections were held in Cambodia and the functioning of any international oversight mechanism.

As the JIM process faltered, the negotiation framework was enlarged in the nineteen-nation Paris International Conference on Cambodia (PICC), co-chaired by Indonesia and France with strong Australian input.[27] Between the first sessions of the PICC, 30 July–30 August 1989, which ended in deadlock, and its reconvening in September 1991, at which a peace accord was formalized, the agenda had been seized by the permanent members of the UN Security Council. The great power dynamics in the regional conflict had undergone significant change in the decade of the struggle over Cambodia's future. This was largely due to Soviet Premier Mikhail Gorbachev's emphasis on rebuilding the USSR's economy and restructuring the state. For this, détente and normalization of relations with the PRC were important. At a 15–18 May 1989 Sino–Soviet summit meeting, Gorbachev and his Chinese counterpart, Deng Xiaoping, agreed to a basis for national reconciliation in Cambodia, internationally supervised elections, and the convening of an international conference. It was the decoupling of the Sino–Soviet relationship from the Southeast Asian conflict that promoted great power consensus on the terms of settlement.

Following the collapse of the first PICC, the UN Security Council's Permanent Five produced a framework agreement for a comprehensive settlement that would allow all of the external participants to step back from the Cambodian imbroglio to let the Khmer people settle their own future. The settlement proposals were approved on 18 August 1990 by the Security Council and endorsed by acclamation at the UNGA on 15 October.[28] The Cambodian factions threatened by isolation from their external supporters had little option but to accept, although grudgingly, the KR and Hun Sen and his renamed State of Kampuchea. The comprehensive political settlement was ratified at the October 1991 second session of the PICC.[29] The Third Indochina War was over. It remained for the United Nations Transitional Authority in Cambodia (UNTAC) to secure the peace in Cambodia.

After more than a decade, both ASEAN and Vietnam got largely what they wanted. ASEAN's goals as laid out in the 1981 ICK Declaration had essentially been achieved. Vietnam was out of Cambodia. The UN through UNTAC and its peacekeepers organized and implemented a generally fair and free election. Under UNTAC, the KR was marginalized, refusing to compete in the internationally dictated political framework. It eventually surrendered to the new Cambodian government. It left, however, the problem of accountability for the crimes of its ruling years, a problem that is still being wrestled with by the international community (chapter 8). For Vietnam, a hostile Cambodia with strategic links to China no longer was a threat and the door to economic development opened. Hun Sen was a winner as well. Although UNTAC was technically in charge in Cambodia, Hun Sen's government remained in place as day-to-day administrators, boosting his political fortunes in post-UNTAC Cambodia (chapters 2 and 8). As Thai, Singaporean, and Malaysian businessmen and investors competed for advantage in a peaceful Indochina, formal ASEAN–Vietnam reconciliation began with Vietnam's accession to the Treaty of Amity and Cooperation in 1992 and the granting to it of official ASEAN "observer" status. Vietnam became ASEAN's seventh member in 1995.

For the United States, USSR, and PRC, the Cold War strategic triangle that had made ASEAN, Cambodia, and Vietnam surrogates in a Southeast Asian conflict zone was succeeded by détente and a replacement of American containment policy in Southeast Asia by growing economic interdependencies as China and Vietnam abandoned their failed command economies for market-oriented economies. With a diminished Soviet presence in Vietnam, China established full diplomatic relations with Vietnam in 1991. As noted in chapter 2, U.S.–Vietnam diplomatic relations were established in 1995. The Cold War in Southeast Asia was over.

Southeast Asia at the End of the Cold War

The political cohesiveness that allowed ASEAN to present a common front in the struggle to oust Vietnam from Cambodia originated in perceptions of a direct threat to the regional international order. It was politically defensive and did not derive from any inherent regional integrative process. Although ultimately diplomatically successful, the success was more a function of the real capabilities and interests of the external partners linked to the regional protagonists than to the capabilities of the ASEAN states. Second, the experience of the Third Indochina War revealed that there was no common ASEAN strategic perception. ASEAN states had disparate strategic orientations toward the United States and China. Third, it became clear that when an ASEAN state decided that its national interests were jeopardized by consensual ASEAN policy, national interests would take priority.

With the ending of the Cold War and the Third Indochina War—the sources of ASEAN's original political cement—the question was what new cement might bind the multiple and diverse national interests of the member states in the ASEAN framework. ASEAN's first effort to grapple with the tasks of cooperation in the absence of an explicit external security threat was contained in the Singapore Declaration of 1992 issued by the ASEAN leaders at their fourth summit meeting. In it, they boldly pledged "to move towards a higher plane of political and economic cooperation to secure regional peace and prosperity."[30] A new relevance had to be found for ASEAN in the challenges of a transforming regional and global international economic order. For more than a decade and a half, ASEAN has sought with only moderate success to reach that "higher plane" (chapter 4). The optimism that economic growth might now control ASEAN's trajectory was undermined in the wreckage of the 1997–1998 financial crisis in which it was every ASEAN country for itself (chapter 7).

The search for a "higher plane" takes place in a fundamentally altered great-power presence in the regional international environment. The crumbling and ultimate disappearance of the USSR left the United States and PRC to establish new political relations with the countries of the region in support of interests divorced from Cold War and Third Indochina War alliances and alignments. What was delicately called in ASEAN's 1992 Singapore Declaration "changing circumstances" allowed the grouping to reassert the ZOPFAN, enhanced by a Southeast Asian Nuclear Weapons-Free Zone (SEANWFZ). The SEANWFZ had been mooted by Malaysia in the 1970s and promoted by Indonesia in the 1980s. The models were the 1963 Treaty of Tlatco declaring Latin America a nuclear free zone and the 1985 Treaty of Rarotonga establishing the South Pacific Nuclear Free Zone (SPNFZ). ASEAN's version had been stymied by U.S.-allied Philippines and Thai objections. Now, with the Russian and American military footprints substantially reduced in the region, the time seemed ripe. The Treaty on the Southeast Asian Nuclear Weapons-Free Zone was signed at the fifth ASEAN Summit in Bangkok on 15 December 1995, entering into force in 1997.[31] Like the ZOPFAN, it was not self-enforcing, calling for the nuclear powers to accede through a separate protocol. This they have proved reluctant to do, including the United States.

The changed post–Cold War strategic environment was underlined by the 1991 termination of U.S. basing rights in the Philippines, a key element in the Cold War U.S. security posture in Southeast Asia. In 1986, Philippines President Ferdinand Marcos was forced from office and into exile, toppled by the Corazon Aquino–led "people's power" revolution. A new democratic political order replaced the two-decades-long Marcos presidential dictatorship. The 1947 U.S.–Philippine Military Bases Agreement (MBA) was scheduled to expire in mid-September 1991. A series of difficult negotiations for renewal began in May 1990 that resulted in a package that would have extended the MBA for ten years. The new treaty had to be ratified by a deeply split Philippine Senate. Opposition focused on issues of sovereignty, the nonnuclear provision of the 1987 Philippine Constitution, American support of the Marcos regime, U.S. overflights during an attempted military coup against the Aquino government, and other grist for an enflamed nationalist mill. The treaty was defeated by a vote of 12 to 11. The government presented the United States with a three-year phaseout plan. The United States shortened this to one year, the end of 1992. The ending of the Cold War gave less importance to Subic Bay's strategic value, particularly with the Russians out of Cam Ranh Bay. Many of the functions performed there, other than major ship repair, were picked up elsewhere: Japan, Okinawa, Guam, Singapore, Thailand, and even Malaysia. What was lost was the visible symbol of American commitment to the region.

The disappearance of the USSR and the lower profile of the United States gave greater relative importance to the emergence of China as an important actor in Southeast Asia with a full range of national interests: economic, political, and security. China was at peace with all of the ASEAN states, had been their strategic ally in the Third Indochina War, and shares many of the social and cultural interests of the developing countries of Southeast Asia. For the first time since World War II, the U.S. preponderance of power in Southeast Asia might be challenged by a power whose reach, while not yet global, is East Asian regional with the full measure of capabilities. The USSR's regional capability had been one dimensional—military. Japan had been one dimensional—economic. The United States is multidimensional, but so too now is China in its economic, political, and even in relative terms, military capabilities. This is the new dynamic in great power relations in Southeast Asia. How it is being managed by the regional actors will be explored in the chapters to follow.

Notes

1. George F. Kennan, "The Sources of Soviet Conduct," *Foreign Affairs* 25, no. 4 (1947): 566–82.

2. Viet Minh is an abbreviation of Vietnam Doc Lap Dong Minh Hoi (League for the Independence of Vietnam).

3. NSC, "United States Objectives and Course of Action with Respect to Southeast Asia [April 1952]," document #2 in *The Pentagon Papers as published by the New York Times* (New York: Bantam Books, Inc., 1971), 27–31.

4. The domino theory postulated the geostrategic consequences for what then was designated the "free world" if Indochina should fall to communism. President Dwight D. Eisenhower stated it at a 7 April 1954 news conference in response to a question about the strategic importance of Indochina to the United States. He framed his answer in terms of what he called "the falling domino principle," in which the first falling domino in a row of dominoes will certainly and quickly lead to the fall of the last domino. He enumerated the order as first Indochina, and then Burma, Thailand, the Peninsula (Malaya and Singapore), and Indonesia, with the consequent threat to the defensive island chain from Japan, Taiwan, and the Philippines, to Australia and New Zealand.

5. "Final Declaration at Geneva Conference and US Statement Renouncing Use of Force," document #14, *The Pentagon Papers*, 49–53.

6. 6 UST 81, *Treaties and Other International Acts Series* 3170.

7. The agreement between American Secretary of State Dean Rusk and Thai Foreign Minister Thanat Khoman was an executive branch interpretation of the Manila Treaty. This interpretation was restated by every American government through the end of the Third Indochina War.

8. The communiqué can be found as appendix C in Russell H. Fifield, *The Diplomacy of Southeast Asia: 1945–1958* (New York: Harper & Brothers, 1958), 512–19. For details of the conference see George McTurnan Kahin, *The Asian African Conference; Bandung, Indonesia, April 1955* (Ithaca, NY: Cornell University Southeast Asia Program, 1956).

9. Accessed at www.smpke.jpm.my/WebNotesApp/PMmain.nsf/faMainPM.

10. Paul M. Kattenburg, *The Vietnam Trauma in American Foreign Policy: 1945–1975* (New Brunswick, NJ: Transaction, 1980), 108–10.

11. "Southeast Asia Resolution," Public Law 88-408. It was called the "Tonkin Gulf" resolution because it followed an alleged attack by DRV torpedo boats on U.S. destroyers off North Vietnam's Tonkin Gulf coast.

12. U.S. Department of State, *Aggression from the North: The Record of North Viet-Nam's Campaign to Conquer South Viet-Nam* (Washington, D.C.: U.S. Government Printing Office, 1965).

13. "Agreement on Ending the War and Restoring Peace in Vietnam," 27 January 1973, 24 UST 4–23, *Treaties and Other International Acts Series* 7542.

14. The Nixon Doctrine was enunciated at a 25 July 1969 press conference on Guam (hence Guam Doctrine) following a meeting with South Vietnam's President Nguyen Van Thieu. It was reiterated in Nixon's address to the nation on Vietnam on 3 November 1969. The texts can be found in *Public Papers of the Presidents of the United States. Richard Nixon*, Vol. 1, 1969 (Washington, D.C.: U.S. Government Printing Office, 1971).

15. Bernard G. Gordon, *The Dimensions of Conflict in Southeast Asia* (Englewood Cliffs, N.J.: Prentice-Hall, 1966), 102.

16. The "Bangkok Declaration," accessed at www.aseansec.org/1212.htm.

17. Tan Sri Ghazali Shafie, "ASEAN Today and Tomorrow," *Foreign Affairs Malaysia*, 14, no. 3 (1981): 335.

18. "Kuala Lumpur Declaration of a Zone of Peace, Freedom and Neutrality," 17 November 1971, accessed at www.aseansec.org/1215.htm.

19. The full texts of the respective communiqués are collected in Appendices 8, 13, and 16 of Leo Suryadinata, *China and the ASEAN States: The Ethnic Chinese Dimension* (Singapore: Singapore University Press, 1985), 183–85, 198–200, 207–9.

20. Accessed at www.aseansec.org/1216.htm.

21. Accessed at www.aseansec.org/1217.htm.

22. The declassified documents were released by the National Security Archive at George Washington University and can be accessed at www.gwu.edu/~nsarchiv/NSAEBB/NSAEBB62.

23. Alan Renouf, *The Frightened Country* (Melbourne, Australia: Macmillan, 1979), 441–42.

24. "Joint Statement by the ASEAN Foreign Ministers on the Situation on the Thai-Kampuchean Border," Bangkok, 25 June 1980, accessed at www.aseansec.org/1611.htm.

25. "Declaration on Kampuchea," *UN Monthly Chronicle*, 18, no. 9 (1981): 37–39.

26. "ASEAN Statement on the Vietnam-China Border War," Bangkok, 20 February 1979, as reported in Foreign Broadcast Information Service, *Daily Report: Asia and Pacific*, 23 February 1979, A-1. This statement is not found in the open documents archived by the ASEAN Secretariat.

27. In addition to the ASEAN 6, Laos, Vietnam, PRK and CGDK, the PICC involved the five permanent members of the UN Security Council (Great Britain, China, France, U.S., USSR), Australia, Canada, India, and Japan.

28. The framework agreement for the Comprehensive Political Settlement in Cambodia is contained in the *Official Records of the Security Council Forty-fifth Year, Supplement for August-September 1990*, document S/216879, annex.

29. "Final Act of the Paris Conference on Cambodia." 23 October 1991, accessed at www.usip.org/library/pa/cambodia/final_act_1023991.html.

30. "Singapore Declaration of 1992," accessed at www.aseansec.org/5120.htm.

31. The SEANWFZ treaty can be accessed at www.aseansec.org/5181.htm.

Suggestions for Further Reading

An overview of American Cold War policy in the Pacific region is Robert McMahon, *The Limits of Empire* (New York: Columbia University Press, 1999). There is a voluminous literature on the U.S. war in Vietnam. A good place to start is David L. Anderson, *The Columbia Guide to the Vietnam War* (New York: Columbia University Press, 2002). A balanced short survey is Gary Hess, *Vietnam and the United States: Origins and Legacy* (Boston: Twayne, 1990). His bibliographic essay is a useful overview of the range of materials on the major topics.

For the causes and diplomacy of the Third Indochinese War, see David W. P. Elliott, ed., *The Third Indochina Conflict* (Boulder, Colo.: Westview, 1981); Donald E. Weatherbee, ed., *Southeast Asia Divided: The ASEAN-Indochina Crisis* (Boulder, Colo.: Westview, 1985); Nayan Chanda, *Brother Enemy: The War after the War* (New York: Macmillan, 1986). For the negotiations to end the war, see A. Acharya, P. Lizée, and S. Peou, *Cambodia—The 1989 Paris Peace Conference: Background Analysis and Documents* (Millwood, N.Y.: Kraus International, 1991). For the view of a senior American participant in the diplomacy ending the war, see Richard H. Solomon, *Exiting Indochina: U.S. Leadership of the Cambodian Settlement and Normalization with Vietnam* (Washington: United States Institute of Peace, 2000). New access to Russian, Chinese, and Vietnamese sources is utilized in Odd Arne Westad and Sophie Quinn-Judge, eds., *The Third Indochina War: Conflict between China, Vietnam and Cambodia* (London: Routledge, 2006).

American intervention in Indonesia's regional rebellion is the subject of George McT. Kahin and Audrey Kahin, *Subversion as Foreign Policy: The Secret Eisenhower and Dulles Debacle in Indonesia* (New York: The New Press, 1995). For the West New Guinea dispute, see John Saltford, *The United Nations and the Indonesian Takeover of West Papua, 1962–1969: The Anatomy of a Betrayal* (London: RoutledgeCurzon, 2004). Indonesia's confrontation with Malaysia is dealt with in J. A. C. Mackie, *Konfrontasi: The Indonesia—Malaysia Dispute, 1963–1966* (Kuala Lumpur: Oxford University Press, 1974).

4

ASEAN and Regionalism in Southeast Asia

THE CONCEPT OF REGIONALISM IN INTERNATIONAL RELATIONS in Southeast Asia signifies the formal association of three or more of the nation-states in the geographic region in political, economic, or other functionally related multilateral structures promoting international cooperation. The purpose is to further national interest through a more efficient allocation of resources in those areas of state activities where complementary interests can be harmonized by collective decision making in terms of maximizing national interest through regional cooperation. It also enhances through a kind of pooling process the capabilities of the individual states in their relations with extraregional powers with greater capabilities. In ASEAN this is called "regional resilience." It is argued in chapter 1 that it is the cooperative association of national interests in regional or subregional political/economic structures that represents the link between the state and regional levels of analysis. Very importantly, that link has no operational regional policy relevance unless and until collective decisions at the regional level are translated into the national policies of the member states.

We have already identified the Association of Southeast Asian Nations (ASEAN) as the most significant expression of the regionalist urge in Southeast Asia. After the EU, ASEAN is often deemed to be the most successful regional grouping in the developing world. Former UN Secretary-General General Kofi Annan noted that "ASEAN is not only a well-functioning indispensable reality in the region, it is a real force to be reckoned with far beyond the region."[1] Unfortunately, however, the all-too-often comparison with the EU leads to disappointed expectations about ASEAN. The European experience has been one of supranational integration requiring derogations of sovereignty and delegations of authority, neither of which the member states of ASEAN have yet been prepared to do. A question to be raised in this chapter, and to be examined more fully in the chapters to follow, is how ASEAN's successes and failures are to be measured and what kind of force it might be beyond the Southeast Asian region. ASEAN regionalism as an international process in Southeast Asia is taking place in the context of a wider East Asia and Pacific economic regionalism (chapter 7). ASEAN's future depends in part on what continuing value its member states will put on a Southeast Asia–centered organizational unit as they are integrated into more inclusive, expansive, and sometimes competitive regionalist patterns of state interaction. As ASEAN states recognize that their national interests require institutional engagements transcending the geographic limits of ASEAN, what will this mean for the claim of ASEAN's "centrality?"

ASEAN Enters into Its Fifth Decade

ASEAN celebrated the fortieth anniversary of its founding "Bangkok Declaration" in 2007. Certainly one of the factors that enter into any evaluation of ASEAN's success as a regionalist enterprise is its durability over time. Chapter 3 discussed ASEAN's 1967 origins and development in the aftermath of Indonesia's confrontation with Malaysia, the uncertainties of the Cold War, and the Second Indochina War followed by the Third Indochina War. In the course of time, ASEAN has become a fixture in the international relations of the region. That it has survived the conflicting interests and divergent strategic perceptions of its members is attributable to the conscious efforts of its political managers to focus on noncontentious interest areas so that no member would feel its national interests threatened by collective decisions. This is at the heart of the so-called ASEAN way: consensus decision making that does not diminish sovereignty or interfere in the domestic arrangements of the member states. ASEAN's regionalism is a loose regionalism in which there is no regional organizational authority over the member states' policies or behavior.

Other factors have contributed to ASEAN's longevity despite the multiple national diversities outlined in chapter 1 that militate against meaningful regionalism. Leadership has been important. From its inception through its first three decades, Indonesia quietly set the ASEAN course at a pace comfortable to all. ASEAN has been an important foreign policy tool for Indonesia. The most comprehensive analysis of Indonesian policy toward ASEAN came to the conclusion that Jakarta had an implicit veto in ASEAN because, as the Indonesian foreign policy expert put it baldly, if not diplomatically, ASEAN needed Indonesia more than Indonesia needed ASEAN.[2] Indonesia's strategy was shaped by two goals. Through ASEAN, it sought to prevent alterations in the regional status quo that might inhibit the realization of Indonesia's full potential and ambitions. In the ASEAN multilateral setting it could increase its capabilities in a way that was not threatening, but at the same time, given the ASEAN way, not limit its options.

Indonesia's policy in ASEAN was set by President Suharto, who became ASEAN's senior and most influential statesman. In a sense, Jakarta was not only ASEAN's official headquarters but, as well, the unofficial repository of ASEAN's policy continuity. One of the great discontinuities in post-Suharto Indonesia was the implicit downgrading of ASEAN in the eyes of Suharto's three immediate successors. Their preoccupation was state survival, not regional cooperation. Nor did the successors have the personal stake in ASEAN's progress that Suharto, an ASEAN founding father, had. This carried serious implications for ASEAN's future. In many respects the ASEAN way was defined as an Indonesian way. One veteran observer of Southeast Asian international politics even linked ASEAN's continued existence to Indonesia's future unity and stability.[3] The relative success of President Susilo Bambang Yudhoyono, elected in 2004, in consolidating democracy and stability in Indonesia (chapter 1) suggests that Indonesia has turned a corner and it can reclaim its regional primacy. This is important since, as a respected former editor of the *Far Eastern Economic Review* wrote, "without Indonesia's presence and leadership, Southeast Asia's chemistry is thrown out of balance and it becomes a region diminished in the eyes of the world."[4]

Another reason for ASEAN's persistence has been that once reconciliation with postconfrontation Indonesia was achieved in 1967, the regionalist stimulus did not originate internally, but externally. If ASEAN's lasting power had depended on substantive progress in regional economic and social cooperation, it probably would not have survived into the new millennium. To date, ASEAN's compelling raison d'être is in being a diplomatic caucus of weaker powers in a regional international system dominated by stronger powers. ASEAN's cement has not been a cooperative, let alone integrative, economic, social, or cultural process. Its cement has been political solidarity in facing external challenge. As those challenges have changed, so too has ASEAN.

As outlined in chapter 3, for more than half of ASEAN's lifetime, the Cold War challenge was proximate: the Second and Third Indochina Wars, pitting first the United States and then ASEAN against what each in turn defined as Russian-backed Vietnam's aggression. The creation of ASEAN itself, followed by its two major regional political/security initiatives—the Zone of Peace, Freedom, and Neutrality (ZOPFAN) and the Treaty on a Southeast Asian Nuclear Weapons–Free Zone (SEANWFZ)—were declaratory efforts to assert some degree of control over the region's strategic environment. With the exception of the domestic radical Islamist groups' connections to international terrorism represented by al-Qaeda (chapter 6), today's external strategic challenges are more remote and less politically tangible, especially China's long-term regional role and the impacts of the processes of globalization—what Thomas Friedman so deftly illuminated as the new dominant international system.[5]

For liberals, ASEAN still retains its unfulfilled integrative promise. For realists, it has become part of the balance of power. For Southeast Asian leaderships, ASEAN is a diplomatic tool. ASEAN is one of the foreign and economic policy outputs of the policy systems of its member states processing national interests. Policymakers and analysts, although differing in their approaches to ASEAN and evaluations of its achievements, would agree that after so long a period of time and with so much effort and prestige invested in it, ASEAN's disappearance would be regionally destabilizing. Although the breakup of ASEAN because of intramural conflict cannot be ruled out completely, the real issue is ASEAN's continued relevance in light of the new challenges. Can it adapt to new regional and international circumstances? Will the tools of the ASEAN way—consensus, sovereignty, and noninterference—suffice in an international environment characterized by complex interdependence? In part, ASEAN's contemporary problem of relevance derives from a dilution through membership expansion of the cohering factors that kept the original ASEAN 5 together.

From Five to Ten: Is More, Better?

When looking for examples of ASEAN's achievements, some observers, particularly in the ASEAN states, nominate its membership expansion to include (with the exception of newly independent Timor-Leste) all of the sovereign states of Southeast Asia as ASEAN's greatest achievement. The 1967 "Bangkok Declaration" left ASEAN membership open to all states in Southeast Asia subscribing to its aims, principles, and purposes. Brunei joined at independence in 1984. Vietnam's admission in 1995 gave final closure to the political gulf between communist and noncommunist Southeast Asia. Membership had been offered as an incentive to Vietnam in the negotiations for terminating the Third Indochina War. Laos was granted observer status in 1992, Cambodia in 1994, and finally Myanmar in 1996. The 1995 ASEAN Summit decided to achieve an inclusive "one Southeast Asia" by the year 2000. The subsequent 1996 informal summit meeting advanced the date to admit the three candidate members simultaneously at the 1997 ASEAN Ministerial Meeting (AMM). This allowed the leaders of the candidate members to join their counterparts at the informal summit scheduled for Kuala Lumpur in November 1997. Because Laos and Cambodia had a longer lead-time for technical preparation for membership, the linking of Myanmar's admission to them was unexpected. It had to do with opposition to Myanmar's membership both in democratic ASEAN circles as well as the West because of the junta's atrocious human rights record (chapter 8). The packaging of Myanmar with Laos and Cambodia held the membership of the latter two hostage. ASEAN made it clear that Myanmar's internal politics were not relevant to the question of membership. As it turned out, it was Hun Sen's 1997 coup in Cambodia that presented a challenge to the ASEAN way.

Myanmar

ASEAN accepted Myanmar as a full member in 1997, recognizing that this would tarnish its image with its major international partners by giving the ASEAN seal of approval to the Myanmar junta. The strongest advocate for Myanmar's membership was Malaysia's Prime Minister Mahathir, the junta's best ASEAN friend. In his welcoming keynote address to the 1997 Kuala Lumpur AMM that admitted Myanmar, he said of Western objections to Myanmar's membership that "ASEAN must resist and reject such attempts at coercion."[6] ASEAN's two-pronged defense of its act was logically inconsistent. On the one hand, it was argued that ASEAN did not interfere in the domestic affairs of other nations and that Myanmar's internal politics were not relevant to the question of ASEAN membership. The second argument was that by "constructive engagement" along a broad range of interests in an ASEAN framework, the junta would be moved in the direction of political change and greater respect for human rights. This turned back on the United States its defense of "constructive engagement" with China. From the realpolitik vantage, the Southeast Asian leaders believed that if they admitted Vietnam, Laos, and Cambodia to ASEAN and isolated Myanmar, the junta would become a Chinese client. Also, there was resentment of the Clinton administration's insistent human rights campaign. ASEAN's refusal to cave in to the American pressure illustrated the diminished American political leverage resulting from the end of Cold War security concerns.

ASEAN's institutional relations with the United States and the EU have suffered because of Myanmar. In ASEAN-controlled settings and agendas, such as the annual AMM Post-Ministerial Conferences (PMC) and ASEAN Regional Forum (ARF), the Western representatives have no choice but to sit with the Myanmar foreign minister and senior officials, either that or boycott ASEAN. They lose no opportunity, however, to openly chide the Myanmar regime on its rights record, to the discomfiture of the junta's ASEAN partners. The real prospect of a Western boycott if Myanmar had assumed the chair of ASEAN in 2006, as was its right by alphabetical rotation, led ASEAN to persuade Myanmar to step aside in favor of the Philippines. American Secretary of State Condoleezza Rice's absence from the 2005 PMC and the ARF meeting was interpreted as a sign of U.S. displeasure at Myanmar's impending assumption of ASEAN leadership. In signing the 2006 ASEAN–U.S. Trade and Investment Framework Agreement (TIFA), the United States specified that it did not change the U.S. economic sanctions on Myanmar. After the junta's September 2007 crackdown on Buddhist monks, President George W. Bush cancelled the proposed 2008 Crawford, Texas, U.S.–ASEAN summit because it would have included Myanmar. Formal ASEAN–EU institutional engagements have been slowed, even paralyzed, by issues of Myanmar's involvement. ASEAN–EU negotiations for a free trade agreement have been stalled over the EU's refusal to include Myanmar in any deal.

Myanmar's ASEAN membership, rather than an asset, has become a cancer eating away at ASEAN's credibility in the community of democratic nations. ASEAN's rhetorical commitments to democratic values and human rights are mocked by the ASEAN way and solidarity with the junta. Bilateral overtures from ASEAN partners for dialogue with the junta on political change are coolly received and rebuffed. ASEAN's constructive engagement has served to buffer the junta from total isolation from the West. There is frustration within ASEAN about the junta's unwillingness to moderate its policy, at the least to release Aung San Suu Kyi. The Malaysian foreign minister has warned that it had reached the point where ASEAN could no longer defend Myanmar if the country made no attempt to cooperate and help itself.[7] The junta's intransigence in the face of ASEAN's entreaties recognizes that ASEAN has no levers to force change other than Myanmar's stake in ASEAN itself. That stake is being devalued as Myanmar is wooed politically and bolstered economically by China and India.

Cambodia

Two weeks before Cambodia's scheduled induction into ASEAN in July 1997, Co-Prime Minister Hun Sen's security forces hunted down the FUNCINPEC supporters of Co-Prime Minister Prince Ranariddh, violently ending the UNTAC-sponsored power-sharing agreement that followed the 1993 election (chapter 2). Beneath the façade of coalition, a struggle for power had the country teetering on the brink of a new civil war as Hun Sen's Cambodian People's Party (CPP) and FUNCINPEC jockeyed in anticipation of the scheduled 1998 elections. Both sides dallied with defectors from the Khmer Rouge to bolster their forces. As rumors of coups swirled, Hun Sen struck a preemptive blow at his erstwhile co-prime minister. Ranariddh fled the country and FUNCINPEC loyalist supporters took up arms in north and northwestern Cambodia to resist Hun Sen's quasi-coup d'état.

The ASEAN foreign ministers were stunned. At a hastily convened meeting they reaffirmed their commitment to noninterference in the internal affairs of other states but then interfered by deciding "that in light of the unfortunate circumstances which have resulted from the use of force the wisest course of action is to delay the admission of Cambodia into ASEAN until a later date."[8] ASEAN saw political stability in continental Southeast Asia at risk. The foreign ministers designated their colleagues from Indonesia, the Philippines, and Thailand to act on ASEAN's behalf as mediators. The ASEAN troika's goal was to guarantee that free and fair elections would be held in Cambodia with the participation of Ranariddh and his party. ASEAN's hand was strengthened by donor nations that withheld aid for nonhumanitarian needs. Cambodia's UN seat was vacant as the General Assembly's Credentials Committee would not decide between a Hun Sen or Ranariddh-backed delegation.

Hun Sen was forced to accept ASEAN-monitored elections in 1998. They were narrowly won by the CPP amid turmoil, intimidation, and vote-rigging. The ASEAN troika, apparently believing a little democracy was better than no democracy, hammered out a new coalition government in which Hun Sen became sole prime minister and Ranariddh the speaker of the National Assembly. With its requirements fulfilled, ASEAN admitted Cambodia to membership in 1999. Prime Minister Hun Sen's rehabilitation was made complete in 2002, when he chaired in Phnom Penh the ASEAN Summit. Hun Sen ultimately forced Ranariddh out of legal politics in 2006.

Why did ASEAN act differently in the Cambodian case—delaying membership and requiring a monitored election—than in the Myanmar case? The fact that internal politics were relevant to membership in Cambodia's case and not Myanmar's was based more on strategic realities than principle. A new civil war in Cambodia would have had political and strategic consequences for the three bordering ASEAN states that Myanmar did not pose. Thailand certainly was not prepared to deal with another flood of Cambodian refugees. ASEAN and the international donor consortium did not want to see the efforts at reconstruction of the shattered society wasted. The ASEAN position on Cambodia was not based on democratic ideology. ASEAN wished to undo the act of force that had led to political instability in the continental heart of the region. Finally, after taking so much heat on Myanmar, ASEAN did not want its international image further sullied by ignoring the events in Cambodia.

A Tiered ASEAN

ASEAN's membership expansion came with costs for cooperation in terms of programmatic coherence and political community. The original ASEAN was, with the exception of Thailand, part of what chapter 1 described as maritime Southeast Asia. Countries with continental interests dominate the expanded ASEAN, focused on contiguity with and economic access to China. The original ASEAN members shared an anticommunist ideology, experiences with communist insurgency, and security bonds with the West. No new integral ideological cement binds the disparate national units of the expanded ASEAN. Table 1.3 in chapter 1 indicates the magnitude of the economic gap separating the core states from the newer members, collectively termed the CLMV countries (Cambodia, Laos, Myanmar, and Vietnam). This has led to intra-ASEAN issues testing the ideal of equality in economic decision making, and the need for special dispensations for the economically second-tier members, including longer target dates for the CLMV to achieve ASEAN's collective economic goals (chapter 7).

It was understood that a widening of the economic division between the two tiers as the "little tigers" outperformed the economic laggards could undermine ASEAN solidarity. ASEAN tried to address the problem of bridging the development gap between the core members and the CLMV countries, launching in 2002 an "Initiative for ASEAN Integration" (IAI). A six-year IAI work plan was drawn with four priority sectors: infrastructure, human resources development, information and communications technology, and regional economic integration. A 2006 update listed 132 IAI work plan projects. The ASEAN 6 had contributed $28.2 million (76 percent from Singapore) to the IAI and external donors $16.9 million.[9] The IAI did not address the structural differences between the political economies of the core group and the CLMV countries, nor did it provide for integrative institutional cooperation.

More immediate concerns for the prospective solidarity of the ASEAN 10 are the political differences that divide ASEAN members, both in terms of their domestic political systems and their strategic perceptions. The overarching similarities of political economies and security concerns of the core members made the original ASEAN possible. The question is whether the greater dissimilarities in the expanded ASEAN lead to division rather than consensus and to even greater obstacles to cooperation than those that prevailed in the past. Although ASEAN can rightfully claim that all of Southeast Asia has been brought under ASEAN's normative tent, this is no predictor of the real policy choices to be made by the individual states in reaction to collective decisions. Furthermore, in an ASEAN 10 those collective decisions lowered the common denominator threshold for policy action.

ASEAN historically has been a political grouping reacting to a threat environment dominated by state actors with greater capabilities than ASEAN can collectively deploy, let alone the member states individually. In a search for security defined traditionally, the Core 5 maintained a high level of externally focused solidarity. The new threat environment is more complex and nontraditional with a multidimensional array of political, economic, social, and cultural challenges. It remains to be seen whether an ASEAN 10 can maintain the kind of solidarity that will be necessary to transform ASEAN from a balance-of-power mechanism to a political/economic community as it embarked in 2008 on a reinvention of itself in the new ASEAN Charter. ASEAN's already diminished consensual solidarity might be further attenuated either through future expansion (Timor-Leste and PNG) or functional absorption into wider forms of regionalism.

ASEAN's Organizational Evolution

How ASEAN's record as a manifestation of regionalism is to be judged depends on the critics' analytical vantage. There is no question but that it has shown remarkable political staying power and has contributed to regional stability. If, however, the measure is real achievements in areas of functional cooperation spelled out in the "Bangkok Declaration," then for its first four decades ASEAN fell far short of its aspirations. Efforts to reconcile competitive claims of self-interest and regional cooperation were disappointing and concrete achievements elusive. Evolving behavioral patterns or structural forms that would lead toward ASEAN's visionary goals have not matched the rhetorical harmony of ASEAN communiqués and declarations. It is difficult to identify any specific concrete economic, social, technical, or cultural function that ASEAN performs that in any clearly recognizable form has contributed to the economic growth and development of the member states. ASEAN's real achievement is its contribution to a regional international political order that has promoted a climate for economic assistance, trade, and foreign direct investment (FDI) supporting national development programs.

One explanation for the lack of functional economic and social progress during ASEAN's first three decades is that the political demands of the regional security environment diverted political resources away from ASEAN's nonpolitical tasks. This assumes that if there were no external security challenges, national elites would have pursued patterns of closer functional cooperation. This is not self-evident. It also ignores the fact that decision making about forms and substance of regional functional cooperation is itself political, especially given linkages to domestic interests. The retort can be made that rather than inhibiting economic and social regionalism, the emphasis on political cooperation in facing external security challenges was a necessary prerequisite for cooperation in other policy areas.

It can be argued that the spillover linking the different dimensions of state activities in ASEAN's cooperative regionalism is from the political to the nonpolitical. This is the reverse of that generally understood from liberal functionalist integration theory that sees political cooperation as resulting from functional cooperation. The problem for ASEAN's regionalists was dual: connecting the international political processes to the regional cooperative process and connecting regional cooperation to national development strategies. It was not for want of study that nonpolitical cooperation faltered. ASEAN's documentary history is rife with academic studies, policy papers, conference reports, and workshops seeking to give flesh to the bare bones of the "Bangkok Declaration." This was particularly true of what emerged as the key substantive issue area: economic cooperation in a regional environment of economic competition (chapter 7). In the words of a former ASEAN secretary-general, to make real progress would have required "almost a new vision and a new sense of dedication on the part of the ASEAN heads of government. Vision, dedication and above all, a fresh infusion of political will."[10] While vision, dedication, and political will may have been absent, there has been no shortage of unfulfilled plans and programs laying out blueprints for ASEAN's development. That they did not eventuate in structures and institutions giving effect to them is the result of the primacy of national interests over the regionalists' goal.

Until the 1992 Singapore Summit, the machinery devised by ASEAN founders to carry out its mission was relatively simple, reflecting, perhaps, the low expectations of the foreign ministers for a decentralized consultative grouping. The foreign ministers' control was institutionalized in their annual ministerial meeting (AMM), ASEAN's collective executive. The chairmanship of the AMM rotates through ASEAN's ten capitals. As noted above, this caused a diplomatic crisis in 2006 when it was Myanmar's turn to assume the chair. The junta was persuaded to pass. Meetings of the ASEAN foreign ministers are not limited to the AMM. Special meetings can be held as occasion demands, for example, the January 1979 meeting to formulate the official ASEAN position on the Vietnam invasion of Cambodia (chapter 3), or the ASEAN position on Hun Sen's 1997 Cambodian coup (above). Between AMMs, the incoming AMM chair chaired the ASEAN Standing Committee (ASC) and was official spokesperson for ASEAN. The ASC was composed of the foreign minister, who was chair, and the ASEAN ambassadors accredited to the host country. In fact, regular direct contact is maintained among the foreign ministers and their senior officials, and the role of the ASC was diminished.

In ASEAN's first decade, the functional tasks of devising cooperative activities below the political level of consultation fell to permanent and ad hoc committees of officials and experts. By 1969, eleven permanent committees dealing with economic, social, and cultural matters had been established. Based in different ASEAN countries, the committees worked in bureaucratic isolation and despite manifest functional overlaps, there was no horizontal integrative mechanism. Although the committees generated numerous plans, projects, and cooperative schemes, there were few approvals and little project implementation. Notably missing from the regionalist orientations of the functional committees was any agency to connect ASEAN's economic development planning to the national development priorities and programs of its member states. This was a fatal pill for future ASEAN initiatives. ASEAN's bureaucratic backstopping was decentralized in national secretariats tasked with carrying out the work of the organization on behalf of their country as well as servicing the AMM and other committees. The national secretariats had no horizontal links with each other or to any centralizing coordinating body above them. Their focus is indicated by the fact that all of the national secretariats are housed in the member nations' foreign ministries.

The "Bangkok Declaration" was not an enforceable treaty. The structure of ASEAN was one of a voluntary association with no binding obligations on the member states. There was no delegation of authority to ASEAN and decision making was by consensual unanimity. ASEAN adopted Indonesian terminology to explain the process: *musyawarah-mufakat* ("consultation and consensus"). This meant that ASEAN moved at the pace of its slowest member. The objective was to avoid compromising fragile political cohesion by conflicts over concrete functional programs and projects where competitive national interests would come into play. Disappointed integrationists blamed the failure in progress in building regional cooperative programs and institutions on the leadership's lack of "political will." In fact, the absence of substantial steps toward functional regionalism was an expression of the AMM's political will.

The 1976 Bali Summit and Its 1977 Kuala Lumpur Follow-up

The heads of government of the five ASEAN states met as ASEAN leaders for their first summit in 1976. This was prompted, as noted in chapter 3, by the communist victories in Indochina. The political centerpieces of the summit were the "Declaration of ASEAN Concord" and the "Treaty of Amity and Cooperation." The summit also tinkered with the organizational structure. The lack of an administrative link at the ASEAN level was partially remedied. A secretariat was established with a secretary-general of the ASEAN Secretariat appointed on a rotating basis for a two-year term (extended to three in 1985) heading it. The post had no executive or policy role. Its charge was to keep the paperwork flowing. The secretariat was headquartered in Jakarta. ASEAN's lack of institutional autonomy was embarrassingly displayed when

Indonesia dismissed the first secretary-general, an Indonesian national, for domestic Indonesian political reasons.

At Bali, the leaders adopted an economic agenda based on the UN blueprint and sought to promote trade liberalization through an ASEAN Preferential Tariff Arrangement (PTA), the precursor to the 1992 AFTA. A new prominence for ASEAN's economic ministers was underlined at the Kuala Lumpur Summit, with their status becoming co-equal with the foreign ministers and their reporting line going directly to the heads of government rather than through the AMM. The economic development-related functional committees were brought directly under the economic ministers. This reflected growing dissatisfaction with the pace of economic cooperation.

The 1992 ASEAN Singapore Summit

With their "Singapore Declaration" of a new will to move to a higher plane of cooperation, the ASEAN heads of government strengthened ASEAN's bureaucratic structures. The leaders showed their determination to take nominal charge of the organization by institutionalizing the ASEAN summits. It was decided to have a formal summit every three years with an informal summit in the intervening years. The distinction between formal and informal ended with the fourth informal summit in Singapore in 2000. The summit is held in that year's ASEAN chair's country. At the summits, the heads of government review ASEAN affairs, ratify and endorse the various proposals and initiatives that are to be undertaken in the name of ASEAN, and take note of regional and global events having bearing on ASEAN interests.

The 1992 Singapore Summit reorganized the bureaucratic structure for ASEAN economic cooperation. It dissolved the existing ASEAN economic committees and tasked the Senior Economic Officials' Meeting (SEOM) with handling all aspects of ASEAN economic cooperation. It also established a ministerial-level council to oversee the implementation of the AFTA. The AMM, ASEAN economic ministers' meeting (AEMM), and ASEAN finance ministers' meeting (AFMM) became the leading organs of ASEAN. These gatherings were paralleled by a burgeoning number of other functional ministerial meetings and councils. At the consultative level, at least, ASEAN's work program comprehended nearly all aspects of a state's national policy concerns.

Finally, the ASEAN leaders at Singapore addressed the problem of continuity and direction within ASEAN itself. The secretary-general of the ASEAN Secretariat was designated the secretary-general of ASEAN with ministerial status and a five-year term. The secretary-general's mandate was expanded to initiate, advise, coordinate, and implement ASEAN activities. The secretary-general does this with a relatively small staff. As of 1 January 2008, there were ninety-nine openly recruited professional staff. There is a quota system for the openly recruited officers, since each member country has to have professional representation in the secretariat. The professional staff is supported by locally recruited staffers. Most of the bureaucratic burden of ASEAN still rests with the ten national secretariats and relevant national ministries. The task of staffing the literally hundreds of ASEAN intergovernmental sessions, committee meetings, workshops, seminars, training programs, and so on, puts an enormous strain on the bureaucratic human resources pool of ASEAN's second-tier members.

The 2003 "Reinvention" of ASEAN

From Singapore 1992 to Bali 2003

The Singapore Declaration's goal of moving ASEAN to a higher plane of cooperation engendered numerous studies and papers attempting to lay out projects and programs to give effect to the new emphasis on the economic and social side of ASEAN. The most ambitious was the 1997 ASEAN Vision 2020 set out by the heads of government at the Kuala Lumpur informal summit in which they pledged to move toward close economic integration.[11] A year later, at the Hanoi Summit, the leaders adopted a detailed plan of action designed to implement Vision 2020. The "Hanoi Action Plan" was peppered with statements of intentions to "foster," "promote," "study," and "strengthen" what are essentially intergovernmental cooperative activities, not regional integrative structures.[12] However positive the intentions might have been, the ASEAN vision was overshadowed by the economic crisis at the end of the decade and the political turmoil that accompanied it.

The financial crisis of 1997–1998 challenged the political leaders of Southeast Asia as no other crisis had since the end of the Indochina wars (chapter 7). They quickly learned that multilateral frameworks for regional economic collaboration provided no cushions for the shocks to their economies as the value of their currencies plunged and economies fueled by debt unrelated to assets hollowed out. There was no collective lifeboat. It was every nation for itself in a series of ongoing bilateral negotiations between governments, international agencies, banks, and other creditors. At the same time that the political elite faced external pressures, they had to cope with the domestic dislocations occurring after the sudden reversal of years of rapid growth, rising living standards, and expectations of a better future. Political anger, generated throughout the region, focused on both the remote structures of global capitalism and more narrowly on domestic individuals, groups, and classes who had benefited the most from Southeast Asia's integration into the global economy but who now appeared to be the authors of economic disaster.

ASEAN's failure to construct a regional response to the Crash of '97 shook the foundations of the grouping as each country groped for solutions, sometimes at the cost of neighbors. Unilateralism, not regionalism, reigned supreme under the watchful eye of the IMF. Questions were raised about the relevance of ASEAN during a time of great economic crisis. As the regional economies slowly emerged from the wreckage, they were pummeled by the economic impact of the Severe Acute Respiratory Syndrome (SARS) (chapter 8) and fears of terrorism (chapter 6). There were hints that a two-tiered ASEAN might become a three-tier ASEAN. In the first years of the new millennium, Singapore and Thailand, frustrated by the slow pace of ASEAN trade liberalization, stood apart as they looked to bilateral FTAs with their major extraregional partners for the stimulus to economic growth (chapter 7). This contributed to an unraveling of the ASEAN consensus on AFTA, even as a booming China drew FDI away from Southeast Asia and competed with Southeast Asia in the global marketplace.

The decrescendo of ASEAN economic cooperation coincided with the political tumult over Myanmar's repressive government. By embracing the Yangon regime, ASEAN distanced itself from its Western democratic dialogue partners. What little collective bargaining power ASEAN might have had in its dealings with Europe and North America was diminished by its growing organizational inability to deal with political issues of great concern to its major dialogue partners—with the exception of China (chapter 8). The war on terrorism and war in Iraq deepened existing differences in strategic perceptions between the Philippines, Singapore, and Thailand and the rest of ASEAN. These three countries joined the U.S.-sponsored "Coalition of the Willing." The domestic political need for governments in Malaysia and Indonesia to placate the Islamic sensitivities of their Muslim populations accentuated the cultural gulf in ASEAN.

What some observers perceived as an erosion of ASEAN's underpinnings and its political devaluation in Europe and North America coincided with a leadership void in ASEAN. Indonesia's President Suharto was off the stage and his successors were preoccupied with domestic stability. Prime Minister Mahathir in Malaysia was a polarizing figure and on his way out. Thailand's Prime Minister Thaksin Shinawatra was an unknown quantity who seemed to have his eye on a larger international stage. Philippine presidents fended off mob rule and coup attempts. Singapore's Prime Minister Goh Chok Tong had always functioned in the shadow of his predecessor Senior Minister Lee Kuan Yew. The CLMV countries did not have leaders with international stature or respect. In these circumstances, how could ASEAN again be reinvented?

The 2003 Bali Summit and the "Bali Concord II" ("ASEAN Concord II")

In 2003, ASEAN's chairmanship passed from Prime Minister Hun Sen's Cambodia to President Megawati Sukarnoputri's Indonesia. This was the first opportunity for a post-Suharto Indonesian leadership to play an important role in shaping the region's future. A Bali ASEAN Summit was capped by the signing of the "Bali Concord II," signifying a rededication to the political, economic, and social goals expressed more than a quarter of a century earlier at the first Bali Summit (chapter 3). The goal was to create "a dynamic, cohesive, resilient and integrated ASEAN Community by the year 2020."[13] This ASEAN Community is to be supported by the three pillars of an ASEAN Security Community (ASC), an ASEAN Economic Community (AEC), and an ASEAN Socio-Cultural Community (ASCC).

The ASC concept was vigorously promoted by Indonesia. It allowed Jakarta to reclaim its position as the strategic center for regional security. The goal is heightened political and security cooperation. The Indonesian proponents underline that it is not a military alliance or a defense pact. It does not provide for new regional security structures. It is based on existing instruments like ZOPFAN, SEANWFZ, and TAC. Working through the ARF, it will incorporate ASEAN's extraregional friends. Rather than an organization or institution, it is conceived as a future *condition* of peaceful relations for which the ASEAN states should strive. The ASC's most problematic aspect is the assumption that it will be underpinned by democracy and respect for human rights. The blueprint for the ASC is to be presented to the November 2008 ASEAN Summit.

Singapore and Thailand pressed for the AEC to meet the growing competition from India and China. The goal was to establish ASEAN as a single market and production base through the free flow of goods, services, investment, and capital by the year 2020. An impatient Singapore and Thailand had pushed for a 2015 deadline. In 2006, the target was in fact reset to 2015. The AEC will be achieved largely through carrying out the stalled implementation of existing agreements on AFTA, services, and investment (chapter 7). Certainly it will require a level of integration, cooperation, and liberalization that has been absent in ASEAN's past. Whether political leaderships in the ASEAN states will have either the will or capability to overcome domestic protectionist interests is problematic. Also, how the AEC can be articulated with other, broader regional free trade areas that ASEAN embraces remains to be seen (chapter 7).

Of the three communities, the ASCC proposal is the most nebulous, but paradoxically perhaps the most achievable. It builds on the ASEAN Vision 2020 and the 2000 AMM resolve to achieve a "socially cohesive and caring

ASEAN."[14] It is intended to foster cooperation in addressing a grab bag of social and cultural problems associated with rural poverty, population growth, unemployment, human resources development, education, environment, and health. The programs are broadly conceived as the human security element of comprehensive security (chapter 8). William Tow has written that "the fate of human security in East and Southeast Asia over the longer term is most likely to be determined by the extent to which it becomes an integral part of *regional* institution building."[15] The ASCC is an initial approach to this.

The kinds of problems to be dealt with in the framework of the ASCC are commonly those of low politics, not involving competing vital national interests—very different from the agendas of the ASC and AEC. The development of common regional policies in these areas where the issues are often technical, scientific, educational, or managerial does not require great political investment and compromise.[16] Furthermore, it is in these functional areas of relations that partnership with external donors and their agencies such as USAID, NZAID, AusAID, to mention but three, as well as international agencies such as the UNDP, UNICEF, and WHO, can be productive. It is also in this area that the special expertise of the NGO communities can be called upon.

By pledging in the Bali Concord II affirmative steps to tighten their internal ties through the AEC, ASC, and ASCC, the ASEAN states hoped to regain collective leverage with their external partners. The Bali Concord II was described by its authors as a historic moment for ASEAN, but there have been many such moments in ASEAN's history, since forgotten. All of the ideas and proposals embraced in the new community frameworks already existed in one form or another in ASEAN's lengthy documentary and rhetorical record. However, in the articulation of an AEC, ASC, and ASCC, for the first time the leaders of ASEAN officially introduced the concept of an ASEAN community as an integrative endpoint for intensified intergovernmental cooperation in ASEAN. Some flesh was given to the bare outlines of the three communities by the acceptance of the work plans for the communities in the 2004 Vientiane summit's Vientiane Action Program (VAP).[17]

The ASEAN Charter

If the goal of an ASEAN community is to be realized, it will require a degree of national political wills and capabilities that heretofore have been absent. The test will be in implementing the plans of action designed to give substance to the frameworks adopted at Bali. These will be set within and limited by ASEAN's operating principles. It was clear to the ASEAN elite that the weak institutional base of ASEAN was unfitted to the task of community building. Accordingly the foreign ministers at the 2004 AMM called for the creation of a new ASEAN charter for the establishment of an effective and efficient institutional framework for ASEAN. The charter would also give a new, more coherent collective face to the organization whose credibility and relevance had been serious diminished in the eyes of the West because of its inability and unwillingness to bring about change in Myanmar. The goal was a more formally structured rules-based organization. At their 2005 AMM, the foreign ministers agreed to a draft text of a "Declaration on the Establishment of an ASEAN Charter."[18] This was promulgated by the heads of government at their 2005 Kuala Lumpur Summit. The declaration promised a forward-looking rules-based organization in a normative framework of democracy, transparency, and good governance. At the same time, it enshrined the ASEAN way of consensus decision making, respect for sovereignty, and noninterference.

The task of reconciling the ideal basis of a new charter to the reality of the ASEAN way was given to an Eminent Persons Group (EPG) that was charged with providing recommendations for the key elements to be included in the charter. The EPG was made up of former high officials of ASEAN governments. As the EPG met, rumors and leaks swirled around possible innovations in the ASEAN way with respect to voting, accountability, a human rights mechanism, compliance, and even sanctions. The EPG's report was given to the heads of government at their January 2007 Cebu, Philippines, summit (postponed from November 2006). They in turn passed the report on to a high-level senior officials' task force that actually fashioned the final draft of the charter. The charter was presented to the heads of government for approval at the 2007 Singapore summit. The official task force—operating by consensus—massaged out of the EPG proposals anything that was unacceptable to the least democratic members. What remained was essentially a restructuring of ASEAN's organizational wiring diagram.

In the new ASEAN the supreme policymaking body is the ASEAN summit of heads of government. This will meet biannually and, if necessary, on an ad hoc basis. Below the summit, an ASEAN Coordinating Council comprised of the ASEAN foreign ministers will manage ASEAN affairs in general and coordinate the work of the three ASEAN Community Councils: an ASC Council, an AEC Council, and an ASSC Council. The community councils will meet biannually, chaired by an appropriate minister from the member state holding the ASEAN chairmanship. The community councils will have under their purview the relevant ASEAN Sectoral Ministerial Bodies, which will have under their purview the relevant senior officials and subsidiary bodies. The work of ASEAN will be supported by its secretary-general, who is ASEAN's chief administrative officer, and four deputy secretaries-general of different nationalities than the secretary-general and from four different ASEAN states. A new Committee of Permanent Representatives based in Jakarta has been created consisting of a permanent representative with the rank of ambassador from each member state. The organizational link between ASEAN and the national level of the memberships will be the ASEAN National Secretariats in each state. Table 4.1 gives an overview of ASEAN's new structure. The ASEAN charter will come into force thirty days after instruments of ratification have been deposited with the secretary-general. Although no time limit for ratification was set, it was hoped that the ASEAN charter could be in force by the 2008 ASEAN Summit. With the Philippines' insistence that its ratification awaited the release of Aung San Suu Kyi (chapter 8) and the Indonesian parliament expressing skepticism over the charter's relevance to Indonesia's democratic national interests, that date may not be achievable.

On its face, the ASEAN charter, in explicitly confirming all previous ASEAN decisions, declarations, and initiatives, has simply rearranged the boxes on a table of organization. What had been trumpeted as a landmark breakthrough has been dismissed by many critics as old wine in new bottles. The charter once again burnishes the principle of noninterference in the internal affairs of ASEAN members and upholds the right of every member state to lead its national existence free from external interference or coercion. Decision making will remain consensual. Regimes like those in Myanmar, Cambodia, and Laos could sign off on a document that touts democracy, the rule of law, and fundamental freedoms because there is no way to hold them accountable within the organization. Even a toothless human rights mechanism was pushed off to a future date (chapter 8). In the absence of a compliance mechanism, any member can pick and choose from the ASEAN plate of norms and values those that it will adhere to with reference to its perception of national interests. Because of the operating rules of ASEAN, the ASEAN democratic agenda will continue to be blocked by the antidemocrats. In a scathing commentary, a leading Thai academic said that the "scarcely relevant" charter laid bare ASEAN's limitations, and that its runaway ambitions had turned into "folly."[19] The charter project, in hindsight, he continued, "was misguided and naively conceived, broached by misplaced overconfidence and manifested in utter disappointment." This may be too harsh a judgment, but it illustrates again ASEAN's historical problem of creating expectations that are dashed by the reality of intra-ASEAN relations.

TABLE 4.1
ASEAN's Basic Structure

ASEAN Summit

ASEAN Coordinating Council

ASEAN Community Councils

Political-Security Council	Economic Council	Socio-Cultural Council
ASEAN Foreign Ministers Meeting (AMM)	ASEAN Economic Ministers Meeting (AEM)	ASEAN Ministers Responsible for Information (AMRI)
Commission on the Southeast Asia Nuclear Weapons-Free Zone (SEANWFZ)	ASEAN Free Trade Area (AFTA) Council	ASEAN Ministers Responsible for Culture and Arts (AMCA)
ASEAN Defense Ministers Meeting (ADMM)	ASEAN Investment Area (AIA) Council	ASEAN Education Ministers Meeting(ASED)
ASEAN Law Ministers Meeting (ALAWMM)	ASEAN Finance Ministers Meeting (AFMM)	ASEAN Ministerial Meeting on Disaster Management (AMMDM)
ASEAN Ministerial Meeting on Transnational Crime (AMMTC)	ASEAN Ministers Meeting on Agriculture and Forestry (AMAF)	ASEAN Ministerial Meeting on the Environment (AMME)
ASEAN Regional Forum (ARF)	ASEAN Ministers on Energy Meeting (AMEM)	Conference of the Parties to the ASEAN Agreement on Transboundary Haze Pollution (COP)
	ASEAN Ministerial Meeting on Minerals (AMMin)	ASEAN Health Ministers Meeting(AHMM)
	ASEAN Ministerial Meeting on Science and Technology (AMMST)	ASEAN Labour Ministers Meeting (ALMM)
	ASEAN Telecommunications and Information Technology Ministers Meeting (TELMIN)	ASEAN Ministers on Rural Development and Poverty Eradication (AMRDPE)
	ASEAN Transport Ministers Meeting (ATM)	ASEAN Ministerial Meeting on Social Welfare and Development (AMMSWD)
	Meeting of the ASEAN Tourism Ministers (M-ATM)	ASEAN Ministerial Meeting on Youth (AMMY)
	ASEAN Mekong Basin Development Cooperation (AMBDC)	ASEAN Conference on Civil Service Matters (ACCSM)

ASEAN Secretary-General

Committee of Permanent Representatives to ASEAN

ASEAN National Secretariats

ASEAN's External Relations

The decision to expand the member states' bilateral connections with important economic and strategic partners to a collective forum was made at the 1977 second Kuala Lumpur ASEAN Summit. This associational relationship with important external partners was formalized as the ASEAN dialogue process.

The Dialogue Partners

At the 1977 summit, the five ASEAN heads of government met with the prime ministers of Australia, Japan, and New Zealand. The following year, 1988, following the annual AMM, the ASEAN foreign minister met in a Post-Ministerial Conference (PMC) with their counterparts from Canada, the EU, and the United States, in addition to Australia, Japan, and New Zealand as official "dialogue partners." Since then four other dialogue partners have joined: the Republic of Korea in 1991, and in 1996, China, India, and Russia. The administrator of the United Nations Development Program (UNDP) also is invited to the PMC as a guest of the host chair.

The PMC takes place in two phases. First, the ASEAN foreign ministers meet with their dialogue partner counterparts as a group (ASEAN + 10) in a closed session of wide-ranging discussion of international economic, political, and security issues. This is followed by separate sessions between the ASEAN ministers and each dialogue partner (ASEAN + 1) to examine their bilateral relationship. Eight of the dialogues take place in a declaratory partnership framework that takes in all functional levels of ASEAN's proposed three communities. It should be understood that these relatively brief and scripted engagements are the product of intensive planning and coordination at the senior official level. The original agenda of the dialogues was restricted to matters of functional cooperation. ASEAN resisted early efforts to broaden the PMC's scope to include political and security matters. However, as these kinds of regional issues bulked larger for some of the partners, and to maintain relevance, the dialogues expanded to cover regional security. It was this aspect of the PMC that was the genesis of the annual separate security dialogue in the ASEAN Regional Forum (chapter 5). Between the PMCs, dialogues continue at different levels of official contact including the ASEAN committees in the dialogue partners' capitals. The ASEAN committees, so-called outposts of ASEAN, are made up of the accredited ASEAN ambassadors to the particular country. There are also ASEAN committees at the Brussels headquarters of the EU and the United Nations European headquarters in Geneva. Each dialogue has an ASEAN country coordinator. The dialogue process for China, Japan,

---

BOX 4.1
ASEAN's Partnership Agreements

ASEAN–China Strategic Partnership for Peace and Prosperity (2003)
ASEAN–Japan Tokyo Declaration for a Dynamic and Enduring ASEAN–Japan
  Partnership (2003)
ASEAN–Russia Partnership for Peace and Security, and Prosperity and Devel-
  opment in the Asia-Pacific Region (2003)
ASEAN–Republic of Korea Comprehensive Cooperation Partnership (2004)
ASEAN–India Partnership for Peace, Progress and Shared Prosperity (2004)
ASEAN–United States Enhanced Partnership (2005)
ASEAN–Australia Comprehensive Partnership (2007)
ASEAN–EU Enhanced Partnership (2007)

India, and South Korea has been enhanced by including them at the annual
ASEAN Summit in a series of ASEAN + 1 summits. New Zealand and Australia held a commemorative summit with ASEAN in 2004. The EU and
ASEAN held a commemorative summit in 2007. An ASEAN–Russia summit
was held in 2005. Of the dialogue partners, only Canada and the United States
have not had an official summit meeting with the ASEAN heads of government. A summit meeting hosted by the United States celebrating thirty years
of the U.S.–ASEAN dialogue was scheduled for 2007 but was cancelled. The
reason given was the president's preoccupation with Middle East issues. An effort to reschedule it in 2008 failed after the September 2007 Myanmar assault
on Buddhist monks and the U.S. refusal to sit down with the junta's prime
minister (chapter 8).

ASEAN's dialogue process complements the member states' interests in
their bilateral relations with the dialogue states, which in functional political
and economic terms are more immediately important. The undertakings at
the ASEAN level are translated into action at the bilateral level. In a number
of cases, the dialogue partners have negotiated at the bilateral level programs
of strategic cooperation that mirror broad statements of partnership with
ASEAN at the regional level. The dialogue partners also have to take into account how problems at the bilateral level might influence the dialogue at the
regional level where ASEAN solidarity rules.

ASEAN + 3 (APT)

Since 1997, three of the dialogue partners—China, the Republic of Korea,
and Japan—have developed a special relationship with ASEAN, formalized as

the ASEAN + 3 grouping. The external stimulus was the financial crisis of 1997 and the effort to find a regional mechanism to deal with it (chapter 7). Since then, the pattern of collaboration and consultation has expanded to nearly every area of state interaction. In 1998, the APT heads of government commissioned an "eminent persons" East Asian Vision Group (EAVG) to report on measures to intensify intergovernmental cooperative links between Southeast Asia and Northeast Asia. Even before the EAVG had completed its study, the six heads of government in a Joint Statement on East Asia Cooperation adopted at the 1999 ASEAN + 3 summit agreed to institutionalize the APT.[20] The EAVG's report was presented to an East Asia Study Group (EASG) set up in November 2000 made up of senior officials. Working from the EAVG's report, the EASG made programmatic recommendations to the heads of government at the 2002 APT summit meeting.[21] The visionary ultimate goal in an undefined future is an East Asia Community. The 2003 APT summit endorsed the EASG strategy to implement short-term measures as well as agreeing to study the feasibility of an East Asia Free Trade Area. The APT consultative structures have penetrated ASEAN's operations at most consultative levels. An APT summit meeting in addition to the ASEAN + 1 summits with China, South Korea, and Japan has become part of the annual ASEAN summit. Important ASEAN ministerial meetings now have parallel APT formats, preceded by APT senior officials' meetings. There is an APT unit in the ASEAN secretariat.

ASEAN's strategy in the APT is to enhance Southeast Asia's significance as a grouping to the Northeast Asian powers. Like its other external regional associations, ASEAN insists on its central agenda-setting role. In the APT framework, ASEAN also is balancing the growing influence of China in other bilateral and ASEAN relationships with the consensus mechanism that includes South Korea and Japan. The risk is that the development of the APT could rival ASEAN itself, or at least present a new array of possible programmatic overlaps. There is also a concern that if the APT should lead to an alternative broader integrative regionalist institution, ASEAN's stand-alone image would be diminished for other external partners. Already, the expansive APT vision has some of the accouterments of the East Asia Economic Group (EAEG) propounded by Malaysia in the early 1990s as a regional alternative to the EU or NAFTA (chapter 7). The EAEG expressly excluded the United States, Canada, Australia, and New Zealand. It has been argued that given the stagnation of ASEAN and APEC, "there is good reason to believe that the APT will emerge as the key organization in East Asia."[22] A more critical view places the APT grouping in the same international structural context as ASEAN itself, calling it "reactionary regionalism" arising not from any internal dynamic but to mediate and moderate external influences on the region.[23]

The East Asia Summit

A new adjunct to the growing complex of summitry around the annual ASEAN Summit was added in December 2005 when the first meeting of the East Asia Summit (EAS) was held. The idea for the EAS was mooted by Malaysia's Prime Minister Abdullah as a first step toward the EAVG's goal of an East Asia Community. The proposed membership format was the ASEAN nations with China, South Korea, and Japan. It differed from the ASEAN + 3 in that the ten ASEAN nations are associated as East Asian individual states, not as ASEAN. Both Japan and Indonesia offered resistance to this structure. Japan feared that China would be dominant in it. Indonesia, as it had with Mahathir's EAEG, opposed the exclusivity of a new grouping that was essentially a deconstruction of the APT. Consensus demanded a broader invitation list, so that at the inaugural EAS in Kuala Lumpur in addition to the APT countries, Australia, India, and New Zealand were present along with Russian President Vladimir Putin as a guest of the EAS. The United States was excluded since it had not acceded to the Treaty of Amity and Cooperation in Southeast Asia (TAC), a ticket of admission. China's interest in the EAS format waned as the membership expanded, since its role would be diluted. The second EAS froze membership at the original sixteen until at least 2008, leaving Russia and the EU knocking on the door, and the United States rethinking its position on the TAC. The question of EAS membership is tied to what its institutional function might be in the regional international structure. Is it to be an APT plus or an APEC minus? In either case, it is moving away from being a first step toward the EAVG's goal of an East Asia Community.

As it stands after the first three EAS gatherings, the summit presents one more opportunity for dialogue at a fairly high level of generalization. The topics have included maritime security, energy security, terrorism, pandemic diseases, and climate change. The second EAS agreed to back a feasibility study for an East Asia Free Trade Area. The third EAS in November 2007 issued a declaration on climate change echoing the Kyoto Protocol.

ASEAN and Europe

ASEAN has transformed its dialogue process with Europe into a formal organizational relationship although not as penetrating or elaborate as the ASEAN + 3. The twenty-seven-nation EU is ASEAN's second largest export market and its third largest trading partner. Europe is also viewed by ASEAN as a participant, albeit somewhat politically remote, in the balance of power with China, the United States, and Japan. To further complement its member states' economic and political interests with Europe, ASEAN has established a consultative process with the EU in addition to the PMC dialogues.

ASEAN–EU Ministerial Meeting (AEMM)

The first AEMM took place in 1978 and was institutionalized in the 1980 "EC-ASEAN Cooperation Agreement."[24] The AEMM meets every two years, alternating between Southeast Asia and Europe. A Joint Cooperation Committee monitors the progress of ASEAN-EU economic cooperation, and since 1995 an annual meeting of ASEAN-EU senior officials convenes. Between these meetings, the ASEAN Brussels Committee represents ASEAN at EU headquarters.

In addition to trade and market issues, there is a political exchange that since 1997 has been preoccupied by the Myanmar junta's assault on democracy. The EU's unwillingness to sit with ASEAN partner Myanmar has been a source of contention. The thirteenth AEMM scheduled for Germany in 1999 was scrapped because of the European ban on visas for the Myanmar officials. It took place the following year in Laos. The EU gave ground in 2003 at the fourteenth AEMM in Brussels when a Myanmar deputy foreign minister was allowed to participate in a discussion of the situation in Myanmar. The full and frank discussion about the situation in Myanmar was continued at the fifteenth AEMM in Jakarta in 2005 and sixteenth AMM in Nuremberg, Germany, in 2007, but the issue of Myanmar's place at the table had been settled at the 2004 Asia–Europe Meeting (ASEM) discussed below. The 2007 AEMM celebrated the thirtieth anniversary of ASEAN–EU formal relations and was marked by the adoption of the "Nuremberg Declaration of an ASEAN–EU Enhanced Partnership" revitalizing the 1980 cooperation agreement.

Asia–Europe Meeting (ASEM)

A new Asia–Europe forum was launched in 1996 with the first ASEM summit meeting.[25] The ASEM Summit meets every two years, alternating between Europe and Asia. ASEM VII was scheduled for Beijing in October 2008. In between summits, meetings of foreign ministers and other relevant ministers and senior officials maintain programmatic continuity. In its original format, the participants were the EU, the then seven ASEAN members, China, Japan, and South Korea. In 2004, the European side of the ASEM was faced with the problem of adding ten new EU states to the ASEM. ASEAN linked this to membership for its missing members, Cambodia, Laos, and Myanmar. The Europeans had been unwilling to accept a package admission of the three because of Myanmar. This became a central issue at the ASEM's fifth foreign ministers' meeting hosted by Indonesia in Bali in July 2003. At that time, the EU ministers allegedly reneged on a gentlemen's agreement to bring the missing ASEAN states into the ASEM. This had become politically impossible for the Europeans after the brutal May 2003 attack on Aung San Suu Kyi's followers, known as the Depayin massacre (chapter 8).

Recognizing that both the ASEM and AEMM processes were at stake, a diplomatic compromise was reached over Myanmar's participation. The 2004 ASEM V in Brussels expanded the grouping by admitting the EC ten and the ASEAN three. Myanmar's membership was given a political asterisk, however, with the expectation that its participation in the ASEM Summit would be lower than head of government. Even then, the Finnish government was reluctant to give the Myanmar foreign minister a visa to attend ASEM VII in Helsinki in 2006 and had to be persuaded by the European Commission to do so. At the Helsinki ASEM, the membership was again expanded with the ASEAN Secretariat, Bulgaria, India, Mongolia, Pakistan, and Romania officially joining ASEM VIII in 2008 in Beijing. Russia has been lobbying ASEAN since 2004 to support its membership in the ASEM. This could be balanced from the Asian side by Australia and New Zealand, both members of the East Asia Summit with the ASEAN + 3 countries and India.

In a sense, the ASEM is an external deployment to Europe of the ASEAN + 3. Europe's interests in Asia go well beyond ASEAN, but ASEAN did not want to see Europe engaged in a Northeast Asia dialogue that excluded ASEAN. For the Europeans, the ASEM was conceived as a balance to APEC, from which it is excluded. The EU accepts ASEAN's position that the AEMM is the cornerstone of the EU's cooperation and dialogue with Asia. This is not unlike the case of the ASEAN Regional Forum (ARF) in which ASEAN is the focal point of the broader East Asia and Pacific security dialogue (chapter 5).

Transregional Links

ASEAN member states belong to a number of other regional groupings that are not institutionally linked to ASEAN in a dialogue format. ASEAN is cognizant of them. An ASEAN state's membership reflects national interests that are not fully served through ASEAN membership. The discussion of wider East Asian and Pacific economic regionalism such as APEC or the proposed East Asia Community is in chapter 7.

The Asian Cooperation Dialogue (ACD)

In an express desire to bridge the missing institutional link between Northeast Asia and South Asia, Thailand's Prime Minister Thaksin launched the Asian Cooperation Dialogue in 2002. The notion was that ASEAN could be the bridge. It also reflected Thaksin's itch for a larger stage then ASEAN. Thai Foreign Minister Surakiart presented the scheme at the 2001 Hanoi thirty-forth

AMM and the 2002 foreign ministers' informal retreat. Despite a lukewarm ASEAN reception, Bangkok pressed forward toward the inaugural ACD foreign ministers' meeting in June 2002. Eighteen countries were represented: the ASEAN 10, Bahrain, Bangladesh, China, India, Japan, Pakistan, Qatar, and South Korea. Joining in 2003 were Kazakhstan, Kuwait, Oman, and Sri Lanka, followed by Bhutan, Iran, Mongolia, and the United Arab Emirates in 2004. Russia and Saudi Arabia were admitted in 2005 and Tajikistan and Uzbekistan in 2006, for a total of thirty members. The overlap in the ACD of ASEAN and the members of the Shanghai Cooperation Organization (SCO) is one of the few structured links between Southeast Asia and Central Asia.[26] The annual formal ministerial meeting is supplemented by a ministerial meeting on the sidelines of the United Nations General Assembly session in September. A first ACD summit has been proposed for 2009.

As conceived and elaborated by Prime Minister Thaksin, the ACD is meant to be an informal forum for Asian foreign ministers to exchange views and promote cooperation to strengthen the "voice of Asia."[27] In addition to dialogue, the ACD has identified nineteen areas of possible functional economic and technical cooperation with identified country prime movers and co-prime movers. Given the ACD's large geographic footprint and the numerous competitive foreign policy agendas contained within it, it can be suggested that the grouping's agenda is going to be difficult to manage beyond the boundaries of another "talk shop." The 2007 sixth ACD ministerial meeting in Korea commissioned a senior officials study group to present a future's plan at the 2008 meeting covering four areas: end goals, funding, secretariat, and track II participation. Although Foreign Minister Surakiart pointedly used the term "Asian way," as opposed to ASEAN way, in describing the ACD, it is doubtful that the ACD will challenge ASEAN's regional primacy.

Bay of Bengal Initiative for Multi-Sectoral Economic Cooperation (BIMSTEC)

In 1997, Bangladesh, India, Myanmar, Sri Lanka, and Thailand joined in a cooperative format to promote trade, investment, and tourism.[28] It has identified thirteen areas for functional cooperation. It was called the BIMST-EC (Economic Cooperation) after the first letters of the names of its members. Maldives, Nepal, and Bhutan have since joined. BIMSTEC can be viewed as the conjunction of New Delhi's look east policy and Bangkok's look west policy. In BIMSTEC, India has also isolated Pakistan from the other members of the South Asia Association for Regional Cooperation (SAARC). BIMSTEC also provides a multilateral link to Myanmar not shared by China.

BIMSTEC held its first summit meeting, hosted by Thailand, in 2004 and adopted the present name. A second summit meeting, to be hosted by India, was put off from 2006 to 2007, and then to 2008 and beyond. Annual meetings of foreign ministers and trade and finance ministers provide policy guidance for senior officials' meetings and working and experts groups in areas promoting functional cooperation. The most significant undertaking has been negotiating a BIMSTEC free trade agreement with a 2017 target date (chapter 7).

Mekong–Ganga Cooperation (MGC)

The Mekong–Ganga Cooperation grouping was founded in 2000 and links India to the five continental Southeast Asian states—Myanmar, Thailand, Laos, Cambodia, and Vietnam. The original proposed name was the Mekong–Ganga Suvarnabhumi, but the notion of the "Golden Peninsula" redolent of Thai historical ambition was rejected by Laos. India's multilateral linking to Laos, Cambodia, and Vietnam, which are not members of BIMSTEC, through the MGC, gives it a political/economic presence in the entire Mekong Basin region where China has been an important strategic development partner (discussed below). The MGC's policy organ is a foreign ministers' meeting that piggybacks on the annual ASEAN ministerial meeting (AMM) when the AMM host is a MGC member. It adopted a program of action at its second ministerial meeting in Hanoi in 2001 with four principal thrusts: education, tourism, culture, and transportation. Emphasis has been given to improving transportation links in an east-west highway corridor.

Indian Ocean Rim Association for Regional Cooperation (IOR-ARC)

Since March 1997, The Indian Ocean Rim Association for Regional Cooperation links nineteen Indian Ocean littoral states in Southeast Asia, South Asia, the Middle East, and Africa. In addition to ASEAN members Indonesia, Malaysia, Singapore, and Thailand, IOR-ARC membership includes Australia, Bangladesh, India, Iran, Kenya, Madagascar, Mauritius, Mozambique, Oman, South Africa, Arabia, Sri Lanka, Tanzania, the United Arab Emirates, and Yemen. The IOR-ARC dialogue partners are China, Egypt, Great Britain, France, Japan, and Qatar. The purpose of the IOR-ARC is to promote trade and investment among members. Policy guidance is given by the IOR Council of Ministers, which meets every two years in an IOR country and annually on the margins of the UN General Assembly. Three working groups have been established: a working group on trade and investment, a business forum group, and an academic group.

Southwest Pacific Dialogue

At Indonesian initiative, a formal Southwest Pacific Dialogue was established in 2002 at the foreign minister level between Australia, Indonesia, New Zealand, Papua New Guinea, the Philippines, and Timor-Leste. It has been institutionalized on the margin of the annual ASEAN ministerial meeting. This allows PNG and Timor-Leste, which are not ASEAN dialogue partners, to have a structured format for exchange of views with countries that share common regional concerns with them.

Subregional Multilateral Frameworks

The Mini-ASEANs

The recommendations of the 1972 original UN developmental blueprint for ASEAN noted the advantages to be gained by the crossing of national frontiers in ASEAN to enhance the productive use of different and potentially complementary endowments of raw materials, skills, and other resources in different geographic areas. This concept was vigorously promoted by the Asian Development Bank (ADB) before the Crash of '97.[29] The terms "growth zones" or geometric metaphors—triangles, quadrangles, even hexagons— were applied to these areas. The key to the strategy is the mobilization of complementary factor endowments in the contiguous national territories. The theory is that freed from the barriers of national sovereignty, market forces would lead to productive and efficient utilization of the disparate economic factors. The governments of the different national territories are expected to facilitate the transnational integration of economic factors by providing infrastructure development, legal frameworks, and incentives to encourage the flow of private and quasi-private investment for zonal development.

The ADB model and most of the literature supporting it has been of an "all things being equal" nature; that is, if unhampered by the intervention of noneconomic variables, where the transnational economic complementarities exist, economic rationality would lead naturally to localized or subregional integration. In the ASEAN experience, at least, the process seems reversed. The growth zones exist by virtue of political proclamation, not market forces. In the 1990s, four such subregional growth zones had officially been endorsed by ASEAN: the Indonesia–Malaysia–Singapore Growth Triangle (IMS-GT or alternatively SI-JORI); The Indonesia–Malaysia–Thailand Growth Triangle (IMT-GT); the Brunei–Indonesia–Malaysia–Philippines East ASEAN Growth Area (BIMP-EAGA); and the Greater Mekong Subregion (GMS) Growth Zone or "growth hexagon."

The IMS-GT or SIJORI

The Indonesia–Malaysia–Singapore growth zone is the only Southeast Asian subregional growth zone that begins to approximate the theoretical model. Actually, the political endorsement of the IMS-GT in the MOU between the three countries formalized at a governmental level the existing pattern of economic relations. Singapore's economy had long been linked to the proximate geographic regions of Malaysia's Johor State (the JO in SIJORI) and Indonesia's Riau Archipelago. Singapore had capital, technology, and entrepreneurial skills. Johor and the Riau Archipelago, especially the island of Batam, had land, labor, and water. Singapore was the hub of two spokes to economic hinterlands that themselves remained largely unconnected. The GT formula semi-disguised Singapore's economic dominance.

Although the economic raison d'être for the IMS-GT had limited geographic scope (Singapore, Johor, Riau), domestic politics demanded its expansion. West Sumatra was included in the original 1994 MOU giving political form to the IMS-GT. In 1996, Malaysia's Malacca, Negri Sembilan, and Pahang states were added. A year later five additional Indonesian provinces sought inclusion: Jambi, Bengkulu, South Sumatra, Lampung, and West Kalimantan. Economically, however, the IMS-GT despite its political scope was still SIJORI. Rather than accept a boundary-less transnational melding with Singapore as the centerpiece, both Indonesia and Malaysia embarked on efforts to compete with Singapore at their ends of the spokes, rather than complement. The political luster of the IMS-GT wore off as noneconomic irritants have intruded to cool bilateral relations between Malaysia and Singapore and Indonesia and Singapore (chapter 5). Symbiotic economic ties still link the three economies but without governmental cheerleading.

IMT-GT

In the Indonesia–Malaysia–Thailand GT, the political structure was erected without reference to the "naturalness" of economic forces in what appears to be the mistaken belief that if politics leads, investment and development will follow. Although politically modeled on the IMS-GT, The IMT-GT had few complementarities and no Singapore-like financial and transportation hub. It geographically embraced the two Indonesian provinces of North Sumatra and Aceh; the four northern Malaysian states of Kedah, Penang, Perak, and Perlis; and five provinces of southern Thailand: Narathiwat, Pattani, Satun, Songkhla, and Yala. Malaysia provided the impetus for this "northern triangle" in an effort to balance developmentally Singapore's dominance in the "southern triangle." It has been expanded to include the ten provinces on

Sumatra, the fourteen provinces of peninsular Thailand, and eight Malaysian states. Officially launched in July 1993, neither Indonesia nor Thailand invested much political capital, let alone public investment in infrastructure that might help attract private capital. The ADB seemed to show more enthusiasm for it than the national partners.[30] In addition to the negative economic impact of the Crash of '97, the internal war in Aceh and the spillover into "growth zone" diplomacy of bilateral disputes over boundaries, smuggling, illegal immigration, and Muslim separatist activities in southern Thailand have further impeded cooperation among the "triangle" partners.

The IMT-GT quickly became moribund. It lacked an operating framework and coherent strategy. Part of the problem was competitive, as opposed to complementary, isthmian development programs of Thailand and Malaysia. Both projected a rail-oil-gas land bridge between the Andaman Sea and the Gulf of Thailand. The Malaysian scheme clashed head-on with Thai Prime Minister Thaksin Shinawatra's Southern Seaboard Development Project aimed at making Thailand a petrochemical player in Southeast Asia. The Thaksin government basically shelved its interest in the IMT-GT. New life was breathed into the project in December 2005 with the first IMT-GT summit meeting on the margins of the ASEAN Summit. It was agreed that the IMT-GT needed to be revitalized and refocused. At a second summit in January 2007, the IMT heads of government adopted the ADB report and action plan for 2007–2011.[31]

BIMP-EAGA

The Brunei–Indonesia–Malaysia–Philippines East Asian Growth Area was officially launched in March 1994 at a ministerial meeting in Davao City, the Philippines. Its promoter was Philippine President Fidel Ramos. Its geographical scope contains the Sultanate of Brunei; Indonesia's Kalimantan provinces, Sulawesi, Malukus, and Papua provinces; East Malaysia's Sabah and Sarawak states and the Federal Territory of Labuan; and the Philippines' Mindanao and Palawan islands. Technical assistance has been provided by the ADB.[32] The goal is to move the subregion from dependence on resource extraction to value-added industry. Its formal structure includes annual summit meetings and annual senior official/ministerial meetings. It has working groups in four areas: transport and infrastructure, natural resources, tourism, and small and medium business enterprise.

The BIMP-EAGA has been described as "an association of neglected regions."[33] With the exception of Brunei, the territories are at the margins of their countries, far from any energizing core hub. The Philippines' effort to make Davao on Mindanao a gateway to BIMP-EAGA has been frustrated by Muslim insurgency. The Sulawesi–Sulu Sea maritime environment is rife with transnational criminal activity (chapter 6). Indonesian official support was only pro forma. Even more so than the IMT-GT, the region has poor infrastructure, particularly direct transportation links, and lack of economic complementarities. Governments have not made public investments that would attract private capital. Given the relative remoteness of the zone from market and transportation centers, major investments in infrastructure could prove to be financial white elephants. So far, BIMP-EAGA has proved a relative economic failure in developmental achievements.

The Mekong River Basin

The end of the Indochina wars ushered in a time of hope and aspiration for internationally cooperative development of Southeast Asia's greatest underutilized economic resource, the Mekong River. Its natural potentials have been limited by the economic, political, and strategic competitions of its six riparian states: Laos, Myanmar, Thailand, Cambodia, Vietnam, and China's Yunnan Province. It is also a region of ethnic pluralism and weak central administrative capacity. It is removed from major markets and has not attracted major investment. With regional peace, new opportunities opened for economic development in a region with some of the lowest per capita GDPs in the world.

Mekong River Commission

The first institutional effort at comprehensive development planning in the Mekong basin was the 1957 UN-sponsored Mekong Committee. The original committee was made up of Thailand, Cambodia, and South Vietnam. After the wars, and following a process of UN Development Program (UNDP) consultation and negotiation, Cambodia, Laos, Thailand, and Vietnam signed in 1995 an Agreement on Cooperation for the Sustainable Development of the Mekong River Basin. A new Mekong River Commission was set up to be the implementing agency with its headquarters now in Vientiane. In 1996, Myanmar and China assumed observer status. The MRC's mission is to "promote and coordinate sustainable management and development of water and related resources" for the benefit of the riparian countries.[34] NGOs concerned about the environmental aspects of the Mekong's management have charged that the MRC is in a crisis of legitimacy and relevancy because of its inaction and failure to address the threats to the river and its people (chapter 8).

Greater Mekong Subregion (GMS)

In 1992, Cambodia, China, Laos, Myanmar, Thailand, and Vietnam agreed to a program of subregional cooperation to enhance economic relations between them and to provide international recognition of a subregional growth zone. From the birth of the Greater Mekong Subregion growth zone, the Asian Development Bank has been the lead agent for coordination, promoting co-financing, obtaining ODA, strategic planning, and technical assistance.[35] The fourth triennial GMS Summit was held in March 2008. At the summit, Chinese premier Wen Jiabao sought to reassure the downstream Mekong states that China's upstream activities will not harm the interests of its Southeast Asian partners on the river (chapter 9). General policy guidance in the various functional areas of activity is given by annual ministerial meetings. In 2001, the tenth ministerial meeting adopted a ten-year development strategy for the GMS.[36] The proposed programs in the so-called growth hexagon are in the transportation, energy, natural resource management, human resource development, trade, investment, and tourism sectors. At the end of 2006, twenty-eight infrastructure projects had cost $6.8 billion. Priority has been given to roads and bridges tying the countries together in a transportation network. China has had particular interest in linking Yunnan to continental Southeast Asia. The GMS approved a cost-sharing agreement in 2007 for the last link in the north-south corridor. This is a third bridge across the Mekong that will go from Chiang Khong in Thailand to Huaysay in Laos, completing by 2010 a road direct from Yunnan to Bangkok. A highlight of the fourth summit was the ceremonial opening of the final Laos section of the road.

In an effort to link ASEAN—particularly Singapore and Malaysia—to the GMS, the 1995 ASEAN Summit created the ASEAN–Mekong Basin Development Corporation (AMBDC). From the Singapore and Kuala Lumpur vantage point, Thailand's status in the MRC and GMS gave it an advantaged gateway into the Mekong zone. The backbone for the AMBDC was a proposed railway corridor from Singapore to Kunming, Yunnan through peninsular Malaysia, Thailand, and Laos, with branches connecting Cambodia and Myanmar. After a decade of little planning progress, ASEAN decided in 2006 to scrap the autonomous AMBDC Council, criticizing it as ineffective and inefficient, and bring oversight of the AMBDC back to the ASEAN finance ministers.

Ayeyawady–Chao Phraya–Mekong Economic Cooperation Strategy (ACMECS)

Mekong basin development fits fully into Bangkok's "Thailand plus" foreign economic strategy. Already in 1993, Thailand had initiated with China, Lao PDR, and Myanmar, the "Quadripartite Economic Cooperation Plan," popularly called the "Golden Quadrangle," for the development of the upper reaches of the Mekong. In 2003, Thai Prime Minister Thaksin Shinawatra promoted a new development plan called the Ayeyawady–Chao Phraya–Mekong Economic

Cooperation Strategy (ACMECS) linking Thailand, Cambodia, the LPDR, and Vietnam and named after the region's principal rivers. The ACMECS, was formalized at a November 2003 summit meeting with the Bagan, Myanmar, declaration.[37] It is institutionalized in biennial summits and annual ministerial meetings. This Thai-centered, core–periphery geoeconomic structure ostensibly would promote mutual benefits through cross-border cooperation and enterprise. A darker view was one of Thai exploitation of weaker partners.

CLMV Cooperation

A 2004 summit of the heads of government of Cambodia, Lao PDR, Myanmar, and Vietnam, followed by an informal summit on the margin of the 2005 Kuala Lumpur ASEAN Summit produced an action plan for CLMV enhanced economic cooperation and integration. It called for closer cooperation and integration in eight functional economic sectors. The third CLMV summit in 2006 projected the formation of a joint coordination mechanism. The fourth summit in October 2007 was postponed because of flooding in Vietnam. The explicit goal for closer CLMV cooperation was to help close the development gap between the CLMV countries and the more developed ASEAN partners. It also laid the basis for a new approach for ODA under the broader GMS umbrella. It might be called sub-GMS cooperation. The question has been raised as to how to articulate the CLMV summit process with the ACMECS.

CLV Development Triangle

Even more sub-GMS, the Cambodia–Laos–Vietnam Development Triangle is specifically tied to the availability of Japanese ODA. The heads of government of the CLV countries had prepared a Master Plan for the CLV Development Triangle to be presented at a CLV–Japan summit on the margin of the 2004 ASEAN Summit in Vientiane. The target areas were the border provinces of the three states. Japan is the most important strategic partner of the GMS, having pledged in 2004 $1.5 billion for Mekong development over three years. In January 2007, Japan announced a new Mekong–Japan Partnership Program under which $40 million in new ODA would go the CLMV countries of which $20 million would go to the CLV Development Triangle.[38]

In January 2008, Japan held the first Mekong–Japan foreign ministerial meeting. Japan's Mekong initiatives have been complicated by the Myanmar issue. Tokyo cancelled $5 million in development assistance to Myanmar in October 2007 after a Japanese journalist was killed in the military crackdown on Buddhist monks (chapter 8). Japan's overtures to the CLV countries are part of its race against China for influence in the region. Tokyo's wooing of the CLV leaders is designed to heighten Japan's political presence as well as economic.

Even though ASEAN regionalism and subregionalism have not fulfilled the promises and expectations of academic enthusiasts and theoreticians, they have involved and habituated governments to patterns of discussion, consultation, and cooperation in a wide variety of low politics functional transactions. Up to now, the significance of these transactions has not really been economic, but like the other manifestations of Southeast Asian regionalism, they are a political contribution to the incremental building of confidence and trust necessary for a peaceful and stable regional international environment.

Notes

1. Kofi Annan, speech to the Indonesian Council on World Affairs, 16 February 2000, accessed at www.un.org/News/Press/docs/2000/20000215.sgsm7303.doc.html.

2. Dewi Fortuna Anwar, *Indonesia in ASEAN: Foreign Policy and Regionalism* (Singapore: Institute of Southeast Asian Studies, 2000).

3. "James Clad, "Fin de Siecle, Fin de l'ASEAN?" CSIS-Pacific Forum *PacNet Newsletter* no. 9, 3 March 2000.

4. Michael Vatikiotis, "Susilo, Regional Affairs and Lessons from Sukarno," *The Jakarta Post*, 3 November 2004.

5. Thomas L. Friedman, *The Lexus and the Olive Tree* (New York: Anchor, 2000).

6. Accessed at www.aseansec.org/3992.htm.

7. "Burma 'Holding SE Asia Hostage'," *BBC News*, 21 July 2006.

8. ASEAN Foreign Ministers' Press Statement after specially convened Kuala Lumpur meeting 10 July 1997, as reported in *The Straits Times*, 11 July 1997.

9. Details of the IAI can be found in *Bridging the Development Gap among the Older and New Members of ASEAN* at www.aseansec.org/14683.htm and *Initiative for ASEAN Integration (IAI): Work Plan for the CLMV Countries* (www.aseansec .org/14680.htm). The 2006 data is from *Report of IAI Work Plans Update (As of 1 September 2006)* at www.aseansec.org/iai_update.doc.

10. Narcisco G. Reyes, "The ASEAN Summit Syndrome," *Foreign Relations Journal* [Manila] 1, no. 2 (1986): 73.

11. "ASEAN Vision 2020" can be accessed at www.aseansec.org/1814.htm.

12. "Hanoi Plan of Action" can be accessed at www.aseansec.org/10382.htm.

13. "Declaration of ASEAN Concord II (Bali Concord II)," 7 October 2002, at www.aseansec.org/15160.htm.

14. "Joint Declaration for a Socially Cohesive and Caring ASEAN," Bangkok, 25 July 2000, at www.aseansec.org/661.htm.

15. Willam Tow, "Alternative Security Models: Implications for ASEAN," in Andrew T. H. Tan and J. D. Kenneth Boutin, eds., *Non-Traditional Security Issues* (Singapore: Select Publishers for Institute of Defence and Strategic Studies, 2001), 269.

16. The ASCC's work plan and specific measures can be accessed at www.aseansec .org/16832.htm and www.aseansec.org/16835.htm.

17. The text and appendices of the Vientiane Action Program can be accessed at www.aseansec.org/VAP-10th%20ASEAN%20Summit.pdf.

18. The text of the "Declaration on the Establishment of an ASEAN Charter" can be accessed at www.aseansec.org/18030.htm.

19. Thitinan Pongsudhirak, "ASEAN's Bang Ends in a Whimper," *Bangkok Post*, 28 November 2007.

20. The "Joint Statement on East Asia Cooperation," accessed at www.aseansec.org/ 5469.htm.

21. The EAVG study can be accessed at www.aseansec.org/pdf/east_asia_vision.pdf. The EASG report is at www.aseansec.org/viewpdf.asp?file=/pdf/easg.pdf.

22. Richard Stubbs, "ASEAN Plus Three: Emerging East Asian Regionalism," *Asian Survey* 42, no. 3 (2002): 453.

23. Mark Beeson, "ASEAN Plus Three and the Rise of Reactionary Regionalism," *Contemporary Southeast Asia* 25, no. 2 (2003): 251–68.

24. The EU–ASEAN home page is ec.europa.eu/external_relations/asean/intro/ index.htm.

25. The ASEM home page is ec.europa.eu/external_relations/asem/intro/index.htm.

26. The Shanghai Cooperation Organization was created in 2001 by Russia, China, Kazakhstan, Kyrgyzstan, and Tajikistan.

27. The ACD home page is www.acddialogue.com/index.php.

28. The BIMSTEC homepage is www.bimstec.org.

29. Myo Thant, Min Tang, and Hiroshi Kakazu, eds., *Growth Triangles in Asia: A New Approach to Regional Economic Cooperation* (Manila: Asian Development Bank, 1994).

30. ADB, *Indonesia-Malaysia-Thailand Growth Triangle: Theory and Practice* (Manila: Asian Development Bank, 1996).

31. ADB, *Building a Dynamic Future: The Indonesia–Malaysia–Thailand (IMT-GT) Roadmap for Development 2007–2011*, available online at www.adb.org/IMT-GT/road map.asp.

32. ADB activities and documents with respect to BIMP-EAGA can be accessed at www.adb.org/BIMP/default.asp.

33. C. P. F. Luhulima, "A Strategic Overview of BIMP-EAGA," *The Indonesian Quarterly*, 24, no. 1 (1996): 65.

34. The Mekong River Commission's website is www.mrcmekong.org.

35. ADB, *Cooperation in the Greater Mekong Subregion* (Manila: Asian Development Bank, 1996).

36. ADB, *Building on Success: A Strategic Framework for the Next Ten Years of the Greater Mekong Subregion Economic Cooperation Program* (Manila: Asian Development Bank, 2002). This is also available as a pdf file at www.adb.org/Documents/ Books/Building_Success/default.asp.

37. "Bagan Declaration," 12 November 2003, at www.thaigov.go.th/news/speech/ thaksin/sp12nov03.htm.

38. The Mekong–Japan Partnership is outlined at www.mofa.go.jp/regions/asia-pac/ mejibg/goal.pdf.

Suggestions for Further Reading

An historical overview of the Southeast Asia region is given by Nicholas Tarling, *Regionalism in Southeast Asia: To Foster the Political Will* (New York: Routledge, 2006). A positive and comprehensive discussion of ASEAN is Rodolfo C. Severino, *Southeast Asia in Search of an ASEAN Community* (Singapore: Institute of Southeast Asia Studies, 2006). A critical look at the ASEAN way is David Martin Jones and M. L. R. Smith, *ASEAN and East Asian International Relations: Regional Delusion* (Cheltenham, UK: Edward Elgar, 2006). Shaun Narine, *Explaining ASEAN: Regionalism in Southeast Asia* (Boulder, Colo.: Lynne Rienner, 2002) is another good survey of ASEAN's development. Sharon Siddique and Sree Kumar, eds., *The 2nd ASEAN Reader* (Singapore: Institute of Southeast Asian Studies, 2003), is a major compendium of articles on all aspects of ASEAN's regionalism. *ASEAN at 40: Progress, Prospects and Challenges* is a special issue of *Contemporary Southeast Asia* 29, no. 3 (2007). The historical development of ASEAN is traced in Alison Broinowski, ed., *Understanding ASEAN* (New York, St. Martin's, 1982); Ronald D. Palmer and Thomas J. Reckford, *Building ASEAN: 20 Years of Southeast Asian Cooperation* (New York: Praeger, 1987); Linda G. Martin, *The ASEAN Success Story* (Honolulu: University of Hawaii Press, 1987); and Alison Broinowski, ed., *ASEAN into the 1990s* (London: Macmillan, 1990).

5

Conflict and Conflict Resolution in Southeast Asia

N ATION-STATES OFTEN FIND THEMSELVES IN COMPETITION and even conflict in pursuit of national interests. Southeast Asian states are no different. In the international system, there are a variety of mechanisms to manage conflicting interests: diplomacy, mediation, arbitration, adjudication, and the coercive threat or use of force. The highest level of interstate conflict is war. The patterns of conflict in Southeast Asia are complex. During the Cold War, great power conflict overlaid Southeast Asian interstate relations (chapter 2). In the present Southeast Asian conflict environment, Islamist terrorism is the latest face of great power-linked violence. The terrorism dimension of conflict will be examined in the next chapter.

Although states' interest in ASEAN's integrity may buffer the intensity of national interest competition, it has not eliminated it. Since the end of the Cold War, local and regional conflicts of interest have threatened the stability of the Southeast Asian international order. As was noted in chapter 1, the ASEAN states are not free from historic and ethnic antagonisms. These rivalries take on new meanings in contemporary nationalism. Added to this are bilateral territorial disputes, in part the legacy of imperialism. The welter of competitive overlapping claims to sovereignty and jurisdiction in the South China Sea has led to fears of escalating armed conflict and tests ASEAN cohesion in the face of growing Chinese power. Separatist struggles in Indonesia, the Philippines, and Thailand have political spillover into regional international relations. This chapter examines the management of conflict in Southeast Asia. In particular, it addresses the question of whether a normative platform for the nonuse of force in conflict resolution has been established through ASEAN and its outreach to its external partners in the ASEAN Regional Forum (ARF).

The ASEAN Way

The ASEAN way describes what is claimed to be Southeast Asia's distinctive approach to interstate relations. It assumes a common interest in a peaceful, harmonious, and stable regional international order in which ASEAN states interact with each other on the basis of their shared acceptance of common behavioral norms. Two Indonesian words have become part of ASEAN's diplomatic vocabulary to denote how interests are to be managed in the ASEAN way: *musjawarah*, meaning "consultation," and *mufakat*, "consensus." It is not a problem-solving mechanism. It is a conflict-avoidance system relying on informal negotiations in loose settings as opposed to adversarial modes in legally grounded institutions. The application of the ASEAN way has two strategic goals. The first is to not allow bilateral disputes between ASEAN states to disrupt wider regional stability and the functioning of ASEAN itself. The second is to not let bilateral issues between ASEAN states and non-ASEAN states negatively affect intra-ASEAN relations.

There is no question but that Southeast Asian states' interest in maintaining the cooperative framework of ASEAN has resulted in a regional security environment in which the possibility of armed conflict between member states has been substantially reduced. Through ASEAN, the member states have provided incentives and mechanisms to contain intramural conflict. This kind of security system has been described as a "security complex," meaning durable and relatively self-contained patterns of security relationships generated by the local states themselves.[1] ASEAN has also been analyzed as an example of cooperative security: being an association for political and security cooperation that concentrates on conflict avoidance and management.[2] With a focus on common regional security interests, the cooperative security process emphasizes dialogue, consultation, and flexibility in dealing with competitive interests. As a practical matter, it is difficult to distinguish the mechanisms of the ASEAN way from diplomacy.

The assertion that ASEAN is a norm-based security regime, let alone a security community, remains to be demonstrated. As noted in chapter 1, "regime theory" has been used to inform the constructivist approach to ASEAN as a security community in which the leaders are socialized to a norms-based regional collective identity—an ASEAN identity. Peace and amity follow since everyone is on the same page of rules of interstate behavior. As Amitav Acharya argues from the constructivist perspective, "the main

reasons for ASEAN's successes and failures can be found in looking at the nature and *quality* of its socialization process and the norms that underpin it"
[italics in the original].[3] Alan Collins, who argues that ASEAN has pursued a
form of common security, commented in an understated fashion that
"whether ASEAN members strictly abide by the norms of the ASEAN way is
questionable."[4]

From a realist perspective, the debate engendered by consideration of
ASEAN as an emerging security community resting on the connection between the socialization process and norms ignores a crucial variable—that is
the appreciation of national interest. For example, questions of the threat or
use of force or nonuse of force in particular situations described below may
be better explained not by reference to the ASEAN way, but policymakers' appreciations of relative power in a rational cost-benefit analysis in the political
context of the vitality of the national interest at stake. If in fact there is an expectation that ASEAN states will not use force against one another to promote
interest, how are we to explain defense spending for conventional force build-
ups in the absence of an extraregional military threat? Force modernization
and acquisitions of high-technology weapons platforms since recovery from
the financial crisis of 1997–1998 have marked the leading defense programs in
Southeast Asia.[5] Reviewing Southeast Asian military procurement programs
for the *Military Balance 2008*, the director-general of London's highly respected International Institute for Strategic Studies (IISS) attributed the emphasis on improving conventional warfare capabilities in part to bilateral tensions among the members of ASEAN, noting that "Southeast Asia's military
establishments are evidently watching their neighbours' defence programmes
closely, and in some cases reacting to them."[6]

In examining conflicting interests among the Southeast Asian states, the
most difficult and sensitive relate to the traditional concerns of national security managers: defense from a threat to sovereignty, territorial integrity, and
the political system—often defined in terms of the ruling elite. The most direct threat is one that seeks to deny sovereignty, contest territory, or overturn
authority. In decision making at this level of state interaction, ethno-nation-
alism is likely to be a more potent ideational force then the purported ASEAN
identity-based shared norms and values.

Treaty of Amity and Cooperation in Southeast Asia (TAC)

The 1976 Treaty of Amity and Cooperation in Southeast Asia seeks to reg-
ulate the behavior of signatory states in the settlement of disputes between
them. The TAC is the regional international legal framework within which the
normative rules expressed in the ASEAN way have been institutionalized in a

---

BOX 5.1
Principles Set Forth in Article 2 of the
Treaty of Amity and Cooperation in Southeast Asia

- Mutual respect for independence, sovereignty, equality, territorial integrity, and national identity.
- The right of every state to lead its national existence free from external interference, subversion, or coercion.
- Noninterference in the internal affairs of one another.
- Renunciation of the threat or use of force.
- Effective cooperation among themselves.

---

theoretically binding treaty obligation.[7] Article 18 of the treaty kept the TAC open to accession by other Southeast Asian states. When ASEAN membership expanded, accession to the TAC became a requirement for membership. A 1998 amending protocol opened the TAC to accession by states outside of Southeast Asia. Papua New Guinea—with an eye to Indonesia—was the first non–Southeast Asian state to accept the TAC. Since then, Australia, Bangladesh, China, France, India, Japan, New Zealand, Pakistan, Russia, South Korea, Sri Lanka, Timor-Leste, and in 2008 even North Korea have acceded. The EU is expected to accede in 2008. The United States is reconsidering its unwillingness to sign and has acknowledged the TAC as a code of conduct to promote regional peace and stability.

The TAC High Council

Where the TAC broke new ground was in providing a mechanism for the pacific settlement of disputes. Article 14 called for the establishment of a High Council consisting of ministerial level representatives from each contracting party. The unique concept of a High Council to help devise ASEAN solutions to intra-ASEAN problems has essentially remained a concept. It was not until July 2001 that the AMM laid out the rules of procedure for the Council, some fifteen years after the TAC. The High Council has taken cognizance of no dispute. There are a number of reasons why ASEAN's foreign ministers felt no urgency to make concrete the pacific settlement provisions of the TAC. There was a reluctance to assign to a new continuing ASEAN ministerial body formal functions that the foreign ministers themselves in informal and ad hoc fashion had occasionally assumed. According to Malaysia's Foreign Minister Syed Hamid, the High Council was never used for dispute settlement because "each of the nations in it has interests of its own. The council will not have a legal basis, but only a political one because of the many conflicting interests."[8] Even if the High Council should be invoked in the future, the TAC's article 18 states that its pacific settlement provisions will apply only if all parties to the dispute agree to their application. Moreover, the High Council's decision making is stipulated to be consensual.

Even if the High Council is by institutional design an ineffectual dispute resolution mechanism, it continues to be valued by ASEAN as an important element in conflict management. The framework for the ASEAN Security Community proposed in the Bali Concord II (chapter 4) states: "the High Council of the TAC shall be an important component in the ASEAN Security Community since it reflects ASEAN's commitment to resolve all differences, disputes, and conflicts peacefully." The new ASEAN charter states that disputes not concerning the interpretation or application of any ASEAN instruments shall be resolved in accordance with the TAC and its rules of procedure (article 24:2). Even if the TAC settlement mechanism cannot be applied, the other signatories are not precluded from offering assistance to settle disputes. ASEAN states do not rely on the TAC for the methods they have developed of informal intervention in the name of the ASEAN way.

The ASEAN Modes of Conflict Resolution

The preferred approach of the ASEAN way is quiet, informal diplomacy through which no party wins or loses but accepts outcomes that will not rupture regional harmony and stability. This is exemplified in another Indonesian formulation, the so-called *empat mata* ("four eyes") format of informal bilateral summits to address issues that have not been compromised at lower bureaucratic working levels. This requires both mutual respect and trust, which is not always present. The most successful practitioner of the art of *empat mata* was Indonesia's President Suharto. He had the statesmanlike standing to intervene as a conciliating third party in other ASEAN nations' bilateral affairs without seeming to interfere. Since his 1998 disappearance from the ASEAN scene, no ASEAN leader has emerged to play a similar role in intra-ASEAN affairs.

This does not mean that there is no realization by ASEAN leaders that events in one ASEAN country or between ASEAN countries can have serious negative affects on other ASEAN countries or the viability of the association. The problem has been how to overcome the internalized barrier of noninterference. In 1997, faced with a coup in Cambodia (chapter 4), Malaysia's Deputy Prime Minister Anwar Ibrahim advanced the concept of "constructive engagement" through which ASEAN could become cognizant of a regional problem and cooperate in finding a solution. A year later, faced by the crisis for democracy in Myanmar (chapter 4), Thailand's Foreign Minister Surin Pitsuwan proposed a policy of "flexible engagement" that would allow ASEAN to place on its agenda a member state's domestic policies that challenged regional harmony and stability. Both initiatives were received coldly and not acted on. The underlying objection was that constructive or flexible engagement might be disruptive of the ASEAN way and come back to haunt any ASEAN state.

The 1997 internal Cambodian political crisis did require ASEAN intervention since Cambodia was a candidate member of ASEAN. A special foreign ministers' meeting created an ASEAN "troika" consisting of the foreign ministers of Indonesia, Thailand, and the Philippines to act for ASEAN in seeking a peaceful and democratic resolution to the situation. Following up on the Cambodia troika, Thailand's Prime Minister Chuan Leekpai persuaded his colleagues at the 1999 ASEAN Informal Summit to establish the ASEAN Troika as an ad hoc ministerial body. This scheme was fleshed out in a "concept paper" adopted at the July 2000 AMM.[9] The troika, consisting of past, present, and incoming chairs of ASEAN, could be called into existence by consensus in the event a situation of common concern arose likely to disturb regional peace and harmony. It would be specifically barred from addressing issues that constitute the internal affairs of ASEAN member countries and would act in accordance with ASEAN core principles of consensus and noninterference. In September 2000, Thai Foreign Minister Surin sought to activate the troika to discuss the situation in Myanmar. Surin was concerned that ASEAN's external relations were being seriously damaged by the junta. Vietnam, chairing ASEAN, refused to act, calling the problem a Myanmar internal affair. The troika has been inactive since then.

ASEAN member states have been pursuing constructive engagement with Myanmar. Since 2003, briefings by Myanmar's foreign minister have been noted by the AMM. The ASEAN counterparts have encouraged Myanmar to move on its roadmap. Under unrelenting Western pressure, ASEAN leaders have traveled to Myanmar on bilateral visits in the name of dialogue and cooperation only to be rebuffed by the junta. In 2006, in an effort to keep constructive engagement with Myanmar alive, Malaysian Foreign Minister Syed Hamid journeyed to Myanmar as ASEAN's special representative. He was snubbed and cut his trip short. The junta has made it clear that as far as it is concerned, ASEAN's constructive engagement as a way to foster political change in Myanmar is no more welcome than the pressure from the West or the UN (chapter 8).

Intra-ASEAN Disputes and Conflicts in Southeast Asia

Continuing intramural conflicts hindering the goal of cooperation in the common interest raise questions about the validity of the basic premises of the ASEAN way. ASEAN's incapacity to move to a politically integrative level above noninterference and respect for domestic sovereignty suggests that notwithstanding claims of community, interstate relations in the ASEAN region are not really different from relations among states in any world region, governed by calculations of national interest and relative power, particularly when historic and ethnic passions collide with contemporary interests.

Thailand and Its Neighbors

Thailand's position at the geostrategic center of continental Southeast Asia has led to centuries of conflict along its Burmese, Laotian, and Cambodian frontiers. Thailand's contemporary borders are those imposed by European imperialism in the nineteenth and early twentieth centuries. Although the modern state is reconciled to its territorial loss, the motives propelling a "golden peninsula" vision of a Bangkok-centered subregional political economy are suspected by Thailand's relatively weaker neighbors (chapter 4).

Thailand–Laos

Since the 1975 Pathet Lao victory in Laos, Thailand–LPDR relations have been irritated by conflict over the Mekong River border set by the 1907 Franco-Siamese treaty. This escalated into local fire-fights as the two sides pushed back at each other. Finally in 1987, a dispute over three villages turned into a pitched military battle at the village of Ban Rom Klao, with over a thousand casualties.[10] It was not until 1997 that Bangkok and Vientiane agreed to a joint border commission. Border demarcation is expected to be completed in 2008. Thailand and the LPDR have also worked to defuse the issue of refugee ethnic Hmong anti-LPDR activity (chapter 8). This has been undertaken in the framework of a joint border committee. At the first meeting between new Thai Prime Minister Samak Sundaravej and Lao PDR President Choummaly Sayasone in March 2008, the two leaders congratulated themselves on the close cooperation between the countries' border provinces.[11] In Laos, Thailand and China are competing for strategic economic opportunities in the exploitation of the LPDR's forest and hydropower resources (chapter 8).

Thailand–Myanmar

Decades of ethnic warfare in Myanmar have brought Burmese armies up to, and across, Thailand's northern and western frontiers and occasional indiscriminate shelling of Thai villages allegedly harboring ethnic rebels on the Thai side of the border. The local Thai military, with a harder line than Bangkok's, push back. With the armies came first a wave of ethnic refugees and then exiled democracy advocates. What has most concerned the Thais has been the uninterrupted flow of narcotics into Thailand from Myanmar (chapter 6). A frustrated Prime Minister Thaksin warned Yangon in August 2003 that if Myanmar did not shut down the methamphetamine labs, Thailand would—a threat that the aggrieved Myanmar junta claimed was harmful to relations. The Thaksin government's effort to prevent its problems with Myanmar from leading to a breach in relations is less a working of the ASEAN way then a desire to prevent disruption of Thai business activities in Myanmar. This includes the human rights issue in Myanmar. According to Foreign Minister Noppadon, "Thailand has no choice but to put national economic interests first in dealing with Burma."[12]

Thailand–Cambodia

Cambodian historical concern about possible Thai designs on its western provinces is the background to the only case in which one ASEAN state has suspended diplomatic relations with another. Latent Cambodian anti-Thai sentiment was inflamed in January 2003 in a paroxysm of violence. The pretext was an alleged remark by a Thai soap opera actress that Angkor Wat, the ancient Khmer temple at the heart of Cambodia's nationalism, belonged to Thailand. Cambodian politicians, including Prime Minister Hun Sen, whipped up a nationalist fervor that culminated in mob attacks on the Thai embassy and Thai business establishments. The Thai government reacted decisively. Thai air force transports and troops were rushed to Phnom Penh's airport to evacuate Thai citizens. Hundreds of others streamed back across the Thai–Cambodian border. Thailand recalled its ambassador and expelled the Cambodian ambassador. The border was sealed and Thai economic assistance was terminated. Thailand demanded an apology and reparations. Relations remained frozen until Cambodia delivered $5.9 million to compensate for the destruction of the embassy and agreed to negotiate compensation of the business losses through payment in kind and tax benefits.

The Thai–Cambodian clash was an unparalleled internal diplomatic crisis for ASEAN, but there was no ASEAN reaction as such. While ASEAN stayed mute, the United States condemned the attacks and called for Cambodia to re-spect its international obligations. Significantly, China's vice-minister for for-eign affairs summoned the Thai and Cambodian ambassadors, telling them that China hoped that normal relations could be reestablished as soon as pos-sible. China's unprecedented diplomatic intervention into a bilateral dispute within ASEAN signaled its growing political interests in mainland Southeast Asia.

In 2008, the historical past again inflamed Thai–Cambodian relations, this time over the twelfth-century Preah Vihear temple situated at the Thai–Cam-bodian border on the ridgeline of the Dangrek Mountains high above the Cambodian plain. In 1962, the World Court ended a long dispute between Thailand and Cambodia over where the temple was located by awarding it to Cambodia. Thai nationalism never fully recovered from this. Access to Preah Vihear is from the Thai side. In 2007, Cambodia applied to UNESCO to reg-ister the temple as a World Heritage site. Thailand sought to block the request until Cambodia agreed to joint management of the heritage park. The Thais met UNESCO's 2008 approval of the Cambodian request by massing military at the disputed site. Cambodia's Prime Minister Hun Sen rode nationalist anger at Thailand to a massive electoral victory in July. As war drums beat, Cambodia's tentative exploration of the possibility for UN or ASEAN inter-vention gave way to Thai insistence that only bilateral mechanisms would be acceptable in defusing the confrontation.

The most important Thai–Cambodian bilateral dispute is over their mar-itime boundaries in the Gulf of Thailand, where a 10,400 square mile (26,000 sq km) overlapping claims area (OCA) is potentially rich in natural gas and oil reserves.[13] Both Thailand and Cambodia have awarded exploration blocks in the OCA. In 2001, Bangkok and Phnom Penh agreed in principle to joint development, with the model being the Malaysia–Thailand Joint Authority (MTJA). They have not yet been able to agree on production and revenue sharing.[14] Regular talks broke down after the 2003 diplomatic crisis and after resumption were interrupted again by the Thai coup. In March 2008, Thai Foreign Minister Noppadon announced that the government would reopen negotiations with Cambodia on joint development in the OCA with the em-phasis on how to divide benefits from the project.

Malaysia–Singapore

The most contentious bilateral relationship in ASEAN is that between Malaysia and Singapore. Although geographically linked by a causeway across the Johor Strait, the cultural and political gulf between the two is enormous.

Ever since separation in 1965, their leaders have viewed each other with suspicion. The long list of disputes over material interests is set in an economic rivalry in which each country views the other's development policies as "beggar your neighbor." The ethnic factor is fully in play, with each unsure of the loyalties of their respective Chinese and Malay minorities. During the late stages of Malaysian Prime Minister Mahathir's rule, the political exchanges were insultingly vituperative. Although the tone changed in the Abdullah government, the rivalry was not far beneath the surface.

Three main issues have emerged as the lightning rods: Singapore's land reclamation project in the Johor Strait, the security of Singapore's water supply, and the territorial issue of sovereignty over the islet of Pedra Branca, which is discussed below in the section on territorial disputes. Singapore has added to its land area by land reclamation. Eighteen percent of Singapore's land area is reclaimed, with another 15 percent enlargement projected in the future. The most controversial reclamation project is in waters bordering Malaysia's Johor state. Malaysia vigorously protested, claiming environmental damage and hazards to navigation. Singapore, on the other hand, viewed the issue as one more Malaysian effort to curtail Singapore's development. In September 2003, Malaysia submitted its case to the Hamburg, Germany-based International Tribunal for the Law of the Sea (ITLOS), requesting a provisional suspension of all Singapore land reclamation activities. In October 2003, the ITLOS handed down a decision. While not ordering Singapore to cease its work, the ITLOS called for the two states to establish a group of independent experts to monitor the project and cautioned Singapore "not to conduct its land reclamation in ways that might cause irreparable prejudice to the rights of Malaysia."[15] The experts group reported in December 2004 in a way that both sides could claim victory. On the basis of the report, Singapore and Malaysia reached a 2005 settlement allowing the reclamation projects to go forward with Singapore cooperating with Malaysia to limit any adverse impacts.[16]

The water issue is much more serious. Singapore's primary source of water is Malaysia. The terms and pricing of supply of untreated water were fixed in water agreements in 1961 and 1962 to run to 2011 and 2061 and became part of the 1965 Separation Agreement. Negotiations over an increase in the price of raw water began in 1998 as part of a package of outstanding bilateral issues. In 2002, Malaysia pushed the water question to the top of its Singapore agenda. Malaysia insists on the right of review of the price as well as raising questions about the terms of any renewal of water agreements. For Singapore, the issue is not price, which can be negotiated, but Malaysia's alleged unilateralism in forcing the issue and throwing into doubt an assured supply of water in the future. From Singapore's point of view, any breach of the water agree-

ments calls into question the Separation Agreement itself. Singapore has reduced the water issue to the question of the very survival of the state. Even in
the post-Mahathir improved political atmosphere, the water issue hangs over
the future. As the clock is running out to 2011, talks are in abeyance.
Malaysia's bargaining position has been strengthened with the opening of
Johor's own water treatment plant, no longer depending on treated water
from Singapore.

During the Mahathir years, the escalating political tension over the water
question and Pedra Branca was accompanied by a strident belligerency in
which voices on each side of the causeway raised the possibility of war. Although both governments downplayed such a possibility, jingoistic speeches
and newspaper columns in Malaysia promised Singapore a "bloody nose" if it
used a "forward defense" strategy in Malaysia. Responding to a remark by
Malaysia's foreign minister that Singapore had two choices, compromise or go
to war, Singapore's foreign minister responded, "Loose talk of war is irre-
sponsible and dangerous. It whips up emotion that could become difficult to
control."[17] Malaysia's current military procurement program, which for the
first time is building an offensive capability, seems designed to make sure
Malaysia has the power to give a "bloody nose." The two nations seem caught
in a classic security dilemma, where war can occur between two parties when
neither desires such an outcome. At its core is each actor's uncertainty about
the intentions of the other.

Territorial Disputes

The criteria of a modern state include legally bounded territory, a concept that
was brought to Southeast Asia by Western imperialism. Colonial rulers, by
treaty and agreement, drew lines on maps showing the limits of sovereign authority, but at the margins of imperial authority the real borders on the
ground were often fuzzy and ambiguous. Along hundreds of miles of their
borders, the map lines had never been physically demarcated through survey
and physical marking. Where the international border ran through transnational ethnic communities, it had little impact on either political loyalties or
local economic activity. In some cases, new state authority refused to accept
the demarcations. For example, one of the irritants in Vietnam–Cambodian
relations in the prelude to the Third Indochina War was Cambodian moving
of French-placed border markers.

The problem of territoriality and sovereign claims in Southeast Asia is aggravated in the maritime zones of states. There, the states seek to draw the
most extensive straight baselines seaward from their utmost extreme coastal

points, or in the case of an archipelago, their furthest lying islands. The marine extension of baselines set the geographic parameters for a state's twelve-mile territorial sea and, beyond that, its two-hundred-mile exclusive economic zone (EEZ). This explains the contests over what otherwise would be unimportant islands or rocks in waters between, for example, Cambodia and Vietnam or Cambodia and Thailand. In terms of maritime zone disputes, the most significant for Southeast Asia are those around the Spratly Islands, in the heart of the South China Sea. Before turning to this, however, four other cases of disputed sovereignty in Southeast Asia shed light on the possibilities and limits for conflict resolution where territory and maritime jurisdiction are at stake.[18]

The Philippines' Sabah Claim

Malaysian sovereignty over its North Borneo Sabah state has been disputed by the Philippines from the creation of the federation in 1963 (chapter 3). The basis of the Philippine position is an 1878 agreement between the Sultan of Sulu and the proprietors of the North Borneo Company transferring the administration of the North Borneo territory to the company. The Philippines insists that once the British decided to relinquish the rights originally held by the company, those rights reverted to the Philippines as sovereign successor of the Sultan of Sulu, and could not be transferred to another state. By constitutional law and domestic legislation, the Philippines maintained that it had acquired "dominion and sovereignty" in North Borneo by historic right and legal title.

Although President Marcos verbally renounced the Sabah claim at the 1977 ASEAN Summit in Kuala Lumpur, this was never followed up by either constitutional amendment or statute.[19] In 2001, the claim was again advanced in the International Court of Justice as the basis for a Philippines' legal intervention in the Malaysia–Indonesia dispute over Sipidan and Ligatan (discussed below). What is important is that the two countries did not let the issue develop into a major crisis. Manila did not forcefully pursue its claim, and the two governments managed to localize the occasional flare-up. Diplomatic relations were proper, but cool, and they were normalized to the operation of ASEAN. For years, there were no Malaysian high-level visits to Manila. Malaysia's concern about the flow of Filipino illegal immigrants to Sabah was balanced by Manila's suspicion that Sabah is a sanctuary for Mindanao Muslim insurgents. In 2002, angry over Malaysia's treatment of Filipino illegal immigrants in Sabah, Philippines President Arroyo created a committee to "restudy" the claim.

Four factors have been at play in politically containing the Sabah problem. First, Manila did not have the real power capabilities to press its claim aggressively. Second, the United States explicitly excluded Sabah from the workings of the U.S.–Philippines alliance. Third, Malaysia as a member of the Organization of the Islamic Conference (OIC) could negatively affect the Philippines' relations in the Middle East and its access to oil. Finally, there was Indonesian diplomacy, particularly *empat mata* encounters between President Suharto and his Malaysian and Philippine counterparts that counseled restraint. Both parties seem reasonably satisfied to let the issue remain in the background of their wider range of ASEAN engagements.

Malaysia–Indonesia: Ligitan and Sipidan

Ligitan and Sipidan are two small islands on Borneo's northeast coast off the land border between Malaysia's Sabah state and Indonesia's East Kalimantan province. They came into dispute between the two nations in 1969 during continental shelf discussions. The islands' geopolitical significance is as points from which baselines can run defining territorial waters and EEZ. The smoldering quarrel over the islands irritated Malaysian–Indonesian relations for more than three decades. Although no shots were fired, Indonesia's navy patrolled in the vicinity of the islands and secret landings were made to demonstrate occupancy. Kuala Lumpur in turn beefed up its security forces in southeastern Sabah.

Prime Minister Mahathir and President Suharto, in an *empat mata* setting, agreed in 1996 to settle the dispute once and for all. It was decided to refer the matter to the International Court of Justice (ICJ). The Ligitan and Sipidan dispute was the first time two ASEAN member nations had referred a bilateral dispute to an external agency for settlement. The TAC mechanism was explicitly excluded. The case went to the ICJ in November 1998. To Malaysia's anger and dismay, the Philippines sought to intervene in the case as an interested party. The Philippines claimed that the legal status of North Borneo (Sabah) was a matter of legitimate concern to the government of the Philippines. The Court refused the intervention without ruling on the merits of the Philippines' claim to sovereignty in North Borneo.

The Court handed down its decision in favor of Malaysia on 17 December 2002. The basis of the ruling was a continuous pattern of legislative, administrative, and judicial authority by Malaysia itself and as a successor state to British authority that had not been previously objected to by either the Netherlands or Indonesia; to use the Court's legal term, the *effectivités*.[20] The ICJ decision did not resolve the maritime boundary between Malaysia and

Indonesia in the Sulawesi Sea. It in fact complicated it for Indonesia, since the two islands are south of what Indonesia had drawn as its baseline. A necessary component for the successfully adjudicated outcome of the Ligitan and Sipadan dispute was strong leadership on both sides willing to settle the problem judicially and that had the domestic political capacity to abide by a possibly adverse decision.

As it was, the decision was not well received by Indonesian politicians. Although the government of President Megawati had not initiated the ICJ case, it did suffer a nationalist backlash demanding that urgent steps be taken to ensure Indonesian sovereignty on the margins of its archipelago. The government immediately reinforced its show of sovereignty over Miangas Island on the maritime boundary between Indonesia and the Philippines north of Sulawesi. It is the northern limit of Indonesian territorial baselines. A 1928 arbitration with the United States awarded the island to the Netherlands. The Philippines still claims, however, that the island, which it calls Las Palmas, is in the Philippines' historic territorial waters. The island is important in fixing the unresolved continental shelf overlap between Mindanao and Indonesia's Sangihe Talaud archipelago to which Miangas is administratively connected.

Malaysia–Singapore: Pedra Branca (Pulau Batu Putih)

The tiny islet of Pedra Branca ("White Rock") and the nearby Middle Rock and South Ledge lie where the Singapore Strait meets the South China Sea. In 1851, the British Straits Settlement government built the Horsburgh lighthouse on it. For more than 150 years, first the Straits Settlement and then Singapore administered it as part of its sovereign territory. In 1979, the territory, called in Malay Pulau Batu Putih ("White Rock"), appeared on a new Malaysian map as part of Malaysia's Johor state. Singapore immediately protested, but Malaysia claimed that the Johor Sultanate had exercised sovereignty over the territory from 1513. By 2002, Malaysia's aggressive pressing of its sovereignty over Pedra Branca had become the centerpiece of a nationalist campaign that included a list of issues including the water talks.

Singapore's insistence on maintaining the status quo over Pedra Branca was denounced by Malaysian Defense Minister Najib as belligerency and a betrayal of the "ASEAN way."[21] Malaysian naval patrols faced off with the Singapore Maritime Police. There was real danger of an armed clash that could have disastrous political spillover effects. The escalation of the crisis by Malaysia was by design, adding to Singapore's sense of crisis and Malaysian intimidation in the water negotiations. It also bolstered domestically the Malaysian government, challenged on the one hand by Islamic conservatives and on the other by the uncertainties of the transition from Prime Minister Mahathir to Abdullah Badawi. ASEAN was silent.

In 1994, Malaysia accepted in principle a Singapore suggestion that the issue of sovereignty be submitted to the ICJ. It was not until 2003, however, that Malaysia and Singapore signed an agreement to refer the dispute to the ICJ. Why would Malaysia finally go to the ICJ? Coming off the Ligitan–Sipidan victory, Kuala Lumpur might have felt emboldened. Also the government may have felt boxed in by the precedent it had set by accepting ICJ jurisdiction in that case. The written proceedings were submitted to the court by the end of 2005 and the oral proceedings took place from 6 to 23 November 2007, at which time the court took the case under deliberation.[22]

If the measures used by the justices in the Ligitan–Sipidan case are applied, namely in the absence of clear title by treaties the *effectivités* are important, then it was likely that Singapore's possession of Pedra Branca would be confirmed. This was the decision handed down by the court in May 2008. The domestic role played by the dispute, however, raises questions about whether the Malaysian government could respond with political equanimity to an adverse decision by the ICJ. Malaysia's unease at the possible outcome of international adjudication seemed indicated by Prime Minister Abdullah's remarks on his first visit to Singapore as head of the Malaysian government in 2004, when he stressed that the two countries should work through bilateral dialogue to solve problems rather than invite third parties or arbitral procedures.

Malaysia–Indonesia: the Ambalat Block

Since 2005, Malaysia and Indonesia have been embroiled in another dispute in which they have alternately flexed military muscle and diplomatic talk. It began in February 2005 when Malaysia granted an oil exploration concession in the Ambalat Block area of the Sulawesi Sea in an Indonesian–Malaysian overlapping maritime zone where Indonesia had earlier granted exploration concessions. Malaysia's claims were based on its own 1979 map that Indonesia never had accepted. Indonesia's claim was based on the Anglo-Dutch Convention of 1891, which the ICJ had found inconclusive with respect to the waters around Sipidan and Ligitan.

Indonesia's protest to Malaysia was quickly followed by a military buildup on both sides, even as they spoke of diplomatic solutions. Gunboat diplomacy became a game of naval chicken between Indonesian and Malaysian warships backed up by jet fighters. The possibility of exploration came to a halt. Nationalists in both countries whipped up frenzy. With his predecessor President Megawati burned by the Sipidan–Ligitan ICJ decision, President Yudhoyono's

political space on the issue was narrow, pressed as he was by nationalist politicians and a military that did not want to back down to the Malaysians. In an
escalation of the crisis, the Indonesian navy seized Malaysia's Karang Unarang
reef, on which it built a "light house."

Three rounds of talks in 2005 ended with neither side willing to compromise. It became quickly clear, however, that after Sipidan and Ligitan, Indonesia would never submit the dispute to arbitration or adjudication, even
though both sides agreed that the 1982 United Nations Convention on the
Law of the Sea (UNCLOS) would be the basis for settlement. No attention at
all was paid to ASEAN's TAC mechanism. Even as talks were going on, it was
revealed that the Indonesian government was conferring with parliamentarians in preparing a $580 million budget to finance military operations to de-
fend the Ambalat block.[23] The dangers of a serious incident were illustrated by
a collision of Malaysian and Indonesian naval ships maneuvering off Karang
Unarang in April 2005. Political and military leaders of both countries called
for restraint in the rules of engagement. Both navies continued patrolling the
disputed waters and Indonesia mounted shows of force near the Malaysian
border of amphibious landing capabilities, one involving forty vessels and five
thousand personnel in December 2005.

It took summit diplomacy between Yudhoyono and his Malaysian counterpart Prime Minister Abdullah to move the conflict away from sovereign claims
to productive economic potential. In a January 2006 meeting, while admitting
that there had been no breakthrough, the two heads of government for the
first time publicly discussed the possibility of joint development in disputed
maritime zones. Even as technical talks about a joint development area went
on, aggressive naval patrolling continued. Despite government entreaties, the
concessionaires stayed away. In March 2008, the Indonesian president called
on the Ambalat Block negotiating teams to work more effectively and bring
the matter to a conclusion.[24]

The South China Sea Conflict Zone

The South China Sea is at the heart of Southeast Asia. It is technically a "semi-
enclosed sea" in which, according to the UNCLOS, the littoral states are encouraged to "cooperate with each other in the exercise of their rights and the
performances of their duties."[25] The geographic core of the competition is the
Spratly Islands archipelago consisting of more than a hundred islets, reefs, and
rocks extending over 250,000 square miles (400,000 sq km) of the central
South China Sea. Competition, rather than cooperation, has been the prevailing characteristic of the relations among the littoral states, with each one seek-

ing to give real effect to its sovereign and jurisdictional claims. The contested areas of the South China Sea are also part of the strategic waterway through which the sea routes from East Asia to the Middle East pass. The United States has deemed freedom of transit of American naval vessels through the South China Sea a vital security interest. The United States takes no position on the legal merits of individual claims to sovereignty but wants peaceful resolution of the disputes so as to avoid clashes that might lead to wider conflict.

The most important resources at stake in the competition for sovereignty are oil and natural gas reserves. The presumption of vast energy resources in the contested South China Sea offshore basin is largely based on extrapolation from the existing proved reserves being worked in uncontested areas on the South China Sea littoral by Brunei, Malaysia, the Philippines, Vietnam, and Indonesia. There, proven reserves are estimated to be 7 billion barrels of oil, currently producing 2.5 million barrels a day, more than half of them Malaysian.[26] Because there has been essentially no exploration in the central South China Sea, there are no reliable figures for proven reserves. Very optimistic—but highly speculative—Chinese estimates run from 105 billion barrels to 213 billion barrels. At the low end of the estimates, the U.S. Geological Survey has offered the figure of a 28-billion-barrel reserve. The demand for natural gas to fuel the region is also rapidly increasing. In the Spratly Islands area alone, the Chinese estimate natural gas reserves of nine hundred trillion cubic feet and in the entire South China Sea, two thousand trillion cubic feet. Even though the Chinese estimates of oil and gas reserves are considered optimistic, the lure of tapping these potential reserves raises the stakes in the territorial and jurisdictional contest, particularly as energy demands and price increase.

China's claim to sovereignty over the South China Sea is like a palimpsest over the patchwork of overlapping claims of the ASEAN rivals. Fewer than half of the Spratlys have been occupied or garrisoned. China, Malaysia, the Philippines, Vietnam, and Taiwan have physically staked their claims. The small forces or isolated markers are designed to give proof to claims of sovereignty. This is reinforced by naval and air surveillance. Brunei's claim reaches out to the Louisa Reef, but it has no military presence.

The foundation for the claims of both China and Vietnam is historical presence; for China going back to the Han Dynasty, twenty-three centuries ago; for Vietnam, a colonial inheritance. The Malaysia and Brunei claims are continental shelf extension-based. The Philippine claims reference discovery and proximity and date only from the 1950s. Part of the reluctance to apply law to settle South China Sea disputes, notwithstanding commitment to the UNCLOS, is the legal tenuousness of some of the claims. Until there is a resolution of the sovereignty questions and resultant jurisdictional overlaps, large-scale exploration and exploitation of the sea's potential resources will be delayed. The question is how the resolution will be achieved.

Since 1974, China has shown willingness to use force to defend its territorial claims. That year, it forcefully displaced South Vietnam from the Paracel Islands (called Xisha by China) to the north of the Spratly group. Since then it has expanded its presence in the Spratlys (called Nansha by China), making deep inroads into Vietnam and Philippines claimed territories. In 1988, the Chinese navy sank three Vietnamese vessels near Fiery Cross Reef. In 1995, the Philippines discovered a Chinese military base at Mischief Reef, deep inside the Philippines EEZ. The Philippines is a relatively soft target for the aggressive moves by rival claimants since its naval assets are few and defensive capabilities degraded. It had long been understood that U.S. security obligations to the Philippines do not extend beyond the treaty boundaries transferring the Philippines from Spain. This is ambiguous, however, in the case of the South China Sea. President Arroyo stated in April 2004 that before the U.S. training of the Philippines Armed Forces shifted to fighting the Abu Sayyaf group, the focus was defense of the Spratlys against China.[27] There have also been clashes between Malaysia and the Philippines and Vietnam and the Philippines. The possibility of escalating conflict, particularly as China's naval and long-range air assets grow, is a destabilizing element in the regional international order.

China's publication and expansive interpretation of its 1992 "Law on the Territorial Sea and Contiguous Zone of the People's Republic of China" spurred ASEAN to a regional response.[28] ASEAN's strategy is to maintain the status quo in the South China Sea without alienating China. ASEAN seized the political agenda with its 1992 "Declaration on the South China Sea."[29] In it, ASEAN emphasized the necessity to resolve by peaceful means and without resort to force all of the sovereignty and jurisdictional disputes. It put Beijing on notice that a unified ASEAN position was emerging from which ASEAN would view the bilateral issues through regionalist eyes. The declaration suggested that functional cooperative activities could be undertaken without prejudicing the sovereignty and jurisdictional problems in areas such as pollution, navigation, piracy, and other transnational issues. Finally, it called for the application of the principles embodied in the TAC as a basis for establishing a code of international conduct over the South China Sea. The drafting of such a code has become the major focus of the ASEAN–China dialogue on the South China Sea, even as China's creeping jurisdictional expansion continues.

Indonesia spearheaded the effort to establish parameters for functional cooperation. It has initiated and chaired since 1990 annual and officially nongovernmental "Workshops on Managing Potential Conflict in the South China Sea." The goal of the workshop process has been to find areas of functional cooperation that would lead to confidence-building measures and habits of cooperation that could eventually produce a political atmosphere conducive to finding solutions to the territorial and jurisdictional disputes.[30] China has participated in the workshops, but with the proviso that they did not discuss matters of sovereignty or territorial jurisdiction. Nor would China allow any multilateral project that might suggest the legitimacy of international intervention in Chinese sovereign territory. The workshop process has not been able to move from its "talk shop" informality to intergovernmental functional cooperation, let alone create habits of cooperation that could translate to the political level.

Toward a Code of Conduct

ASEAN members learned from the 1995 Mischief Reef affair how instrumentally ineffective their 1992 declaration was in reining in Chinese ambitions. It did not slow down China's "salami strategy" of slice by slice, stone marker pillar by navigation buoy, expanding its physical claim to jurisdiction over the contested waters. For more than a decade, ASEAN and China have been working on fashioning a "Code of Conduct on the South China Sea" to which both sides could agree. ASEAN wants a code that will have a restraining influence on Chinese unilateral acts to change the status quo. China, in turn, requires a text that does not undermine its sovereign claims nor unduly close its options in defending its claims. The Chinese have not retreated from their insistence that the issues of sovereignty and jurisdiction are not matters for multilateral disposition but are bilateral. On the other hand, faced with ASEAN's concerns, they have accepted both with ASEAN and in the ARF that questions of peace and security can be addressed in general terms.

A draft of a code of conduct acceptable to all parties is still elusive. It is understood, however, that any code will be voluntary and not legally binding, providing political guidance rather than regulating behavior. The best that ASEAN could attain by 2002 was a "Declaration on the Conduct of Parties in the South China Sea" that enunciated again commitment to international law, the UNCLOS, and voluntary adherence to the principles of peace, self-restraint, functional cooperation, and consultation.[31] ASEAN acknowledges that the declaration has yet to be fully implemented but nevertheless continues to reaffirm in ASEAN + China and ARF settings that the adoption of a "code of conduct" on the basis of consensus is still a goal.[32] Why can a consensus "declaration" on conduct be reached but not a code? A code is a regulatory statement against which behavior can be evaluated and accountability demanded, even if not enforceable. A declaration, on the other hand, is an expression of intentions that may or may not be fulfilled.

It is doubtful that any nonbinding code of conduct will significantly alter state behavior. The history of China's diplomacy in South China Sea competition is one of declarations of cooperation followed by unilateral acts revising the status quo followed by new declarations of cooperation. Despite China's promise to respect the status quo as promised in the 2002 Declaration, Chinese research vessels and warships continued to intrude into Philippine waters, laying down markers on unmarked reefs. China and Vietnam have faced off over petroleum drilling concessions. Chinese threats forced a British–American–Vietnam oil consortium to abandon development of a gas field off southern Vietnam. The Chinese have driven away Vietnamese fishing vessels from the Spratlys, sinking three in July 2007. Vietnamese anti-China public protests over China's alleged infringement of Vietnam's sovereignty in the disputed maritime zones provoked a stern warning to Hanoi that friendly bilateral ties were at stake. In November 2007, China again politically reasserted its claim to all of the contested area by creating as part of Hainan Province a new county/city administrative structure named Sansha Shi for the Paracels, Spratlys, and Macclesfield Bank. The contest in the South China Sea is fraught with political and nationalist tensions.

Prospects for Joint Development

After more than a quarter of a century, it is abundantly clear that China is not going to scale back its claims nor cease its activities to enforce these claims. The fact that China ratified the TAC in 2003 may raise the political costs of future Chinese unilateralism but does not alter the fundamental structure of the competition. In the words of the Indonesian scholar/diplomat who conceived the workshop process, "it is basically a scramble for resources."[33] Real national interest and relative power are in the foreground of this scramble, while UNCLOS and ASEAN norms are relegated to a rhetorical background. It is also unlikely that China will retreat from its insistence on bilateralism in resolving disputes. As China's energy requirements grow, the search for settlement becomes even more urgent for concerned Southeast Asian states. Realistically and pragmatically, this means that ASEAN claimants will have to find a framework that does not depend on the exclusivity of sovereign claims. The solution most often discussed is to put aside sovereign claims and to agree to cooperate in exploration and exploitation of resources in disputed areas through joint development mechanisms.[34]

A model for joint development exists in the Gulf of Thailand, where Malaysia and Thailand are exploiting natural gas fields under their 2,800 square mile (7,250 sq km) overlap. A 1979 MOU on joint exploration and exploitation led to the creation in 1991 of the Malaysia–Thailand Joint Authority (MTJA), operating on a 50-50 cost and benefits basis. As noted in chapter 3, Australia and East Timor resolved their Timor Sea overlap problem through joint development. The MTJA model has been envisaged as the way Thailand and Cambodia might manage the exploitation of the oil and gas reserves under their Gulf of Thailand overlap. Joint production has been suggested as a possibility in the Brunei–Malaysia overlap. The two countries have been negotiating a settlement. In a joint communiqué in August 2007, Prime Minister Abdullah Badawi and Sultan Hassanal Bolkiah said they hoped for an agreement soon but that details still remained to be worked out. Also, as noted above, Malaysia and Indonesia have been engaged in technical discussion about joint development of the Ambalat Block.

China will not discuss a multilateral joint development framework within which each would share equally, but has indicated willingness to consider joint development on a bilateral basis. On 1 September 2004, Philippine President Arroyo oversaw the signing in China of an "Agreement on Joint Marine Seismic Undertaking in Certain Areas of the South China Sea" (JMSU) between the China National Offshore Oil Corporation (CNOOC) and Philippines National Oil Corporation (PNOC). Such an undertaking could only be in anticipation of joint exploration and development. The other ASEAN claimants were stunned. The Philippines had been the primary mover for ASEAN's coordinated efforts to maintain the status quo in the region, yet had cut a deal with China without consultation. Vietnam accused the Philippines of violating the Philippine-inspired 2002 declaration. However, it only took six months for the pressure of the reality of the Sino-Philippine accord to bring Vietnam on board. In March 2005, the bilateral seismic survey became tripartite when Vietnam's state-owned PetroVietnam joined the JMSU in what Arroyo hailed as "a diplomatic breakthrough for peace and security in the region."[35] Chinese President Hu Jintao, visiting Manila shortly after the signing, said that China and the Philippines "have taken the lead in the groundbreaking joint development in the South China Sea."[36]

There may have been hidden costs for the Philippines in the agreement. In January 2008, details of the scope of the vague "certain areas of the South China Sea" that the Philippines agreed to explore jointly were made public.[37] The nearly 58,000 square mile (143,000 sq km) JMSU zone included more than 9,000 square miles (24,000 sq km) of indisputably Philippine waters that have never been claimed by China or Vietnam. After blindsiding ASEAN, the Arroyo government now was charged by angry politicians and editorialists with not only relinquishing its Spratly claims but selling out the country's sovereignty. In return for giving China the deal, it was alleged that China promised $8 billion in loans and grants, thus adding to the scandals engulfing the Arroyo administration over its dealings with China. The controversy erupted just as the Philippine Congress was readying a measure confirming that the Philippines national territory included its Spratlys claim. China has warned Manila that the move could hurt friendly relations and mutually beneficial co-operation.[38]

In the tripartite agreement China directed its salami strategy to ASEAN solidarity, slicing off the countries one by one. Overtures have been made to Malaysia and Brunei. China would be the big economic winner in this process since it claims all of the central South China Sea and would share benefits from all of the claimed ASEAN states' zones. China would be a political winner too, by eliminating an irritant in its relations in South East Asia. The Southeast Asian states would not be losers, however. Joint development would be better than the current atmosphere of intimidating threat scaring off investment, concessionaires, and contractors. In terms of the national interests of the ASEAN claimants, in the face of the power disparities in the South China Sea, joint development is better than no development and the continued creep of a real Chinese presence and military power in the contested region.

The International Dimensions of Ethnic Conflict

Chapter 1 noted the ethnic/religious map of Southeast Asia and its lack of conformity to the political map. This has led to conflict between ethnic minorities caught in the political framework of the modern state that usually is controlled by the dominant ethnic group: Shans, Karens, Chins, and other minorities in a Myanmar dominated by ethnic Burmese, or Indonesian outer-island minorities bound in a Java-centric state. Then there are ethnic groups that have been cut off from their own people by the borders of the modern state; for example, the Khmer minority in delta Vietnam or the Malay Muslims in the southern provinces of Thailand. Conflict ensues when minorities, either encapsulated in the state or transborder, add a political sense of "nationalism" to their identity and begin demanding self-determination.

Ethnic and religious conflict impacts international relations in Southeast Asia when it alters the patterns of relations between nations either bilaterally or in ASEAN's multilateral framework. Southeast Asian nations cannot ignore events that touch on their national identity or sovereignty. Thailand must react, for example, when Myanmar troops cross the border in pursuit of ethnic rebels or lob mortar rounds into Thai border villages. As already noted, the Lao PDR is outraged when Hmong dissidents operating from the

Thai side of the Mekong explode bombs in Vientiane. Malaysia's border relations with Thailand have to take into account Malay sympathy for the Muslim minority in Thailand. Nor can Southeast Asia in its collective expressions through ASEAN be indifferent to wider international concerns about the political and human rights issues raised in ethnic conflict, Myanmar being the most notorious case (chapter 8).

On the whole, Southeast Asian governments have managed ethnic conflicts well in the sense that they have not allowed them to disturb unduly the normal flow of regional relations. There are, however, two areas of ethnic conflict in addition to Myanmar that have the potential to disrupt regional stability and the ASEAN way. These are the separatist conflicts in Thailand and the Philippines. Indonesia was once on this list, but the Yudhoyono government and the Aceh separatists have settled their conflict. There is now the question of whether the resolution of the Aceh conflict can be a model for other conflicts.

Muslim Separatism in the Philippines

For more than three decades, the Philippines, an overwhelmingly Christian country, has faced armed Islamic insurgency in a war in its south, during which more than 150,000 people have died. The Muslim cause has been the creation of an independent Moro nation (*bangsamoro*) and has had two principal political/military organizations claiming leadership: the Moro National Liberation Front (MNLF) and the Moro Islamic Liberation Front (MILF). A splinter group, the Abu Sayyaf Group (ASG), has complicated the politics of peacemaking. The existence of links between the Philippine separatist groups and foreign Islamist terrorist groups like Jema'ah Islamiyah (JI) and al-Qaeda has made the conflict a front in the war on terror (chapter 6). Highly visible American military support to the Philippines Armed Forces has made the United States a political stakeholder in the Philippine government's relations with two Moro liberation forces.

In 1973, the MNLF revolted against the Marcos dictatorship, continuing Muslim centuries-long resistance to Manila's authority. The MNLF enjoyed the favor of the Organization of the Islamic Conference (OIC). Indonesia and Malaysia, both members of the OIC, helped ward off sanctions against Manila, but at the same time pressed for concessions to Muslim aspirations. With the good offices of Libya, the Tripoli Agreement was reached in 1976 that provided for Muslim autonomy in those provinces and cities where there was a Muslim majority. During Corazon Aquino's administration, legislation was passed for an Autonomous Region in Muslim Mindanao (ARMM), but it was

---

BOX 5.2
The Bangsamoro

The Muslim minority in the Philippines numbers 4.5 million, or about 5 percent of the total population. The Muslims are concentrated in the extreme south, being a majority in four provinces in southwestern Mindanao and the Sulu Archipelago and a minority in western and southeastern Mindanao. The Muslim population is collectively called Moro, a Spanish label derived from "moor." Once a term of opprobrium, today it is used proudly to distinguish not only a people but their sense of nationhood (*bangsa*). The Moros can be broadly thought of as the northern extension of the Malay Islamic culture, but this is not an ethnic definition of a community. The Bangsamoro consists of ten ethnic-linguistic groups. When, as in recent years, they are pressed by external non-Muslim forces, the commonality of Islam prevails over ethnic distinctions. Historically, it was Moro sultanates that gave supravillage political structure to precolonial Philippines. The Spanish aggressively spread crusading Christianity southwards from Luzon, not completing the pacification of Mindanao until shortly before the United States displaced Spain as sovereign. American authority was imposed in the course of a fierce struggle against the Moros, who resisted the displacement of customary law and traditional authority in a secular colonial state. After Philippines' independence, the Moros continued to resist efforts to assimilate the south to rule from Manila. Large-scale migrations of Christian Filipinos after 1950 added religious tensions that exacerbated underlying political and economic tensions in a Manila-centric system that favored the newcomers. Marcos's martial-law regime was the last straw.

---

not until 1996 in the Ramos administration that a final peace settlement was reached, brokered by Indonesia and signed in Jakarta. An elected ARMM government took office with MNLF leader Nur Misuari as its first governor. The MILF, the MNLF's competitor for Muslim political allegiance, did not accept the formula for autonomy. Many of the MNLF's insurgent warriors deserted the ranks and went over to the MILF with their weapons.

The ARMM did not live up to its promise. Manila did not deliver economic and social development funds; Islamic law was not enforced; and the ARMM was not allowed its own security force. The MILF extended its sway over much of the countryside. In November 2002, Nur Misuari went into revolt, but the torch of the armed struggle had already passed to the 12,500 fighters-strong MILF. One of President Gloria Arroyo's promises when she came to office in 2001 was peace in the south. Manila enlisted Kuala Lumpur's OIC-blessed good offices. A MILF–Philippines ceasefire was worked out in Kuala Lumpur at the end of 2001, only to be shattered in February 2003. The MILF declared an all-out war, and President Arroyo officially labeled the MILF a terrorist organization, putting a bounty on the leadership. She continued to look to Kuala Lumpur to facilitate talks with the MILF. Malaysia agreed to host peace talks, but not if Manila treated MILF negotiators as terrorist fugitives. Kuala Lumpur also accepted that any peace settlement would have to respect the territorial integrity of the Philippines.

In anticipation of resumed peace, a ceasefire was put in place in July 2003, overseen by a Malaysia-led small international monitoring team (IMT). Members of the IMT included Brunei and Libya with support from Japan and Canada. Despite local breakdowns, the general cease-fire held. In 2003 there had been 132 clashes between the Philippine military and the MILF; in 2007, only 17. The peace talks began in Kuala Lumpur in September 2003 with both sides pledged to find an acceptable political settlement. The United States promised diplomatic and financial support to the peace process, proposing as much as $30 million in development funds for the region. The U.S. State Department funded a United States Institute of Peace (USIP) project in support of the Malaysian mediation. Japan and Australia also made important commitments of economic support.

There were two major issues in the negotiations: the geographic scope of the Moro's "ancestral domain" and the control of its resources. In November 2007, a draft agreement was reached that would create a new autonomous region known as the Bangsamoro Judicial Entity, which would expand the ARMM by a thousand villages, including non-Muslim villages, in six rather than four provinces. As a kind of sideshow to the negotiations with the MILF, the Philippines restarted its peace negotiations with the MNLF, still facilitated by Indonesia as the chair of the OIC Peace Committee for Southern Philippines (PCSP). An OIC–Philippines–MNLF meeting in November 2007 agreed to a framework to rejuvenate the1996 peace agreement. Libya actively sought to reconcile the MILF and MNLF, and in December 2007 Seif el-Islam el-Qaddafi, son of Libya's leader Muammar el-Qaddafi, brought the two parties together. According to the MILF's spokesperson, "We promised to iron out whatever differences we have had in the past not later than September 2008 and come up with a single road map."[39] Reconciliation does not mean unification, and there remains the problem of division of loyalties and territorial and resources control.

The hope that peace was at hand was quickly dashed in December 2007 when the government insisted that it would require a constitutional amendment to "dismember" the country, a position that the MILF rejected out of hand, threatening to resume hostilities. Malaysian and American intervention sought to get the peace process back on track. The American ambassador to the Philippines made an unprecedented visit to the MILF head at his headquarters. At a ten-thousand-person gathering of the MILF in March 2008,

Moro leaders, while still committed to a peaceful solution, expressed doubt that it could be accomplished in an Arroyo administration, caught up as it was in politics and corruption.[40] A frustrated Malaysia, citing lack of progress in the talks, announced in April 2008 its phased pullout from the IMT, beginning in May and to be completed by September. Brunei announced it would follow the Malaysian lead. The concern was that as long as Manila stalled, MILF extremists allied with the JI and other radical Islamists would push for a new round of hostilities.

Pattani Muslim Separatism in Thailand

In 2004, the long simmering tinderbox of discontent of the Muslim population of South Thailand ignited. By the beginning of 2008, the death toll was 2,900. The flash point was a January 2004 raid on an army barracks in Narathiwat province and coordinated attacks on other government targets. Three major rebel groups are known to be involved as well as smaller splinter groups: the Pattani United Liberation Organization (PULO); the Barisan Revolusi Nasional-Coordinate (BRN-C, National Revolutionary Front-Coordinate); and the Gerakan Mujahideen Islam Pattani (GMIP, Pattani Islamic Warriors Movement). There is an umbrella United Front for Independent Pattani (Bersatu). The origins and political orientations of the insurgent groups are different, with PULO being Malay nationalist, BRN-C more Islamist, and GMIP with its roots in the Afghan *mujahideen* and links to al-Qaeda. The armed strength of the insurgents is variously estimated at three thousand to five thousand, with active supporters numbering ten thousand to twelve thousand.[41]

Gasoline was thrown on the fire by the April 2004 killing at Tak Bai village in Narathiwat of thirty-two armed militants in the Thai security forces' storming of the Krue Se mosque in Pattani Province and the October 2004 deaths of eighty-five protesters being transported to a holding camp by the army. As the Thaksin Shinawatra government poured troops into the south— up to forty thousand military and paramilitary—the spiraling tit-for-tat warfare intensified. The terrified Buddhist minority and an intimidated Muslim population were caught between the insurgents and the army. The formation of local militia and vigilante groups deepened insecurity in the stricken provinces. Critical elements of the government's social infrastructure—health workers, teachers, local officials, Buddhist monks—fled the region. Thaksin's failure to resolve the crisis was used by the Thai junta as one of the justifications for the September 2006 coup. The generals proved no better able to tackle the problem. When the junta turned the government over to a new elected Samak government in January 2008, the situation had worsened, be-

---

BOX 5.3
The Pattani Muslims

Thailand's Muslim population is more than three million, the great majority of whom are ethnic Malays living in the far south of the country. They are concentrated in the provinces of Satun, Yala, Pattani, and Narathiwat, which, with the northern Malayan provinces, were part of the old Pattani Sultanate. The sultanate had been tributary to the king of Siam in the nineteenth century and was annexed in 1902. The contemporary territorial framework is a result of a 1909 Anglo–Siamese treaty in which the Thais relinquished all claims to the northern Malay states but retained sovereignty over the Malay population north of the border. Thailand seized its lost Malay provinces during World War II but was forced to return to the 1909 border in 1945. The Thai Malay Muslims, occupied in traditional subsistence agriculture, plantation agriculture, and fisheries, have resisted assimilation into a culturally Buddhist Thai state that aggressively defined a Thai identity in its language, educational, and administrative policies. There are numerous kinship ties across the border in Malaysia and dual citizenship is not uncommon. A rising political consciousness among the Thai Malay Muslims, complementing their sense of economic and social deprivation, has its roots in the emergence in the 1940s of the National Front for the Liberation of Pattani (BNPP, Barisan Nasional Pembebasan Pattani). Its leaders were drawn from the descendents of the old sultanate's aristocracy.

---

coming "more dangerous, more deadly, and more threatening to the security of the nation and its neighbors."[42]

The neighbor with the greatest interest is Malaysia. The various Islamic insurgent groups have had long political ties with Malay Muslims across the border. Thai officials were quick to charge that the Thai Muslim insurgents were operating from safe havens in Malaysia. Even though sharp words have been exchanged between Bangkok and Kuala Lumpur over whether Malaysia is functioning as a sanctuary for terrorism, a high-level security dialogue has called for greater cooperation. While Thai security forces clamped down on the southern provinces, their Malaysian counterparts across the border swept up suspected rebels. Joint Thai-Malaysian military patrols along the border were instituted for the first time since the ending of the communist insurgency more than two decades ago.

Malaysia's security concerns are not just that of spillover of the war on the border but the opportunity opened for a regional Islamist terrorist group such JI or al-Qaeda to get a foothold on the peninsula. Moreover the recreation of a strongly Islamic greater Pattani state has grave implications for loyalties in Malaysia's northern tier. The strategic problem for Thailand became more

critical after the Malaysian elections in March 2008 put Malaysian Islamist opposition party PAS (Partai Islam se-Malaysia)-dominated governments in
power in the three states abutting the Thai border. Junta Prime Minister
Surayud met Malaysia's Prime Minister Abdullah in February 2007, at which
time the question of possible Malaysian mediation with the insurgents was
raised. The problem is who to negotiate with. PULO spokesmen in exile claim
talks between the separatists and Thai security officers had taken place outside
of Thailand since 2005, with Jakarta being one of the venues. The older generation Thai Muslim leaders, now gathered under the umbrella of Bersatu, are
not the commanders on the ground. Even if a Malaysian prime minister could
break through the constraints of domestic politics to agree to act as an honest
broker it would be difficult to get the Thai establishment to agree. Bangkok
would be uncomfortable having a predominantly Muslim country, even an
ASEAN partner, in an interventionist role, no matter how limited, between the
state and a group of rebellious Muslim citizens.

The ASEAN way is not yet relevant in this kind of situation. After the Tak
Bai incident, Prime Minister Abdullah and Indonesia's President Yudhoyono
wanted to discuss southern Thailand as a possible regional security issue at the
2004 Vientiane ASEAN Summit. Prime Minister Thaksin threatened to walk
out and return to Bangkok. Because of ASEAN's golden rule, ASEAN has not
taken cognizance of the conflict in South Thailand despite the implications—
including expanded terrorist threats—for the ASEAN Security Community.
Moreover, up to 2008, Bangkok has been successful in diplomatically warding
off OIC intervention. In his first meeting with Malaysia's Prime Minister Abdullah in April 2008, Thai Prime Minister Samak implicitly linked Malaysia's
dependency on Thai rice imports to Kuala Lumpur's security cooperation on
the border, requesting the extradition of two alleged insurgent leaders.[43] Given
the 2008 Malaysian election outcome, this would be politically difficult for the
Malaysian leader.

Officials in Bangkok are speaking of at least a decade before the situation in
the south returns to "normal." If by normal is meant the status quo ante of a
passive Muslim population under centralized Bangkok control, this seems unlikely with the politicization and even radicalization of ever larger numbers of
the Muslim community. The insurgents have promised the war will worsen if
the southern Muslims are not given self-determination. It is doubtful that the
postjunta elected Thai government will approach the crisis in the South in a
fresh or innovative manner. Prime Minister Samak has alleged that the instiga-
tors of the southern violence are "from outside the country," seemingly ignoring its indigenous roots.[44] Samak immediately dismissed the idea floated by his
interior minister that some form of autonomy should be considered. But the
idea is out there to be seized upon by the OIC and Muslim oil-producing countries even if ASEAN remains silent.

Indonesia

Indonesia has confronted ethnic and religious insurgency since the foundation of the independent state. The Darul Islam revolt on Java and the Christian-based separatism of the Republic of the South Moluccas immediately challenged the republic's legitimacy and integrity. As noted in chapter 2, regionalist and ethnic rebellion in Sumatra and East Indonesia between 1957 and 1962 had clandestine support from the United States. The Suharto regime's repressive security state effectively, if ruthlessly, quenched dissidence. The collapse of that state has seen a recrudescence of ethnic and sectarian violence ranging from ethnic gang brawling and church bombings to horrific local ethnic cleansing in Maluku and South Sulawesi. For the regional international order, the most critical areas of Indonesia's internal security problems were at its provincial extremities in Aceh and Papua.[45] The goals of the Free Aceh Movement (GAM) and the Free Papua Organization (OPM) were independence from Indonesia. East Timor's independence revitalized the aspirations of these longstanding separatist movements. Jakarta had committed to use whatever force was necessary to ensure that there was not another East Timor. Intervening political forces including democratization and international attention worked to modify this policy.

Aceh

The war in Aceh that began in 1976 was only the last phase of the struggle of the Acehnese people to throw off "alien" rule, beginning with the Dutch and continuing into Indonesia's independence. The Acehnese are strongly Islamic, but religion was not the only—and perhaps not the most important—issue on the GAM (Gerakan Aceh Merdeka, Free Aceh Movement) separatist agenda. The Acehnese resented the fact that Javanese and other migrant Indonesians enjoyed the greatest benefits from the exploitation of Aceh's oil and natural gas reserves. In the course of the struggle between Aceh demands for self-determination and Indonesian insistence on the integrity of the unitary republic, more than ten thousand lives were lost and the human rights of the population ignored by both sides.

The transition to a democratic Indonesia after the collapse of the Suharto government provided the opening for moving away from a purely military strategy toward Aceh. During the Habibie presidency, laws on decentralization were passed giving Aceh and other provinces greater control over resources. The Wahid government began the negotiating process with GAM, facilitated by the Swiss Henri Dunant Center. In 2001, the Megawati government granted "special autonomy" to Aceh that included the introduction of *sjariah* (Islamic) law. In December 2002, the government and GAM reached a mediated

---

BOX 5.4
Aceh's Struggle

Aceh historically was a fiercely independent Muslim sultanate at the northern end of Sumatra. Among the first territories in Southeast Asia to become Islamized, its ethnicity is closely bound up in its Islamic identity. Between 1873 and 1903, the Dutch forcefully extinguished Aceh's independence at great human cost in the Aceh War, although local resistance continued. After World War II, the Acehnese struggled for autonomy in the new Republic of Indonesia, feeling betrayed by the secular nationalism underpinning the new state. Acehnese dissidents supported the Darul Islam revolt and the later regionalist rebellions in Sumatra. In 1959, Aceh was given the status of a "special territory" but this did not quell resentment of rule from Jakarta. From an Acehnese vantage, the Javanese-dominated central government had replaced the Dutch as colonial rulers to be resisted. The Free Aceh Movement (GAM) was founded in 1976, and under the leadership of Tengku Hasan di Tiro, a claimed descendant of the last Sultan of Aceh, began anew armed struggle. The succeeding low-intensity war was marked by counterinsurgent military operations, arbitrary arrests, and exiles. The GAM's political leadership was in European exile. Despite the Indonesian government's determined efforts to crush the GAM militarily, its local field commanders proved resilient and were connected to the people.

"Framework Agreement" for the cessation of hostilities to be monitored by a Joint Security Commission that included a small group of foreign monitors, primarily Thai and Filipino military officers. A Japan–U.S–EU.–led Tokyo Conference on Peace and Reconstruction in Aceh promised a special aid package for the beleaguered province. Not surprisingly, the settlement collapsed within four months. Jakarta flooded the province with thousands of troops, declared martial law, and in May 2003 began an all-out offensive to wipe out GAM once and for all.

Jakarta hoped to deflect foreign criticism of the action by labeling GAM a terrorist organization. Indonesia worked diligently within ASEAN and with donor nations to obtain declarations of support for Indonesia's national unity. After the start of the 2003 military campaign, the ASEAN foreign ministers reaffirmed their support for Indonesia's sovereignty and territorial integrity, recognizing the Indonesian efforts—implicitly the military campaign—to restore peace and order in Aceh.[46] International insistence on Indonesian territorial integrity recognized that the breakup of Indonesia would be regionally destabilizing. The vision of the possible international outcome was more of a Balkans case than a USSR, since in a failed Indonesia there would be no Russia. A success for separatism in Indonesia would be a model for separatist movements elsewhere in the region. A weakened Indonesia would present even more fertile ground for Islamic radicalism and terrorism. Although Jakarta considered the war in Aceh to be an issue of sovereign concern, it was effectively internationalized because of Indonesia's importance to the future of the region's international order.

As the months wore on, the government's timetable for victory became longer and longer, with martial law extended into 2004. Malaysia braced for a cross-strait flow of refugees. Donor nations feared that an East Timor-like human disaster was in the offing. In November 2003, the conveners of the Tokyo conference on Aceh issued a "Joint Statement on Aceh" expressing concern about the extension of the military emergency in the province and its implications for the well-being of the people of Aceh.[47] Jakarta denounced what it called foreign "meddling," pointing out that the role of the Tokyo conference co-chairs had ended with the breakdown of the peace talks.

At the end of 2004, GAM and the people of Aceh were faced with two human disasters. The first was the military campaign the Indonesian army was carrying out. The second was the devastation brought to Aceh by the December 2004 tsunami (chapter 8). The only way the people and economy of Aceh were going to recover would be in a stable political environment in which economic resources could be mobilized for Aceh's recovery and rehabilitation. The new Yudhoyono government began a new round of negotiations with the GAM, facilitated this time by the Finnish Crisis Management Initiative (CMI) led by former Finnish president Martti Ahtisaari. On 15 August 2005 a memorandum of agreement was signed ending the separatist war—not with independence but with self-government and greater autonomy for Aceh. The demilitarization measures of the MOU were overseen by the Aceh Monitoring Mission (AMM), a program of the EU's European Defense and Security Policy. Joining them were monitors from Thailand, Malaysia, Singapore, the Philippines, and Brunei. Indonesia's parliament passed the necessary autonomy legislation in July 2006, and in December 2006 Aceh's first directly elected governor was picked—a former GAM military commander.

The circumstances that led to the resolution of the Aceh conflict do not seem to fit other cases of ethnic conflict in Southeast Asia. The Indonesian government and GAM did not have a deep religious divide—unlike Thailand, the Philippines, and other ethnic minorities spread throughout the region. Nor is it likely that another intervening variable as dramatic as the 2004 tsunami can be expected. Another analyst has pointed to a kind of "double defeat" of the contending militaries forcing strategies to change. From 2003,

GAM was losing the armed struggle in the province, but the Indonesian military was under pressure to reduce its role in a democratic society.[48] It is doubtful that any of Yudhoyono's post-Suharto predecessors, even if they had the political will, would have had the political capability that he did in exerting command over the military and police making them hew to the negotiating line.

Papua

The former Netherlands' territory of West New Guinea became an Indonesian province in 1967. This followed a threatened Indonesian war against the Dutch. American and UN intervention led to a transfer of sovereignty to Indonesia (chapter 3). Since then, an episodic, low-intensity armed struggle has been waged by the OPM (Organisasi Papua Merdeka, Free Papua Movement) against Indonesian rule. Although the armed strength of the OPM numbers only in the low hundreds, its existence provides a nationalist core for a widely shared aspiration for self-determination. An aggressive Indonesian transmigration policy has relegated the indigenous Melanesian peoples to the economic and social margins of the society. Papuan nationalists view the Indonesian and foreign exploitation of the province's resources as a pillaging of their national patrimony. Harsh and abusive civil-military relations have aggravated the tensions. For the OPM and its Papuan supporters, Indonesia has turned Papua into an internal colony.

Papuan nationalists took heart in the turmoil of the post-Suharto democratic transition. In November 1999, thousands of Papuans rallied for independence. Indonesian President Abdurrahman Wahid, while apologizing for past human rights violations, ruled out independence as an option, a position crystallized in the government of his successor President Megawati. The 2002 special autonomy granted Aceh also included Papua. In violation of the special autonomy, the province has been split in two between Papua and West Papua. The motive was to weaken Papuan nationalism and dilute the impact of greater local control over resources. The beneficiaries of autonomy are not the Papuans, but the Indonesian migrant population. In 2008 new waves of protests demanded an end to special autonomy and a self-determination referendum.[49]

With the exception of Vanuatu, Jakarta has been able to deny the OPM any international personality. In Vila, Vanuatu's capital, there is a West Papuan People's Representative Office that houses the secretariat of the West Papua National Coalition for Liberation, formed in 2008. The ASEAN states, ASEAN's dialogue partners, and the ARF members are committed to the maintenance of Indonesia's territorial integrity. Indonesia has been able to

---

BOX 5.5
Papua's Struggle

In the nineteenth century, European imperialism partitioned the island of New Guinea. Up to World War I, the eastern half was a German colony and the western came under the Netherlands' sovereignty. After World War I, the German territory, Papua New Guinea (PNG), became a British League of Nations mandate administered by Australia, and after World War II, a UN trust territory administered by Australia. It gained independence in 1974. Although Netherlands New Guinea had been administered separately from the Netherlands East Indies, independent Indonesia claimed it as part of its colonial legacy from the Dutch. As the Dutch began a belated effort to prepare the racially Melanesian population of the territory for self-government, Indonesia prepared to use force if necessary to wrest what it called West Irian (Irian Barat) from the Dutch. With no support from its Western allies and militarily unable to sustain a war in Asia, the Dutch accepted an American-brokered face-saving compromise. In October 1962, the Netherlands transferred the territory to an interim UN administration. Eight months later, in May 1963, administrative control was transferred to Indonesia with the promise that an act of self-determination would take place by 1969. That year, following an indirect and coerced "act of free choice," dubbed by critics an "act of no choice," the territory was integrated into Indonesia as its twenty-sixth province, Irian Jaya, and now two provinces, Papua and West Papua. Deprived of self-determination and self-government, the Melanesian nationalist activists of the OPM began the armed resistance to what they termed Indonesian colonialism.

---

neutralize support from across the PNG's border for their Melanesian brothers. In the 2006 Lombok Pact, Australia promised not to allow Indonesian separatist groups to operate from Australia (chapter 2). Nevertheless, continuing patterns of injustice and human rights abuse by the Indonesian military against Papuan nationalists will rally Western liberal politicians and NGO advocacy groups to the cause of self-determination for Papua. The 2007–2008 chairman of the U.S. House of Representative foreign affairs subcommittee on Asia championed self-determination for Papua, and Congress withheld a portion of fiscal year 2008 U.S. security assistance to Indonesia until the secretary of state could report on the status of human rights in Papua. In his 2007 Independence Day State Address, President Yudhoyono sternly warned that Indonesia would not tolerate any effort, from within or without, to violate the sovereignty and unity of the state by fostering separatism. One of the lessons from Aceh, however, is that it is possible to move from a limited special autonomy to a more federal status without threatening territorial integrity or sovereignty.

The ASEAN Regional Forum (ARF)

The ASEAN members have sought to engage their external partners in the ASEAN way of conflict resolution: with its strengths—multilateral consultation and declaratory acceptance of norms of behavior—and limitations of consensus and noninterference. The institutional framework for this is the ASEAN Regional Forum. The ARF is a foreign ministerial grouping of twenty-seven states in the Asia-Pacific region. In addition to the ASEAN 10, the membership consists of ASEAN's ten formal dialogue partners and Bangladesh, Papua New Guinea, Mongolia, North Korea, Pakistan, Sri Lanka, and Timor-Leste. Future membership is on hold, although Kazakhstan, Kyrgyzstan, and Afghanistan are knocking on the door. The purpose of the ARF is to foster dialogue on issues of regional peace and security in order to promote confidence building and transparency. It is the only multilateral political/security forum linking Northeast Asia, Southeast Asia, and South Asia. The annual ARF meeting is an adjunct to the ASEAN ministerial meeting (AMM). The chairman of the AMM is also the chairman of the ARF. Although initially resisting a formal role for defense officials and military officers in the ARF process, beginning with the 2002 ARF they now meet separately the day before the foreign ministers. The ARF has no independent bureaucratic structure. It is supported by the ASEAN Secretariat. Its official record is the "Chairman's Statement," a consensual document released at the conclusion of the meeting.

Development of the ARF

The ARF is a product of the 1990s post–Cold War redistribution of power in East Asia in a new strategic order characterized by three major structural factors: the collapse of the Soviet Union, the rise of China, and questions about the scope and intensity of future U.S. commitments. In adjusting to the post–Cold War regional international environment, the ASEAN states had two political imperatives with respect to external powers. The first was the need to engage a rising China in a functionally comprehensive network of relationships, including security, which would give Beijing a stake in regional multilateralism. The second was to find a vehicle to guarantee continued U.S. involvement in the Southeast Asian security environment to balance China, but not in a way that would threaten it.

Through the ARF, the ASEAN states have involved themselves in the security problems of Northeast Asia, preempting the possible emergence of a separate Northeast Asia security dialogue. The 1992 Singapore ASEAN

Summit called for an intensified post-ministerial conference (PMC) on political and security matters. The first enhanced PMC took place after the 1993 AMM. That meeting agreed to constitute the ARF in a separate consultative framework but maintaining a contextual ASEAN identity. The first formal ARF meeting took place in Bangkok on 15 July 1994. Input from regional institutes of strategic and international studies and "think tanks," linked together as ASEAN ISIS, intellectually backstopped the official process.

For China, participation in the ARF solidified its political role in Southeast Asia in a format independent of a policy framework dominated by the United States or Japan. It was a politically cost-free way to show Southeast Asia China's nonthreatening and cooperative face. In fact, the China–ASEAN connection has meant that the Taiwan issue or other questions of concern about China such as Tibet are excluded from multilateral scrutiny. For the United States, the Clinton administration's decision to accept an embryonic regionalization of U.S. security interests in the ARF's setting coincided with the notional vision of "community," expressed as well through APEC. ARF membership is relatively cost free for the United States also. The American pattern of cooperative security in East and Southeast Asia is still based on its core military alliances and other bilateral security partnerships unconstrained by multilateral obligations.

The "Concept Paper" for the ARF, endorsed at its second, 1995 meeting, assigned a "pivotal role" to ASEAN, which had undertaken the "obligation to be the primary driving force of ARF."[50] That role for ASEAN is ritually endorsed at the ARF's annual meetings. ASEAN's primacy is in part because the well-established ASEAN structure was convenient for the institutional add-on of the ARF. ASEAN's success in developing cooperative modes in other areas of functional cooperation with its external partners made ASEAN a natural home for the ARF. The ASEAN connection alleviates concerns that one or another of the regional great powers could self-interestedly manipulate the ARF. At the same time, however, arguments have been made that ARF would have greater impact if it were independent of the ASEAN way and an agenda that critics see as skewed by ASEAN's deference to China. With ASEAN in charge, it is assured that the ARF moves forward "at a pace comfortable to all" with decision making by consensus and noninterference. This has meant that in terms of addressing conflict and security issues, ARF has not moved forward beyond a "talk shop." The annual ARF Chairman's Statement is a vanilla confection of a laundry list of expressions of "concern about" or "welcoming of" events and situations at a level of generalization that hides the deep disagreements among the conferees. It has been vetted in every foreign office and thoroughly massaged at senior officials' meetings before the foreign ministers ever see it.

ARF's Activities

An innovative aspect of the ARF is the organization of its Track II component. This consists of a network of national nonofficial groups in ARF member states who are linked in the Councils for Security Cooperation in the Asia-Pacific (CSCAP). CSCAP, established in 1993, predating ARF itself, provides a platform for a continuing structured expert dialogue between regional security-oriented institutions and individuals on topics supporting the ARF's agenda of confidence building and security cooperation.[51] Freed from the official restraints of politics and diplomacy, Track II can openly address sensitive issues that governments avoid.

It was agreed at the 1995 session that cooperative activities within ARF would be built in a three-stage process: (1) the promotion of confidence building; (2) development of preventive diplomacy; and (3) the elaboration of approaches to conflict. The ARF's institutional concentration has been on the first stage, primarily through twice annual meetings of an Inter-sessional Support Group (ISG) on Confidence Building Measures and Preventive Diplomacy. In 2001 ARF adopted a "Paper on Concept and Principles of Preventative Diplomacy."[52] The concept paper was hailed as a major achievement in the evolution of the ARF. The paper, recognizing the overlap between confidence building and preventive diplomacy, tried to define preventive diplomacy and suggest principles to guide its practice. Measures such as efforts to build mutual trust and confidence, norm building, and enhancing channels of communication were identified, but without structural forms or applications to real conflicts.

Since 2001, terrorism has been prominent on the ARF agenda. There is an Inter-sessional Meeting (ISM) on Counter-Terrorism and Transnational Crime. There is an ISM on Disaster Relief, which, given its functional nature, has moved more quickly in program development. Direction is given by a "shepherds' group of nations" (Australia, China, the EU, Indonesia, Malaysia, and the United States) that are ready to take the lead in preparing for emergency disaster relief. A proposed new ISM on Non-proliferation was taken under consideration at the 2007 meeting. The formal ISG and ISMs meet biannually, alternating between the ASEAN and non-ASEAN co-chair countries. There are also numerous seminars and workshops throughout the inter-sessional year. Since 2004, there has been an annual ARF Security Policy Conference (ASPC) of senior defense and military officials to promote transparency. This is also the case with the publication of the annual *ASEAN*

Regional Forum Security Outlook (ASO) that consists of voluntary country submissions. The 2007 ASO had thirteen submissions of which four were Southeast Asian: Indonesia, Philippines, Singapore, and Thailand.[53]

Strengthening ARF

The ASEAN drivers of the ARF process recognize that some participants are uncomfortable with the inability of ARF to transform the grouping from deliberation to preventive diplomacy. In 2001, the ARF authorized a registry for an Expert and Eminent Persons (EEP) group to provide input on how to strengthen ASEAN for the future. The actual registry was not in place until 2005. The EEPs held their first plenary meeting in Korea in 2006 and their second in Manila in 2007. Proposals by the EEPs go to the Senior Officials Meeting, which assesses their practicability before passing them on to the foreign ministers. Any proposal will have to pass the ASEAN way test of consensus, noninterference, and moving forward at the pace of the slowest member.

In an effort to give some semblance of organizational continuity and focus, the 2001 ARF adopted a concept paper on the "Enhanced Role of the ARF Chair."[54] This set out principles and procedures for the chair's role in good offices and coordination between ARF meetings. This was prompted by the ASEAN ministers' sense that ASEAN was becoming marginalized in the ARF. The Southeast Asian ARF Chair is essentially a bystander in the wider diplomatic setting of East Asia and the Pacific. One Indonesian analyst observed that ASEAN stood on the sidelines, becoming a spectator or cheerleader to the actions of the other participants.[55] In a new effort to give the ARF chair a more proactive role in preventive diplomacy, the 2007 ARF adopted terms of reference for an institution known as the ARF "friends of the chair" (FOC). This turned the ASEAN troika (chapter 4) into an ARF quartet. The FOC was conceived as a quick-reaction group to be activated on an ad hoc basis by the ARF chair in times of emergency or threats to regional peace and security. The friends of the chair are designated as the past chair, the incoming chair, and a foreign minister of a non-ASEAN country. At China's insistence, the ARF chair will have to inform the ARF member countries in advance of his convening of the FOC. This suggests that based on ARF's rule of consensus, China or any other member holds a veto. Even if the FOC goes into operation, it cannot be interventionist. The discussion about the FOC or any effort to give ARF a greater role in conflict resolution begs the question of whether ARF under any leadership, ASEAN or otherwise, has the institutional gravitas to really influence outcome in Asian conflict zones.[56] Tinkering with the ARF's mechanism may not be enough to meet the challenge of its relevancy to the central problems of security in East Asia and the Pacific. Looming on the ARF's horizon is the prospect under study of transforming the six-party talks on the nuclear proliferation issues in Korea into a permanent Northeast Asian security forum.

Notes

1. Barry Buzan, "The Southeast Asian Security Complex," *Contemporary Southeast Asia* 10, no. 1 (1992): 2.

2. The most comprehensive analysis of ASEAN as a cooperative security association is Ralf Emmers, *Cooperative Security and the Balance of Power in ASEAN and the ARF* (London: RoutledgeCurzon, 2003).

3. Amitav Acharya, *Constructing a Security Community in Southeast Asia: ASEAN and the Problem of Regional Order* (London: Routledge, 2001), 18.

4. Alan Collins, *Security and Southeast Asia: Domestic, Regional and Global Issues* (Boulder, Colo.: Lynne Rienner, 2003), 137.

5. Robert Hartfield and Brian Job, "Raising the Risks of War: Defence Spending Trends and Competitive Arms Processes in East Asia," working paper 44, University of British Columbia Center of International Studies, March 2005.

6. John Chipman, Press Statement on the launch of *The Military Balance 2008*, accessed at www.iiss.org/publications/the-military-balance/military-balance-2008-press-statement.

7. The text of the treaty is at www.aseansec.org/1217.htm.

8. As reported by *Bernama* [Malaysian National News Agency], 20 December 2002.

9. "The ASEAN Troika," concept paper adopted at the thirty-third AMM, Bangkok, 24–25 July 2000, accessed at www.aseansec.org/3637.htm.

10. Ronald Bruce St, John, "The Land Boundaries of Indochina: Cambodia, Laos and Vietnam," *Boundary and Territory Briefing* 2, no. 6 (1998): 39.

11. "New Thai PM Visits Laos," *Vientiane Times*, 3 March 2008, as reported by *Asia News Network*.

12. As quoted in Achara Ashayagachat, "New Approach to Burma, says Noppadon," *Bangkok Post*, 26 February 2008.

13. For the overlapping jurisdictions in the Gulf of Thailand and the possibilities for joint development, see Clive Schofield, "Unlocking the Seabed Resources of the Gulf of Thailand," *Contemporary Southeast Asia* 20, no. 2 (2007): 286–308.

14. Andrew Symon, "Cambodia, Thailand Struggle over Petroleum," *Asia Times Online*, 14 June 2007.

15. Full documentation of the case can be found at the court's website, www.itlos.org.

16. "Malaysia and Singapore Compromise over Long Disputed Waters," accessed at www.parlimen.gov.my/transfer/Malaysia_and_Singapore.pdf.

17. Prof. S. Jayakumar, parliamentary speech, 25 January 2003.

18. For a review of territorial disputes between ASEAN states see Ramses Amer, "The Association of South-East Asian Nations and the Management of Territorial Disputes," *Boundary and Security Bulletin* 9, no. 4 (Winter 2001–2002): 81–96.

19. The 1973 constitution defines the Philippines national territory as the archipelago and "all of the other territories belonging to the Philippines by historic or legal claim." The 1987 constitution states that in addition to the archipelago, the national territory includes "all other territories over which the Philippines has sovereignty or jurisdiction."

20. Links to the full documentation of the ICJ adjudication of *Sovereignty Over Pulau Ligitan and Pulau Sipidan (Indonesia/Malaysia)* can be accessed at www.icj-cij .org/docket/files/102/7714.pdf.

21. "We'll Defend 'Sovereignty' Over Pedra Branca: Najib," *The Straits Times Interactive*, 15 January 2003.

22. The full proceedings can be accessed through the case link at www.icj-cij.org.

23. Tony Hotland, "Legislators Criticize Juwono over Ambalat Disclosure," *The Jakarta Post*, 30 March 2005.

24. Deborah Loh, "Malaysia and Indonesia on Common Ground," *New Straits Times*, 9 March 2008.

25. *United Nations Convention of the Law of the Sea*, Article 123, "Cooperation of States Bordering Enclosed or Semi-enclosed Seas," accessed at www.un.org/Depts/los/ convention_agreements/texts/unclos/closindx.htm.

26. The statistical data on South China Sea energy resources is that given by the U.S. Energy Information Administration of the Department of Energy updated to March 2006 and accessed at www.eia.doe.gov/cabs/South_China_Sea/Background .html.

27. "War Games with US Targeted China: Arroyo," *The Straits Times Interactive*, 5 April 2004.

28. The English language text of the Chinese Territorial Sea Law can be accessed at www.un.org/Depts/los/LEGISLATIONANDTREATIES/PDFFILES/CHN_1992_Law. pdf.

29. "ASEAN Declaration on the South China Sea," 22 July 1992, accessed at www.aseansec.org/3634.htm.

30. A retrospective view after sixteen years of the workshop process is given in the conference report "The South China Sea: Towards a Cooperative Management Regime," S. Rajaratnam School of International Studies, Nanyang Technical University, Singapore, 16–17 May 2007.

31. "Declaration on the Conduct of Parties in the South China Sea," 4 November 2002, accessed at www.aseansec.org/13165.htm.

32. Paragraph 8 of the "Chairman's Statement of the 11th ASEAN–China Summit," 20 November 2007, accessed at www.aseansec.org/21105.htm; paragraph 17 of the "Chairman's Statement 14th ASEAN Regional Forum," 2 August 2007, accessed at www.aseansec.org/20808.htm.

33. Hasjim Djalal, "South China Sea Island Disputes," *The Raffles Bulletin of Zoology*, Supplement no. 8 (*The Biodiversity of the South China Sea*), 2000, accessed at www.rmbr.nus.edu.sg/latest/RBZs8-SCS/djalal.html.

34. Various cooperative schemes are discussed in Mark J. Valencia, Jan M. Van Dyke, and Noel Ludwig, *Sharing the Resources of the South China Sea* (Honolulu: University of Hawaii Press, 1999).

35. As quoted in Luz Baguioro, "Three Nations Sign Pact for Joint Spratlys Survey," *The Straits Times*, 15 March 2005.

36. As quoted in Aurea Calica, "GMA, Hu Vow to Turn South China Sea into 'Area of Cooperation,'" *The Philippine Star*, 29 March 2005.

37. Barry Wain, "Manila's Bungle in the South China Sea," *Far Eastern Economic Review* 171, no. 1 (2008), 45–48.

38. "Spratly Issue Worries China, Saying It Could Spoil Relations," *The Manila Times*, 13 March 2008.

39. As quoted by Carlos H. Conde, "Philippine Muslim Rebel Groups Agree to Reconcile," *International Herald Tribune*, 14 December 2007.

40. "Philippine Rebels Say Peace Deal with Manila Unlikely," *The Straits Times*, 11 March 2008.

41. For a discussion of the separatist groups, see Carin Zissis, "The Muslim Insurgency in Southern Thailand," Council of Foreign Relations, *Backgrounder*, 1 February 2007, accessed at www.cfr.org/publication/12531/muslim_insurgency_in_southern_thailand.html.

42. Editorial, "Peace Remains Only a Dream," *Bangkok Post*, 7 January 2008.

43. "KL to Consider Call for Return of Top Rebels," *Bangkok Post*, 25 April 2008.

44. "Thai PM Blames Foreign Militants for Separatist Unrest," *The Straits Times*, 7 March 2008.

45. For concise discussions of the general problems of separatism in Aceh and Papua see Anthony L. Smith, "Conflict in Aceh: The Consequences of a Broken Social Contract," *Harvard Asia Quarterly* 6, no. 1 (Winter 2002): 47–55, and David Webster, "'Already sovereign as a people,' a Foundational Movement in West Papuan Nationalism," *Pacific Affairs* 74, no. 4 (Winter 2001–2002): 507–28.

46. Aceh was the subject of paragraph 17 of the "Joint Communiqué of the 36th ASEAN Ministerial Meeting," 16–17 June 2003, accessed at www.aseansec.org/14833.htm.

47. U.S. Embassy [Jakarta] Press Release, "Joint Statement on Aceh by the EU, Japan, and the U.S.," 6 November 2003, accessed at www.usembassyjakarta.org/press_rel/aceh_jsc.html.

48. Kirsten E. Schulze, "From the Battlefield to the Negotiating Table: GAM and the Indonesian Government 1999– 2000," *Asian Security* 3, no. 2 (2007): 80–98.

49. Nethy Dharma Somba, "Papuans 'Fed Up' with Special Autonomy," *The Jakarta Post*, 8 March 2008.

50. "The ASEAN Regional Forum: A Concept Paper," accessed at www.aseansec.org/3635.htm.

51. The CSCAP web page can be accessed at www.cscap.org.

52. "ASEAN Regional Forum (ARF): Concept and Principles of Preventive Diplomacy," accessed at www.aseansec.org/3742.htm.

53. The annual *ARF Security Outlook* can be accessed at www.aseanregionalforum.org through the link to library/publications.

54. "Enhanced Role of the ARF Chair (Shared perspectives among the ARF members)," accessed at www.aseansec.org/3647.htm.

55. Kornelius Purba, "ARF Phnom Penh Meeting: ASEAN is the Cheerleader," *The Jakarta Post*, 13 June 2003.

56. A more positive conclusion from a "constructivist" perspective is in Dominik Heller, "The Relevance of the ASEAN Regional Forum (ARF) for Regional Security in the Asia-Pacific," *Contemporary Southeast Asia* 27, no. 1 (2005): 141–42. See also, Hiro Katsumata, "Establishment of the ASEAN Regional Forum: Constructing a 'Talking Shop' or a 'Norm Brewery,'" *The Pacific Review* 19, no. 2 (2006) 181–98.

Suggestions for Further Reading

Already noted in the chapter, the books by Amitav Acharya, *Constructing a Security Community in Southeast Asia: ASEAN and the Problem of Regional Order* (New York: Routledge, 2001), and Ralf Emmers, *Cooperative Security and the Balance of Power in ASEAN and the ARF* (New York: Routledge, 2003), are comprehensive examinations of many of the issues raised in this chapter but from two different theoretical perspectives. Allen Collins, *Security and Southeast Asia: Domestic, Regional, and Global Issues* (Boulder, Colo.: Lynne Rienner, 2003), gives special attention to the South China Sea and the war on terrorism. In addition, for the South China Sea dispute, see Lee Lai To, *China and the South China Sea Dialogues* (Westport, Conn.: Praeger, 1999), and Mark J. Valencia, "Building Confidence and Security in the South China Sea: The Way Forward," in Andrew T. H. Tan and J. D. Boutin, eds., *Non-Traditional Security Issues in Southeast Asia* (Singapore: Select Publishing for the Institute of Defense and Strategic Studies, 2001), 528–69. For the ASEAN way see Jurgen Haacke, *ASEAN's Diplomatic and Security Culture: Origins, Development and Prospects* (New York: Routledge, 2003). For the origins of the ASEAN Regional Forum see Michael Leifer, *The ASEAN Regional Forum: Extending ASEAN's Model of Regional Security* (London: International Institute for Strategic Studies *Adelphi Paper* no. 302, 1996).

Ethnic conflict is treated in Wan Kadir Che Man, *Muslim Separatism: The Moros of Southern Philippines and the Malays of Southern Thailand* (Singapore: Oxford University Press, 1995); Thomas M. McKenna, *Muslim Rulers and Rebels: Everyday Politics and Separatism in the Southern Philippines* (Berkeley: University of California Press, 1998); Anthony Reid, ed., *Verandah of Violence: The Background to the Aceh Problem* (Seattle: University of Washington Press, 2006); Damien Kingsbury and Harry Aveling, eds., *Autonomy and Disintegration in Indonesia* (London: RoutledgeCurzon, 2003); Duncan McCargo, ed., *Rethinking Thailand's Southern Violence* (Singapore: National University of Singapore Press, 2007). The journal *Asian Security* 3, no. 2 (2007) deals with the ethnic conflicts discussed in the chapter. Detailed reports on the ethnic insurgencies can be found at the International Crisis Group's country links on its website www.icg.org.

6

Transnational Violence and Crime in Southeast Asia

TRADITIONAL THREATS TO STATE SOVEREIGNTY, territorial integrity and juris- dictional claims, and to the integrity of the political system were examined in chapter 5. The sources of threat were either from other states in the international system or domestic claimants to an alternative, separate state identity. This is the traditional security arena in which threats are state-based and the responses are political, diplomatic, or coercive. Another category of threat requiring like responses originates from nonstate actors whose activities against the state's security and stability have no boundaries in terms of the international system but whose hostile acts affect the way the bounded states relate to one another in the international system. This chapter will focus on two such manifestations of transnational threat that have loomed large in contemporary Southeast Asia: terrorism and transnational organized crime. The challenge for the state actors is to find mechanisms to meet this new order of threat for which the national compartments of sovereignty and exclusive jurisdiction can be obstacles to effective countermeasures.

Terrorism

After the horrific destruction of New York's World Trade Center on 11 September 2001, Washington announced that Southeast Asia was the second front in a global war on terror. Southeast Asian leaders enlisted in that war with varying degrees of enthusiasm. Philippines President Gloria Macapagal-Arroyo was the first regional leader to call President George W. Bush with support. In-donesian President Megawati Sukarnoputri, visiting Washington shortly after 9/11, endorsed President Bush's call to arms against terrorists. On her return to Jakarta, however, she lapsed into her typical silent withdrawal from crisis. Malaysia and Singapore used their longstanding internal security acts to round up suspected terrorists. Thailand's Prime Minister Thaksin Shinawatra made an initial false step by suggesting neutrality, but quickly reversed himself, de-claring Thailand an ally. In bilateral and multilateral settings such as Asia-Pa-cific Economic Cooperation (APEC) summits, the United States confirmed the primacy of counterterrorism for U.S. interests in Southeast Asia.

The joining of the United States and vulnerable Southeast Asian states in a joint struggle against an elusive terrorist enemy meant that, after more than a quarter of a century, security again was the United States' greatest regional concern. The difference was that the American war in Indochina had visible state-based Cold War enemies (chapter 3). The protagonists of terror are linked in a shadowy network of groups and individuals articulating a virulent Wahhabist brand of radical Islam and deliberately directing deadly force against innocent civilians (see box 6.1). The subsequent American connection of the "war on terror" to the invasion of Iraq did not lead to an expansion of the security consensus on terrorism in Southeast Asia; just the opposite. Malaysia and Indonesia expressly opposed the war in Iraq. Only traditional se-curity partners the Philippines, Thailand, and Singapore supported the United States. All, however, continued cooperation in counterterrorism. Their support for counterterrorism was not based on American perceptions of its national interests, but of their own interests. The terrorist enemies were a threat to their own national institutions and ideology as well as eroding the investment climate. In the local context, the grievances are not just those of Islam.[1] For the United States, the war against al-Qaeda and its allies extends from Europe, through the Middle East and South Asia, to Southeast Asia. For Southeast Asians, however, it is localized, the states' antagonists being domes-tic radical Islamists and separatists. That which links the local Southeast Asian states' counterterrorist campaigns to each other and the United States is the networking of terrorists in the Jema'ah Islamiyah (JI).

Jema'ah Islamiyah ("Islamic Community")

The JI's Indonesian roots go back to the failed 1950s Darul Islam (DI) re-volt against the new pluralist Indonesian state. The DI's goal of an Islamic state remains alive as the ideological underpinning of fundamentalist clerics. Rhetorical militancy was accompanied in the late 1970s and early 1980s by

---

BOX 6.1
Wahhabism

Wahhabism is the primary religious stream inspiring Islamic terrorists. It is a fundamentalist Sunni Islamic movement that aggressively seeks to restore Islam to its original seventh century purity of belief and practice as set forth in the Koran and the authoritative statements of the Prophet Mohammad (*hadith*) as handed down by tradition. The Wahhabi ideological origins are in the teachings of revered religious scholar Ibn Abd al Wahab (1703–1792) to the Bedouins of the Arabian Peninsula. It is the religion of contemporary Saudi Arabia, which has been accused of propagating it through the funding of Muslim institutions in other Muslim countries. Although of historically different origins, Wahhabism and Salafiyya, another conservative Islamic revival movement, have similar puritanical goals. With a pan-Islamic dynamic, Wahhabists insist on the strict enforcement of Islamic law in a community where there is no boundary between the state and religion. Although violence or holy war (*jihad)* is not necessarily intrinsic to Wahhabism, its morphing in the form of contemporary terrorism had its roots in the resistance war against the Soviet Union in Afghanistan. Thousands of Muslim volunteer fighters (*mujahideen*) were radicalized in mosques and schools funded by Saudi Arabia.

---

occasional acts of violence and terrorism. One of the most prominent radical teachers in Central Java at that time was Abu Bakar Ba'asjir, whose Islamic boarding school (*pesantran*) became famous for his fiery incitements to struggle for an Islamic state and the establishment of a new caliphate uniting under one political-religious ruler all Muslims in Southeast Asia. Many of Ba'asjir's students went on to teach in or found other *pesantrans*. Strong countermeasures by the Suharto government scattered the militants. A number went to jail and others, including Ba'asjir, fled into exile, many to Malaysia. It was in Malaysia in the mid-1990s that the JI was established. In the post-Suharto period, Ba'asjir and other JI members returned to Indonesia to take up the struggle. A widespread network of JI cells was developed with al-Qaeda connections. Ba'asjir emerged as the leading public voice of an Islamist agenda for Indonesia as a senior member of the Indonesian Mujahideen Council (MMI, Majelis Mujahideen Indonesia). From that platform, he praised al-Qaeda's terrorist attacks on Western targets. Although Ba'asjir claims that the JI does not exist, JI terrorists acknowledge him as their inspiration.[2]

JI's link to al-Qaeda was forged by the Southeast Asian *mujahideen* (Soldiers of Islam) who joined the resistance to the Soviet Union's invasion and occupation of Afghanistan, 1979–1989. Under the sway of the Taliban, Southeast Asian mujahideen received training and indoctrination in al-Qaeda training camps. Returning to Southeast Asia with new lethal skills and radical incentive, the JI veterans became the terrorist backbone of regional Islamic fundamentalism with ties to radical Muslim groups throughout Southeast Asia. As good intelligence and counterterrorist roundups decimated JI's senior leadership, it has become more an ideological umbrella under which loosely networked cells find common cause than an organizational entity with a hierarchical table of organization. It was through the JI that al-Qaeda established its foothold in Southeast Asia.[3] From the strategic point of view, the al-Qaeda link raised the JI's sights from the struggle for Islam in Southeast Asia to the global struggle of Islam against the West in general and the United States in particular. By its conflating the American war on terrorism with a "war on Islam," the JI gained a powerful psychological weapon that it used to portray itself as the defender of the faith for all Muslims.

The Regional Response

At their November 2001 ASEAN Summit, the ASEAN heads of government adopted an "ASEAN Declaration on Joint Action to Counter Terrorism."[4] They expressed their commitment to combat terrorism, adding that cooperative joint practical counterterrorism measures should "be in line with specific circumstances in the region and in each member country." In practical terms the regional cooperative measures suggested were not new, but efforts to strengthen the capacity of the existing bilateral and regional frameworks for fighting transnational crime (discussed below). Throughout the document, the leaders emphasized that the United Nations should play the major role at the international level. The leaders urged all ASEAN states to accede to the twelve major international conventions on terrorism. The importance of the UN and international law is a theme that appeared in subsequent ASEAN statements and reflected regional uneasiness about the United States as a "global policeman." A second ASEAN joint declaration at the 2002 ASEAN Summit deploring recent terrorist bombing attacks in Indonesia and the Philippines called for an intensified counterterrorist cooperation and coordination within the region.[5] It also expressed concern about impacts on the regional economy because of international perceptions of insecurity. It urged the international community to avoid issuing alarming travel warnings and to support restoring business confidence.

The ASEAN Regional Forum (ARF) put terrorism on its agenda in 2002 when it adopted a "Statement on Measures against Terrorist Financing" and set up an intersessional meeting on counterterrorism and crime (ISM-CTTC) that first met in March 2003. As examples of the topics covered by the ISM-CTTC, the 2007 fifth ISM-CTTC had as its theme the promotion of intercivilizational dialogue and the sixth in February 2008, social participation in counterterrorism.[6] Terrorism has become an item on the ASEAN + 3 dialogue. In August 2002, the United States and ASEAN signed a "Joint Declaration for Cooperation to Combat Terrorism" that included the usual commitments to greater information flow, intelligence sharing, and capacity building.[7] A similar undertaking came out of the January 2003 ASEAN–EU ministerial meeting. On a broader scale of participation, Indonesia and Australia co-hosted the February 2004 Bali Ministerial Meeting on Counter-Terrorism that brought together ASEAN and China, the EU, Fiji, France, Russia, South Korea, Timor-Leste, the United Kingdom, and the United States. The participants basically reaffirmed the existing commitments to combat terrorism.[8]

Common to all of ASEAN pronouncements about counterterrorism is the explicit rejection of an identification of terrorism with religion. In the words of the 2002 declaration, "We deplore the tendency in some quarters to identify terrorism with particular religions or ethnic groups." The Bali ministerial meeting "emphasized the importance of avoiding the identification of terrorism with any particular religion or ethnic group." It is politically understood that what ASEAN calls "terrorist elements" are in fact the Islamist extremists of JI and its ilk. ASEAN's identification of terrorism with acts rather than actors and assigning causation in general terms to social and economic circumstances rather than ideology and political goals reflects a consensual awareness of the political sensitivity of counterterrorism in the region's large Muslim population.

As a follow-up to the Bali meeting, the ministers established an ad hoc working group of senior legal officials to study the adequacy of existing regional legal frameworks for combating terrorism. It was not until November 2004 that eight ASEAN countries (not including Thailand and Myanmar) agreed to a Treaty on Mutual Legal Assistance in Criminal Matters, which previously had been a matter of a varying mix of bilateral arrangements.[9] The treaty specifically stated, however, that it did not apply to extradition, long a sensitive issue in ASEAN. In January 2007, the ASEAN Summit gave their counterterrorism cooperation a legal underpinning with the signing of the ASEAN Convention on Counter-Terrorism.[10] Up to then ASEAN had been the only major geopolitical global region without a legally binding agreement on terrorism.[11] The possibility of a convention had first been raised in the 2001 declaration on counterterrorism. Unlike the ASEAN charter, which set a requirement of ten ratifications to come in force, the counterterrorism convention required only six. It was intended to provide a legally binding framework for regional cooperation to counter, prevent, and

suppress terrorism. Although hailed as a breakthrough, it created no new instrumentalities or mechanisms, being essentially a codification of the developing pattern of legal and enforcement assistance measures.[12] Missing from
it, however, is a guarantee of extradition. Article 15 of the treaty states that
in the absence of a bilateral extradition treaty, the requested party may *at its
option* consider the convention as a legal basis for extradition of someone
who has committed terrorist acts. If criminal justice is to be part of the proposed ASEAN Security Community, an ASEAN extradition treaty will be a
necessary step.

As part of capacity building, new regional institutions have been set up to
provide legal and law enforcement training and networking facilities. Malaysia
established the Southeast Asia Regional Center for Counter-Terrorism
(SEARCCT) to develop and organize capacity building programs. Since it
opened its doors in July 2003 through November 2007, 1,596 officials (1,352
ASEAN nationals) had passed through forty-six courses.[13] The United States
had discussed such a regional institution with Malaysia, but Malaysian opposition to the U.S. role in the Middle East prevented any formal American partnership. The United States has been the major provider of training resources.
An Indonesia–Australia Jakarta Center for Law Enforcement Cooperation
(JCLEC) was established in 2004 as a resource for Southeast Asia in the fight
against terrorism.[14] The secretariat is in Jakarta but the training base is the Indonesian Police Academy in Semarang.

Under the symbolic and rhetorical expressions of ASEAN's will to combat
terrorism, the real struggle is at the national level, where al-Qaeda and JI have
left their influence throughout the region in local JI cells' links to local organizations such the Kumpulan Mujahideen Malaysia (KMM, Malaysia Mujahideen Group) or some of the component movements in Thailand's rebellious south. The major battlegrounds have been in Indonesia and the
Philippines' south.[15]

Indonesia and the JI

On 12 October 2002, two bomb attacks at tourist bars on the island of Bali
killed nearly two hundred innocents, many of them young Australians. What
made the Bali attack singular was not just the number of casualties but the fact
that the investigation clearly demonstrated the connection between the JI and
al-Qaeda, something even President Megawati could not deny. In the months
following 9/11, Indonesia had resisted American, Australian, Malaysian, and
Singaporean pressure—based on good intelligence—to act against the JI.
Known JI plotters were not arrested, including Hambali (aka Riduan Is-

mudin), JI's underground operational leader and Southeast Asia's most wanted terrorist. Hambali was arrested in Thailand in 2004 and turned over to the United States for imprisonment in Guantanamo. Good police work, with foreign expert forensic cooperation and intelligence, wrapped up the JI cell that carried out the Bali operation. Three of the bombers were tried and sentenced to death in 2003. In March 2008, they launched another appeal of the convictions.

Abu Bakar Ba'asjir was tried and convicted of treason in the Bali bombings, but the conviction was overturned on appeal. He was rearrested for conspiracy in the Bali bombings, found guilty, and served twenty-five months of a thirty-month sentence. His conspiracy conviction was overturned in 2006, effectively clearing him of any involvement in the terrorist attack. He has reclaimed his spot as a leading Muslim vocal opponent of the United States, Indonesia's relations with the United States, and the war on terror. Nor has the JI as an organization been banned in Indonesia.

The more the United States pressed the Indonesian government, the more the JI could accuse the government of caving into the Americans. It was the radical Muslims' manipulation of Islamic symbols to inflame Indonesia's Muslim populations that made Megawati's government timid about directly challenging the terrorists. The depth of Indonesian Muslims' sympathy for the JI tactics, if not its goals, was not deep, particularly as innocent Indonesians became the JI's victims. In East Indonesia, JI-influenced groups poured gasoline on the fire of sectarian violence that caused thousands of lives to be lost and half a million internally displaced people. In August 2003, a suicide bombing attack at a Marriott hotel in Jakarta killed eleven. In September 2004, a truck bomb outside the Australian embassy killed eleven and wounded two hundred. In October 2005, three suicide bombers killed twenty people in attacks on restaurants in Bali. Since then, the news has not been of attacks, but of the capture or killing of key JI operatives.

The electoral mandate given to President Susilo Bambang Yudhoyono in 2004 opened a political window for a stronger counterterrorism campaign in Indonesia. With Western intelligence, training, and technical skills well in the background and enhanced Indonesian capabilities in the forefront, the Yudhoyono government moved decisively against the terrorists. In January 2006, the United States ended all restrictions on security assistance to Indonesia that had been imposed because of Indonesia's record in East Timor. Since then a bilateral security relationship has resumed with a priority on counterterrorism. Indonesia's normalization of security relations with Australia in 2006 provides additional access to security assistance. Although no victory has been declared, there has not been a major terrorist incident in Indonesia since the

October 2005 Bali attacks. In 2007, a series of arrests effectively decapitated the JI's leadership. Although JI as a movement has been seriously weakened and its influence diminished, scattered diehard militants still have a capacity to strike back.

The Philippines

The Abu Sayyaf Group (ASG) is the smallest and most violent of the Muslim insurgent groups in the Philippines' southern provinces. The Abu Sayyaf ("Bearer of the Sword") is a splinter group of Islamic extremists based in the Sulu Archipelago but operating as well in Muslim Mindanao. Its professed separatist goal is the creation of an Islamic state. The ASG's first terrorist attack was the killing of two American evangelists in 1991. Its most notorious attack was the sinking of *Superferry 14* in Manila Bay in 2004, killing over one hundred passengers and crew. The ASG was placed on the U.S. State Department's Foreign Terrorist Organizations (FTO) list in 1997. ASG's links to the JI and al-Qaeda have made it a major target of the war on terror. Through the ASG, the foreign terrorist organizations have also been able to penetrate the extremist wings of the main Muslim separatist organizations, the Moro Islamic Liberation Front (MILF) and the Moro National Liberation Front (MNLF) (chapter 5).[16] The ASG and ASG-connected MILF units have provided training facilities for JI terrorists from Indonesia. The American war on terror and the Philippines' war on Muslim separatism in its south have coincided in the battle against the Abu Sayyaf Group.[17]

The ASG's founder was Abdurajak Janjalani, who brought back from Afghanistan a virulent Wahhabist ideology. Abdurajak was killed in a 1998 shootout. His younger brother, Khadaffi Jajalani, succeeded him. He was killed in 2006. His successor, Abu Sulamein, was shot to death in a firefight with the army in January 2007. Despite leadership losses, the ASG regroups and fights back. In July 2007, a clash between the ASG and Philippine marines left fourteen marines dead. Ten of the recovered bodies were beheaded. Over the years, the ASG has financed itself by banditry, piracy, extortion, and kidnappings for ransom. In May 2001, the ASG kidnapped twenty people from a Philippine resort, including three Americans. One American was beheaded. The other two were husband and wife Christian missionaries. A year later, the husband and a Filipina hostage nurse were killed in an American-backed Philippine army rescue.[18] The ASG strength at the end of 2006 was estimated at two to three hundred, down from its top estimated strength of one thousand. Like the JI, however, a weakened ASG is still dangerous. It takes only a few terrorists to wreak great havoc. The political threat is that ASG attacks will provoke retaliations damaging to the precarious cease-fire with the MILF (chapter 5).

When President Arroyo traveled to the United States in November 2001 to celebrate the fiftieth anniversary of the U.S.–Philippines Mutual Defense Treaty (MDT), she and President Bush issued a joint statement in which the two leaders pledged military cooperation to end the terrorist activities of the ASG.[19] They promised a vigorous plan to strengthen the Philippine security forces' capacity to combat terror. The way had been paved by the 1999 passage by the Philippine Senate of a Visiting Forces Agreement (VFA) that provided a new legal framework for American military personnel in the Philippines, absent since the termination of the bases agreement in 1991. It allowed a resumption of joint exercising and training, particularly the combined annual Balikatan ("shoulder-to-shoulder") exercise. The VFA was complemented in 2002 by a Mutual Logistics Support Agreement. In the American war on terror, the Philippines outstrips by far all other Southeast Asian security assistance recipients.[20]

The stationing of a unit of American Special Forces in the south to advise and assist the Philippine Armed Forces in counterterrorism operations against the ASG has been at the point of the U.S.–Philippines counterterrorism alliance. This is the only place in Southeast Asia that American forces have been deployed to support in the field counterterrorism measures. They were first deployed in the January 2002 "Balikatan" exercise as Joint Task Force 510 and after August 2002 as Joint Special Operation Task Force-Philippines (JSOTF-P). The JSOTF-P assists and advises at the strategic and operational levels in tactics, intelligence, and psychological warfare. The JSOTF-P has been credited with helping the AFP make significant gains against the ASG.[21] Although technically only advisors, the JSOTF-P's role at the battalion and company levels of the AFP sometimes blurs the distinction between advice and operational involvement. Nationalist critics of the Arroyo government's close security arrangement with the United States accuse her of violating the constitutional ban on foreign bases, troops, or facilities without a treaty ratified by the Philippine Senate. The government's answer is that the U.S. role is legal under the MDT.

Since 9/11, ASEAN and its dialogue partners have slowly put in place at the regional level a cooperative framework of mutual national commitments to combat what they agree is the common threat of terrorism. While activity at the regional level may have created a climate of consultative confidence, it has been at the national level where the terrorist enemies have been engaged. Where the threat has been most critical, in Indonesia and the Philippines, robust security partnerships have been important in enhancing counterterrorism capabilities. The future problem country may be Thailand, where the deteriorating security situation in the south provides a fertile field for cultivating recruits to terrorism (chapter 5). Unlike the case of Indonesia and the Philippines, the key bilateral ally will not be the United States or Australia. It will be Malaysia and its willingness and capability to prevent its side of the common border from being a Thai–Muslim terrorist haven.

Transnational Crime

The United Nations Convention against Transnational Organized Crime (TOC) is the main international instrument in the fight against transnational crime. It was adopted in 2000 and went into force in 2003.[22] Its goal is to promote greater international cooperation against the broadening and expanding loose criminal syndicates and networks around the world from further exploiting the opportunities that globalization has opened for them. There is a long list of different activities like drug trafficking, trafficking in persons, trafficking in firearms, smuggling, money laundering, counterfeiting currency, counterfeiting documents, and so on, which meet the definition of transnational organized crime (see box 6.2). All of these forms of criminal activities are taking place in Southeast Asia. Although the primary responsibility for crime fighting rests with the national authorities, the ASEAN states have sought to foster cooperation among themselves and with dialogue partners.

ASEAN's Declaratory Anticrime Regime

The call for cooperation in fighting transnational crime has been on ASEAN's agenda since at least 1976, when the Bali Concord I urged intensi-

---

BOX 6.2
TOC Definition of Transnational Crime (from Article 3)

A crime is a transnational crime if:

- It is committed in more than one state;
- It is committed in one state but a substantial part of the preparation, planning, and   direction or control takes place in another state;
- It is committed in one state but involves a criminal group that engages in criminal activities in more than one state;
- It is committed in one state but has substantial effect in another state.

fied cooperation in eradicating narcotics trafficking. Since then, the ASEAN ministerial meetings (AMM) and summits regularly appeal for cooperation in transnational crime prevention. The felt need to publicly stress enhanced cooperation in what might be called a declaratory anticrime ASEAN regime papered over the very slow progress in building cooperative institutions and structures for effective enforcement of existing national laws. Poor national police capabilities, weak judicial systems, and corruption seemed to give the edge to the criminals. Another major problem has been an absence of any harmonization of criminal codes and an unwillingness to extradite or render accused nationals to the jurisdictions of another state.

The first ASEAN effort to establish a regional framework for fighting transnational crime was the 1997 "ASEAN Declaration on Transnational Crime" issued at a meeting of ASEAN interior or home affairs ministers.[23] Besides the usual exhortations for cooperation and coordination, the declaration called for the creation of an ASEAN Ministers' Meeting on Transnational Crime (AMMTC) meeting every two years. It is supported by an annual meeting of the Senior Officials' Meeting on Transnational Crime (SOMTC). The task of the AMMTC is to coordinate the activities of the relevant working bodies including the ASEAN Senior Officials on Drug Matters (ASOD) and the ASEAN Chiefs of Police (ASEANAPOL) as well as other ASEAN bodies such as finance ministers, law ministers, customs, and immigration. ASEANAPOL has been meeting annually since 1981. The first AMMTC commissioned an experts' group to draw up a plan of action to expand to the regional level the national and bilateral efforts at combating transnational crime. The plan of action was approved by the second AMMTC and a work plan for implementation was adopted in 2002.

A central thread in the effort to enhance regional capabilities has been the insistence on more open communication and intelligence sharing among the national agencies involved in the common fight against crime. ASEAN itself, however, does not have an institutional capability to coordinate or act as a clearinghouse. After a decade of communiqués, declarations, work programs, and other tools to encourage greater cooperation, the AMMTC at its 2007 meeting had what was described as a candid exchange of views on the need for "a more feasible and substantive line of communication amongst our relevant national organs for the expeditious and substantive exchange of intelligence and information."[24] The most successful example of formal information sharing has been the promotion by ASEANAPOL of its electronic ASEANAPOL database system (e-ADS), which links to Interpol's global database.

ASEAN has expanded the AMMTC to include China, Japan, and South Korea. At the 2002 ASEAN + China Summit, China and ASEAN jointly declared cooperation in the field of nontraditional security issues, giving priority to transnational crime.[25] A memorandum of agreement on a five-year work plan for cooperation between ASEAN and China was put in place in 2004. China also suggested in 2002 that the ASEAN + 3 format be expanded to include an AMMTC + 3. The first plus three transnational crime meeting was in January 2004. The following year, the AMMTC + 3 endorsed in principle a work plan, which at the time of the 2007 AMMTC + 3 still remained under study to identify the modalities of implementation and the priorities. China has also pressed ASEAN to institutionalize an AMMTC + China. In an "informal" 2007 AMMTC + China consultation, the ASEAN side agreed that the SOMTC + China should study the question of a separate AMMTC + China and report back. In intra-ASEAN dealings and between ASEAN and dialogue partners, three areas of transnational crime have received particular attention: piracy, trafficking in narcotics, and trafficking in persons.

Piracy

The greatest security threat to international trade moving through the Southeast Asian region's waterways is piracy. Piracy was one of the concerns listed in ASEAN's 1997 Declaration on Transnational Crime. Piracy is also on the ASEAN Regional Forum's agenda with its ARF "Statement on Cooperation against Piracy and Other Threats to Security."[26] The perennial problem of piracy received greater international attention when after 9/11 it was connected to the threat of terrorism.[27] A sudden increase in incidents after 1998 became very worrisome to ship owners and regional national security managers. From 99 reported attacks in Southeast Asia in 1998, the number mounted to 167 in 1999 and 257 in 2000.[28] Most of the attacks take place in sovereign territorial waters and are not acts of piracy as defined by UNCLOS, but rather armed robbery against ships, which technically falls under the national law of the nation where the attack occurs.[29] For reporting purposes, the International Maritime Board's (IMB) Piracy Reporting Center based in Kuala Lumpur uses a broader definition: "Piracy is an act of boarding or attempt to board any vessel with the intent to commit theft or any other crime and with the intent or capability to use force in the furtherance of that act." While not a binding international law definition, certainly for policy response it better characterizes the maritime threat in Southeast Asia.

The pirates launch themselves from hiding places on the coastlines of Indonesia, Malaysia, and the Philippines to prey on commercial vessels and their crews. Approaching in fast speed boats, armed gangs swarm on board to rob, kidnap for ransom, or even hijack the vessel. The increase in piracy after 1998 has been attributed to a number of factors including the political and economic regional instabilities following the Crash of '97 (chapter 7). The fact that the majority of the hit-and-run pirates can flee back into territorial waters left enforcement to national authorities who often were unable or unwilling to pursue or arrest. There is evidence that maritime authorities have even been complicit. Other attacks originate from criminal syndicates that hijack ships for their cargo and hold the crews for ransom. Even as the opportunistic attacks of small gangs have been declining as antipiracy shipboard measures have improved, the criminally organized attacks of heavily armed men have been more threatening.

Focus on the Straits

The perceived threat of terrorism and piracy was threefold. Terrorists as pirates could seek to generate financial support for their activities through robbery and ransom. Terrorists could hazard or impede navigation by sinking ships, which in the case of oil tankers would cause coastal environmental damage. Finally, there was a threat scenario in which terrorists could use a seized ship as a weapon against regional ports. A pirate-seized liquid natural gas carrier would be a powerful bomb. It was the dramatic impress of the terrorist threat that focused renewed attention on the strategic vulnerability of the straits of Malacca and Singapore.

One of the busiest maritime thoroughfares in the world, more than sixty thousand vessels a years ply the straits carrying more 40 percent of world trade, including 80 percent of the energy supplies of China, Japan, and South Korea. Navigation is slow and ships are confined to designated traffic lanes. At its narrowest point in the Phillips Channel, the Singapore Strait is only 1.5 miles wide. The port of Singapore is the world's largest container transshipment port, handling in 2007 one-fifth of all global container movements. Any incident or event that might impede passage through the straits or threaten the security of Singapore's port would disrupt regional economies and would have global consequences for trade. It was the incidence of piracy and the threat of terrorism that prompted Lloyd's Market Association to give the Malacca Strait a war-risk insurance rating in 2005. The littoral states insist that the security of the straits is their sovereign responsibility. The war-risk rating added to the pressures on them from China, India, Japan, and the United States to tighten security. Japan has been in the vanguard of the major users to fashion a framework for cooperative security.

Regional Cooperation Agreement on Combating Piracy and Armed Robbery against Ships in Asia (ReCAAP)

Once Japan had identified piracy in Southeast Asia as a threat to its vital commerce, it took the lead in attempting to build a regional multilateral maritime security regime in which it could have both a political and enforcement role.[30] Prime Minister Keizo Obuchi put the problem of piracy on the ASEAN + 3 table at the 1999 Manila Summit, proposing a meeting of officials with direct responsibilities for combating piracy. In April 2000, Japan hosted a Conference on Combating Piracy and Armed Robbery against Ships, billed as the first regional conference on the piracy problem. The participants were the heads of coast guards and maritime policy officials of sixteen states and one special area: the ten ASEAN states, Bangladesh, China, Hong Kong, India, Japan, South Korea, and Sri Lanka. In a document called "Asia Anti-Piracy Challenges 2000," the participants agreed to greater cooperation to meet the common threat. Tokyo quickly followed up by sending an expert mission to the Philippines, Malaysia, Indonesia, and Singapore to identify specific areas of cooperation. A Japanese Coast Guard vessel was sent on an exercise mission to India, Malaysia, and the Philippines.

A second conference was held in Tokyo in October 2001, the Asia Cooperation Conference on Combating Piracy and Armed Robbery against Ships. The concept of a formal regional cooperation agreement was sponsored by Prime Minister Junichiro Koizumi. After three years of negotiation, the "Regional Cooperation Agreement on Combating Piracy and Armed Robbery against Ships in Asia" (ReCAAP) was finalized in November 2004.[31] It went into force for fourteen signatories in September 2006. Indonesia and Malaysia, although promising to cooperate, have withheld their signature, apparently concerned about the scope of the agreement in territorial waters.[32]

ReCAAP reinforces existing obligations to take measures to prevent and suppress piracy and armed attacks against ships. Its major innovation was the establishment of an Information Sharing Center (ISC) located in Singapore, which was launched in November 2006. The center's purpose is to share information so as to help improve national responses and enable the development of operational coordination. The first executive director of the ISC was Japanese and Japan provided the funding. It is unclear how the ISC will relate to the IMB Piracy Reporting Center. The jurisdictional and territorial sensitivities that have inhibited operational cooperation are reflected in the agreement. Article 2:4 acknowledges that the agreement does not prejudice the position of any party to disputes concerning territorial sovereignty or the application of the UNCLOS. Article 2:5 states that nothing in the agreement authorizes a party to exercise jurisdiction or perform functions in the territory of another party that are exclusively reserved to the other by its national laws.

The Malacca Strait Patrols

ReCAAP and other declaratory statements did not provide for an on-water surveillance, prevention, and enforcement presence. Malaysia and Indonesia began so-called coordinated patrols in 2002 in their own territorial waters. In 2004, Singapore joined the coordinated patrols called the Malacca Strait Security Initiative (MSSI). In the arrangement, the national units operated independently under their own national commands and stayed in their own territorial waters. MSSI did not add to Indonesian capabilities in its national waters from where the majority of the attacks came. Despite the coordinated patrols, the IMB reported thirty-eight attacks in 2004, up from twenty-eight in 2003. In 2004, the United States floated a Regional Maritime Security Initiative (RMSI) that would have a special U.S. force join the antiterrorism and antipiracy patrolling. Although endorsed by Singapore, it was flatly rejected by Malaysia and Indonesia as an encroachment on their sovereignty. Behind the scenes, China did not want the United States to become directly involved in guarding a waterway vital for its oil imports.

In 2005, the MSSI countries launched an "eye-in- the-sky" project for aerial reconnaissance with missions flown in turn by aircraft from the three states. To give even greater cooperation to the Malacca Strait Coordinated Patrol Network, the participating services hammered out in April 2006 the terms of reference and standard operating procedures for the management and coordination of the air and sea patrols. The question of hot pursuit is based on bilateral agreements between Indonesia and Malaysia and Indonesia and Singapore.

The possibility of transforming the coordinated patrols into joint patrols was raised as early as 2004 but because of the "sensitivities" of the subject has always been simply a matter for future consideration.[33] One of the sensitivities is that joint patrolling would ignore the territorial boundaries that have allowed fleeing pirates to find sanctuary in friendly waters. A second sensitivity is that joint patrolling would underline the disparate naval, coast guard, and marine capabilities among the three participants. Thailand has expressed interest since 2005 in joining the coordinated patrol network but its association has been on an ad hoc basis. Thailand Prime Minister Samak Sundarajev raised the subject again in early 2008. The hesitation on the part of his ASEAN colleagues was in part connected to concerns about becoming involved in the insurgency in South Thailand.

Although continuing to rule out a physical foreign military presence for straits security, Malaysia and Indonesia have called on the user community for assistance in obtaining naval and coast guard assets, technical assistance, and intelligence sharing. The United States, for example, has worked with Indonesia to establish a radar warning system along the Sumatran coast of the Malacca Strait. Both the United States and Japan have donated fast patrol craft dedicated to straits security. In 2007, Japan's coast guard opened an Office of Piracy Countermeasures to expand cooperation with Southeast Asian coast guards. The commitment made by the littoral states to antipiracy cooperation and a real decline in pirate incidents in the straits region led Lloyd's to lift the war-risk rating in August 2006. The IMB reported eleven attacks in the Malacca Strait in 2006, a five-year low. There were only seven attacks in 2007. In lifting the war-risk rating, Lloyd's stated that "evidence has shown that not only has the situation improved within the area but that the measures are long term."[34] The Malacca Strait was pirate-free in 2007. The steady decline reported in 2007 for all of Southeast Asia including Indonesia and the straits was, according to the IMB, the "cumulative result of increased vigilance and patrolling by the littoral states" as well as precautions taken on board.

The Sulu and Sulawesi Seas Zone

The focus on the Malacca Strait is because its security is of vital global interest. It is not, however, the only hotbed of piracy in Southeast Asia. The maritime zone of the Sulu and Sulawesi Seas in the tri-border area of Malaysia, Indonesia, and the Philippines is a center of criminal activity—piracy; smuggling; trafficking in drugs, people, and weapons; kidnapping—with connections to terrorism and ethnic insurgency.[35] The maritime tri-border zone lies at the center of ASEAN's BIMP-EAGA subregional growth zone (chapter 4). Until greater prevention and enforcement capabilities are created and deployed, the region will remain better known for its criminal and terrorist activity than its commercial prospects. Of particular concern to Indonesia and Malaysia is the passage by sea of JI terrorists from ASG and MILF training sites to Sulawesi, Kalimantan, and Sabah. In March 2008, Indonesia went on border alert in East Kalimantan in anticipation of three hundred JI members returning from training in the Philippines.

The common security interests of the three countries led them to develop a framework for cooperation in border security and combating transnational crime in their territories. They signed an Agreement on Information Exchange and Establishment of Common Procedures in May 2002.[36] Although protocols for cooperation may be in place, the operational limit is real capacity to police the maritime zones. A 2006 Philippine initiative for a coordinated patrol system similar to that in the Malacca Strait made no headway. Significant Malaysian and Indonesian maritime enforcement assets are already assigned to Malacca Strait security. Furthermore, Indonesia and Malaysia are involved in a naval standoff in the Sulawesi Sea in the Ambalat Block dispute (chapter 5). The small Philippine navy is built around obsolescent hulls. Its very limited offshore capabilities are directed to its South China Sea EEZ and Spratlys claim. Since 2001, the United States has worked with the Philippine navy Special Forces, supplying and training with small inshore patrol craft to build up a counterterrorist capability in the Philippines' southern, internal waters. In 2007, the Philippines announced a plan called Coast Watch South to establish a chain of seventeen coastal watch stations from the southern end of Palawan to Davao in Mindanao. The stations are supposed to have fast patrol boats and helicopter support. The United States will provide the radar installations and Australia has promised up to thirty new high-speed airboats for riverine and coastal estuary use.

Narcotics Production and Trafficking

The production and distribution of illicit drugs has long been recognized as a major criminal activity in Southeast Asia with socially devastating, economically undermining, and politically corrupting consequences. The two categories of drugs of concern are opiates and methamphetamine-type stimulants (ATS). The use of injectable heroin—processed from opium—has contributed to the spread of HIV/AIDS in Southeast Asia (chapter 8). Crystal methamphetamine, known as "ice," is a purer and more addictive form of methamphetamine. Although the principal responsibility for combating the domestic impacts of crime and addiction falls to the national governments, interdicting the trade requires interstate cooperation and international assistance. At the global level, the narcotics trade is tracked by the United Nations Office on Drugs and Crime (UNODC). At the national level, capabilities have been assisted by foreign assistance for counternarcotics programs, including support from drug enforcement agents from the U.S. Drug Enforcement Agency (DEA) and the Australian Federal Police (AFP), among others.

The Golden Triangle

Historically, the remote highlands and mountains at the heart of continental Southeast Asia where Myanmar, Laos, and Thailand border one another had been the major source of the opium from which morphine and then heroin is processed. This has been romantically called the Golden Triangle. On the temperate slopes, opium poppies were cultivated at the nations' margins by poor farmers, many of whom were ethnic minorities. The raw opium was purchased by middlemen, often ethnic Chinese, taken to opium refineries for processing into heroin, and then into the Southeast Asian and international drug markets. At its height, the trade financed ethnic insurgent armies, warlords, criminal syndicates, and politicians. In the second half of the twentieth century the Golden Triangle was the world's largest source of opium. In the first years of the twenty-first century, the cultivation of opium poppies in the Golden Triangle has been reduced by 81 percent.[37] From 33 percent of global production of opium in 1998, production of opium in the Golden Triangle in 2007 was only 5 percent, most of that in Myanmar. Table 6.1 shows the dramatic decline in cultivation and production. According to the UNODC, Laos and Thailand have reduced poppy cultivation to such an extent that opium production is negligible and no longer finds its way to international markets. The Thai program of crop eradication, provision of alternative livelihood, and law enforcement has been so successful that the UNODC points to it as a model for its neighbors.

One of those neighbors is Myanmar. Although Myanmar's cultivation has dramatically declined, it still is the world's second largest producer of opium and the source for most of the heroin in Southeast Asia. The increase in cultivation and production of opium in 2007 hopefully is not a trend. It reflects in part the Myanmar government's strategy of ceasefires with ethnic minorities, allowing a continuation of traditional drug activities. It also underlines again the impoverishment of the Myanmar state and its inability to create alternative livelihoods. The junta itself has been accused of involvement in drug production and distribution.

Even as the long war in Southeast Asia against opium and its derivatives is being won, the threat of ATS is growing. The center of production of methamphetamines is in the minority states of Myanmar. Drug gangs in their secret labs along the Myanmar–China and Myanmar–Thailand border are producing hundreds of millions of tablets annually for markets in Thailand, China,

TABLE 6.1
Golden Triangle Poppy Cultivation in Hectares (Hectare=2.47 Acres)

Country	1998	2006	2007
Lao PDR	26,800	2,500	1,500
Myanmar	130,300	21,500	27,700
Thailand	1,486	157	205
Total	157,900	24,157	29,405

Source: UNODC, Opium Poppy Cultivation in Southeast Asia: Lao PDR, Myanmar, Thailand (October 2007).

India, and onward distribution by criminal syndicates, often with links to expatriate Southeast Asian minority communities. After U.S.–Thailand joint counternarcotics operations disrupted drug trafficking operations along the Thai–Shan States border in the middle 1990s, the drug center moved north to the area controlled by the United Wa State Army (UWSA) adjacent to China's Yunnan Province. The UWSA is the largest producer of ATS in Southeast Asia. The UWSA's 2006 pledge to stop poppy cultivation has been more than offset by its ATS labs. In 2002, a tablet form of Wa-produced methamphetamine called "yaba" appeared in the United States. In January 2005 an indictment was unsealed in New York against seven UWSA drug lords.

The Myanmar counternarcotics program is headed by its Central Committee for Drug Abuse Control (CCDAC). The CCDAC partners with the UNODC in eradication programs, including a large swath of Wa Special Region 2, with funding from Australia, Japan, and Germany. The United States was involved but pulled out when the UWSA threatened the lives of American DEA field agents because of the 2005 indictments. According to U.S. authorities, the CCDAC cooperates regularly and shares information on investigations with the DEA and the AFP as well as having border intelligence and law enforcement ties with Chinese, Thai, and Indian counterparts.[38] Even so, in the fiscal year 2008 annual "Presidential Determination of Major Drug Transit or Illicit Drug Producing Countries," Myanmar was singled out with Venezuela as failing demonstrably to adhere to their counternarcotics obligations.[39] Myanmar's designation was in part because it had not taken into custody the Wa criminals named in the American 2005 indictment. Nor has Myanmar cut off access to the legal precursors for synthesizing methamphetamines. American support for counternarcotics activity and crop eradication in Myanmar has been seriously limited by the suspension since 1988 of direct bilateral contributions because of the American sanctions against the junta. U.S. support is indirect through UNODC and other multilateral frameworks.

Laos continues to be designated a major drug transit state. Because of its central location and new roads and bridges connecting it to China, Vietnam, and Thailand, Laos will remain an important route for drug traffickers. Of course, the Golden Triangle is not the only location where illicit drugs are produced in Southeast Asia. The second largest source of methamphetamines in Southeast Asia is the Philippines, where the local "shabu" is fabricated for domestic consumption and trafficking to Indonesia, the Canadian and American west coasts, and Australia. It is alleged that elements of the MILF and the ASG are involved in the trade. Drug consumption and trafficking are also problems for Cambodia, Malaysia, and Indonesia, although they are not considered major producing countries.

The Regional Framework for Counternarcotics

The problem of drug abuse and trafficking has been on the ASEAN de-claratory agenda since 1976, catalogued as an element in fighting transna-tional crime in general. The commitment to counternarcotics made in the second ASEAN Summit's Bali Concord was followed quickly in September 1976 by a "Declaration of Principles to Combat the Abuse of Narcotic Drugs." To implement the principles, an ASEAN Drug Experts' group began meeting and in 1984 produced an "ASEAN Regional Policy and Strategy in the Pre-vention and Control of Drug Abuse and Illicit Traffic." The policy and strat-egy document was significant in that it went beyond the issues of health and social policy. It recognized that narcotics consumption and trafficking were threats to national security and political stability.[40] The experts' group became the ASEAN Senior Officials on Drug Matters (ASOD), tasked with coordinat-ing ASEAN cooperation. In their 1997 "Vision 2020" statement, the ASEAN heads of government identified for the first time the goal of an eventual drug-free ASEAN. This was given programmatic endorsement in the 1998 AMM's "Joint Declaration for a Drug Free ASEAN 2020." Two years later, the 2000 AMM advanced the drug-free target to 2015.

The goal of a drug-free ASEAN by 2015, as in ASEAN's other endeavors, de-pends on the uneven capabilities of its member states. This will require polit-ical will by leaders of member states as well as support from donor nations and agencies. ASEAN structured a memorandum of agreement in 2002 on technical cooperation with UNODC. The ASEAN + 10, ASEAN + 3, and es-pecially ASEAN + 1 dialogues have promoted cooperation, funding support, and technical assistance with its partners. This has been very important pro-grammatically in winning financial and technical support for national drug prevention, drug abuse, and drug enforcement activities. A symbolic demon-stration of cooperation with its major partners was the "Bangkok Political De-claration in Pursuit of a Drug-Free ASEAN 2015" that was issued by an Octo-ber 2002 international conference on a drug-free ASEAN sponsored by ASEAN and the UNODOC.[41]

The most structured effort at multilateralism that followed from the con-ference is the "ASEAN and China Cooperative Operations in Response to Dangerous Drugs" (ACCORD) adopted in October 2000.[42] The 2000 work plan for the ACCORD was revised at a 2005 second ACCORD conference in Beijing with priority given to the growing ATS problem. The 2005 meeting also endorsed an initiative for regional joint action against ATS-related crimes including trafficking. It proposed greater cooperation among enforcement agencies. An examination of the level of regional cooperation actually reached by the ACCORD shows that it falls short of its goals. After six years, Ralf Emmers pointed out that cooperation in the ACCORD framework is primarily national and bilateral. He noted that "policy implementation at a multilateral and collective level has not yet been attained."[43] The ACCORD has been driven by China as part of China's strategy to combat the influx of drugs to Yunnan and beyond. Already in 1993 China had executed memorandums of agreement with the LPDR, Myanmar, and Thailand on collaborative efforts to control the flow of opiates.

The Judicial Framework

Where police capabilities exist and are not compromised by corruption of the justice system, in Southeast Asia the punishment for the criminal possession of drugs or trafficking in illicit substances is harsh and unremitting, far more severe then in most Western democracies. Southeast Asia's treatment of drug offenders has become a matter of concern for human rights NGOs around the world. Singapore has the strictest drugs laws in the region. It has executed by hanging more people than any other Southeast Asian country, most of them for drug offences. The death penalty is mandatory for anyone found with fifteen grams (0.5 oz) of heroin. Its policy came under scrutiny in 2005, when it hanged a twenty-five-year-old Australian citizen of Vietnamese descent who had been arrested in 2002 carrying 400 grams (14 oz) of heroin from Cambodia to Australia.

Despite Australian diplomatic efforts to have the Singapore government commute the sentence and a personal representation by Prime Minister John Howard to Prime Minister Lee Hsien Loong for clemency, the execution went forward as scheduled. The Australian attorney-general denounced it as "barbaric." Australian parliamentarians demanded diplomatic reprisals and the powerful Australian trade unions threatened a boycott of Singapore ships and planes. Howard rejected calls for retaliation against one of Australia's most important allies in Southeast Asia. He said that the execution should serve as a warning to other young Australians—and other Westerners. "Don't imagine for a moment," he said, "that you can risk carrying drugs anywhere in Asia without suffering the most severe consequences."[44] The death penalty is applied for drug offences in Vietnam, Malaysia, and Indonesia. However these countries are not as concerned about the inflexible integrity of their legal systems as with their wider foreign policy concerns. The death penalty may be applied but is commonly commuted to life imprisonment, which then often is reduced. For example nine Australians, known as the "Bali 9" were arrested in Indonesia in 2005 in a conspiracy to carry 8.2 kg (18 lbs) of heroin to Australia. In the judicial process of trials, appeals, and counterappeals, at one point six of the nine were condemned to execution by firing squad. By February 2008, only three were still to face the firing squad, five had life in prison sentences, and one a twenty-year sentence. In October 2004, a young Australian woman was arrested at the Bali airport for having 4.1 kg (9 lbs) of marijuana in her baggage. She was sentenced to twenty years' imprisonment. Her final appeal was turned down in 2008 and her hopes to be exchanged to an Australian prison seemed dashed by Indonesia's unwillingness to do deals with convicted drug criminals and expectation that, once back in Australia, she would be released.

In 2003, Thai Prime Minister Thaksin, frustrated by the flow of ATS tablets from Myanmar to the country, threatened the junta that if it did not close down the labs, Thailand would. The threat was followed, not by use of force against the ASEAN neighbor, but rather the alleged criminal trafficking syndicates in Thailand. In February 2003, Thaksin launched an all-out war on drugs. He demanded quick results, giving the bureaucracy and police three months to eradicate drug dealing. Summary justice was meted out, and when deaths were challenged they were explained away as self-defense or the result of drug gang warfare. One of the charges the junta raised against Thaksin in justifying the 2006 coup was the pattern of extrajudicial killings during the war on drugs.

Human rights groups charged that at least 2,500 extrajudicial killings had occurred. A five-month investigation in 2007 reported that in the February to April 2003 three-month period, there were 2,599 murder cases of which 1,370, more than half, were related to drug dealing. Even though Thaksin's order to eradicate the dealers had been carried out, the panel came to no conclusion as to accountability or criminal liability.[45] When Prime Minister Samak Sundarajev announced in February 2008 a new campaign against the drug trade, it was feared that impunity again would be attached to the government agents. Samak said he would use the same tactics that were used in 2003, adding "I will not set a target for how many people should die," although his interior minister suggested three thousand to four thousand bodies.[46] The new war on drugs kicked off on 1 April.

Trafficking in Persons (TIP)

Modern-day slavery is trafficking in persons who are forced, defrauded, or coerced into labor or sexual exploitation. It is estimated that up to eight hundred thousand people—80 percent women and children—are trafficked across national borders. Perhaps nearly a third of them originate in Southeast Asia. The transnational aspect of TIP does not count the probably millions of women and children who are trafficked within their own countries. Although great attention has been given to sexual exploitation, the victims include domestic workers like maids, factory laborers, child labor, and in Myanmar even child soldiers. The abuse, violence, and indignities visited on the victims of the traffickers are a gross violation of human rights. The task of combating trafficking is complex, involving the protection of the victims, enforcement of antitrafficking laws, effective prosecution of criminals, supervision of labor recruitment, and the political will to challenge all of the employers who profit from the human trade. Trafficking also has huge social costs in terms of gender rights, minority rights, child welfare, and public health.

All of the Southeast Asian states are touched to some extent by human trafficking, either as states of origin, transit, or destination, or in the worst cases, all three. With greater awareness of the scope of the problem, particularly following the economic and political instabilities following the Crash of '97 (chapter 7), and pressed by domestic and foreign NGOs and governments, the Southeast Asian states put in place a variety of national laws and regulations in pursuit of the three Ps of antitrafficking—prevention, prosecution, and protection. It is incorporated in ASEAN's 1997 "Declaration on Transnational Crime" and is on the work programs of the AMMTC. The problem has been to give real substance to the declaratory and regulatory superstructure. This has required inputs of ODA on a bilateral basis to help build capabilities. The global benchmark for assessing the antitrafficking efforts a country is making is the implementation of the legally binding provisions of the UN Protocol to Prevent, Suppress and Punish Trafficking in Persons Especially Women and Children. It was an optional supplement to the Convention on Transnational Organized Crime discussed above. Commonly called the Palermo Protocol, after the city in Italy where they met to give their final approval in December 2000, the protocol, which entered into force in 2003, provided the first globally approved and legally binding definition of trafficking in persons (box 6.3). The Palermo Protocol had three principle thrusts:

- To facilitate convergence in national approaches with regard to the establishment of domestic criminal offences;
- To promote efficient international cooperation in investigating and prosecuting trafficking in persons crimes;
- To protect and assist the victims of trafficking in persons with full respect for their human rights.

BOX 6.3
International Definition of Trafficking in Persons

Palermo Protocol, Article 3(a)
"Trafficking in persons" shall mean the recruitment, transportation, transfer, harboring or receipt of persons, by means of the threat or use of force or other forms of coercion, of abduction, of fraud, of deception, of the abuse of power or of a position of vulnerability or of the giving or receiving of payments or benefits to achieve the consent of a person having control over another person, for the purpose of exploitation. Exploitation shall include at a minimum, the exploitation of the prostitution of others or other forms of sexual exploitation, forced labor or services, slavery or practices similar to slavery, servitude or the removal of organs.

The Palermo Protocol was particularly important in the attention it gave to victims' rights, calling on the signatories to provide for the physical, psychological, and social recovery of victims of trafficking including shelter, medical care, and counseling. This victims-first approach was in sharp contrast to culturally, politically, and legally unsympathetic Southeast Asian societies. In many cases, the victims were seen as at best illegal immigrants or even criminals themselves, for whom jail rather than shelter was appropriate. Only the Philippines in Southeast Asia has ratified the Palermo Protocol. The status of Southeast Asian signatures, accessions, and ratifications to the major TIP-related international agreements is documented in table 6.2.

One measure of how successful the Southeast Asian states have been is their place in the annual *Trafficking in Persons Report* prepared by the State Department's Office to Monitor and Combat Trafficking in Persons.[47] The TIP report is mandated by the U.S. Congress and is based on compliance with the Trafficking in Victims Protection Act of 2000 as strengthened in 2003 (TVPA). There are three tiers of placement. Tier 1, countries that fully comply with the act's minimum standards for the elimination of trafficking, has no Southeast Asian states. Tier 2, countries not in full compliance but making significant efforts to comply, includes Indonesia, Laos, the Philippines, Singapore, Thailand, and Vietnam. A Tier 2 "watch list" of countries that require special scrutiny, names Cambodia. Two Southeast Asian countries, Malaysia and Myanmar, are on tier 3—countries that neither satisfy minimum standards nor are making a significant effort to come into compliance. Tier 3 countries are subject by the TVPA to certain foreign security assistance sanctions to be invoked by the "Presidential Determination with Respect to Foreign Governments' Efforts Regarding Trafficking

TABLE 6.2
TIP Relevant International Conventions

Country	Palermo Protocol to Suppress & Punish Trafficking in Persons	ILO Conv. 182 Elimination of Worst Forms of Child Labor	Optional Protocol to the Conv. on the Rights of the Child, on the Sale of Children, Prostitution, and Child Pornography	Optional Protocol to the Conv. of the Rights of Child in Armed Conflict	ILO Conv. 29, Forced Labor	ILO Conv. 105, Abolition of Forced Labor
Brunei			A			
Cambodia	S	R	R	R	R	R
Indonesia	S	R	S	S	R	R
Lao PDR	A	S	A	A	R	
Malaysia	S				R	
Myanmar	A					
Philippines	R	R	R	R	R	R
Singapore		R		S	R	
Thailand	S	R	A	A	R	R
Timor-Leste			A	A		
Vietnam		R	R	R	R	

Note: S=signature, A=accession, R=ratification.
Source: U.S. Department of State, 2007 *Trafficking in Persons Report.*

in Persons." The 2007 Presidential Determination invoked sanctions on Myanmar—already under the U.S. human rights sanction regime (chapter 8)—but waivered sanctions on Malaysia as justified by national interest in security cooperation with Malaysia in the war on terror and peacekeeping operations.[48]

The transnational characteristics of TIP cannot be combated by building national capabilities. In addition to declaratory statements from multinational fora, there has been some multilateral institution building in which Southeast Asian nations, donor countries, and NGOs have been brought together in the common effort to eradicate TIP. We will mention here only three of the most prominent.

ARTIP

The Asia Regional Trafficking in Persons Project (ARTIP) is an Australian-funded five-year program to promote more effective and capable criminal justice systems of governments in the Asia region.[49] Inaugurated in 2006, the initial partner countries were Cambodia, Lao PDR, Myanmar, and Thailand. Indonesia joined in 2007, and it is expected that the program will be expanded to other ASEAN countries at a rate of one a year. ARTIP is based on the premise that an effective criminal justice response to trafficking is a key to ending the impunity for traffickers and security and justice for victims. ARTIP builds on its predecessor, the 2003–2006 Asia Regional Cooperation to Prevent People Trafficking (ARCPPT), which sought to facilitate a more coordinated approach to the crime of trafficking with Cambodia, Lao PDR, Myanmar, and Thailand.

The COMMIT Process

The Coordinated Mekong Ministerial Initiative against Trafficking (COMMIT) is the first regional instrument that has made a serious effort to institutionalize a multisectoral approach to combat trafficking in persons within the Greater Mekong Subregion as well as from the GMS to other destinations. The COMMIT Process began in 2003 with a series of informal discussions and roundtables among GMS government representatives. It was formalized in a memorandum of understanding signed at the October 2004 first COMMIT inter-ministerial meeting by Cambodia, China, Lao PDR, Myanmar, Thailand, and Vietnam. The coordinating body for COMMIT is the United Nations Inter-Agency Project on Human Trafficking in the Greater Mekong Sub-Region (UNIAP).[50] Box 6.4 identifies the specific forms of trafficking that COMMIT addresses. The MOU was followed by a subregional plan of action with eleven thematic projects that link COMMIT to the other major regional anti-

---

BOX 6.4
Trafficking in Persons within the Greater Mekong Subregion

- Trafficking from Cambodia, China, Laos, and Myanmar to Thailand for labor exploitation, including the sex trade.
- Trafficking of children from Cambodia to Thailand and Vietnam for begging and lately from Vietnam to Cambodia, Laos, and Thailand for the same purpose.
- Trafficking of women and girls from Vietnam, Laos, and Myanmar to China for forced marriages and boys for adoption.
- Domestic trafficking of kidnapped children in China for adoption and of women and girls for forced marriages.
- Trafficking of women and girls from Vietnam to Cambodia for the sex trade.

Source: Susu Thathun, Project Director, UNIAP, accessed at www.fmreview.org/text/FMR/ 25/10.doc.

---

trafficking actors—UN agencies, NGOs, and intergovernmental organizations. The second COMMIT inter-ministerial meeting took place in March 2008 to approve an expanded subregional plan of action emphasizing commitment to a trafficking-free GMS.

The Bali Process

The Bali Process broadens the regional consultative framework for collaboration on the illegal movement of people to the Asia-Pacific. It was initiated at the Regional Ministerial Conference on People Smuggling, Trafficking in Persons and Related Transnational Crimes held in Bali in February 2002. Co-chaired by Australia and Indonesia, its stimulus was the flow of people originating in South Asia and the Middle East to Australia through Indonesia. The initial bilateral cooperation has become a regional consultative process of forty-two Asia-Pacific countries together with nineteen "participating countries," and eleven other Bali process organizations such UNODC, Interpol, International Labor Organization (ILO), and so on.[51] The steering group is composed of Australia, Indonesia, New Zealand, Thailand, the International Organization for Migrants (IOM), and the UNHRC. Two country coordinators lead programmatic activities in two thematic areas: Regional and International Cooperation on Policy Issues and Law Enforcement (Thailand) and Regional and International Cooperation on Policy Issues and Legal Frameworks (New Zealand). A second ministerial conference was held in Bali in 2003, and the process continues under the policy guidance of an annual Bali Process Senior Officials' Meeting and the coordination of the IOM.

The Bali Process was designed to demonstrate political commitment to the common purpose of cooperating in combating trafficking in persons and people smuggling. In February 2008, co-chairs Australia and Indonesia convened a side event at the Vienna Forum to Fight Human Trafficking to review the outcomes of the Bali Process. They concluded that it was a model for regional cooperation against human trafficking in the Asia-Pacific region and beyond.[52] Its contribution is strengthening and facilitating nonbinding and informal cooperation among policymakers and practitioners, international organizations, and NGOs.

Although most of the Southeast Asian states are working to enhance their antitrafficking capabilities and are improving their treatment of the victims of trafficking, a reading of the country narratives in the State Department's TIP report shows how far there is to go. The policy problem can be explained as how to convert the normative statements and "soft mechanisms of cooperation" into strengthening the three Ps.[53] The UNODC, the custodian of the Palermo Protocol, admits that "translating it into reality remains problematic. Very few criminals are convicted and most victims are probably never identified or assisted."[54]

Notes

1. This is a point made by Natasha Hamilton-Hart, "Terror in Southeast Asia: Expert Analysis, Myopia, and Fantasy," *The Pacific Review* 18, no. 3 (2005): 303–25.

2. The most detailed analyses of the Jema'ah Islamiyah have been done by Sidney Jones for the International Crisis Group. Beginning with "Violence and Radical Islam" (October 2001) through "Jemaah Islamiyah's Publishing Industry" (February 2008), she and her colleagues have produced a series of studies that rival or even excel the intelligence production of Western embassies or of Indonesia's own state intelligence agencies. They can be accessed through the Indonesia country link at www.crisis-group.org.

3. For a survey of the JI and its links see Greg Barton, *Struggle in Indonesia: Jemaah Islamiyah and the Soul of Islam* (Sydney, Australia: University of New South Wales Press, 2004).

4. The text of the "ASEAN Declaration on Joint Action to Counter Terrorism" can be accessed at www.aseansec.org/5620.htm.

5. The text of the Phnom Penh "Declaration on Terrorism" can be accessed at www.aseansec.org/13154.htm.

6. The ISM-CTTC co-chairs' statements can be read as annexes to the annual ARF chair's statements, accessed at www.aseanregionalforum.org.

7. The ASEAN–U.S. declaration can be accessed at www.aseansec.org/7424.htm.

8. The co-chairs' statement on the Bali Regional Ministerial Meeting on Terrorism can be accessed at www.aseansec.org/16000.htm.

9. The text of the treaty can be accessed at www.aseansec.org/17363.pdf.

10. The text of the "Convention on Counter-Terrorism" can be accessed at www.aseansec.org/19250.htm.

11. For a discussion of the modeling for an ASEAN counterterrorism treaty see Gregory Rose and Diana Nestorovska, "Toward an ASEAN Counter-Terrorism Treaty," *Singapore Year Book of International Law 2005* (Singapore: National University School of Law, 2005), 157–89.

12. "ASEAN's Accord on Counter-Terrorism a Major Step Forward," *The Nation* [Bangkok], 19 February 2007; "Convention on Counter Terrorism Opens New Chapter," *Bernama* [Malaysian National News Agency], 13 January 2007.

13. The SEARCCT website is www.searcct.gov.my.

14. The JCLEC website is www.jclec.com.

15. The U.S. Department of State has published since 2004 an annual *Country Report on Terrorism* (CRT) with information compiled by the National Counterterrorism Center. This is released at the end of April for the previous year. An HTML version of the 2007 CRT can be accessed at www.state.gov/s/ct/rls/crt/2007. The CRT replaced the previous annual publication since 2000 of *Patterns of Global Terrorism*.

16. Where the ASG fits into the MNLF–MILF–ASG triangle is discussed in Douglas Bakshian, "Winding Down the Mindanao War," *Far Eastern Economic Review* 170, no.10 (2007): 47–51.

17. Rommel C. Banlaoi, "The Role of Philippine-American Relations in the Global Campaign against Terrorism: Implications for Regional Security," *Contemporary Southeast Asia* 24, no. 2 (2002): 294–312.

18. The kidnapping of the Burnhams is the background for an analysis of the ASG by Mark Bowden, "Jihadists in Paradise," *Atlantic Monthly* (March 2007), accessed at www.theatlantic.com/doc/200703/bowden-jihad.

19. Office of the Press Secretary, "Joint Statement between the United States of America and the Republic of the Philippines," 20 November 2001, accessed at www.whitehouse.gov/news/releases/2001/11/20011120-13.html.

20. Press Release, "GMA [Gloria Macapagal-Arroyo] Cites Benefits of Strong RP–U.S. Military Partnership," Office of the President of the Republic, 5 March 2004, accessed at www.op.gov.ph/news.asp?newsid=4589.

21. Donald Greenlees, "Philippine Military, with U.S. Help, Checks Rebels," *International Herald Tribune*, 17 February 2007.

22. The text of the TOC convention can be accessed at www.unodc.org/pdf/crime/a_res_55/res5525e.pdf.

23. The ASEAN "Declaration on Transnational Crime" can be accessed at www.aseansec.org/5640.htm.

24. "Joint Communiqué of the Sixth ASEAN Ministerial Meeting on Transnational Crime (AMMTC)," 6 November 2007, accessed at www.aseansec.org/21038.htm.

25. "Joint Declaration of ASEAN and China on Cooperation in the Field of Non-Traditional Security Issues," 4 November 2004, accessed at www.aseansec.org/13185.htm.

26. The ARF statement on piracy can be accessed at www.aseansec.org/14837.htm.

27. Adam J. Young and Mark J. Valencia, "Conflation of Piracy and Terrorism in Southeast Asia: Rectitude and Utility," *Contemporary Southeast Asia* 25, no. 2 (2003): 269–83.

28. Piracy statistics are from the annual piracy reports of the International Maritime Bureau Piracy Reporting Center established in Kuala Lumpur in 1992. It offers weekly, quarterly, and annual reports on worldwide piracy. The IMB was founded by the International Chamber of Commerce Commercial Crimes Services in 1981 to be the focal point for the fight against maritime crime. The IMB's website can be accessed at www.icc-ccs.org/imb/overview.php.

29. For discussions of the application of the UNCLOS definition of piracy in Southeast Asia see Zou Keyuan, "Implementing the United Nations Convention on the Law of the Sea in East Asia: Issues and Trends," in *Singapore Year Book of International Law 2005* (Singapore: Singapore National University School of Law, 2005), 45–49.

30. John F. Bradford, "Japanese Anti-Piracy Initiatives in Southeast Asia," *Contemporary Southeast Asia* 26, no. 3 (2004): 480–505.

31. The text of the ReCAAP can be accessed at www.mofa.go.jp/mofaj/gaiko/kaiyo/pdfs/kyotei_s.pdf.

32. Yoshiro Sato, *Southeast Asian Receptiveness to Japanese Maritime Security Cooperation* (Honolulu: Asia Pacific Center for Strategic Studies, September 2003): 3, posted at www.apcss.org.

33. The term "sensitivities" was used by Malaysian defense chief Najib in commenting on the prospect for joint patrolling in "KL: Joint Patrols with RI, S'pore in Malacca Can Be Examined," *The Jakarta Post*, 17 April 2007.

34. As cited in "Lloyd's Removal of War-Risk Rating on Malacca Straits Hailed" by the Associated Press at business.inq7.net/money/breakingnews/view_artifle.php?article_id=14271.

35. A concise overview of the threats in the tri-border region is Ian Storey, "The Tri-border Sea Area: Maritime Southeast Asia's Ungoverned Space," *Terrorism Monitor* 5, no. 19 (11 October 2007), online at www.jamestown.org/terrorism/news/article.php?articleid=2373708.

36. The text of the agreement can be accessed at www.aseansec.org/17346.pdf.

37. The statistics on opium production in this section are drawn from the United Nations Office on Drugs and Crime (UNODC), *World Drug Report 2007* and UNODC's *Opium Poppy Cultivation in Southeast Asia: Lao PDR, Myanmar, Thailand* (October 2007).

38. United States Department of State, *International Narcotics Control and Strategy Report*, 28 February 2008, 279.

39. The text of the "Presidential Determination" can be accessed at www.whitehouse.gov/news/releases/2007/09/20070917-1.html.

40. For the development of ASEAN's policy framework see "Cooperation on Drugs and Narcotics Overview," at www.aseansec.org/5682.htm.

41. The text of the declaration can be accessed at www.aseansec.org/5714.htm.

42. Details about ACCORD can be found at its website www.accordplan.net.

43. Ralf Emmers, "International Regime Building in ASEAN: Cooperation against the Illicit Trafficking and Abuse of Drugs," *Contemporary Southeast Asia* 29, no. 3 (2007): 518.

44. As quoted in "Australian Executed in Singapore," *BBC News*, 12 December 2005.

45. Piyanuch Thammakasetchai, "'War on Drugs' Probe Draws a Blank," *The Nation*, 16 January 2008.

46. As quoted in "Thailand PM Targets Drug dealers," *BBC News*, 23 February 2008.

47. TIP reports from 2001 to the present can be accessed at www.state.gov/g/tip/rls/tiprpt.

48. The 2007 "Presidential Determination" can be accessed at www.state.gov/g/tip/rls/psrl/07/93704.html.

49. The ARTIP website is www.artipproject.org.

50. The UNIAP website is www.no-trafficking.org.

51. The Bali Process website is www.baliprocess.net.

52. "The Bali Process: A Model for Regional Cooperation in the Fight against Human Trafficking," accessed at www.baliprocess.net/index.asp?pageID=2145831461.

53. Ralf Emmers, Beth Greener-Barcham, and Nicholas Thomas, "Institutional Arrangements to Counter Human Trafficking in the Asia Pacific," *Contemporary Southeast Asia* 28, no. 3 (2006): 505.

54. The quote is from the UNODC website at www.unodc.org/documents/human-trafficking/Act-Against-Human-Trafficking.pdf.

Suggestions for Further Reading

There is a growing and often sensational body of literature on terrorism in Southeast Asia. A representative sample includes: Gregory Abuza, *Militant Islam in Southeast Asia: Crucible of Terror* (Boulder, Colo.: Lynne Rienner, 2003); Rohan Gunaratna, *Inside Al Qaeda: Global Network of Terror* (New York: Columbia University Press, 2002); Mike Millard, *Jihad in Paradise: Islam and Politics in Southeast As*ia (Armonk, N.Y.: M. E. Sharpe, 2004); Kumar Ramakrishna and See Seng Tan, eds., *After Bali: The Threat of Terrorism in Southeast Asia* (Singapore: Institute of Defence and Strategic Studies and World Scientific, 2003); Paul J. Smith, ed., *Terrorism and Violence in Southeast Asia: Transnational Challenges to States and Regional Stability* (Armonk, N.Y.: M. E. Sharpe, 2005).

A sample of studies of various aspects of transnational crime would include Allen Dupont, *East Asia Imperiled: Transnational Challenges to Security* (Cambridge, UK: Cambridge University Press, 2005); James O. Finckenauer and Ko-lin Chin, *Asian Transnational Organized Crime* (Hauppauge, N.Y.: Nova Scientific, 2006); Bertil Lintner, *Blood: The Criminal Underworld of Asia*

(London: Palgrave Macmillan, 2003); Derek Johnson and Mark Valencia, *Piracy in Southeast Asia: Status, Issues, and Response* (Singapore: Institute of Southeast Asian Studies, 2005); Adam J. Young, *Contemporary Maritime Piracy in Southeast Asia: History, Causes, and Remedies* (Singapore: Institute of Southeast Asian Studies, 2007). The classic study of the historical drug trade in the Golden Triangle is Alfred A. McCoy, *The Politics of Heroin in Southeast Asia* (New York: Harper & Row, 1972).

7

Southeast Asia in the Regional and International Economies

A S THE SOUTHEAST ASIAN COUNTRIES CAME TO INDEPENDENCE in the immediate post–World War II era, their economies remained closely tied to their former colonial rulers. With the exception of Singapore, the largest exports were the primary commodities of the agriculture and mining sectors of their economies, most of which remained in the hands of their European owners. The majorities of the populations were engaged in subsistence agriculture. Manufactured capital and consumer goods were imported. The political goal of all the new states of Southeast Asia was to promote real economic growth so as to end the low-level equilibrium of agricultural poverty. The question was how to break out of dependency in an international exchange relationship in which exported low cost primary commodities came back as higher cost, value-added manufactured goods. This seemed to condemn the exporting states to low growth and poverty. Their answer was economic development, which came to mean industrialization.

The Southeast Asian states first adopted an industrialization strategy of import substitution that would allow them to close the exchange gap. The problem was that the domestic markets were not large enough to support industrialization platforms for real economic growth based only on import substitution. Economic development came only when capital was invested in growth strategies of export-led industrialization. It was this strategy of trade that produced Southeast Asia's "little tigers." But these "little tigers" were only kittens if compared to Japan, South Korea, and Taiwan. The policy problem for Southeast Asia has been how to maintain and defend its access to a share of international trade and investment, particularly with a dragon prowling among them. Their answer is to build a bigger production and market platform through ASEAN's regional economic integration.

Intra-ASEAN Regionalism and AFTA

At the 2003 Bali Summit, ASEAN's leaders announced the ASEAN Community project, which included an ASEAN Economic Community (AEC). This is to be in place by 2015 (chapter 4). The goal is establishing ASEAN as a single market and production base, thus strengthening its competitiveness in the global economy. A little more than three years later, ASEAN advanced the AEC calendar to 2010. The haste was not because scheduled intermediate program targets were being met earlier than expected. It was because the ASEAN countries felt themselves increasingly squeezed between a rising China and a rising India, both of which were expanding their global markets and attracting capital at, it was feared, ASEAN's expense. The AEC builds on programs and agreements that have been in place for years. One critic put it quite bluntly: "The Southeast Asian nations had over 30 years to build an 'ASEAN house,' and they have squandered the opportunity. Had ASEAN evolved along the lines envisioned by its founders, it would not have displayed the disarray with which its members confronted the rise of China."[1]

From Competition to Cooperation

For the first quarter of a century of ASEAN's organizational evolution, the contending pulls of maintaining solidarity in the face of external security threats and giving substance to the "Bangkok Declaration" promise of regional functional cooperation resulted in politics being in command (chapter 4). The foreign ministers who drove ASEAN gave little priority to matters of real economic cooperation. Even if they had, the members' national economic development plans were competitive rather than complementary, and access to assistance, investment, and markets was viewed as a zero-sum game. Initial efforts to reconcile national self-interest and regional cooperation were disappointing and concrete achievement elusive. In discussing the cooperative efforts, it should be remembered that until 1985, the group was the ASEAN 5, and from 1985 to 1995, an ASEAN 6, and, finally, with the addition of the CLMV countries, an ASEAN 10. The dynamics of negotiating intra-ASEAN economic cooperation have changed as the membership has expanded.

The UN Blueprint

The first proposals to give policy flesh to the bare bones of the "Bangkok Declaration" came in the recommendations of a United Nations team of economists commissioned in 1969 by the ASEAN foreign ministers, and whose work was completed in 1972.[2] Adopted in principle by the governments at the 1976 Bali Summit, the strategy called for industrialization based on market sharing and resource pooling. At its heart was an ambitious package of large-scale industries. This was the genesis of the ill-fated ASEAN Industrial Projects (AIP) scheme.[3] Only two of the proposed five came on stream and these had already been slated as national projects. There was a proposal for a system of "complementarity agreements" in the ASEAN Industrial Complementation (AIC) scheme, through which specified manufacturing activities were to be horizontally integrated across state boundaries. The automotive industry was chosen as an appropriate industry for initial regionalization. This was quickly derailed by Malaysia's decision to build its own automobile, the Proton Saga, with Japan's Mitsubishi Corporation. An ASEAN Industrial Joint Venture (AIJV) initiative was started in 1983. The AIJVs were private undertakings from the ASEAN region (but with non-ASEAN equity participation) that would be given a 50 percent tariff preference in intra-ASEAN trading (raised to 75 percent in 1986). The AIJV concept got off to a slow start and quickly bogged down in ASEAN and national bureaucratic mazes where, according to the chairman of the ASEAN Private Sector Committee on the Implementation of the AIJV, "the merits of the AIJVs are not well perceived in all capital cities in ASEAN."[4]

The ASEAN Task Force

As national jealousies and overlapping bureaucracies stymied progress, criticism of ASEAN's slow pace toward functional cooperation mounted. The ASEAN Chamber of Commerce and Industry (ASEAN CCI) reviewed ASEAN's performance in 1981 and found it wanting, describing a "decrescendo" since the Bali Summit.[5] In response to the critics, the ASEAN ministerial meeting (AMM) commissioned in 1982 an ASEAN Task Force on ASEAN Cooperation. The mandate was to appraise ASEAN's progress, identify policy measures that would maximize the attainment of ASEAN's objectives, and define new directions for cooperation. The task force reported its recommendations to the 1983 AMM, which then parceled them out to various committees for consideration. This set the stage for the relative indifference of the foreign ministers at the 1984 AMM, when they endorsed the effort in principle, accepted some politically easy recommendations, and then consigned the meat of the report to "further study"; a limbo from which it was never resurrected.

The report's recommendations did not deviate significantly from the UN strategy adopted at Bali. The report emphasized that ASEAN regionalism had no supranational objectives—that its aim was cooperation, not integration. What was troublesome to the task force—and put it at odds with the foreign ministers' persuasion—was the degree of vigor to be applied to cooperation. In the words of the report: "Behind all aspects of cooperation lies the political will to cooperate. . . . Regional interests are usually accorded priority only if they coincide with or promote national interest."[6] As one observer noted, cooperation that demanded sacrifices from the members could not flourish given the differing national outlooks and priorities.[7] These "outlooks and priorities" were embedded in competitive national development plans taking place behind high tariff and nontariff barriers to protect national markets. Indonesia consistently resisted the regionalization of its economy for fear of penetration by the economically stronger ASEAN states. A particular bogey to Indonesia and Malaysia was vibrant and open-to-the-world Singapore.

The Preferential Tariff Arrangements (PTA)

As noted, the original UN blueprint also called for market sharing as a means of liberalizing and expanding intra-ASEAN trade. The initial effort was the 1977 Preferential Trade Arrangement (PTA). This mechanism called for negotiations on a bilateral or multilateral basis of an ASEAN margin of tariff preference that would then apply on a most-favored-nation basis to all ASEAN states.[8] In implementing the PTA, protracted negotiations over goods to be included and goods that could be excluded had the effect of seriously limiting its trade significance. By the 1986 Manila ASEAN Summit, only 5 percent of items offered under the PTA were actively traded. How minimal the impact was is suggested by the fact that PTA-traded goods accounted for just 2 percent of intra-ASEAN trade, which itself was only 17 percent of ASEAN total trade.[9]

Philippine President Corazon Aquino opened the 1986 AMM in Manila by scolding the foreign ministers for lack of progress in economic cooperation. "After 19 years of existence," she said, "ASEAN should already be evaluating the impact of regional economic cooperation instead of endlessly discussing how to get it off the ground."[10] While the foreign ministers concentrated their attention on the diplomacy of the Third Indochina War, their economic ministerial counterparts had a new focus. Driven essentially by what today would be called Track II nonofficial circles, by 1985, discussions on ASEAN's future began to center on the process of moving from PTA arrangements to an ASEAN Free Trade Area with ultimately a goal of an ASEAN common market. Under the sponsorship of the ASEAN CCI, a "Group of 14," a veritable who's who of ASEAN economic and financial brain power, began to chart a course toward economic integration, offering concrete recommendations to foster the organizational process.[11] The Group of 14's 1997 final report made trade liberalization the highest priority for ASEAN.[12] Other studies followed in increasing volume and influence. By the end of the 1980s, trade had become the central issue for ASEAN's attentive public. The practical policy aspects of free trade dominated the ASEAN official, academic, and business dialogue. The breakthrough was the decoupling of the idea of ASEAN free trade from the goal of an ASEAN common market. This was necessary if Indonesia were to be brought on board.

The ASEAN Free Trade Area

The January 1992 Singapore summit meeting of the ASEAN heads of government, only the fourth summit in twenty-five years, was the first opportunity for ASEAN member nations to respond collectively to the dramatic restructuring of the regional international environment (chapter 3). The Third Indochina War had been officially closed. Cold War imperatives no longer dominated ASEAN's policy plate. Not since the 1976 Bali Summit had expectations been so high for the prospect of a purposeful and progressive restructuring of ASEAN and a meaningful redirection of its agenda. A sense of urgency was felt. A summit without new initiatives would be a failed summit. One of ASEAN's most distinguished statesmen opined that the summit gave the leaders "the opportunity to evolve a consensus on the steps which ASEAN must take to strengthen its cooperation and to be relevant to the world of the 1990s."[13] The relevancy was to be found in the first step toward regional economic integration. The politics of foreign policy was no longer in command.

What was called at the time a landmark in ASEAN's history was reached with the signing in Singapore of a "Framework Agreement on Enhancing ASEAN Economic Cooperation."[14] This would lead ASEAN to the pledged higher economic plane. The way forward was the establishment of an ASEAN Free Trade Area (AFTA) to be phased in over a period of fifteen years (2008). Up until the 2003 Bali II Summit with its proposed ASEAN Economic Community, AFTA was the economic cement of ASEAN, no matter how weak when compared to the political cement of the Third Indochina War. The implementing mechanism for the AFTA was a system of common effective preferential tariffs (CEPT) that would progressively lower tariffs on intra-ASEAN trade in goods to 0–5 percent over the fifteen-year period (see box 7.1). The tariff cuts moved forward on both "fast" and "normal" tracks. The CEPT scheme went into effect on 1 January 1993.[15] The AFTA did not affect the ASEAN member states' bilateral or multilateral trading relations. Each member state maintained its own national tariff regime and trade regulations for non-ASEAN trading partners.

The AFTA was not treaty-based. It was an enabling mechanism for voluntary commitments to consensual goals. The Philippines had circulated the draft of a comprehensive ASEAN Treaty of Economic Cooperation that included not

---

BOX 7.1
CEPT

The implementing mechanism of the ASEAN Free Trade Area was the common effective preferential tariff (CEPT). This was a tariff preferential to ASEAN members applied to goods identified for inclusion in the CEPT scheme and meeting rules of ASEAN origin. Local content was defined as "substantial transformation" in terms of value added of at least 40 percent of ASEAN content. The CEPT scheme covered all manufactured products, including capital goods, and processed agricultural goods. Initially excluded goods in the "temporary" and "sensitive" categories were to be phased into the tariff lines of the CEPT scheme over time.

---

only goods but also services, capital, and labor. This was quickly shunted aside. The CEPT scheme of progressive and reciprocal tariff reductions phased in over time fell between the push for free trade and Indonesia's reluctance to open its domestic markets to a feared flood of ASEAN manufactured consumer and capital goods. AFTA was initially hedged with conditions, qualifications, and escape clauses, such as an ASEAN minus X formula, which would allow nonparticipation in specific circumstances. The loopholes reflected consensual accommodation of national domestic political demands. Like the PTA, the AFTA had lengthy exclusion lists in three categories: temporary, to protect certain domestic producers; sensitive, which were basically the political lightning rods of raw agricultural products, including rice; and general, based on national security, health, morals, historic importance, and other internationally recognized criteria. Only about 1 percent of all ASEAN tariff lines fall in the general exclusion category. The temporary and sensitive categories for exclusions had time limits for later inclusion in the CEPT scheme.

In 1995, the target tariff level of 0–5 percent for the ASEAN 6 was advanced to 2003 and then again in 1998, to 2002. The late-entering CLMV countries were given longer deadlines: 2006 for Vietnam, 2008 for Laos and Myanmar, and 2010 for Cambodia. The CEPT agreement was amended in January 2003 by a protocol that set a target for elimination of all intra-ASEAN import duties by 2010 for the ASEAN 6 and 2015 for the CLMV countries. By 2005, 99.77 percent of the ASEAN 6 tariff lines under the CEPT scheme had achieved the target of 0–5 percent; 65 percent were at 0 percent; and the ASEAN 6 average tariff was 1.74 percent as compared to the 1993 average of 12.76 percent. For the CLMV countries, more than 90 percent of their goods had been brought under the CEPT scheme of which 77.88 percent had achieved the 0–5 percent tariff range.[16] In 2008, 94 percent of all goods in intra-ASEAN trade were in the CEPT 0–5 percent tariff range.

AFTA Plus

Even as the scope of AFTA was broadened as more goods came into the CEPT system and the pace of tariff reductions accelerated, other measures were introduced to facilitate trade in goods, including agreements on customs nomenclature, valuation, and the development of common product certification standards. While the CEPT scheme itself related to tariff barriers, the AFTA framework also called for the elimination of nontariff barriers and quantitative restrictions. Trade in goods is only one part of intra-ASEAN economic transactions. The ASEAN states also worked to create a more comprehensive program of cooperation in other sectors of the regional economy.

The services sector is a large and expanding component of GDP in ASEAN countries. In 1995, the ASEAN economic ministers signed the "ASEAN Framework Agreement in Services" (AFAS), under which measures for intraregional liberalization of trade in services would be negotiated.[17] The goal is to provide national treatment for services suppliers among ASEAN countries. A 2003 protocol to the AFAS applied the ASEAN minus X formula, allowing the liberalization of specific services without having to extend the benefit to nonparticipating countries. Since 1996, there have been four rounds of negotiations with six packages of commitments covering financial services, construction, maritime transport, air transport, health services, telecommunication, and tourism. Also under the AFAS, mutual recognition agreements (MRA) are being negotiated to facilitate the flow of professional services. As of November 2007, four MRAs had been concluded: engineering, nursing, architecture, and surveying. MRAs for medicine, dentistry, and accountancy were expected in 2008.

In order to stimulate the flow of investment within ASEAN, an ASEAN Investment Area (AIA) was endorsed at the 1995 ASEAN Summit.[18] The AIA agreement covers the manufacturing, agriculture, mining, forestry, and fishery sectors, and services incidental to those sectors. The AIA calls for opening up these sectors to foreign investment and national treatment to foreign investors. Temporary exclusions in the manufacturing sector ended for the ASEAN 6 and Myanmar in 2003 and will end for Vietnam, the LPDR, and Cambodia in 2010. Temporary exclusions in the other sectors will end for the ASEAN 6 plus Cambodia in 2010; for Vietnam, in 2013; and for the LPDR and Myanmar in 2015. The AIA ministers began the task of widening the scope of the AIA to cover investments in services in 2003. The ASEAN minus X formula could be applied.

ASEAN revived the AIJV scheme in its 1996 ASEAN Industrial Cooperation (AICO) scheme, claiming to have learned from the mistakes of the past schemes.[19] The AICO was designed to encourage technology-based industrial cooperation by providing tariff and other incentives to ASEAN-based companies with a minimum of 30 percent ASEAN equity and that engaged in some form of resource sharing. In the case that one of the companies cannot meet the equity requirement, a waiver can be negotiated. A minimum of two companies in two ASEAN states had to participate. The product output of the AICO projects would enjoy the CEPT rate of 0–5 percent tariff. This was reduced in 2002 to 0 percent. The CEPT rule of 40 percent local content applied. The countries in which the AICO companies are operating can offer nontariff incentives. This carries a risk of bidding wars. By 2007, 145 AICO applications had been approved, valued at $1.8 billion.

The regional commitment to cooperative measures promoting economic growth did not address the problem of regionally harmonizing first five and then ten different economic systems with their mix of state and private enterprise, different banking systems, different regulative structures and procedures, different tax systems, and different judicial systems. There are also the structural disincentives of corruption, lack of transparency, and cronyism.

The External Impetus

Expectations about the quantifiable economic benefits and qualitative political benefits of liberalized and expanded intra-ASEAN trade and investment were only a part of the decision making about AFTA and its follow-ons. In terms of directions of trade, there was no anticipation of a significant diversion of trade from ASEAN's principal external markets in Japan, Europe, and the United States to intra-ASEAN markets. There was concern, however, about the future growth of those markets and investment opportunities in ASEAN as a result of protectionism in ASEAN countries' traditional markets. These fears crystallized in exaggerated perceptions of closing Asian market access to the European Union and the North American Free Trade Agreement (NAFTA). In one sense, closer intra-ASEAN economic cooperation was an adjustment to emerging global trading blocs. It also was the beginning of an adjustment to emerging competition with China in trade and the diversion to China of foreign direct investment (FDI).

Another external impetus was the development of the Asia–Pacific Economic Cooperation (APEC) forum. The establishment of APEC in November 1989 as an intergovernmental grouping to promote cooperation among Pacific Rim countries was the maturation of two decades of consultation and diplomacy. Largely moved by Indonesian and Malaysian reservations, ASEAN had resisted the appeals for Pacific regionalism. The concern was that the ASEAN members' voices would be muted and their influence diluted and diminished in a broader grouping dominated by Japan and the United States.[20] Nevertheless, when it became apparent that the ASEAN countries' major Pacific trading partners were going forward with the scheme, the ASEAN 6 joined Australia, Canada, Japan, New Zealand, South Korea, and the United States at the founding APEC ministerial meeting. Technically the membership is not of governments but of economies. The exigencies of the international economy, pressure from domestic economic interests, and diplomacy over-came ASEAN reluctance. Added to these factors was ASEAN's desire not to be left out and viewed as irrelevant. In 1991, the PRC, Hong Kong, and Taiwan were admitted. APEC now has twenty-one members, adding Chile (1994), Mexico (1993), Papua New Guinea (1993), Peru (1998), Russia (1998), and Vietnam (1998). A ten-year moratorium on new members was put in place in 1997, which was extended in 2007 to 2010, leaving ASEAN members Cambo-dia, LPDR, and Myanmar out.

In dramatic opposition to the conceptual underpinnings of APEC, which sought to unite like-minded Pacific Rim countries in pursuit of freer trade in the framework of the World Trade Organization (WTO), a contrary position was expressed in the notion that the East Asian economies had to defend them-selves against Europe and North America. This was the anti-APEC posture of Malaysian Prime Minister Mahathir. In December 1990—without consultation with his ASEAN counterparts—he proposed the formation of an East Asia Economic Group (EAEG).[21] In its original iteration, the EAEG was to be an economic bloc that could negotiate as a unit on issues of international trade. Although any real leverage it might have depended on Japan's inclusion, Ma-hathir denied the EAEG would be a yen bloc. The United States lobbied vigor-ously against the EAEG. In a letter to the Japanese foreign minister, Secretary of State James Baker warned that it would "divide the Pacific in half."[22] This has been a consistent U.S. position on exclusive East Asian arrangements.

In ASEAN, guided by Indonesian President Suharto—who had been in-sulted by Mahathir's unilateralism—the EAEG was downgraded to an ad hoc East Asia Economic Caucus (EAEC) as a "non institutional entity." The 1992 "Singapore Declaration" said that "with respect to an EAEC, ASEAN recog-nizes that consultations on issues of common concern among East Asian economies, as and when the need arises, could contribute to expanding the re-gion's economy and the promotion of an open and free global trading sys-tem." Mahathir may have had the last laugh, however, when in referring to the ASEAN + 3 in 2003, he said "we would be very happy if we stopped hiding be-hind this spurious title and called ourselves the East Asia Economic Group."[23]

To show its commitment to the APEC process, the United States hosted the first APEC leaders' meeting in November 1993, on Blake Island, Washington. Mahathir conspicuously boycotted the meeting. The next year, President Suharto hosted in Bogor, Indonesia, the second of what became annual APEC summits. Suharto's up-front support of the APEC process was a rebuff to Mahathir, who had to choose whether to cause a major breach in ASEAN by staying away, or swallow his pride and take part—which is what he did. The "Bogor Declaration" was APEC's signature undertaking. In it, the leaders resolved to liberalize trade and investment in the Asia–Pacific region, with the goal of free and open trade by 2010 for the developed economies and 2020 for the developing economies. It was viewed as an endorsement of American liberal international economic policy. In Southeast Asia, the APEC program of trade and investment liberalization framework seemed like a larger Pacific regionalist overlay over AFTA. Unlike other ASEAN extraregional engagements, however, ASEAN was not in control of the APEC agenda. ASEAN's strategy was twofold. First, through AFTA and AFTA plus structures it moved to stay ahead of APEC. Second, from within APEC, the ASEAN 6, with Malaysia at the point, resisted efforts to move APEC from loose consultative structures to institution building that might give binding effect to its decisions.

The Crash of '97

The end to a decade of rapid growth by Southeast Asia's "little tigers" came in the financial crisis of 1997–1998. It started with an assault on the Thai currency, the baht, which had been pegged to a basket of currencies dominated by the U.S. dollar. The mid-decade decision by the United States and Japan to let the dollar appreciate against the yen and China's 1994 devaluation of its yuan against the dollar left the exports of Thailand and the other "little tigers" at a competitive disadvantage and their currencies overvalued. In the boom years, awash with capital, the abundant liquidity had been invested in excess productive capacity, real estate, and other speculative ventures. In 1997, as Thai current account deficits widened and the baht weakened, the Thai central bank gave up efforts to defend the baht. On 2 July 1997, without warning to its ASEAN partners, the Thai central bank abandoned the dollar peg and allowed the baht to float. Within two months it had lost 38 percent of its value. This triggered a regional financial shockwave revealing the structural sand on which Southeast Asian bubble economies had been built. The collapse starkly exposed the inadequacies and institutional weaknesses that had been concealed by high economic growth rates. The cumulative impact of currency speculation, nonperforming loans, massive debt, crony capitalism, weak or nonexistent regulative safeguards, and corruption left a trail of institutional and political wreckage in the banking and finance sectors. Thailand, Malaysia, and Indonesia were particularly hard hit, but the impact was felt throughout the region as investment plummeted, liquidity dried up, and confidence failed. Growing economies contracted as output fell and growth rates dropped dramatically and even turned negative. By 1998, Thailand and Indonesia were in deep economic depressions.

The Global Response

The immediate task facing the afflicted countries was recapitalization and restoring investor confidence. The International Monetary Fund took the lead in managing the international response. The IMF coordinated rescue operations by multilateral funding agencies and bilateral assistance packages.[24] The total pledged for Thailand was $17.2 billion and for Indonesia $49.7 billion. Japan was the largest single donor with $4 billion for the Thai package and $5 billion for the Indonesian rescue. Singapore also made $5 billion available for Indonesia. The United States did not participate in the Thailand package. This was a strategic error since it left the impression of an uncaring America. As the financial contagion spread, the United States did not repeat the Thai mistake, pledging as a "second line of defense" $3 billion for the Indonesian package. Thailand finished paying back its IMF debt by 2003 and Indonesia in 2006.

The IMF-organized support programs were contingent on the imposition of an IMF regime of structural reforms, adherence to macroeconomic fundamentals, and budgetary austerity. For Southeast Asian economic nationalists, the IMF conditions were viewed as a kind of economic pax Americana. The United States played an important role in forcing the IMF reforms on a resisting Suharto government in Indonesia. President Clinton dispatched former Vice President Walter Mondale to Jakarta to tell Suharto that the United States would not support Indonesia if it did not accept the IMF terms. Malaysia refused to submit to the political and economic rigors of an IMF package, with Mahathir blaming the crisis on Western capitalists who wanted to take over Asia's distressed economies. Malaysia adopted capital controls and other domestic measures to salvage financial stability. Southeast Asian leaders' distaste for IMF intervention was shown by support for Japan's September 1997 proposal for a $100 billion Asian Monetary Fund. This was viewed as a thinly veiled effort to evade the conditionalities of IMF assistance.[25] The scheme was given the cold shoulder by the World Bank, IMF, EU, and the United States.

The Regional Response

The financial crisis showed that the countries of Southeast Asia and ASEAN were ill-prepared to manage the volatile flows of global capital coursing through the region. National responses of defending currencies were doomed to failure. ASEAN had no collaborative financial mechanisms. In fact, the first meeting of ASEAN finance ministers occurred only three months before the crash. The ASEAN 6—distrustful of the IMF—recognized that they could not construct a financial self-protection framework simply from their own resources. They turned instead to the wider East Asian region for cooperation. It is the response to the financial crisis that is the genesis of the ASEAN + 3. The leaders of China, Japan, and South Korea were invited to attend the 1997 Kuala Lumpur ASEAN Summit. This was repeated the next year at a summit in Hanoi, where China proposed regular meetings between the countries' finance and monetary officials. The emergent ASEAN + 3 was institutionalized in the first "Joint Statement on East Asian Cooperation" at the 1999 Manila summit.[26]

Financial and monetary affairs were among the areas of cooperation addressed. One of the first fruits was the Chiang Mai Initiative (CMI). Meeting on the sidelines of the May 2000 ADB meeting in Chiang Mai, Thailand, the finance ministers of the ASEAN + 3 announced the CMI, the central feature of which established an ASEAN + 3 currency swap arrangement.[27] This was an extension of the 1977 ASEAN swap agreement, which had begun with $200 million available; that was raised in 2002 to $1 billion, and again in 2005, to $2 billion. It was not called on in the financial crisis. The CMI provided for a network of bilateral swap agreements (BSA) for short-term currency exchanges between ASEAN central banks and their three East Asian counterpart institutions. This is designed to alleviate temporary liquidity shortages (box 7.2). Theoretically there could be thirty such BSAs in the ASEAN + 3 network. Through 2007, sixteen had been negotiated among eight countries with $80 billion available.

This initial linking of the financial institutions of the ASEAN states to China, Japan, and South Korea has been viewed by proponents of East Asian economic integration as a possible new first step toward an Asian Monetary Fund (AMF). A possible indicator was the move to expand the CMI mechanism to not only bilateral BSA agreements but also to provide for multilateral swap accords as well. At their 2007 meeting, the ASEAN + 3 finance ministers stated their agreement that "a self-managed reserve pooling arrangement governed by a single contractual agreement is the appropriate form of multilaterism."[28] In 2008, the ASEAN + 3 finance ministers agreed to an $80–100 billion range pool to which ASEAN countries would contribute 20 percent and China, Japan, and South Korea, the

---

BOX 7.2
Currency Swap Agreement

A currency swap agreement allows one country's central bank or monetary authority to exchange its currency for foreign currency—commonly U.S. dollars—from another country's central bank or monetary authority's currency reserves and later reverse the exchange at a future date. It is designed for short-term support for a country facing immediate current account liquidity problems. The swap is reversed at a future date.

balance. The idea of a self-managed currency pooling arrangement suggests a de facto AMF outside the oversight and discipline of the IMF.

One of the objections to an AMF is the potential moral hazard posed by access to pooled reserves without effective structures for monitoring and surveillance of the user's financial health and practices as well as the absence of conditionality. Surveillance was high on the agenda of the IMF-sponsored Manila Framework group of fourteen Pacific region nations' finance and central bank deputies. They first met in November 1997 to promote a new framework to enhance regional financial stability.[29] In 1999, ASEAN established an ASEAN Surveillance Process to exchange information on financial developments and provide an early warning system.[30] Surveillance has also been a topic for the CMI countries' consultations. ASEAN surveillance has many shortcomings. It is "informal and simple" and its peer review takes place in the context of the ASEAN way. Its data is IMF data, massaged and transferred by the ASEAN Secretariat to the ASEAN Surveillance Coordinating Unit made up of finance and central bank officials, who then pass it on to the AFMM for "peer review." The IMF data, of course, is that provided by governments, some of which have serious issues of transparency. It is to be doubted that any eventual CMI surveillance process will be more complex or formal than ASEAN's.

By 1999, the ASEAN states had weathered the worst of the crisis and with international assistance began to regain the lost economic ground, but progress was slow and depended more on global demand and interest rates than national policies in ASEAN countries, let alone ASEAN mechanisms. As a result of the financial crisis and as part of the recovery progress the ASEAN leaders resolved to hasten and deepen their economic cooperation. This was the thrust of the Bali Concord II. The question can be asked, however, if the ASEAN Economic Community—at least in its present design—could mount a common defense if another currency and financial crisis should strike? Or, would it again be every ASEAN country for itself? The fragility of ASEAN's integrative thrust was illustrated in November 2006 when Thailand's central bank suddenly imposed capital controls to limit investment inflows that were putting upward pressure on the baht. This was done unilaterally, without consultation with Thailand's ASEAN partners. The Thai stock market nosedived and markets elsewhere in the region plunged as investors lost confidence. The contagion of the 1997 crash sprang to mind. The Thai finance minister defended the move in terms of national interest. "A small nation like ourselves," he said, "if we don't protect ourselves, who else will protect us?"[31] In the absence of common central institutions such as a common market, a common currency, and a common monetary regulator to which national sovereign interests have been subordinated, the AEC in its present form promises no alteration in the operation of the ASEAN way.

Patterns of ASEAN Trade and Investment

The driving force of ASEAN cooperation has been the desire to expand trade and attract investment. The financial crisis of 1997–1998 was a temporary setback. The structural and macroeconomic policy adjustments in the national economies of those countries most severely affected have strengthened. Their export platforms and AFTA plus have enhanced the region's investment climate. But even as Southeast Asian exports surged again and current accounts strengthened in the early years of the twenty-first century, clouds loomed on the policy horizons. In 2008, economic slowdowns in the United States and Europe and increases in energy costs required downward projections in growth forecasts. More troubling was the question of ASEAN's future place in the global economy as China, with a seemingly inexhaustible supply of cheap labor, seeks to become the world's dominant labor-intensive manufacturing center and India lays its claim to business-processing and information technology.

The gloomiest forecast has China moving up the manufacturing ladder to mid and high levels of technology leading to the deindustrialization of Southeast Asia. Southeast Asia would revert to square one as a primary product exporting region to serve China's resources demand. Another scenario has Southeast Asia reorienting its trade from the United States and Europe to a Chinese consumer market of 1.3 billion that is growing in size and income. In either case, the outcome portends a decoupling of Southeast Asia from Europe and the United States, leaving it as a Chinese economic hinterland. These alarmist projections do not take into account measures that Southeast Asian states can take—and are taking—to sustain their growth. Nor are these projections supported by an empirical base that can demonstrate such an outcome is inevitable or that China's rise is necessarily sustainable at its current rate of ascent.

Trade Patterns

Table 7.1 shows ASEAN merchandise trade and share of trade, including intra-ASEAN, with the region's ten most important trading partners in 2006 (at writing the last accessible cumulation from the ASEAN trade statistics database). ASEAN's share of a quarter of its total trade is up from 19 percent when AFTA was put in place in 1992. The top five accounted for 69.5 percent of the trade, of which more than a third was from Japan and the developed West. Table 7.2 shows ASEAN's trade with its top five partners over the five-year period 2002–2006 and table 7.3 their percentage share of ASEAN's total trade. As can be seen, the rate of China's market growth in the region exceeds that of the other major trading partners. In the five years, China's two-way trade with ASEAN increased by 330 percent. In the same period, the aggregate

TABLE 7.1

Top Ten ASEAN Trade Partners 2006

Country	Trade Value $ Millions*			% Share of Trade		
	Export	Import	Total	Export	Import	Total
Intra-ASEAN	189,176.8	163,594.5	352,771.4	25.2	25.0	25.1
Japan	81,284.9	80,495.6	161,780.5	10.8	23.3	11.5
United States	96,943.5	64,252.5	161,196.0	12.9	9.8	11.5
EU-25	94,471.8	66,118.1	160,589.9	12.6	10.1	11.4
China	65,010.3	74,950.0	139,961.2	8.7	11.5	10.0
South Korea	25,670.0	26,849.7	52,519.6	3.4	4.1	3.7
Australia	23,148.5	13,262.8	36,411.4	3.1	2.0	2.6
India	18,928.1	9,774.6	28.702.7	2.5	1.5	2.0
Taiwan	9,032.0	12,876.9	21,908.9	1.2	2.0	1.6
Hong Kong	13,784.0	6,409.0	20,193.0	1.8	1.0	1.4
Total top ten	617,449.9	518,584.6	1,136,034.6	82.2	79.3	80.9
Others	133,257.9	135,513.2	268,771.1	17.8	20.7	19.1
Total ASEAN trade	750,707.9	654,097.8	1,404,805.7	100.0	100.0	100.0

* In some cases the export + imports = total and cumulative may be off because of rounding to the nearest 0.1 or 0.0.
Source: ASEAN trade statistics as of 14 September 2007, table 20.

total trade of the EU, Japan, and the United States nearly doubled. China passed the United States in ASEAN trade in 2007. Preliminary Chinese figures put China's 2007 trade with ASEAN at as much as $190 billion. The 2007 U.S. figure was $171 billion.

China's regional trade growth spurt is in part a function of its entry into the WTO in 2001. More important, however, has been the phasing in of free trade agreements with ASEAN that are discussed below. As other important trading

TABLE 7.2

Total ASEAN Two-Way Trade with Top Five Trade Partners 2002–2006
(Value in U.S. $ Millions)

Country	2002	2003	2004	2005	2006
Intra-ASEAN	159,908.8	206,731.6	260,697.5	304,893.2	352,771.3
Japan	97,541.1	113,400.6	143,313.0	153,834.3	161,780.5
USA	104,954.4	117,885.7	135,859.7	153,918.3	161,196.0
EU	97,056.8	100,364.6	131,543.1	140,533.7	160,589.9
China	42,759.7	59,629.9	80,066.0	113,393.5	140,053.3
Total ASEAN	713,816.8	824,538.7	1,071,847,8	1,224,889.4	1,404,805.7

Source: ASEAN Statistical Year Book 2006, table V.9 and 2006 ASEAN trade statistics as of 14 September 2007, table 20.

TABLE 7.3
ASEAN Top Five Trade Partners as Percentage of ASEAN Total Trade 2002–2006

Country	2002	2003	2004	2005	2006
Intra-ASEAN	22.4	25.0	24.3	25.0	25.1
Japan	13.7	11.7	13.4	12.6	11.5
USA	14.7	14.3	12.7	12.6	11.5
EU-25	13.6	12.0	12.3	11.5	11.4
China	6.0	7.0	7.5	9.3	10.0

Source: From table 7.2.

partners complete negotiations for ASEAN free trade agreements, any first-up advantage to China will be reduced. There is nothing in the trade data that would suggest as yet a trade diversion to China indicative of an impending decoupling of ASEAN members' economies from their traditional major trade partners. That ASEAN is globally competitive is demonstrated by its growth in exports even in labor-intensive industries. Cambodia is a case in point where its recent strong economic growth is underpinned by the same kind of labor-intensive consumer goods such as textiles that China exports. This is partially explained by an FDI strategy of China plus one so as not to be wholly dependent on China.

ASEAN data presented in the aggregate do not reflect the real patterns of trade in the region. Table 7.4 shows ASEAN trade in 2006 on a country basis. Singapore accounts for more than a third of the total, and by adding Malaysia and Thailand, 75 percent of ASEAN's total trade is accounted for. The distortion in the aggregate data is in part because of Singapore's role as an entrepôt. As noted in chapter 6, Singapore is the world's largest container transship-

TABLE 7.4
Total ASEAN Trade 2006 by Country (Value in U.S. $ Millions)

Country	Exports	Imports	Total	% of ASEAN
Brunei	7,619.4	1,488.9	9,108.3	0.6
Cambodia	3,514.4	2,923.0	6,437.4	0.5
Indonesia	100,796.8	61,065.5	161,864.1	11.5
Lao PDR	402.7	587.5	990.2	0.1
Malaysia	157,226.9	128,316.1	285,543.0	20.3
Myanmar	3,514.8	2,115.5	5,630.2	0.4
Philippines	47,410.1	51,773.7	99,183.6	7.1
Singapore	271,607.9	238,482.0	510,089.9	36.3
Thailand	121,579.5	127,108.8	248,688.3	17.7
Vietnam	37,033.7	40,236.8	77,270.5	5.5
Total ASEAN	750,707.8	654,097.8	1,404,805.7	100.0

Source: ASEAN trade statistics as of 15 August 2007, table 17.

ment port. A significant part of Singapore's intra-ASEAN trade reflects goods being imported from other ASEAN countries for re-exportation or goods being re-exported from Singapore to other ASEAN countries. Malaysia and Indonesia have tried to challenge this with container-handling port facilities in Johor and Batam, respectively.

Investment Patterns

The productive capabilities of the market economies of Southeast Asia require access to capital from international financial institutions like the World Bank and the ADB and foreign direct investment. It is the latter that has played the critical role in the industrial development propelling GDP growth rates. ASEAN's concern that China is sucking up FDI from ASEAN has already been noted. One estimate is that up to 70 percent of new investment in East Asia—excluding Japan—is going to China and only 20 percent to ASEAN.[32] Table 7.5 shows the top ten sources of ASEAN FDI inflow and table 7.6 the percentages of the total flow. The data does not support a conclusion that ASEAN is losing a zero-sum game of attracting FDI. The continued attractiveness of the ASEAN region for FDI is shown in the 2007 A.T. Kearney FDI Confidence Index. This is an annual (since 1998) composite global survey result based on political, economic, and regulatory environments and the investment preferences of major companies in seventeen sectors.[33] China and

TABLE 7.5
Top Ten Sources of ASEAN FDI Inflows 2004–2006 (Value in U.S. $ Millions)

Countries	2004	2005	2006	2004–2006
EU-25	10,046.1	11,139,6	13,361.9	44,955.6
Japan	5,732.1	7,235.8	10,803.3	30,813.7
Intra-ASEAN	2,803.7	3,765.1	6,242.1	19,377.7
USA	5,234.4	3,010.6	3,864.9	13,736.1
Other Latin America*	(60.5)	919.4	1,035.1	3,958.3
Hong Kong	529.6	773.0	1,353.4	3,430.7
South Korea	806.4	5,77.7	1,099.1	3,347.3
Cayman Island	2,029.1	(19.9)	476.4	3,003.7
Taiwan	366.8	(66.8)	668.1	2,417.4
China	731.5	502.1	936.9	2,302.9
Total top ten sources	28,217.1	27,835.4	39,841.2	127,343.3
Others	6,900.1	13,232.4	12,538.3	43,478.5
Total	35,117.2	41,067.8	52,379.5	170,821.0

* Excludes Argentina, Brazil, Mexico, and Panama.
Source: ASEAN Foreign Investment Statistics as of 13 August 2007, table 27.

TABLE 7.6
Top Ten Sources of ASEAN FDI Percentage of Total ASEAN Inflow 2004–2006

Countries	2004	2005	2006	2004–2006
EU-25	28.6	27.1	25.5	26.3
Japan	16.3	17.6	20.6	18.0
Intra-ASEAN	8.0	9.2	11.9	11.3
USA	14.9	7.3	7.4	8.0
Other Latin America*	(0.2)	2.2	2.0	2.3
Hong Kong	1.5	1.9	2.6	2.0
South Korea	2.3	1.4	2.1	2.0
Cayman Island	5.8	0.0	0.9	1.8
Taiwan	1.0	(0.2)	1.3	1.4
China	2.1	1.2	1.8	1.4
Total top ten	80.4	67.8	76.1	74.5
Others	19.6	32.2	23.9	25.5
Total	100.0	100.0	100.0	100.0

* Excludes Argentina, Brazil, Mexico, and Panama.
Source: ASEAN Foreign Investment Statistics as of 13 August 2007, table 27.

India ranked 1 and 2 (China for the fifth year in a row). The other Asian states in rank order were Singapore (7), Vietnam (12), Malaysia (16), Japan (19), Indonesia (21), and South Korea (24). Thailand, previously ranked in the top 25, was dropped because of the poor performance of the junta. Vietnam has been spectacularly successful in attracting new investment. FDI pledges in 2007 were valued at more than $2 billion, a 70 percent increase over 2006, and 1,500 new projects were licensed. The clouds in the investment climate in much of Southeast Asia are domestic political turmoil, shortages of skilled labor, infrastructure inadequacies, uncertain legal frameworks, and corruption.

If ASEAN FDI data is disaggregated on a country basis, the same pattern appears as in the trade data. Table 7.7 shows the 2006 FDI inflow, both intra-ASEAN and extra-ASEAN, to each ASEAN country and its percentage of the total flow. Singapore, Thailand, and Malaysia attracted nearly 80 percent of all FDI in the region. Singapore alone accounted for just short of 46 percent of regional FDI inflow. Singapore's position as the dynamic center of the region's engagement in the international economy has not endeared it to economic nationalists in other ASEAN states, particularly Malaysia and Indonesia. The investments of its sovereign wealth fund Temasek in politically sensitive Indonesian and Thai IT and telecommunication sectors has become a new irritant in the long list of neighbors' complaints about the economic and financial policies of the island republic. Indonesia also accuses Singapore of sheltering corrupt Indonesians who had moved their money to Singapore. It is reported that one-third—eighteen thousand—of individuals in Singapore with a net worth of more than U.S. $1 million are of Indonesian origin. Their

TABLE 7.7
FDI Inflow Intra- and Extra-ASEAN by Country 2006 (Value in U.S. $ Millions)

Country	Intra-ASEAN	Extra-ASEAN	Total	% of ASEAN Total
Brunei	9.7	423.5	433.5	0.1
Cambodia	155.5	327.7	483.4	0.1
Indonesia	1,524.5	4,031.7	5,556.2	10.6
Lao PDR	10.6	176.8	187.4	0.03
Malaysia	467.8	5,591.9	6,059.7	11.5
Myanmar	27.8	115.2	143.0	0.03
Philippines	(95.6)	2,440.6	2,345.0	4.4
Singapore	1,137.7	22,917.7	24,055.4	45.9
Thailand	2,822.1	7,933.9	10,756.1	20.5
Vietnam	181.9	2,178.1	2,360.0	4.5
ASEAN	6,242.1	46,137.4	52,379.7	100.0
ASEAN 5	5,856.6	42,915.8	48,772.4	93.1
BCLMV	385.5	3,221.6	3,607.1	6.9

Source: ASEAN foreign investment statistics as of 13 August 2007, table 25.

total assets have been estimated at U.S. $87 billion.[34] In 2007, Indonesia linked both a defense cooperation agreement with Singapore and sand exports for Singapore's construction industry to the completion of an extradition treaty. It is not clear how Singapore's desire to be the Switzerland of Southeast Asia will fit within the framework of an ASEAN Economic Community.

Economic Regionalism beyond AFTA

Through AFTA and its corollary AFAS and AIA services and investment liberalization programs, the ASEAN nations have sought to expand economic growth through deeper intra-ASEAN integration. Similar patterns of cooperation and structures for integration have been pursued by ASEAN countries with their major extraregional economic partners. Since recovery from the Crash of '97, there has been a rush for bilateral and regional free trade agreements (RTA). This has been led by ASEAN's economic winners Singapore, Malaysia, and Thailand as they seek even greater market access to the wider East Asian and global economy. They have been prompted by uncertainties in the global trade and investment climate. The promise of liberalization of trade through the processes of the WTO has faded. The Doha round of WTO negotiations that began in 2001 has sunk in the quagmire of agriculture and global North–South recriminations. At the same time that global negotiations for trade liberalization have broken down, ASEAN sees the politics of protectionism in Europe and North America as a threat to trade expansion. To secure their economic futures, the ASEAN nations have moved forward on national and regional trade agendas. Outside of AFTA, the member countries are free to manage their own national trade relations and through ASEAN they can engage collectively. The bargains they reach collectively do not exclude better bargains reached bilaterally.

The proliferation of FTAs and RTAs has provoked debate about their economic costs and benefits. On one side, it is warned that the trade-diverting results of and overlapping rules in a patchwork pattern of competitive FTAs and RTAs will make liberalization in the global framework of the WTO or the Pacific region framework of APEC harder to achieve in the future.[35] Alternatively, it has been argued that the growing networks of FTAs and RTAs are necessary building blocks—not needing consensus among 151 nations—to global trade liberalization. The spread of FTAs, with their built-in trade preferences, will provide incentives for the hesitant to catch up. The term "competitive liberalization" was coined to describe this process.[36]

ASEAN's "Noodle Bowl" of FTAs

Since 2002, ASEAN states have signed or are negotiating six regional trade agreements. In the same period ASEAN states have entered into or are negotiating more than sixty bilateral or other multilateral free trade arrangements. Singapore has set the pace, followed by Thailand and Malaysia. By 2008, Singapore had signed thirteen bilateral or multilateral FTAs, with another ten under negotiation. The FTAs have different scopes and depths. The most comprehensive—and the most difficult to negotiate—cover goods trade, services, investment, government procurement, intellectual property rights, and other nontrade items. These are sometimes called "WTO plus" agreements. Table 7.8 lists the important intra-Asian or major partner free trade initiatives.[37] Just a glance at the table shows the lack of participation below the ASEAN RTAs of the CLMV countries. This has led to the warnings that the weaker economies will be marginalized and disadvantaged as the "winners" win more. This also has implications for ASEAN solidarity. Southeast Asia is also a good example of the "spaghetti bowl" effect, translated to Asia as "noodle bowl," of multiple free trade arrangements. The term describes the lack of uniformity in the differing complex rules of trade from one FTA to another, making trade more expensive for business and in the end costing more for the consumer.[38]

If, as economists argue, the opening of the floodgate of FTAs will in fact negatively impact global liberalization of trade and even ASEAN economic integration, why do the political leaders pursue it? In part, because even if the hodgepodge of bilateral and regional FTAs is second best when compared to a WTO framework, it is politically attainable in the lifetime of a government.[39] More di-

TABLE 7.8
ASEAN's Noodle Bowl of FTAs

Signed	Negotiating	Proposed
ASEAN–China	ASEAN–Australia/NZ CER	
ASEAN–Japan	ASEAN–European Union	
ASEAN–South Korea	ASEAN–India	
Brunei–Japan	Malaysia–Australia	Brunei–Pakistan
	Malaysia–New Zealand	Brunei–United States
Indonesia–Japan	Malaysia–United States	
		Indonesia–Australia
Malaysia–Japan	Singapore–China	Indonesia–India
Malaysia–Pakistan	Singapore–Pakistan	Indonesia–New Zealand
		Indonesia–United States
Philippines–Japan	Thailand–India	
	Thailand–South Korea	Malaysia–India
Singapore–Australia	Thailand–United States	Malaysia–South Korea
Singapore–India		
Singapore–Japan	Vietnam–Japan	Philippines–Pakistan
Singapore–New Zealand		Philippines–United States
Singapore–South Korea		
Singapore–United States		Thailand–Pakistan
		Thailand–South Korea
Thailand–Australia		
Thailand–China		
Thailand–India		
Thailand–Japan		
Thailand–New Zealand		

rectly to the political point, there is fear of being left out of the scramble. Prime Minister Thaksin put it bluntly when defending the proposed Thailand–United States FTA. Fearing the competition from Singapore and Malaysia for U.S. markets, he argued "as other countries pursue their own deals . . . we need to move now, before we have no more room to move."[40]

China

The blossoming of ASEAN–China trade depicted in table 7.2 can be linked to the staged implementation of ASEAN's first RTA, which, when completed in 2015, would make the ASEAN–China Free Trade Area (ACFTA) the world's largest in size of population included, with a market of more than 1.7 billion potential consumers. Pushed hard by China, which wanted to open Southeast Asian markets to competitive Chinese agricultural products and manufactures, ASEAN agreed in 2002 to an ASEAN–China Comprehensive Economic Cooperation Framework Agreement, which led first in 2004 to an agreement on trade in goods. The trade deal, effective July 2005, provided for an "early harvest" group of items for immediate tariff reductions and "normal" and "sensitive" tracks for liberalization of trade to zero tariffs for the ASEAN 6 in 2010 and the CLMV countries in 2015. By 2015 more than seven thousand trade items will be at a zero tariff.

The trade strategy was front-loaded with the products that would generate the quickest benefits. For China, this meant flooding Southeast Asian markets with goods from Chinese agricultural and manufacturing sectors that were more competitive than Southeast Asia's. This was particularly true in Myanmar, Laos, Cambodia, and Thailand's northern provinces, which have been inundated with Chinese goods in a kind of legal dumping. Trade became part of the wider Chinese strategy of integrating continental Southeast Asian markets and resources into the development of its southwest Yunnan province. As China and the ASEAN 6 closed in on the 2010 target date for full implantation of the scheme, protectionist urges kicked in and the detailed negotiations went very slowly. The Chinese have called for a "more pragmatic approach" in dealing with the final stages.[41]

The original RTA framework agreement was comprehensive in scope. In addition to the 2004 merchandise agreement, ASEAN and China have agreed to liberalize trade in services and investments. A services agreement went into effect in June 2007 with a package of commitments. Two more rounds of service commitments have to be wrapped up by 2010. Differential treatment and flexibility were offered to the CLMV countries. The goal of achieving an investment agreement by 2010 has been more elusive.

Japan

Japan negotiated its first ever bilateral FTA, called an economic partnership agreement (EPA), with Singapore, which went into effect in 2002. It eliminated tariffs on 98 percent of trade between the two countries. Since then, Japan has negotiated five other EPAs with ASEAN countries: Malaysia (2006), the Philippines (2006), Brunei (2007), Indonesia (2007), and Thailand (2007). It held its first formal negotiation for an EPA with Vietnam in January 2007. Japan's free trade strategy as ASEAN's single largest export market was to build a network of bilateral FTAs in which the economic asymmetry between Japan and an ASEAN country would be a negotiating plus. Rather than a "stringing together" of bilateral pacts, as the ASEAN secretary-general put it, ASEAN wanted a region-wide agreement with Japan.

The signing of ACFTA moved Japan to begin negotiations for an ASEAN RTA. A framework agreement for a regional comprehensive economic partnership was established in 2003. Negotiations for a comprehensive EPA began in 2005. It was originally expected that the agreement would be concluded in 2009, but the 2007 ASEAN–South Korea agreement (discussed below) speeded the process up. The basic agreement was reached by November 2007, and on 14 April 2008 the last ASEAN state signed off on it. The Japan–ASEAN EPA is ASEAN's first comprehensive free trade agreement covering not only merchandise trade but also the services and investment sectors, which have been negotiated separately in the other RTAs in place. Under the pact, Japan will remove tariffs on 90 percent of imports from ASEAN. As in its bilateral FTAs Japan continues to protect its agricultural sector including rice, beef, and dairy products. The ASEAN 6 will phase out tariffs on 90 percent of their imports from Japan, including consumer electronics and autos, over ten years. The CLMV countries have been given fifteen to eighteen years to comply fully.

South Korea

South Korea used its 2005 bilateral FTA with Singapore as a bridge to Southeast Asia. It crossed that bridge with the ASEAN–Republic of Korea Free Trade Agreement covering goods, which was signed in May 2006 and went into effect in July 2006. The timetable for implementation is 2009 for the ASEAN 6 and 2016 for the CLMV countries. An agreement on trade in services was signed in November 2007, and an investment agreement is expected in 2008. The agreement on goods was an ASEAN minus one pact because Thailand refused to sign. The Thais protested South Korea's exclusion of Thai agricultural products, particularly rice, from the FTA cuts. Bilateral talks between Bangkok and Seoul resulted in an April 2008 compromise that permits Thailand to have a slower schedule in reducing tariffs on imports from Korea of certain sensitive products. The ASEAN target is 2010–2012 and the Thais will have until 2016–2018. South Korea's proposed bilateral FTAs with Malaysia and Thailand have had little traction.

Australia and New Zealand

The first bilateral FTA in the Southeast Asian region was between Singapore and New Zealand in 2000. Australia's comprehensive WTO plus FTA with Singapore went into force in 2003. An Australian–Thailand FTA in 2005 opened protected Thailand markets for Australian agricultural, dairy, and meat products markets and was strongly opposed by Thai domestic interests. There was a Thai constitutional challenge to the FTA that failed. Since 2005, both New Zealand and Australia have been negotiating comprehensive FTAs with Malaysia, but Kuala Lumpur resists the inclusion of WTO plus features.

Since 1983, Australia and New Zealand have traded within their own bilateral free trade area in the Australia–New Zealand closer economic relations (CER) agreement. In the context of the CER, Australia and New Zealand are treated as a unit in the negotiations for an ASEAN–CER FTA. Its roots were in earlier discussion about possible links between AFTA and the CER. Negotiations began in 2005 for a comprehensive FTA and, through March 2008, thirteen negotiating sessions had been held. It was hoped by the CER side that the agreement could be concluded by the end of 2008. Progress was slow in issues of market access, rules of origin, and intellectual property rights. The New Zealand trade minister comparing the CER negotiation with ASEAN's China, Japan, and South Korean agreements stated that the latter had "generally been at a lower level of ambition."[42]

India

India hopes to position itself as a fourth major power actor in Southeast Asia and put itself on the same regional footing as China. This includes an Indian RTA with ASEAN. The framework agreement was reached in 2003. At the 2005 ASEAN–India Summit, the ASEAN side noted that the negotiations had not moved forward as expeditiously as hoped. A proposed implementation date was moved forward from January 2006 to January 2007. The major difficulty has been Indian restrictions on major agricultural exports from ASEAN to India. The crucial item has been palm oil, which is Malaysia's and Indonesia's largest export item to India. In July 2006, ASEAN suspended negotiations with India. An Indian special envoy was sent to ASEAN to revive the talks. ASEAN agreed, but with the proviso that India had to make more concessions. The bargaining gaps narrowed through negotiations in 2007 as India brought its exclusion list down from 1,400 items to 489, close enough to ASEAN's target of 400.

In the proposed FTA, 80 percent of the two sides' tariff lines would be gradually reduced to zero by July 2018. Fifteen percent of the tariff lines would be on a sensitive list with tariffs at 0–5 percent. A maximum of 5 percent could be excluded. By November 2007, it was hoped that the agreement could be signed in April 2008, but the palm oil issue still was a sticking point. India would not accept Indonesia's terms for a compromise formula that would decrease Indian market access to Indonesia to make up for continued high tariffs on palm oil. The lengthy and tough negotiations for an ASEAN–India RTA stand in sharp contrast to ACFTA. India's political and economic weight does not tip the balance in Southeast Asia the way China's does. Also, ASEAN has been on a learning curve in its RTA negotiations as it seeks to harmonize the differing interests of its members in tiered implementation formulas and in evaluating the costs and benefits of concessions.

European Union

The EU and ASEAN agreed to begin negotiations for a comprehensive trade pact in May 2007, following a feasibility study showing benefits for both sides. From the EU side, an ASEAN trade agreement was an acknowledgment of the breakdown of the Doha round of WTO negotiations and the growing number of FTAs in Southeast Asia by EU global economic competitors. ASEAN was anxious to strike a deal in advance of EU–China and EU–India trade agreements. The goal was ambitious in its wide-ranging scope and depth. It was soon clear, however, that the harmonizing of interests of ten ASEAN countries and twenty-five EU countries was more difficult than in earlier ASEAN RTAs. A major stumbling block was the unwillingness of some EU states to include Myanmar. By the fourth round of negotiations in April 2008, the ASEAN position on topics such as intellectual property, rules of origin, services, and investment had become conservative, with only Singapore pushing for greater liberalization and other ASEAN countries more defensive. Rather than have the talks collapse, the focus turned to a smaller group of ASEAN countries with the possibility of a future ASEAN minus X–EU trade agreement.

The United States

The Singapore–United States FTA, which went into force in January 2004, was a leading-edge agreement, which became the model for U.S. trade negotiation strategy in the Southeast Asian region. It is a WTO plus deal that expanded market access in goods, services, investment, government procurement, and intellectual property. It was groundbreaking in its environmental protections and guarantees of labor rights. The U.S.–Singapore FTA's scope and depth is more comprehensive than any other FTA signed or proposed by ASEAN or its members. Negotiations for a Thailand–U.S. FTA began in 2004, but were put on hold as a consequence of the 2006 Thai coup that drove Prime Minister Thaksin Shinawatra from office. Thaksin had been an ardent free-trader. The new civilian Thai government said in early 2008 that it was prepared to resume talks but the negotiations would have to start again from scratch. The United States launched FTA negotiations with Malaysia in March 2006. Both sides seemed reasonably confident that a deal could be reached by the end of the year, but that was not to be. Transparent and reciprocal access to government contracts and affirmative action policies of preference for ethnic Malays were sticking points. In January 2008, after a year's delay, a new round of talks encouraged the U.S. chief negotiator, but the Malaysian side was in no rush to resolve the outstanding issues.

As a first fruit of the ASEAN–United States Enhanced Partnership, an "ASEAN–U.S. Trade and Investment Framework Agreement" (TIFA) was signed in August 2006. A TIFA is a necessary initial step toward an FTA. The United States has bilateral TIFAs with every ASEAN state except Myanmar and the Lao PDR. Whether the ASEAN TIFA will lead to a U.S.–ASEAN RTA is problematic. The United States would want included in such an agreement the leading-edge WTO plus provisions of the Singapore FTA model. Washington's insistence has already slowed progress toward the Thai and Malaysian FTAs and would certainly encounter resistance from ASEAN's less advantaged members. Also, the fast-track trade promotion authority (TPA) under which the George W. Bush administration pressed its trade agenda expired in June 2007 and was not renewed by Congress. With the TPA, the president could bring a trade agreement to Congress, which had to vote it up or down within ninety days and without amendment. This gave U.S. negotiating partners confidence that the agreements they made would not be subject to future renegotiation because of congressional intervention. The lack of TPA and congressional protectionist sentiments put even the Thai and Malaysian FTAs under negotiation in jeopardy.

Singapore, Malaysia, and Thailand have signed or are negotiating bilateral trade agreements in Latin America and the Middle East. In addition there are other multilateral FTA frameworks engaging ASEAN countries. Brunei and Singapore are joined with New Zealand and Chile in the Trans-Pacific Strategic Economic Partnership (TP-SEP), better known as the P4. Implemented in 2006, it built on the existing Singapore–New Zealand bilateral agreement. The P4 provides for a three-step phasing out of tariffs by 2015. The United States expressed interest in 2008 in associating itself with the P4 service and investment agreements. In chapter 4, it was noted that Myanmar and Thailand are part of the Bay of Bengal Initiative for Multi-Sectoral Technical and Economic Cooperation (BIMSTEC) grouping with six South Asian states—not including Pakistan. A framework agreement for a BIMSTEC FTA was concluded in 2006 with a proposed 2017 date for full implementation. Indonesia and Malaysia participate in the Preferential Tariff Agreement of the Eight Developing Countries (D-8) grouping that was formed in 1997. The other D-8 members are Bangladesh, Egypt, Iran, Nigeria, Pakistan, and Turkey. Malaysia is also participating in the negotiations for an OIC PTA.

Economic Regionalism beyond ASEAN

The international economic policies of the ASEAN countries have been directed to maximize trade and FDI opportunities. The market-driven expansion of trade and FDI has led to greater intra-ASEAN economic integration—but not a common market—and greater integration of the ASEAN economies with others in East Asia. This has been accomplished through negotiating structures below the global framework of the WTO or the wider trans-Pacific regionalism of APEC. It has been a product of AFTA, bilateral FTAs, and the all-ASEAN FTAs with major trading partners. This has left, however, the inefficiencies of the "noodle bowl" effect that prevent the full realization of market potentialities. There remain competing tariffs, rules of trade and FDI, and regulatory hurdles distorting free cross-border transactions. The all-things-being-equal economic answer seems simple: disentangle the noodles by consolidating the multiple overlapping arrangements into a single uniform regional arrangement. However, it will not be economists doing the disentangling, it will be politicians. There will have to be a demonstrable coincidence of econometric modeling and political appreciations of national interest. The first question is where to start?

An obvious possible starting point would be the ASEAN + 3 grouping, which, as previous chapters have noted, now encompasses nearly every area of functional cooperation. In 2003, the ASEAN + 3 Summit endorsed the proposal of the East Asian Study Group for a future East Asia Free Trade Area (EAFTA) (chapter 4). Such an FTA would solidify Chinese dominance in the ASEAN + 3 processes. In 2005, a joint expert group spearheaded by China launched a feasibility study of an EAFTA. The expert group reported back in August 2006, claiming that the benefits of an EAFTA would exceed those of AFTA, the ASEAN RTAs, or any other bilateral or subregional arrangements.[43] It would make East Asia more competitive internationally. The experts called for comprehensive WTO plus trade, services, and investment agreements, taking as reference points the existing FTAs. They set out a possible schedule that would have negotiations begin in 2009, be completed in 2011, and an agreement implemented in 2016 (CLMV countries, 2020). They left open the possibility to extend the EAFTA at the "appropriate time" to other countries with which ASEAN was negotiating RTAs. The report was taken under advisement, and in 2007 a second-phase sector-by-sector study led by South Korea got underway.

The expert group reference to an "appropriate time" for expansion of an EAFTA was a response to Japanese pressure for a Comprehensive Economic Partnership in East Asia (CEPEA), an FTA that would include all of the participants in the East Asia Summit group: ASEAN, China, Japan, South Korea, Australia, New Zealand, and India. This is referred to as the ASEAN + 6. Japan's initiative is widely viewed as an attempt to dilute China's influence in Southeast Asia. In welcoming the expert group EAFTA report at the January 2007 ASEAN + 3 Summit, the chairman's statement added, "We should continue to examine other possible FTA configurations such as the East Asia Summit."[44] The immediately following East Asia Summit launched a feasibility study of a CEPEA. Econometric modeling shows that an ASEAN + 6 FTA would yield the largest gains to East Asia with losses to nonmembers through trade diversion relatively small. The ASEAN + 3 FTA is less beneficial but provides larger gains than any of the FTAs between ASEAN and individual countries outside the bloc.[45] In either case, enormous negotiating difficulties can be expected given the diversities in levels of development and uneven distribution of costs and benefits once the aggregate gains are broken down by country. There is also the deep political gulf between Japan and China and Japan and Korea that would have to be overcome. Until Japan is able to resolve the large number of sensitive issues with Korea and China, it is difficult to imagine them agreeing on either proposed multilateral FTA.[46]

There is also the question of what impact an EAFTA would have for the ASEAN states on their extraregional trade relations. The ASEAN 6 would not want preferential arrangements in a closed regional framework to jeopardize their access to Europe or the United States. The United States strongly opposes an EAFTA based on closed regionalism rather than the open regionalism of APEC, decrying again the idea of drawing an economic line down the middle of the Pacific. The United States advocates instead a Free Trade Area of the Asia Pacific (FTAAP). Discussed since 2004 in the Track II APEC Business Advisory Council (ABAC) and the Pacific Economic Cooperation Council (PECC), the FTAAP became a part of the APEC agenda when it was urged by President Bush at the 2006 Hanoi APEC leaders' meeting. The "Hanoi Declaration" recognized the difficulties of negotiating such an instrument, but instructed APEC officials to begin feasibility study of an FTAAP as a long-term proposition.[47] In 2007, at their Sydney, Australia, meeting, the APEC leaders declared that "through a range of practical and incremental steps, we will examine the options and prospects for a Free Trade Are of the Asia Pacific." Proponents of the FTAAP see it as both defensive and offensive: defensive in terms of the ASEAN + 3 and ASEAN + 6 and offensive in terms of forcing the pace of global liberalization.[48]

Even as the multiple studies of a next possible level of agreements for a higher stage of East Asian or East Asia and Pacific economic integration are going on, the ASEAN states will continue the implementation of their present agreements and the ongoing negotiations for future agreements. Realistically, the noodle bowl is going to become more tangled, at least until the AEC is in place and the current ASEAN plus one FTAs are fully implemented. In working beyond the current ASEAN-centered frameworks for a higher state of integration at some later date, the ASEAN states will have to consider the costs to ASEAN solidarity and identity if AFTA disintegrates as the member states are absorbed into a wider integrative framework. It is difficult to see how ASEAN could remain a driver of such a process without a central authority to speak for the collective group and conduct negotiations. This would require a degree of political integration and institutionalization that is not promised in the new ASEAN charter. Whatever political cement for ASEAN was produced by the building of AFTA could be less binding in the building of an EAFTA or, even more so, in an FTAAP.

Notes

1. Walden Bello, "China and Southeast Asia: Emerging Problems in an Economic Relationship," Focus on the Global South, 26 December 2006, accessed at www .focusweb.org/china-and-southeast-asia-emerging-problems-in-an-economic-relationship.html.

2. United Nations, *Economic Cooperation among Member Countries of the Association of Southeast Asian Nations*, Report of a United Nations Team, *Journal of Development Planning* 7, (1974).

3. For ASEAN's early industrialization strategies, see Majorie L. Suriyamongkol, *Politics of ASEAN Economic Cooperation* (Singapore: Oxford University Press, 1988).

4. Hamzah Sendut, as quoted in the *Indonesia Times*, 8 August 1986.

5. ASEAN CCI, *Review of ASEAN Development* (Hong Kong: ASEAN CCI, November 1981).

6. The 66-page *Report of the ASEAN Task Force to the ASEAN Ministerial Meeting* was never released as an official ASEAN document. Copies were available through ASEAN national secretariats. There was a press release on the *Recommendations of the ASEAN Task Force in the Seventeenth ASEAN Ministerial Meeting*, Jakarta, 9–10 July 1984. No record of the ASEAN Task Force exists on the official ASEAN website.

7. Susumu Awanohara, "Much Ado about Nothing," *Far Eastern Economic Review*, 24 May 1986: 66.

8. The details of the PTA can be accessed at www.aseansec.org/1376.htm.

9. The data is drawn from Ooi Guat Tin, "ASEAN Preferential Trading Arrangements: An Assessment," and Gerald Tan, "ASEAN Preferential Trading Arrangements: An Overview," both in Noordin Sopiee, Chew Lay See, and Lim Siang Jin, eds., *ASEAN at the Crossroads* (Kuala Lumpur: Institute of Strategic and International Studies, 1989).

10. Corazon Aquino, "Time Is Well Past for Talking," text of speech as given in *The Diplomatic Post* [Manila], July–September 1986: 8.

11. The study papers are compiled in Noordin Sopie, et al., *ASEAN at the Cross Roads* (Kuala Lumpur: Institute of Strategic and International Studies, 1989).

12. ASEAN CCI, *The Way Forward: Report of the Group of Fourteen on ASEAN Economic Cooperation and Integration* (Kuala Lumpur: Institute of Strategic and International Studies, 1987).

13. Tommy Koh, "What Makes the 4th ASEAN Summit Historic," *Straits Times Weekly Overseas Edition*, 25 January 1992.

14. The "Framework Agreement" can be accessed at www.aseansec.org/5125.htm.

15. The "CEPT Agreement" can be accessed at www.aseansec.org/1164.htm.

16. The tariff statistics are as given in the report of the 2006 AFTA Ministerial Council meeting, accessed at www.aseansec.org/20863.htm.

17. The AFAS framework agreement can be accessed at www.aseansec.org/6628.htm.

18. The AIA agreement can be accessed at www.aseansec.org/6466.htm.

19. The AICO agreement can be accessed at www.aseansec.org/1948.htm.

20. APEC is headquartered in Singapore. Its website can be accessed at www.apec.org.

21. On the origins of the EAEG and Mahathir's intentions, see Linda Low, "The East Asia Economic Grouping," *The Pacific Review* 4, no. 4 (1991): 375–82.

22. As quoted by Shim Jae Hoon and Robert Delf, "Bloc politics: APEC Meeting Clouded by Fears of Regionalism," *Far Eastern Economic Review*, 18 November 1991: 26.

23. As quoted in "ASEAN-plus-3 should be called E. Asia Economic Group," *Asian Economic News*, 11 April 2003.

24. The IMF program is outlined in the "Recovery from the Asian Crisis and the Role of the IMF," *IMF Issue Brief*, June 2000, accessed at www.imf.org/external/np/exr/ib/2000/062300.htm.

25. Jürgen Rüland, "ASEAN and the Asian Crisis," in Sharon Siddique and Sree Kumar, eds., *The 2nd ASEAN Reader* (Singapore: Institute of Southeast Asian Studies 2003), 244–45.

26. The ASEAN + 3 first joint statement can be accessed at www.aseansec.org/5469.htm.

27. "Joint Ministerial Statement of the ASEAN + 3 Finance Ministers Meeting," 6 May 2000, accessed at www.aseansec.org/6312.htm.

28. "Joint Ministerial Statement of the 10th ASEAN + 3 Financial Ministers' Meeting," 5 May 2007, accessed at www.mof.go.jp/english/if/as3_070505.htm.

29. The fourteen countries represented were Australia, Brunei, Canada, China, Hong Kong, Indonesia, Japan, South Korea, Malaysia, New Zealand, the Philippines, Singapore, Thailand, and the United States. In addition to the IMF, representatives of the World Bank and the Asian Development Bank participated. The statement of the new framework can be accessed at www.mof.go.jp/english/if/if000a.htm.

30. The "Terms of Understanding on the Establishment of the ASEAN Surveillance Process" can be accessed at www.aseansec.org/739.htm.

31. "Thai Finance Minister Says Capital Controls Were Bid to Save the Country," *Star Online* [Penang], 24 December 2006.

32. Chan Heng Chee [Singapore ambassador to the United States], "China and ASEAN: A Growing Relationship," presentation to the Asia Society Annual Ambassadors Forum and Corporate Conference, Houston, Texas, 3 February 2006, accessed at app.mfa.gov.sg/pr/read_content.asp?View,4416,.

33. Global Business Policy Council, "New Concerns in an Uncertain World: The 2007 A.T. Kearney Foreign Direct Investment Confidence Index," December 2007, accessed at www.atkearney.com/main.taf?p=5,1,1,120,10.

34. Merrill Lynch and Capgemni, *2006 Asia-Pacific Wealth Report*, as reported by Reuters, 10 October 2006.

35. Bernard K. Gordon, "Asia's Trade Blocs Imperil the WTO," *Far Eastern Economic Review* 168, no. 10 (2005): 5–10.

36. C. Fred Bergsten, "Competitive Liberalization and Global Free Trade: A Vision of the Early 21st Century," Peterson Institute of International Economics, Working Paper 96-15, 1996, accessed at www.iie.com/publications/wp/wp.cfm?ResearchID=171.

37. There are two major Internet sources to track free trade arrangements in the Asia-Pacific region by grouping and by country. The first is the ADB's Asia Regional Integration Center at aric.adb.org/FTAbyCountryALL.php. The second is at www.bilaterals.org, which bills itself as "everything that's not happening at the WTO."

38. The now popular description of the growing number of FTAs as a "spaghetti bowl" was first used by Jagdish Bhagwati, "U.S. Trade Policy: The Infatuation with Free Trade Areas," in Jagdish Bhagwati and Anne O. Krueger, eds., *The Dangerous Drift to Preferential Trade Agreements* (Washington, D.C.: AEI, 1995), 1–18.

39. This is the argument made by Barry Desker, "In Defence of FTAs: From Purity to Pragmatism in East Asia," *The Pacific Review* 17, no. 1 (2004): 3–26.

40. As quoted in Tony Allison, "Thailand, US Inch Ahead on Trade Accord," *Asia Times*, 14 January 2006.

41. Vice-Premier Zeng Peiyan as quoted in "China, ASEAN on Crucial Stage in FTA Talks," *China Daily*, 1 November 2007.

42. New Zealand Trade Minister Phil Goff, as quoted in *China View*, at www.chinaview.net, 23 April 2008.

43. Y. Zhang et al., *Towards an East Asia FTA: Modality and Road Map. A Report by the Joint Expert Group for a Feasibility Study on EAFTA* (Jakarta: ASEAN Secretariat, 2006).

44. "Chairman's Statement of the Tenth ASEAN Plus Three Summit," Cebu, Philippines, 14 January 2007, accessed at www.aseansec.org/19315.htm.

45. Masahiro Kawai and Ganeshan Wignaraja, "Regionalism as an Engine of Multilateralism: A Case for a Single East Asian FTA," Manila: ADB Working Paper on Regional Economic Integration, no. 14, 2007. The results were also reported by Kawai and Wignaraja in "A Broad Asian FTA Will Bring Big Gains," *Far Eastern Economic Review* 171, no. 3 (2008): 46–48.

46. Markus Hund, "ASEAN Plus Three: Towards a New Age of Pan-East Asian Regionalism? A Skeptic's Appraisal," *The Pacific Review* 16, no. 3 (2003): 383–417.

47. The declarations of APEC leaders' meetings can be accessed at www. apec.org.

48. C. Fred Bergsten, "Toward a Free Trade Area of the Asia Pacific," Peterson Institute for International Economics, Policy Paper 07-2, 2007, accessed at www.iie.com/publications/interstitial.cfm?ResearchID=710.

Suggestions for Further Reading

The ASEAN Secretariat has an online overview of the ASEAN Free Trade Area titled *Southeast Asia: A Free Trade Area* (www.aseansec.org/pdf/afta.pdf). ASEAN trade and investment statistics as well as other statistics can be accessed

through the statistics link on the ASEAN Secretariats' website (www.aseansec
.org). The U.S.–ASEAN Business Council has on its website a brief overview titled "The ASEAN Free Trade Area and other Areas of ASEAN Economic Cooperation" (www.us-asean.org). For ASEAN's economic evolution see, Simon
S. C. Tay, Jesus P. Estanislao, and Hadi Soesastro, *Reinventing ASEAN* (Singa-
pore: Institute of Southeast Asian Studies, 2001); Sharon Siddique and Sree
Kumar, eds., *The 2nd ASEAN Reader* (Singapore: Institute of Southeast Asian
Studies 2002); Denis Hew Wei-Yen, ed., *Brick by Brick: The Building of an
ASEAN Economic Community* (Singapore: Institute of Southeast Asian Studies,
2007); Helen Nessadura, *Globalization, Domestic Politics, and Regionalism: The
ASEAN Free Trade Area* (London and New York: Routledge, 2003); Swee Hock
Saw, *China–ASEAN Economic Relations* (Singapore: Institute of Southeast
Asian Studies, 2006); Markus Hund, *ASEAN and ASEAN + 3: Manifestation of
Collective Identities in Southeast and East Asia* (Munster, Germany: VDM Ver-
lagshaus Monsenstein und Vannerdat, 2007). Stephen Haggard, *The Political
Economy of the Asian Financial Crisis* (Washington, D.C.: Institute of Interna-
tional Economics, 2000) and T. J. Pempel, *The Politics of the Asian Economic
Crisis* (Ithaca, N.Y.: Cornell University Press) are both good studies of the
Crash of '97. For ASEAN in the context of wider regionalism, consult John
Ravenhill, *APEC and the Construction of Pacific Rim Regionalism* (Cambridge,
U.K.: Cambridge University Press, 2001); Edward J. Lincoln, *East Asian Eco-
nomic Regionalism* (Washington, D.C.: Brookings Institution, 2004); Christo-
pher Dent, *East Asia Regionalism* (London: Routledge, 2008).

8

Human Security in Southeast Asian International Relations

THE INTRODUCTION OF THE CONCEPT OF HUMAN SECURITY as a policy category reflects a paradigm shift from the state to the individual. Human security is a condition in which individuals are safe in their economic and societal circumstances in a setting of equality and justice. The discussion of how human security fits into international relations often is so diffuse that it leads critics to pass it off as a feel-good semantic catch-all. It is more accurate to view it as a topical umbrella under which a variety of policies and programs, domestic and international, addressing specific issue areas affecting an individual's welfare and status, can be systematically interrelated in a holistic way. The emergence of human security as an object of international attention can be traced back to the 1994 United Nations Development Program's report on *New Dimensions of Human Security*.[1] The twin goals were epitomized as *freedom from want* and *freedom from fear*. As the dialogue about human security developed, two major emphases gained currency. Freedom from want was conceived of in terms of a broad human needs-based approach. Freedom from fear became more narrowly focused on defense of human rights in the state.

Human Needs and Human Security

For the 1994 UNDP report, the primary threats to human security were economic and social: poverty, disease, employment, displacement, education, environment, gender inequality, and so on. This also characterized the 2003 major follow-up study by the UN secretary-general's Commission on Human Security titled *Human Security Now: Protecting and Empowering People*, which, with its broad prescriptions, seemed to equate human security with sustainable development.[2] At this level of generalization, it is difficult to operationalize the concept in policy terms for the international community beyond already well-established programs of development and humanitarian assistance by UN agencies, donor governments, and nongovernmental organizations. As is noted in chapter 4, human security is a goal of the prospective ASEAN Socio-Cultural Community (ASCC).

Millennium Development Goals (MDG)

One effort to make more concrete human security was the adoption at the UN's Millennium Summit in 2000 of eight Millennium Development Goals with a target date for achievement of 2015 (see box 8.1). In Southeast Asia, MDG progress is regionally facilitated by the tripartite cooperation of the UNDP, the United Nations Economic and Social Commission for Asia and the Pacific (ESCAP), and the Asian Development Bank (ADB). The MDGs have also been incorporated into the national development programs assisted by bilateral ODA. Progress is regionally evaluated in annual MDG reports.[3] In 2007, at the halfway point, Vietnam, Malaysia, and Thailand were on track toward the 2015 target. On an ADB statistical index, Vietnam scored highest in the Asia-Pacific region. Indonesia, Laos, Myanmar, and the Philippines were falling behind, while Cambodia and Timor-Leste seemed out of the race. Singapore and Brunei, of course, already exceed the developmental goals. The disparities can be further illustrated by a different measurement, the UNDP's Human Development Index (HDI). As table 8.1, shows, the HDI correlates

---

BOX 8.1
The Millennium Development Goals

The UN Millennium Summit in September 2000 adopted the "Millennium Declaration," in which the leaders pledged to a new global partnership to reduce extreme poverty with time-bound targets and a deadline of 2015. The eight Millennium Development Goals (MDG) are:

- Eliminate extreme hunger and poverty;
- Achieve universal primary education;
- Promote gender equality and empower women;
- Reduce child mortality;
- Improve maternal health;
- Combat HIV/AIDS, malaria, and other diseases;
- Ensure environmental sustainability; and
- Develop a global partnership for development.

TABLE 8.1
Southeast Asian per Capita GDP-PPP and HDI Rank

Country	$ Per Capita GDP-PPP	HDI Rank
Singapore	31,400	25
Brunei	25,600	30
Malaysia	12,800	63
Thailand	9,200	78
Philippines	5,000	90
Indonesia	3,900	107
Vietnam	3,100	105
Cambodia	2,800	131
Laos	2,200	130
Myanmar	1,800	132
Timor-Leste	800	150

Sources: GDP-PPP from CIA *World Fact Book,* updated as of December 2007. All entries are 2006 estimates except Brunei and Timor-Leste which are 2005 estimates. HDI Rank from UNDP *Human Development Report 2007–2008,* accessed at www.hdr.undp.org.

with economic development, here measured as per capita gross domestic product expressed in purchasing power parity (PPP).[4]

Governance and Human Development

Human security on the needs side ultimately depends on how the availability of external and internal resources are utilized. This raises the issue of governance; that is, the way in which authority in the state is exercised. The goal of freedom from want requires more than just resources, it require good governance. For human security to be achieved, governments should have both the will and capacity to promote social and economic policies in the interest of the public good and implement those policies fairly and uniformly, inclusive of all elements of the population.

It is an article of faith in the West that good government is democratic government and that human security requires popular political participation. Yet for Southeast Asia, an outcome-oriented view of good governance in terms of satisfying needs is independent of types of political systems and institutional structures since, according to a key ADB proposition, none of them can claim to have any comparative advantage from the point of view of governance.[5] Authoritarian Singapore's place on the HDI index and Vietnam's MDG achievement record are cases in point. The intervening variable between resource availability and human security, at least in terms of freedom from want, is not necessarily democracy but political will.

The issue of corruption is perhaps the most internationally visible test of the assumed requisites of good governance such as rule of law, accountability, and transparency. Corruption encourages inefficiencies in the allocation of scare

TABLE 8.2
2007 Transparency International Corruption Perception Index

Global	Regional	Country	Score
4	2	Singapore	9.3
43	8	Malaysia	5.1
84	14	Thailand	3.3
123	20	East Timor	2.6
123	20	Vietnam	2.6
131	22	Philippines	2.5
143	25	Indonesia	2.3
162	26	Cambodia	2.0
168	29	Laos	1.9
179	32	Myanmar	1.4

Source: Transparency International at www.transparency.org/policy_research/survey_indices/cpi.

economic and social resources intended for the public good. As corruption eats away at government budgets, assistance packages, and regulatory structures, the programmatic basis for human security is undermined. While no country in Southeast Asia is free of corruption, the cluster of Southeast Asian countries at the low end of the 0 to 10 composite Corruption Perception Index (CPI) shown in table 8.2 suggests a connection between corruption, poverty, and human security.

The pervasive corruption characteristic of many Southeast Asian countries presents tough choices for the international donor community. In the case of Cambodia, for example, the Hun Sen government has been unwilling to attack the corruption that is siphoning off funds and wasting natural resources. Reform has not taken place despite the pleas and threats of the donor community. Yet, assistance continues flow, essentially without conditions. To punish Cambodia by cutting off or lowering assistance levels would reduce or end programs designed to enhance human security. It would be devastating to nongovernmental organizations that are the major agents for those programs and that are dependent on external grants for funding. In the case of Myanmar, the government deliberately obstructs the work of UN agencies and NGOs trying to bring humanitarian assistance to the afflicted population. In 2007, the International Committee of the Red Cross shut down field offices in Myanmar, and its president denounced the junta for causing "immense suffering."[6] If China, India, and ASEAN nations that are scrambling for Myanmar's energy resources are unconcerned about the misery of the Burmese people, there is little the UN or the West can do without regime change in Myanmar.

Refugees

One population class whose human security is at particular risk is refugees who have fled their homelands because of war, ethnic oppression, or other threats to their human security. The office of the United Nations High Commissioner for Refugees (UNHCR) is the principal international agency responsible for coordinating the protection for refugees, working in tandem with national governments and NGOs.

The Legacy of the Indochina Wars

Following the communist 1975 victories in Vietnam, Cambodia, and Laos, Southeast Asia was flooded with Indochinese refugees. The largest numbers came from Vietnam. The first wave was people who had worked for the old South Vietnam government or with the Americans. A second wave, including many Sino-Vietnamese, was prompted to leave by the economic policies imposed in the name of socialism. Thousands of Hmong, a Lao ethnic minority who had sided with the United States in the CIA's secret war against the Pathet Lao and its North Vietnam backer, crossed the Mekong into Northeast Thailand. Thousands of Cambodians pushed into neighboring Thai provinces to escape the Khmer Rouge's killing fields. By 1978, UNHCR camps housed 150,000 Cambodians. This doubled after the 1978 Vietnamese invasion. By 1980, an estimated three hundred thousand Cambodians were in UNHCR camps and at least another two hundred thousand strung out, unsupervised, along the border. The Cambodian refugee camps were the recruitment grounds for the Khmer resistance during the Third Indochina War (chapter 3). The unregistered Cambodians outside the UNHCR camps were not eligible for processing for resettlement. Most of them eventually voluntarily returned to Cambodia or were involuntarily repatriated by Thai authorities.

The ASEAN nations saw the refugees as a burden causing economic, social, and political problems. The ethnic Chinese origin of many of the so-called boat people complicated their reception. Thailand received the largest number of Indochinese refugees. Other "countries of first asylum" were the Philippines, Malaysia, Singapore, and Indonesia. Working with the UNHCR, the countries of first asylum agreed to establish transit sites where the UNHCR could register and process refugees for third-country resettlement, but not for resettlement in first asylum countries that insisted on guarantees that they would not be left with "residual problems"—that is, illegal migrants.[7] In that event, Thailand presented the unacceptable alternative of forced repatriation. The United States accepted the largest number of Indochinese. Since 1975, 1.3 million have been admitted to the United States as refugees for permanent resettlement from countries of first asylum or the Vietnam in-country processing programs.[8] Among these are 900,000 Vietnamese, 150,000 Cambodians, and 105,000 Hmong. The last group of 1,500 Vietnamese refugees from a Philippine camp was admitted in 2005. The final group of 15,000 Hmong arrived in the United States in 2004–2005. Australia, Canada, France, and Great Britain also took in significant numbers of refugees.

A Hmong "residual problem" exists in Thailand. In addition to those who were not eligible for third-country resettlement, new arrivals continued to be treated by the UNHCR as refugees while the Thai government claimed they were illegal economic migrants. In 2007, as many as eight thousand Hmong remained in camps. Thai involuntary repatriations of Hmong have been criticized by the UNHCR and human rights advocates around the world. The Laos government opened a resettlement zone north of Vientiane but has not allowed international access to verify—contrary to what the Hmong allege—that the returnees are not being mistreated. The Thai military junta reached an agreement with Lao PDR that complete repatriation would be accomplished in 2008.

The Flight from Myanmar

Even as the Indochinese refugee population in Thailand declines, the number of cross-border refugees from Myanmar has escalated to more than 140,000 in nine Thai-administered camps along the border. Each crackdown in Myanmar sends a new wave of refugees. The largest number is from ethnic minority groups like the Karen and Chin who have resisted Burmese subjugation since independence and have been the targets of brutal military campaigns amounting to ethnic cleansing. A much smaller group is democracy advocates whose antijunta political activities have alarmed the Thai government. While the UNHCR continues to work with the ethnic minorities in the border camps, the Thais have not allowed the UNHCR to process refugee claims by Burmese political dissidents seeking asylum. They remain at risk of being sent back to Myanmar as illegal immigrants. Since the UNHCR's third-country resettlement program for the Myanmar refugees in Thai camps began in January 2005, it has become the world's largest resettlement program, which by December 2007 had sent nearly 21,000 to third countries while nearly 4,000 more had been approved for resettlement and were waiting to leave.[9] More than half went to the United States, which made an open-ended offer to take Myanmar refugees from the Thai camps in 2005. The United States proposed an admission level of 13,000 for FY 2008. Australia and Canada had the next largest intake, each with more than 2,000 Myanmar refugees. As the refugees depart Thailand, more arrive, so the camps stay full.

Malaysia has received the second largest number of refugees in Southeast Asia with more than 43,000. Myanmar refugees account for more than half, with Muslim Rohingyas from Arakan (Rakhine) state and Chins predominant. Unlike Thailand, Malaysia has not signed the 1951 UN Covenant on the Status of Refugees and its 1967 protocol. UNHCR protection is limited in a Malaysian political and economic environment that equates refugees with the thousands of illegal migrant workers in the country. Even UNHCR-certified refugees are subject to harassment, arrest, and deportation. Malaysia fears that if it should abide by international standards it would be swamped with asylum seekers. In Malaysia, the UNHCR does process Myanmar refugees for third-country resettlement. For fiscal year 2008, the United States proposed to accept 4,000. With peace and rebuilding in Indonesia's Aceh Province, the number of Acehnese refugees in Malaysia, which once stood at 12,000, is diminishing. A new refugee problem may emerge, however, as the war in Thailand's southern provinces adjoining Malaysia widens and become more violent (chapter 5).

Vietnam, Cambodia, and the Montagnards

The ethnic tribal minorities of the Vietnam highlands, collectively known as Montagnards (literally "mountaineers"), have not been easily politically assimilated into the post-1975 Vietnamese state. A number of tribesmen allied themselves with the United States during the Second Indochina War under the political umbrella of FULRO (Front Unifié pour la Libération des Races Opprimées, or United Front for the Liberation of Oppressed Races). Many also had become Christians. As the government sought to consolidate its authority over the Montagnards' traditional homelands, protests erupted in 2001 over Vietnamese settlers occupying ancestral land, suppression of native cultures, and closure of churches. To escape a government crackdown, hundreds of Montagnards fled across the border into Cambodia, where they were gathered in two UNHCR camps. A tripartite Cambodia–UNHCR–Vietnam agreement on voluntary repatriation was reached in 2002. Because Vietnam would not allow the UNHCR to monitor the treatment of those who were repatriated, as well as Cambodian and Vietnamese intimidation of the refugees in camps to force them to choose repatriation, the UNHCR withdrew from the agreement. The camps were closed and forced repatriation followed. New refugees were hunted down by Cambodian and Vietnamese security forces. At the end of 2003, Cambodia's treatment of the Montagnards was labeled by the UN human rights envoy in Cambodia as a clear violation of the UN refugee convention.[10]

A new agreement was forged between the UNHCR and Cambodia and Vietnam in January 2005. This allowed the UNHCR to participate again in programs of voluntary repatriation and processing of those eligible for third-country resettlement. The largest group resettled, numbering more than nine hundred, has gone to the United States. Most important, Vietnam accepted UNHCR monitoring missions to Vietnam's Central Highlands. Hanoi's concessions were in part a response to the human rights roadblock thrown up by the United States Congress to Vietnam being accorded permanent normal trade relations (PNTR), a requirement of WTO membership. After visiting Cambodia and Vietnam, including the Central Highlands, in 2007, the senior U.S. official responsible for refugees indicated that both Cambodia and Vietnam had lived up to their commitments on the treatment of the refugees, a conclusion that human rights and refugee advocates contested.[11]

East Timor Refugees in West Timor

The assault on the population by Indonesian army-backed militias following the 1999 East Timor independence vote sent tens of thousands of East Timorese westward into adjoining Indonesian West Timor (chapter 2). The Australian-led International Force for East Timor (INTERFET) that restored order forced pro-Indonesia militias to flee to the same regions. More than a quarter of a million East Timorese arrived in West Timor. The UNHCR began operations in October 1999 with humanitarian relief and the beginning of an ultimately successful voluntary repatriation program. The task was complicated by the volatile refugee mix as the militias continued to terrorize and recruit from the camp populations. A September 2000 militia attack on the UNHCR office in Attambua killed three staff members. The UNHCR halted operations and evacuated its entire staff from West Timor. It did not resume its mission until Indonesia provided enhanced security in 2001. More than 225,000 East Timor refugees returned to independent Timor-Leste. Another 28,000 who could confirm their Indonesian citizenship stayed in West Timor. The UNHCR also found solutions for most of the 4,500 children who had become separated from their families in the upheavals. With its job essentially complete, the UNHCR closed out its operation in West Timor in December 2005. In 2006, in the wake of political violence (chapter 2), the UNHCR was called on for an emergency response to the problem of 150,000 internally displaced people. In 2008, more than 35,000 internally displaced refugees were in fifty-eight camps with both the UN and the East Timor government fearing that they would become permanent dependents.

Papua New Guinea and West Papuan Refugees

There are more than ten thousand Papuan refugees from Indonesia's West Papuan provinces scattered along the PNG side of the border dividing the island. More than three thousand of them are in a UNHCR-PNG government monitored camp. The majority, however, are in a number of border sites outside the UNHCR administrative reach and are dependent on volunteer humanitarian assistance. Third-country resettlement is not an option and the goal is to integrate the refugees into PNG society. The PNG government, while sympathetic to the refugees' plight, is sensitive to the potential problems they pose. The integrity of the PNG border with Indonesia depends on the refugee sites not being used as bases or sanctuaries for the Free Papua Movement (OPM) (chapter 5).

Migrant Labor

Unlike refugees, migrant workers as a class do not have a UN international bureaucracy committed to their welfare and protection. There is a UN special rapporteur on the human rights of migrants. The major multilateral intergovernmental body that monitors migrant movement is the International Organization for Migration (IOM) with 122 member states. Working with governments and regional and national NGOs, the IOM promotes humane and orderly migration. In Southeast Asia, only the Philippines, a major labor exporting country, has ratified the 1990 International Convention on the Protection of the Rights of All Migrant Workers and their Children. It was not until 2007 that ASEAN as a grouping addressed the question of migrant labor, a previously taboo subject because of political sensitivities. It adopted an "ASEAN Declaration on the Protection and Promotion of the Rights of Migrant Labor."[12] The declaration called for ASEAN's relevant bodies to develop an instrument for the protection of migrant labor and for ASEAN's secretary-general to make an annual report on the implementation of the declaration. ASEAN's sudden attention to the issue may be connected to the fact that the Philippines was the host nation and its ministries and national ASEAN secretariat helped prepare for the summit. However, until migrant protection is institutionalized in an ASEAN setting like the Socio-Cultural Community, the framework for real protection will be based on national policies and bilateral diplomacy between labor-exporting and labor-importing countries. The question is how the country of origin's interest in the protection of its citizens can be reconciled with the country of destination's policies, laws, and internal regulations.

In Southeast Asia, developed Singapore and developing Malaysia and Thailand have chronic shortages of unskilled and semiskilled labor, while Indonesia, the Philippines, and Myanmar have large surpluses of labor who are attracted to the more developed labor markets. Part of the labor supply to meet the labor demand is obtained by recruitment of contract laborers who arrive documented and with work permits for fixed periods. In the best cases, this is managed through bilateral agreements. Thailand has agreements with Cambodia, Laos, Myanmar, and Malaysia. Malaysia has agreements with Indonesia, the Philippines, and Thailand. The agreements, however, do not guarantee protection. It is undocumented labor, either arriving directly or overstaying permits, that is at the center of the bilateral political issues. These are epitomized in the strains on the Malaysia–Indonesia relation.

In Malaysia, migrant labor makes up 22 percent of the labor force.[13] Nearly 70 percent—1.3 million—are Indonesians. Of these, nearly half are illegal.

The government, responding to domestic pressure, has enacted tough laws to detain and expel illegal workers, using the baton-wielding volunteer vigilante group RELA (Ikatan Relawan Rakyat, People's Volunteer Corps) to hunt down and detain suspected undocumented laborers. Nearly 70 percent of RELA's targets have been Indonesians. RELA has been accused by international and domestic human rights organizations of systematic murder, battery, and rape as a tactic. RELA finds it difficult to distinguish between legal and illegal migrants or between migrant labor and UNHCR-registered refugees. In a press conference in Indonesia in December 2006, the UN special rapporteur on the human rights of migrant labor claimed that Indonesian migrants faced serious abuse in Malaysia.[14] The vulnerability of the migrants extends to their workplace, where, while the government seems indifferent, they are subjected to abuse and forced labor at the hands of their employers.

The issue came to a head in 2007 after several publicized cases of mistreatment of Indonesians in Malaysia, mistaken by RELA as illegal migrants, raised a storm of anti-Malaysia protests in Indonesia. There were parliamentary threats of downgrading diplomatic relations. Prime Minister Abdullah tried to calm the storm by telephoning President Yudhoyono to apologize. The issue of Indonesian migrant workers was the focus of Yudhoyono's meeting with the Malaysian prime minister in January 2008. In his press conference following the meeting in Kuala Lumpur, Yudhoyono said, "We must determine that Indonesian migrant workers' safety, security, and rights are well protected."[15] In the ASEAN fashion, the two countries set up an eminent persons group to study the problem. A more direct approach would be to renegotiate the bilateral agreements governing recruitment and employment to include the guarantees, if not of the international convention, of the ASEAN declaration on migrants. This could be the consensual foundation for a future ASEAN instrument on the protection of migrant labor.

In Thailand, where there may be as many as two million migrant workers—nearly three-quarters of whom are illegal—the major flow is from Myanmar. As the economic refugees try to eke out a living and send money home to their families, they are subject to the worst forms of exploitation and without any social safety net. The dangers faced by the smuggled migrants were tragically underlined when, in April 2008, fifty-four workers were found suffocated in a sealed seafood container truck. From the Thai point of view the policy issue is one of border security.[16] The Thais correctly identify the problem as misrule in Myanmar, but as long as the Myanmar economic push-factor exists along the 1,500-mile (2,400-km) porous border, the human traffic will continue.

Humanitarian Relief

Southeast Asia is a region where large numbers of its population live under threat of natural disaster: typhoons, flooding, earthquakes, mudslides, and volcanic eruptions. The disastrous May 2008 cyclone that devastated Myanmar's Irawaddy River delta region is but the most recent example. Few of the governments have the human, financial, communications, and logistics capabilities and infrastructure to respond fully from their own resources to large-scale disaster. Bilateral and coordinated multilateral external assistance involving national governments, UN agencies, and NGOs have a vital role to play. Nowhere was this more fully demonstrated than in the response to the earthquake and tsunami of 2004.

On 26 December 2004, on the coast of Indonesia's Aceh Province on the island of Sumatra, a magnitude 9 deep-sea earthquake in the Indian Ocean triggered a devastating tsunami washing the Indian Ocean littoral states. The tsunami caused immense loss of life and massive destruction. More than a quarter of a million people died, over 110,000 in Aceh alone. Hundreds of thousands were displaced as their housing was destroyed, an estimated 700,000 in Aceh. Also in Southeast Asia, peninsular Thailand's west coast was hit, with more than six thousand persons dead or missing and important tourist centers badly damaged. More than two million people were left in desperate straits. The countries affected were overwhelmed by the pressing immediate needs and future tasks of reconstruction and rehabilitation. The international community faced an unprecedented challenge. The response was the mobilization of the largest international humanitarian rescue and relief operation since World War II.

Among the first responders were U.S. fleet elements diverted to Aceh. In all thirteen ships and thousands of sailors spearheaded the immediate relief effort. Utilizing staging facilities in Thailand and Singapore, the American "soft power" deployment was the backbone of the logistical operations that supported the arriving disaster and relief teams from around the world. By the end of 2007, the third anniversary of the tsunami, governments, individuals, and corporations around the world had pledged more than $13 billion for tsunami recovery. To keep the tsunami victims in the spotlight, UN Secretary-General Kofi Annan named former American president Bill Clinton as the UN special envoy for tsunami recovery. Clinton chaired the Global Consortium for Tsunami Recovery. A third of the recovery funds went to Aceh.

Pandemic Disease

The eradication of epidemic disease is built into the MDG goals and is an important element of human security. This component has been called "biosecurity." Southeast Asia is located in what one epidemiologist has called "ground zero" of new epidemics.[17] Recurrent epidemics take a toll not only on the populations but also on economic growth and development, particularly as disease impacts men and women in the most productive years of their lives. Prevention, monitoring, and treatment stress already overburdened health infrastructures even as the mobility of people within and between nations makes containment more difficult. Because disease knows no boundaries, ASEAN has sought to be proactive in seeking to contain infectious diseases.

SARS

The regional vulnerabilities to such biothreats were demonstrated in 2003 with the spread from China to Southeast Asia of severe acute respiratory syndrome (SARS). The spread of the disease was addressed at an emergency ASEAN summit meeting in April 2003, where the heads of government mandated a comprehensive regional response. Although the actual job of fighting the disease fell to the public health officials of the individual states, coordination was carried out by the health ministers of the ASEAN + 3. The international effort was coordinated by the World Health Organization (WHO). Over eight thousand cases were documented by WHO, with a mortality rate of 9 percent. The economic costs of SARS in East Asia were put at $18 billion in nominal GDP terms and overall costs of $60 billion by the ADB.[18] The ASEAN health ministers declared ASEAN to be SARS-free in June 2003, claiming to be the first to make a regionwide response to the epidemic.[19] One important lesson learned from SARS as an emergent disease was the need for transparency. China's attempt to hide the original occurrence delayed the WHO's response.

Avian Flu

Since 2004, a new pandemic threatens the populations and economies of Asia and beyond. It is a particularly virulent form of the H5N1 strain of avian influenza, sometimes identified as HPAI (highly pathogenic avian influenza). It begins in infected domestic and wild fowl and is passed from infected birds to humans. It has a high mortality rate. As of 31 December 2007, Indonesia, Vietnam, and Thailand had reported the largest number of confirmed cases in Southeast Asia. Indonesia had 116 cases with 95 deaths, Vietnam 101 cases and 47 deaths, and Thailand 25 cases and 17 deaths, and the number of cases was growing, particularly in Indonesia, where there were 127 deaths by May 2008. Myanmar's report of only one case is suspect given the regime's total lack of transparency. The only treatment is the patented drug Tamiflu, which Japan is stockpiling for ASEAN in Singapore. Indonesia has resisted supplying bird flu virus samples to international research labs without guarantees of benefits from future commercial vaccines that might be produced.

The disease is contained by removing its source, which means quarantining and culling infected flocks of domestic fowl. Programs of inoculation are both expensive and do not really reach the high density of backyard domestic chickens and ducks. Farmers are reluctant to kill their flocks without adequate compensation. The great fear—a global one, not just Southeast Asian—is that the virus will mutate for human-to-human transmission rather than just bird-to-human. The head of the UN Food and Agriculture Organization said in March 2008 that Indonesia was facing an uphill battle against the virus. The virus was endemic to poultry stocks in all but two of Indonesia's thirty-three provinces. He warned that the high levels of infected birds added to the possibility of the feared mutation triggering a worldwide pandemic.[20]

If there were a global pandemic, the results would be devastating. The WHO presents a frightening prospect. If not contained quickly, a rapidly spreading pandemic could cause more than a billion cases and up to 7.4 million deaths. A one-year pandemic could cost 3 percent of Asian GDP and direct economic costs of $8–12 billion.[21] The public health systems in Southeast Asia have a limited capacity to respond to a pandemic and depend on international cooperation and support. The affected Southeast Asian governments in cooperation with WHO and donor nations are erecting surveillance and response mechanisms at both national and regional levels. The WHO has a "Regional Influenza Preparedness Plan" (2006–2008) and ASEAN has prepared a "Regional Framework for Control and Eradication of Highly Pathogenic Avian Influenza (HPAI) 2006–2008." In three international donor conferences between January 2006 and December 2007, $3 billion was pledged to combat avian flu worldwide. The United States is the single largest donor with a pledge total of $629 million.

HIV/AIDS

The South and Southeast Asian region has had the second highest incidence of HIV/AIDS in the world after sub-Saharan Africa. Southeast Asia is the area where the epidemic is most acute, with 1.6 million persons afflicted, a third of them women.[22] The toll is greatest in the population aged fifteen to forty-nine with a high rate of transmission from injected drugs and unprotected commercial sex. The highest numbers of reported cases are in Thailand (580,000), Myanmar (339,000), and Indonesia (193,000). Indonesia has the most rapid increase in the number of new cases. UNAIDS, the United Nations' HIV/AIDS program, has designated the spread of the disease the greatest threat to development and security facing the ASEAN nations.[23] An ASEAN Task Force on AIDS to coordinate regional policies was established in 1993. A series of multisectoral ASEAN Work Programs, the third, 2006–2010, have sought to connect officials, scientists, NGOs, and external donors in a joint effort to identify strategies for prevention, care, and treatment.

An important problem has been access to antiretroviral treatment, which is hugely expensive. Treatment with the patented antiretrovirals can cost between

$10,000–15,000 per patient per year. The need to combat HIV/AIDS has challenged Western pharmaceutical licensing practices and patent protection from generics, raising serious international intellectual property rights questions. Thailand took the lead in 2007 by issuing compulsory licenses for the production of generic versions of two American patented HIV/AIDS drugs and threatened to break cancer and heart disease patents if the prices were not voluntarily reduced. The U.S. administration and Congress were lobbied by the pharmaceutical industry to act against Thailand's intellectual property "theft." Thailand was put on the U.S. Trade Representative's "priority watch list." Industry concern is that other countries will follow Thailand's example.[24]

Myanmar is of particular concern both for the human security of its population and the threat it poses to the region. An international health conference held in Bangkok warned in 2007 that infectious diseases in Myanmar were beyond the ability of the government to control and were spreading beyond the country's borders. The senior UN representative in Myanmar gave a mid-2007 estimate of 620,000 people in Myanmar as being HIV/AIDS-positive even as UN and NGO health workers had to stop offering HIV/AIDS services because of pressure from the junta.[25] This, he said, together with other diseases and acute poverty, was leading toward a serious humanitarian crisis. Such a crisis would propel ever more refugees into neighboring countries, further straining their already overburdened human security support systems. The draft resolution the U.S. presented to the UN Security Council in January 2007—which received a Russian and Chinese double veto—added HIV/AIDS, avian flu, and drug trafficking to the list of threats Myanmar posed to regional peace and security. Certainly, the Myanmar case is one in which freedom from want and freedom from fear are inextricably connected and shows that needs and rights are both part of human security.

Human Rights and Human Security

The principled value base of the contemporary international human rights regime to which Southeast Asian states belong was first enunciated in the 1945 preamble to the charter of the United Nations reaffirming faith in fundamental human rights, in the dignity and worth of the human person, and the equal rights of men and women. Article 2 of the charter states that a principle of the UN is "sovereign equality," which means that the UN has no authority to intervene in matters essentially within the domestic jurisdiction of a member. The tension between the international goal of protecting human rights and the domestic authority of a sovereign state has been the constant thread in the dialogue between defenders of rights and alleged violators. This tension is replicated at the Southeast Asia regional level in ASEAN's inability to reconcile its claimed commitment to the norms of democracy and human rights with its insistence that state sovereignty and noninterference is the bedrock of the region's international relations.

The International Rights Regime

By accepting membership in the UN, the countries of Southeast Asia accepted its obligations, including human rights and freedoms. The rights and freedoms alluded to in the charter's preamble were spelled out in the "Universal Declaration of Human Rights," adopted by the UN General Assembly in 1948. Although not a treaty, the declaration has been accepted in principle as the measure of what the charter requires. Today, more than one hundred treaties and other international instruments flow from the constituting base of the UN charter and declaration. The core agreements are shown in box 8.2. The normative regulative framework of the UN's human rights system is the standard by which a government's treatment of its own people is measured by other governments. Although human rights are routinely breached around the world, no government willingly acknowledges itself a rights violator. The pattern of the Southeast Asian states' formal acceptance of the international rights regime is uneven. There is no ASEAN consensus on regionalization of the global norms. Table 8.3 shows the status of the ASEAN states signing, acceding to, or ratifying the core agreements giving instrumental effect to human rights. At the international level, the Geneva-based United Nations Human Rights Council (UNHRC) is the principal intergovernmental body tasked with examining, monitoring, and reporting on human rights conditions both in specific countries and on broad themes such as women's rights or freedom of expression. It replaced the heavily criticized Commission on Human Rights (UNCHR) in 2006. The new UNHRC shows little promise, however, of being any more able to curb rights violations and strengthen protection of victims. The forty-seven state members are elected by the United Nations General Assembly by direct majority vote for candidates drawn from five regional membership groupings. The Asian group has thirteen seats, three of which are currently held by ASEAN states. In 2008 these were—with their expiry date of current term—Indonesia (2010), Malaysia (2009), and the Philippines (2010). Just like the old commission, the council's reports and resolutions are subject to coalition and regional bloc political and diplomatic maneuvering, depending on the issues or countries being evaluated.

The High Commissioner for Human Rights (UNHCHR) is the principal human rights officer. Neither the UNHRC nor the UNHCHR has enforcement authority. They can only recommend actions to governments. In extraordinary

---

BOX 8.2
Core International Human Rights Treaties

- Covenant on Economic, Social, and Cultural Rights (CESCR)
- Covenant on Civil and Political Rights (CCPR)
- Convention on the Elimination of All Forms of Racial Discrimination (CERD)
- Convention on the Elimination of All Forms of Discrimination against Women (CEDAW)
- Convention Against Torture and Other Cruel, Inhuman or Degrading Treatment or Punishment (CAT)
- Convention on the Rights of the Child (CRC)
- International Convention on the Protection of the Rights of All Migrant Workers and Members of Their Families (CRMW)
- International Convention for the Protection of All Persons from Enforced Disappearances (*not yet in force*)
- Convention of the Rights of Persons with Disabilities (*not yet in force*)

---

cases "special procedures" can be mandated for human rights oversight in particular countries of concern. Two such situations exist in Southeast Asia: a special rapporteur for Myanmar and a special representative of the secretary-general for human rights in Cambodia. In addition there has been a special envoy of the secretary-general for Myanmar.

Unburdened by the diplomacy of UN consensus seeking, national government structures in Europe and North America have greater effective in-

TABLE 8.3
Status of Southeast Asian Accession, Ratification,
and Signatures to Core International Rights Conventions in Force

Country	CESCR	CCPR	CERD	CEDAW	CAT	CRC	CMRW
Brunei				A		A	
Cambodia	A	A	R	R	A	A	S
Indonesia	A	A	A	R	R	R	S
Laos	R	S	R	R		A	
Malaysia				A		A	
Myanmar				A	A	A	
Philippines	R	R	R	R	A	R	R
Singapore				A		A	
Thailand		A	A	A	A	A	
Timor-Leste	A	A	A	A	A	A	A
Vietnam	A	A	A	R		R	

Note: A=accession, R=ratification, S=signature only, blank=no action
Source: UNHRC Treaty Body Basis.

fluence in promoting the international human rights agenda in Southeast Asia. This is because they do have enforcement mechanisms including sanctions and contingent conditions for aid and trade. Since 1992, all EU trade and cooperation agreements have included the protection of human rights as a condition. The EU, like the United States, has imposed sanctions on Myanmar. The official lead in the United States comes from the State Department's Bureau of Democracy, Rights, and Labor (DRL) headed by an assistant secretary of state. Every year, under a congressional mandate, DRL compiles an exhaustive report on the status of democracy and rights in 194 countries of the world as well as an International Religious Freedom Report.[26] As official statements of the United States government, the reports provoke angry reactions from countries accused of rights violations. Countries found to engage in systematic, ongoing, and egregious violations of religious freedom can be designated by the secretary of state as "countries of particular concern" (CPC) and subject to economic sanctions. In 2007, Myanmar was the only Southeast Asian state of the eight designated CPCs. Vietnam had been a CPC until 2006, when it was dropped prior to President Bush's visit to Hanoi.

In addition to keeping the executive and legislative branches of government alert to human rights issues, the congressionally mandated rights reports provide ammunition to international rights advocacy groups and domestic rights NGOS in offending countries. Congressional interest in a robust American stance on human rights is also expressed in its independent oversight over U.S. policy in rights-related matters through investigations, hearings, and legislation. Congress' control over the budgets for U.S. foreign operations is also a lever on human rights it is willing to use.

The NGO component in the international rights networks is very important. Rights INGOs have been active investigators of rights infringements, marshalling public opinion, and embarrassing governments. They aggressively lobby governments to take steps against offenders. The UNCHR procedures allow for NGO participation. Two of the most influential and credible are Amnesty International and Human Rights Watch.[27] Other groupings are country, case, or issue specific. At the Southeast Asian domestic level, NGOs struggle against hostile government agencies and largely passive publics. The local NGOs exist enmeshed in restrictive regulative and legal constraints. Their "shadow" rights reports to intergovernmental and INGO establishments can balance and embarrass governments' official positions on rights situations. Governments use domestic NGOs' connections to INGOs as proof that they are witting agents of foreign powers. Arrests and imprisonment of rights workers by the more authoritarian regimes are not uncommon.

Regional Views of Human Rights

Despite the UN's rights system's claim to universality, there is no unified view on human rights either globally or in Southeast Asia. To many Southeast Asian elites, the West's emphasis on civil and political rights in a democratic framework is the expression of a particular historical and cultural process in economically developed societies. According to ASEAN leaders, the West's preoccupation with this one category of rights and freedoms ignores economic, social, and cultural rights that are of paramount importance for the full realization of human dignity and individual achievement. The more extreme views see the West's human rights campaign as a kind of political/cultural neocolonialism, particularly when conditionality is applied to trade and aid on the basis of rights judgments. The Western and Asian views were compromised, if not reconciled, at the 1993 United Nations Vienna World Conference on Human Rights. The "Vienna Declaration" stated that "while the significance of national and regional particularities and various historical, cultural and religious backgrounds must be borne in mind," nevertheless "it is the duty of states, regardless of their political, economic and cultural systems, to promote and protect all human rights and freedoms." As for economic development, it was agreed that "while development facilitates the enjoyment of all human rights, the lack of development may not be invoked to justify the abridgement of internationally recognized human rights."[28] The legal context of national sovereignty and noninterference in domestic affairs was not challenged.

One of the recommendations at Vienna was that the UN should establish the office of the high commissioner for human rights. In the General Assembly debate on the post, China, India, Malaysia, and Indonesia took the lead in limiting any powers the UNHCHR might have to investigate and make binding recommendations. The January 1994 authorizing resolution explicitly linked the high commissioner's function to respect for the sovereignty and domestic jurisdiction of the member states. In operational terms this means that the official with principal responsibilities for UN human rights activities and his representatives and envoys can only act with the consent of the state concerned. Another recommendation of the Vienna Conference was the expansion of regional human rights machinery. Asia remains the only UN-defined region without a regional human rights mechanism.

Shortly after the Vienna Conference, ASEAN, still a six-member grouping in 1993, at its annual ministerial meeting reaffirmed its commitment to human rights and freedoms as set out in the "Vienna Declaration." In line with this, the members agreed that ASEAN should consider the establishment of an appropriate mechanism on human rights. There the matter rested for a decade and a half. It was argued by ASEAN officials that a precondition for an ASEAN human rights body was the establishment of national human rights commissions in each ASEAN state. National human rights agencies exist in only four ASEAN countries: the Philippines (1987), Indonesia (1993), Malaysia (1999), and Thailand (1999). As rights watchdogs they are relatively toothless, with little investigative and no juridical power. They can advise and make recommendations to other agencies of government. ASEAN could not mandate that other countries had to have rights bodies nor was it made a condition of later membership for Myanmar, Laos, and Cambodia. The ministers also agreed in 1993 that they should coordinate a "common approach" to human rights; this meant in practice to let each government pursue its own course.

By 2007, two converging policy demands on the nonauthoritarian ASEAN leaderships refocused their attention on the need for some kind of regional human rights regime. The first was civil society demands that human rights be institutionalized in the new charter (chapter 4). The second was the increasing embarrassment to ASEAN of its failure to respond to the shame that Myanmar was bringing to the regional grouping. The 2007 ASEAN charter commits the grouping to adherence to the principles of democracy, the rule of law and good governance, and respect and protection of human rights and fundamental freedoms.[29] In order to meet the requirement of consensus, the drafters had to reject any measures that would hold accountable any ASEAN member for its violations of human rights or would deviate from ASEAN's golden rule of noninterference. This would have been unacceptable certainly to Vietnam, Laos, Cambodia, and, especially, Myanmar. The result was the charter's article 14: "In conformity with the purposes and principles of the ASEAN Charter relating to the promotion and protection of human rights and fundamental freedoms, ASEAN shall establish an ASEAN human rights body." The terms of reference for this body, however, are not in the charter. They were to be determined at a future date by the ASEAN foreign ministers.

The establishment of an ASEAN human rights body was one of the most contentious issues in the charter's drafting. The CLMV opposed any human rights compliance mechanism being included in the charter. No time frame was set for the foreign ministers' diplomatic exercise of getting a lowest common denominator consensus on what the terms of reference of the proposed human rights body might be. With the authoritarian states holding consensus vetoes, it is unlikely that any ASEAN human rights instrument will be approved that will substantially alter the human rights practices of the undemocratic ASEAN states. It was the lack of credibility on the full protection of human rights in ASEAN that led Philippine President Arroyo to warn her heads-of-government colleagues that if Myanmar did not commit to democracy and release Aung San Suu Kyi, the Philippines might not ratify the charter.[30] One of Thailand's most respected political scientists bitterly commented that "ASEAN's highly proclaimed charter has turned into a regional exhibit for Burma's intransigent internal repression and blatant disregard for basic civil liberties."[31]

Human Rights Issues in the ASEAN States

Even a casual perusal of the annual U.S. *Human Rights Report* shows that every Southeast Asian state has a blemished human rights record. While for the victims, each case of abuse is special, it is only due to cases of gross and systematic patterns of denial of rights as government policy that human rights concerns become issues in the way governments treat one another in their international relations. While human rights NGOs and advocacy groups may become energized by their agendas, governments prioritize their policy attention and deployment of political and economic capabilities in terms of perceptions of national interest. Human rights are seldom the highest priority among the ASEAN states or in dealings with the ASEAN states by external states. The exception is Myanmar.

Myanmar

Since 1990, Myanmar has been ruled by a military junta that is at war with its own people. The people view Aung San Suu Kyi, the detained leader of the National League for Democracy (NLD), as holding rightful authority (chapter 2). The government's misrule has devastated the economy and shattered society. In Asia it can only be compared to North Korea in the human insecurity of its citizens in terms of both needs and rights. Myanmar is condemned internationally for its continuous assault on democracy and human rights. Its membership in ASEAN has tarnished the organization, impeded its diplomacy, and mocked the new ASEAN charter's commitment to democracy and human rights (chapter 4). Despite this, the junta has not wavered in its political course in the face of domestic opposition and international pressure. Its case, like those of other outrageously egregious human rights violators—the Sudan in Darfur, for example—tests the limits of what the international community can or is willing to do to force change.

The United States has been in the forefront of the campaign to mobilize the international community against the junta so as to isolate it from sources of material and diplomatic support. The political context of U.S. policy is framed as a "national emergency," first declared by President Clinton in 1997 and annually renewed by Clinton and his successor President Bush. The junta's human rights and antidemocratic policies have been defined as "hostile to U.S. interests" and posing "a continuing unusual and extraordinary threat to the national security and foreign policy of the United States."[32] Under the Burmese Freedom and Democracy Act a variety of U.S. economic and political sanctions are mandated cutting Myanmar off from U.S. markets, exports, and financing. The EU, Canada, Australia, Japan, and South Korea also impose sanctions on Myanmar, including arms embargoes. The EU has imposed a visa ban on named government officials as well as freezing the assets of high-ranking junta members. No other country, however, has put in place the same range of measures as the United States or fully shares Washington's seeming belief that sanctions will force the junta to change course. The junta has had ample access to ASEAN, Chinese, and Indian investment in resource development. Nor have the sanctions limited the operations in Myanmar of Western multinational corporations. The economic pain has been felt by workers, many of them women who have become unemployed because of the closure of factories geared to Western consumers.

Any hope that ASEAN democrats might have had that the junta would be sensitive to the international community were dashed in May 2003, when a junta-instigated mob violently attacked Aung San Suu Kyi's motorcade in northern Myanmar at the village of Depayin, killing up to seventy of her supporters. The junta again swept up opposition figures, including Aung San Suu Kyi, and more than 1,100 of them were still imprisoned in 2008. This led to a new round of Western sanctions against Myanmar and new pressures on ASEAN to deal intramurally with Yangon. For the West, the issue is not just Suu Kyi, but the structure of the junta's antidemocratic rule.

The Yangon regime tried to mollify its ASEAN partners by announcing at the end of August 2003 a vague "road map" that would lead Myanmar on the path to a modern, developed, democratic country. The road map included drafting a new constitution as the basis for a parliamentary system. Even without a timetable or promise to release Suu Kyi, the worried ASEAN partners seized on this as a way out. ASEAN's leaders expressed their satisfaction with the "roadmap" at the 2003 Bali Summit, where they welcomed the "positive developments" in Myanmar. They described the "road map" as a "pragmatic approach" that "deserves understanding and support." They reiterated their opposition to sanctions against Myanmar as "not helpful in promoting peace and stability essential for democracy to take root."[33] The problem was that by 2008, the road map led to a democratic dead end. Myanmar's continuous rebuff of ASEAN's gentle diplomacy finally led ASEAN to the conclusion that moral suasion would not work, that "constructive engagement" meant business as usual for the junta, and that ASEAN solidarity was the priority in dealing with Myanmar. In 2006, ASEAN leaders admitted that they could not change Myanmar and that the real influence would have to come from China and India. It was almost with a sense of relief that they passed the problem of Myanmar off to the United Nations.

The UN had been directly involved in the diplomacy of human rights in Myanmar since 1992, when the UNCHR's first of three special rapporteurs on human rights in Myanmar was appointed. All three reported to the UN the dire circumstances of human rights under military rule. The first rapporteur resigned in 1996 because of lack of support. The second quit in 2000 because the junta would not admit him. The third, Paulo Sergio Pinheiro, was appointed in 2000 and was still serving in 2008. Making a rare country visit in

2003, he reported that the human rights situation in Myanmar had re-gressed.[34] He was barred from the country for the next four years. In 2000, in addition to the special rapporteur, Secretary-General Kofi Annan appointed his own special envoy to try to move the junta diplomatically. The first envoy was Razali Ismail, a Malaysian, who left the post in 2006 after two visits and no results. He was replaced by the former UN undersecretary for political af-fairs, Ibrahim Gambari, who in 2008 was still in the post now called special advisor.

Myanmar is the only country in Southeast Asia to which the United Nations General Assembly through its Third Committee (social, humanitarian, and cultural) and plenary sessions has repeatedly expressed grave concern at on-going systematic violation of human rights and fundamental freedoms. The UNGA's December 2006 resolution 61/232 on the "Situation of Human Rights in Myanmar" was another in an annual litany of Myanmar's abuse of human security.[35] It was very much like the resolutions in the previous years. The in-dictment is long. It includes violations of international humanitarian law committed against civilians such as forced labor, rape and sexual abuse as a weapon, child soldiers, forced displacement of refugees, and physical abuse of prisoners. It affirmed that the will of the people is the basis of authority of the government and that will was clearly expressed in the 1990 elections. The an-nual resolutions call on the government to release all political prisoners, lift all restraints on free political activity, to cease suppression of ethnic minorities, and allow all parties to participate in a political transition process with a clear timetable to democracy.

Resolution 61/232 was passed by a margin of eighty-two countries for, twenty-five against, and forty-five abstentions. This was the first time the Human Rights Council had singled out a country by name. The only other country so treated has been Israel. Only Timor-Leste in Southeast Asia voted in favor. Singapore, the Philippines, and Thailand abstained. The other ASEAN countries voted no with Myanmar. So did India and China. The ASEAN vote breakdown on passage of the draft resolution in the Third Com-mittee was the same. It was passed and forwarded to the General Assembly by a vote of seventy-nine to twenty-eight with thirty abstentions. That vote came after Myanmar had moved to adjourn the debate. On the vote to adjourn, which was lost—sixty-four yes, seventy-seven no, thirty abstain—all ten ASEAN states voted with Myanmar. In 2007, there was a marked difference in ASEAN's voting in the Third Committee on its draft resolution on the situa-tion in Myanmar. On Myanmar's motion to adjourn, Indonesia joined Timor-Leste in voting no and Singapore and the Philippines abstained. The previous year's ASEAN unanimity with Myanmar on the procedural question was bro-ken. This was more evident in the vote to pass the draft resolution. It was passed by a vote of eighty-eight to twenty-four with sixty-six abstentions. ASEAN was split down the middle on support of Myanmar. While not voting yes, Brunei, Indonesia, the Philippines, Singapore, and Thailand abstained. Malaysia joined the CLMV countries in voting no. The draft resolution was forwarded to the GA with the same vote. The GA vote on it was to be on 18 December 2007 but was postponed on a technicality.

What had changed so much in a year to have peeled so many ASEAN votes away from Myanmar? It was not change in Myanmar itself. It was Myanmar's shockingly brutal crackdown in September 2007 on demonstrations by Buddhist monks—the so-called Saffron Revolution—and supporters that generated a new wave of international political revulsion against the junta. As many as 110 were killed, thousands arrested, and an unknown number gone missing. This new wave of repression spurred the UNHRC in a special October session to adopt a resolution deploring violent repression in Myanmar and calling for the release of all political detainees and the lifting of all restraints on freedoms.[36] This was a consensus statement of the forty-seven member body, which included Indonesia, Malaysia, the Philippines, China, and India.

The General Assembly resolutions mandated the continuation of the secretary-general's "good offices" mission and called on the Myanmar government to cooperate with the special advisor and special rapporteur. In the aftermath of the September killings and arrests, Special Advisor Gambari made two trips in October and November 2007 to meet with the junta, trying to press upon them the urgency of a "genuine dialogue" with Aung San Suu Kyi. He proposed a three-way dialogue with himself as the interlocutor between the junta and the leader of the democratic opposition. The junta demurred, but did allow a liaison to her by a relatively low-ranking junta member that led nowhere. Special Rapporteur Pinheiro was also allowed to return on a fact-finding mission to verify deaths, detentions, and harassment of democracy activists. The UN initiatives did not budge the junta. Gambari was told that that "Myanmar will not bow to outside pressure. It will never allow any outside interference to infringe on the sovereignty of the state."[37]

At the urging of the United States and Great Britain, the UN Security Council put the situation in Myanmar on its agenda. In a consensus statement by the president of the Security Council after Special Advisor Gambari's first visit in October, the Security Council deplored the use of violence against peaceful demonstrators, called for the release of all political detainees, and stressed the need for all parties to work together for a peaceful solution, endorsing the proposal for three-way talks leading to national reconciliation.[38] As a consensus statement it was framed at a political level general enough to satisfy permanent members China and Russia and nonpermanent member Indonesia. Secretary-General Ban Ki Moon, frustrated by the junta's refusal to include

Suu Kyi and the NLD in the political process, warned Myanmar that the international community was running out of patience, saying the junta had to stop inflicting suffering on its own people and embrace democracy.[39] He appealed for ASEAN's "special cooperation" because "ASEAN has a special political responsibility in promoting further democratization." If by that he meant ASEAN's obligations under the new ASEAN charter, this promises little. Special Advisor Gambari had been invited by ASEAN to address the leaders at the November 2007 summit meeting that adopted the charter. At Myanmar's insistence, the invitation was withdrawn.

Any Security Council action requires the concurrence of Russia and China. The secretary-general tried to broaden support for his "good offices" mandate by convening an informal fourteen-nation "Group of Friends" on Myanmar.[40] As the "friends," including some ASEAN nations, as well as China, Russia, and the United States, consulted on how to spur democratic change in Myanmar, the junta simply waited out the international community, knowing that China and Russia would not allow the Security Council to endorse enforcement measures. This was made clear in the Security Council's consensus "press statement" on Myanmar in January 2008, affirming the objectives of the Council's October statement and "regretting the slow rate of progress so far towards meeting those objectives."[41] After twenty years without progress toward economic and political reform in Myanmar, it is difficult to see how hortatory injunctions without sanctions will change the junta's course.

Even as the United States, Great Britain, and other Western liberal democracies try to ratchet up pressure on Myanmar, China's position is clear. China claims it has an objective view of Myanmar and will provide constructive assistance toward the junta's efforts to realize national reconciliation and democratic progress. With China's Security Council insurance policy and ASEAN acquiescence, the junta continues to move along its "road map" for a new constitution and political system that excludes Aung San Suu Kyi and the NLD and marginalizes the ethnic minorities. This will not be regime change. The military will still be in command. This seemed clear when it was announced in February 2008 that the constitution was completed and would be submitted to a May referendum. Parliamentary elections would be held in 2010. A place for the NLD and Aung San Suu Kyi in the process was specifically denied. It was only after this political fait accompli that the junta permitted UN envoy Gambari back for a March 2008 visit, during which he was stonewalled on the possibility of a place for the opposition. The UN role seemed ended. ASEAN was satisfied that the timetable for a return to constitutional rule in Myanmar—no matter how democratically flawed—had been set. The junta had its way. For the opposition, there was only despair and resignation.

Cambodia

According to NGO rights watchdogs, a decade after the United Nations Transitional Authority for Cambodia (UNTAC) had handed over authority to the new Cambodian state, there has not been an inch of progress toward the rule of law, the basic foundation of democracy.[42] As part of the transfer, an office of the special representative of the secretary-general for human rights in Cambodia was established. The special representatives since 1993 have copiously documented the abuse of human rights in Cambodia, particularly as Hun Sen mounted attacks on civil society groups and democratic activists after the 2003 elections looking to the 2008 elections.

Yash Ghai, a Kenyan jurist who helped draw up the 1993 Cambodian constitution, was appointed special representative in 2005. He has been extraordinarily vocal in denouncing Hun Sen's campaign to stifle free speech, calling it the beginnings of a totalitarian regime.[43] In his reports through 2007, the UN envoy has regarded human rights violations in Cambodia as the intentional and systematic acts of the government to maintain power. He has underlined the rampant corruption and the abuse of the judicial system in land-grabbing by the elite. The government's response is that Ghai is "stupid," "deranged," a "trouble-maker," and a "tourist," demanding that Secretary-General Ban Ki Moon fire him. The United States has supported Ghai both in words, calling him a strong advocate of human rights, and deed. The American ambassador to Cambodia walked shoulder-to-shoulder with him leading the 10 December 2007 parade celebrating International Human Rights Day.

The Philippines

The case of the popular uprising called the "people's power" revolution against President Ferdinand Marcos's attempts to steal the February 1986 snap election showed that ASEAN's principle of nonintervention in the domestic political affairs of member states is ambiguous. Through the years of the Marcos dictatorship in the Philippines, the ASEAN governments had remained largely unconcerned by the destruction of democracy and human rights abuses of the regime. However, as the popular challenge to Marcos led by Corazon Aquino, widow of the murdered democratic standard bearer Benigno "Ninoy" Aquino, gathered momentum, the implications for possible spillover effects could not be ignored. The ASEAN elite realistically accepted the fact that peaceful succession with all its policy unknowns was preferable to a Marcos attempt to retain power at all costs, which could prove regionally destabilizing.

In an unprecedented departure from previous norms of intra-ASEAN behavior, the ASEAN foreign ministers coordinated a joint statement on the situation that was released simultaneously in their respective capitals on 23 February 1986.[44] Warning that the critical situation in the Philippines portended
bloodshed and civil war, widespread carnage and political turmoil, the
ASEAN ministers called on the parties to restore national unity and solidarity,
hoping that all Philippine leaders would join efforts to bring about a peaceful
solution to the crisis. Even though the foreign ministers refrained from calling
upon Marcos to step down, the fact that they formally and publicly addressed
the issue demonstrated their appreciation of the gravity of the moment. It was
with a sense of relief that ASEAN capitals welcomed the departure of Marcos
for Honolulu exile and congratulated Corazon Aquino on the successful
struggle of the Philippine people.

The three democratic presidential successions that followed Marcos's overthrow came to an end in 2001 when allies of Vice President Gloria Macapagal-
Arroyo toppled popularly elected President Joseph Estrada. Accusing Estrada of
corruption, Arroyo's forces mounted their own people's power mass demonstrations and in a military-backed quasi-coup the Supreme Court declared the presidency vacant and swore Arroyo in. President Arroyo used Marcos-like tactics to
suppress popular opposition against her grasp of power. She was elected in her
own right in 2004 in an election marked by massive fraud and intimidation.
As her legitimacy crumbled and fearing a third "people's power" backlash, she
looked to the military for protection, turning it loose in an emergency decree
copied from Marcos's play-book "to maintain public peace, order, and safety
and to prevent and suppress lawless violence."[45]

Since her election, there has been a wave of extrajudicial killings—more than
nine hundred—of journalists, civil society activists, labor leaders, and leftist
politicians. A UNHRC special rapporteur laid the responsibility for the killings
squarely on the military. This is a conclusion joined by human rights NGOs in
Europe and the United States. The military denies responsibility. Both the EU
and the United States acknowledge that the chain of command ultimately leads
to the president. Fending off U.S. congressional outrage, the responsible State
Department official told a hearing that "[Arroyo] has to take the steps to stop any
involvement by members of the security forces."[46] This assumes that she would
be willing to risk her alliance with the senior military leaders. At the end of 2007,
there had been no steps taken to hold accountable those behind the killings.

Indonesia, ASEAN, and East Timor

Throughout the Suharto government's rule, its real achievements were tarnished by the authoritarian nature of its political system and record of human

rights violations beginning in the bloody aftermath of the 1965 coup and transfer of power from Sukarno. Despite a crescendo of allegations and complaints from global human rights organizations, Indonesia's geostrategic importance during the Cold War and its pivotal role in Southeast Asia politically insulated it. From 1976 the question of East Timor was always in the background of Indonesia's bilateral relations. It assumed new prominence after the November 1991 Dili massacre when troops fired on a funeral procession, killing more than one hundred people. There were worldwide calls for sanctions against Indonesia. Jakarta furiously, and for the most part successfully, resisted efforts to link the East Timor issue to other areas of international relations, particularly international economic relations. Western policy toward Indonesia remained one of "constructive engagement," which meant regime support.

The international situation for Indonesia changed after the 1999 East Timor referendum and the Indonesian army-inspired violence that followed (chapter 2). In the words of the senior UN official in East Timor, the human and material destruction was "a planned and coordinated operation under TNI [Indonesian Armed Forces] direction."[47] The East Timor case was different from the earlier "democratic" crises in the ASEAN region. ASEAN inaction in the face of the grievous human rights issues in East Timor jeopardized its credentials as the steward of stability and security in Southeast Asia. The ASEAN states in the spirit of ASEAN solidarity had resolutely backed Indonesia's governance in East Timor to the very end, no matter the international opprobrium attached to it. The situation in East Timor was never part of ASEAN's discourse. In fact, democratic governments in Bangkok and Manila, under Indonesian pressure, used antidemocratic measures to thwart NGO organizers of international meetings in support of the East Timor struggle for independence. Even as the UN was preparing to intervene to halt the anarchic reign of terror in the province, ASEAN leaders were still muttering the ASEAN mantra of noninterference.

It was only when Indonesia gave its nominal permission for the International Force for East Timor (INTERFET) to enter East Timor that previously mute ASEAN put East Timor on its collective agenda and began consultations on participation. After an informal meeting of the ASEAN foreign ministers at the September 1999 APEC meeting in New Zealand, the chairman of the ASEAN Standing Committee, Thai Foreign Minister Surin Pitsuwan, now ASEAN's secretary-general, traveled to Jakarta to ensure that Indonesia requested ASEAN countries' participation. It was too late to give INTERFET an ASEAN face. INTERFET was led by Australia with a chain of command leading back to UN headquarters in New York. Thailand and the Philippines, freed from the restraints of noninterference by Indonesian acquiescence to the UN mandate, made battalion-sized force contributions to INTERFET and the subsequent UN peacekeeping force. A Singapore infantry platoon was included in the New Zealand (composite) peacekeeping force battalion. A small number of Malaysian language assistants were attached to the Jordanian battalion.[48] The deputy commander of INTERFET was Thai as were the second and third commanders of the peacekeeping force. They were succeeded by a Filipino. The presence of ASEAN uniformed troops as part of the multinational forces had a political as well as military significance, but they were operating not as an ASEAN force. They were national contingents dedicated to an international force in the field in the ASEAN region. ASEAN formally closed its limited involvement in the East Timor affair at the July 2002 AMM. The foreign ministers "commended" Indonesia for its efforts in resolving the East Timor issue and noted the key role of UN Transitional Administration in East Timor (UNTAET) in ensuring the territory's smooth transition to full independence. Nobel Peace Prize co-winner José Ramos-Horta, who became Timor-Leste's first foreign minister, and in 2007 president, scathingly criticized the ASEAN grouping as being "accomplices" of Indonesia. ASEAN inaction in the face of the international challenge presented by East Timor diminished its political credibility and suggested the futility of expecting future ASEAN action with respect to Myanmar.

Malaysia

Malaysia has long been a target of democracy and human rights activists because of the use of government instruments, including a punitive Internal Security Act (ISA), to stifle political opposition. The government makes no apologies for this. In a domestic political context historically conditioned by communist insurgency, racial tension, and fundamentalist Islamic challenges to the ruling moderate Muslim leadership, Western-style democracy, including press freedom, is viewed as inappropriate and potentially destabilizing. Long-serving Prime Minister Mahathir was Southeast Asia's most outspoken critic of the West's human rights agenda, viewing it as a form of political and cultural imperialism designed to slow Malaysia's development and claims to equality.

International attention reached its zenith in 1998 when Prime Minister Mahathir turned on his deputy prime minister and presumed heir apparent Anwar Ibrahim. Anwar had spoken out for political reform and greater democratic opening. Mahathir fired Anwar and had him arrested on corruption and sexual misconduct charges. Held under the ISA, Anwar was beaten by Malaysia's senior police officer. Witnesses in his two trials complained of police coercion and physical abuse. A compliant judge routinely approved the irregularities of the prosecution, which itself was under the whip of a prime minister determined to end Anwar's political career. Anwar was found guilty of corruption and sodomy and sentenced to six to nine years.

The show trials caused a storm of protest in Malaysia and abroad. Street demonstrations in Kuala Lumpur were met by police truncheons and water cannons. Anwar partisans under the banner of reform—*reformasi*—were swept up under the ISA. The pro-Anwar sentiment was channeled into a new political movement led by Anwar's wife, Wan Azizah Ismail. She, like Aung San Suu Kyi in Myanmar and Corazon Aquino in the Philippines, became the symbol of democratic reform. Malaysia issued strong protest notes to the United States, Canada, Australia, New Zealand, and the EU accusing them of meddling in Malaysian affairs. The pro-Anwar sentiments of the democratic Thai, Indonesian, and Philippine governments put a severe strain on intra-ASEAN relations. Mahathir reserved his special anger for American Vice President Al Gore, who took President Clinton's place at the 1998 APEC Kuala Lumpur Summit. There, on the Malaysian prime minister's home turf, Gore seemed to encourage Malaysian dissidence. "From Thailand to South Korea, Eastern Europe to Mexico," he asserted, "democracies have done better in coping with economic crises than nations where freedom is suppressed." He went on, "Among nations suffering economic distress we continue to hear calls for democracy, calls for 'reformasi.' We hear them today—right here, right now— among the brave people of Malaysia."[49]

After 9/11, Malaysia had new justification for aggressive use of the ISA. To the consternation of rights activists, the head of Suhakam, the Malaysian Human Rights Commission, stated "human rights should take a back seat in the war against terrorists."[50] Prime Minister Mahathir was warmly welcomed by President Bush at the White House in May 2002. His friendship, leadership, and support were praised. The ambivalence of the U.S. posture was marked. At the photo-op, with Mahathir seated beside him, President Bush was asked by a reporter whether it was still the position of the United States that Anwar Ibrahim should be released from jail. Bush tersely replied: "Our position has not changed." Then in response to a question about former President Carter's visit to Cuba, Bush characterized Cuba as a place without human rights, with a repressive government, without a free press, concluding that the people of Cuba should demand freedom.[51] The irony was not missed by Malaysian democracy activists.

Malaysian civil society had hoped that the succession of Prime Minister Abdullah Badawi in 2003 would lead to greater democratic opening and respect for human rights. One sign was the release and pardoning of Anwar. Under Abdullah, however, while the style and tone are different, the antidemocratic and repressive practices of the state are little different. Surprisingly, in 2006, it was former Prime Minister Mahathir who charged Abdullah with creating a police state, ignoring the fact that the mechanisms of a draconian internal security regime had been expanded, honed, and tuned by Mahathir himself. In forcefully asserting Malay dominance, Malaysia has to balance its relations with China and India with the tactics it employs in dealing with domestic ethnic Chinese and Indian opposition parties and movements.

Abdullah and the ruling Malay elite find themselves challenged on two fronts. Anwar has reemerged as the leader of a coalition of forces attacking the ruling party's corruption and demanding electoral reforms. At the same time, interethnic relations are being destabilized as a younger generation of non-Malays is demanding political and economic equality and an end to Malay preference. In November 2007, the Anwar-led Bersih (Clean) movement staged the largest protest demonstration seen in Kuala Lumpur since his arrest a decade earlier. Bersih's protest was followed two weeks later by a massive demonstration by Indian Malaysians led by the Hindu Rights Action Force (Hinderaf), a coalition of thirty Indian NGOs. Hinderaf's anger is directed at a system of Malay rule that it claims condemns the Indian population to poverty. The government's reaction to Bersih's and Hinderaf's public opposition was thousands of armed police, tear gas, water cannons, and hundred of arrests under the ISA. Prime Minister Abdullah made it clear he was willing to sacrifice public freedom to maintain political stability. The challenge, however, is clearly to what the European Union's ambassador said as he relinquished his post was a one-party state in which non-Muslims are increasingly marginalized and their rights jeopardized.[52] As noted in chapter 2, in a strange coalition, Anwar partisans and disaffected minorities united with the fundamentalist Muslim party in the 2008 election that weakened Abdullah's government.

Vietnam

The Socialist Republic of Vietnam is organized as a Marxist-Leninist one-party state that does not allow political opposition. Basic democratic liberties are denied. No domestic or international human rights groups are permitted to operate. Since 2001, the issues of religious freedom and the status of ethnic minorities have been joined to become Vietnam's most nagging international human rights problem (see discussion of refugees above). It is not just Montagnard Christians that Vietnam sought to discipline. Control over all religion has been tightened. The Vietnamese communist party is building party cadres within the six official religious organizations to make sure they follow party policy and counter dissent. Vietnam's rebuff of international criticism of its rights and freedoms record has impeded the development of fully normal relationships with the West. It was one of the most serious issues in the PNTR dialogue with the United States. Hanoi made some adjustments in its policies as part of the diplomatic bargaining for its WTO entry. Continuing suppression of dissent and restrictions on NGOs in the post-PNTR, post-WTO agreements have led to charges that the United States was double-crossed. The topic of Vietnam's rights record remains an issue in the U.S.–Vietnam diplomatic dialogue. Hanoi, seeking even closer relations with the United States, is sensitive to these concerns. Visiting the United States in June 2007, Vietnam's President Nguyen Minh Triet indicated a willingness to increase dialogue on the human rights issues with a "determination not to let the differences affect the two countries' overall larger interests."[53]

Accountability for Crimes against Humanity

In Southeast Asia, as elsewhere, international and domestic conflict often sees deadly and cruel force used against defenseless and vulnerable populations. This leads to atrocities, genocide, and other crimes against humanity. The international community has promoted the creation of judicial mechanisms to bring violators of international humanitarian law to account. International criminal tribunals have been established for the former Yugoslavia, Rwanda, and a Special Court in Sierra Leone. In Southeast Asia, despite international pressure, the governments of Cambodia and Indonesia resisted efforts to establish international accountability for alleged crimes against humanity. In Cambodia, prosecution is aimed at the Khmer Rouge leaders held responsible for crimes against humanity during their rule in the 1970s. The targets in Indonesia are the military, police, and civilian officials responsible for the savage attack on the East Timor people following the 1999 independence referendum.

Cambodia and the Khmer Rouge

An estimated 1.7 million Cambodians died from disease, starvation, and mass murder during the Khmer Rouge rule between 1975 and the Vietnamese invasion that ousted them in 1978 (chapter 3). Despite the obvious reluctance of Cambodian Prime Minister Hun Sen, the international donors who underwrite Cambodia's budget have insisted that the aging leadership of the KR be held accountable for their crimes against humanity. Negotiations with the UN for a tribunal began in 1997. The sticking point was who is in charge, Cambodia or the UN. Hun Sen may have feared that a truly independent trial would open old wounds as well as put his and his associates' own Khmer Rouge past under scrutiny. China, perhaps Asia's strongest defender of sovereign rights, backed Cambodian intransigence. An independent trial could throw light on China's own role as the Khmer Rouge's patron during the era of the killing fields. Cambodia's ASEAN partners, especially Myanmar and Indonesia were also uneasy about a UN-supervised trial because of the precedent it might set for the region. Even though genocide is an international crime, Cambodia, clinging to the principle of sovereignty, demanded that any trial be in a Cambodian court based on Cambodian law. The UN and donor nations were distrustful that such a court in a notoriously weak and corrupt judicial system would meet minimum international standards of justice and procedure. They demanded international participation.

In August 2001, the Cambodian National Assembly passed a law establishing a court to try the Khmer Rouge leaders. UN Secretary-General Kofi Annan insisted that any court should be based on a Cambodian–UN memorandum of agreement. After failing to get changes assuring a fair and credible trial by international standards, Annan broke off negotiations in February 2002. In December 2002, the UN General Assembly passed a resolution calling on the secretary-general to resume negotiations with Cambodia to form a tribunal. Negotiations led to a compromise agreement in March 2003 on the establishment of Extraordinary Chambers in the Courts of Cambodia (ECCC). The ECCC consists of two courts: a trial court of three Cambodian and two foreign judges and a supreme court of four Cambodians and three foreigners. Decisions must enjoy the support of at least one international judge. The bench was not sworn in until July 2006, in part because of a dispute over funding, with Cambodia insisting that the international community must pay the entire estimated $56.3 million cost.

Delays continued after the ECCC was sworn in as the foreign and Cambodian judges argued for months over the rules governing the operation of the courts. The first of an expected eight arrest warrants by the ECCC was not handed down until July 2007. While the procedural wrangling was going on, the UN began auditing the ECCC accounts in the face of evidence of blatant corruption undermining the credibility of the process. The United Nations Development Program (UNDP) oversees the financial management of the ECCC and cleared it of wrongdoing in April 2008. A new element was added when a victims unit was established to allow the victims of the Khmer Rouge to be plaintiffs as civil parties. The complexity of the management and funding of the proceedings caused an upward revision of both the cost of the trials and how long it would take. In January 2008, Cambodia presented the donor nations a new budget of $170 million that would extend the life of the ECCC to 2011.

Indonesia and the East Timor Trials

The wanton carnage and human rights abuses that took as many as two thousand lives and displaced hundreds of thousands of people as internal refugees have been fully documented in the October 2005 report submitted to Timor-Leste's parliament by the country's Commission for Reception, Truth, and Reconciliation (CAVR).[54] An outraged international community has demanded for a decade that the perpetrators of the crimes against humanity be held accountable. In a September 1999 special session, the UNCHR voted to investigate the affair. None of the eleven Asian members of the commission voted in favor. UN Secretary-General Kofi Annan appointed an International Commission of Inquiry. The commission reported back to him in January 2000, finding patterns of gross violations of human rights and breaches of humanitarian law by the army and militias. It recommended the establishment of an international human rights tribunal.[55] Parallel to the UN inquiry, the Indonesian National Human Rights Commission formed a Commission to Investigate Violations of Human Rights in East Timor. Its conclusions were very similar to those of the international commission. Unlike the situation in Cambodia, Indonesia was not hard pressed to accept an international tribunal. There was concern that Indonesia's fragile democratization would be put at risk if nationalist passions were unleashed or the TNI closed ranks and withdrew support from the government.

Then Indonesia insisted that national law would be the basis for finalizing the human rights issues with respect to East Timor. President Megawati created an Ad Hoc Human Rights Court in January 2002. The ad hoc court had limited reach. Even though the Indonesian Human Rights Commission traced responsibility for the East Timor outrage up the military chain of command to TNI chief General Wiranto and other senior officers, only eighteen indictments came down for civilian and military personnel who had been on the ground in East Timor. It was clear from the outset that the government was unwilling to challenge the army leadership or public opinion, which felt the accused were national patriots being sacrificed to appease the West. By the end of a weak and flawed pro forma prosecution there were only six convictions, all of which were reversed on appeal.

Even though no international tribunal was formed, the human rights situation in East Timor remained on the UNCHR's agenda. At the 2003 meeting, the chairperson's statement expressed disappointment over the process and outcome of Indonesia's ad hoc rights tribunal but, in a victory for Indonesian diplomacy, agreed to drop the issue from future agendas. In Timor-Leste itself, UNMISET's Serious Crimes Unit aided Timor-Leste's prosecutorial authorities, who issued 380 indictments, of which 270 were for individuals in Indonesia. General Wiranto and six other senior officers were charged with crimes against humanity. There was no possibility, however, that Indonesia would extradite anyone charged. Recognizing that good relations with Indonesia was Timor-Leste's paramount interest, President Xanana Gusmão hastened to reassure Jakarta that Dili had no intention of letting the issue of human rights abuses and crimes against humanity disrupt the development of stable, cooperative, and friendly relations with Indonesia. There was a sigh of relief in Dili when the UNMISET's crimes mandate ended in 2005.

Unrelenting international pressure prompted the formation in January 2005 of a United Nations three-member Commission of Experts to review the prosecution of serious crimes in East Timor in 1999. The commission's July 2005 report found that the Indonesian prosecution was "manifestly inadequate" and showed "an evident lack of political will to prosecute." Furthermore, the commission said the ad hoc court itself did not present a "credible judicial forum." The experts recommended that if Indonesia did not take steps to review the prosecutions and hold those responsible accountable then the Security Council should create an ad hoc international court for East Timor in a third country.[56]

Indonesia and Timor-Leste refused to cooperate with the Commission of Experts and tried to preempt it by establishing in March 2005 their own binational Commission on Truth and Friendship (CTF). Supposedly modeled on South Africa's Truth and Reconciliation Commission, the ten-member— five from each country—CTF had no judicial or subpoena power. Its mandate was to foster reconciliation, even amnesty, but not to prosecute or punish.[57] Victims and human rights advocates called the process a whitewash. According to the UN Committee of Experts, the CTF's terms of reference "contradicted international standards on denial of impunity for serious crimes" and noted the absence of any mechanism to compel truth. The commission began its hearings in February 2007. UN Secretary-General Ban Ki Moon subsequently instructed United Nations officials not to cooperate with the CTF because the UN could not be seen as endorsing crimes against humanity. The CTF missed August 2007 and January 2008 deadlines for presenting its report. According to the Indonesian side, the process of finding a consensus that was unbiased and fair for both Indonesian and East Timor was tough.[58] Reporting on the CTF in January 2008, one NGO put it: "Too much friendship, too little truth."[59]

Notes

1. The UNDP 1994 report can be accessed at hdr.undp.org.
2. The commission's report can be accessed at www.humansecurity-chs.org.

3. Links to the progress reports and all documentation for the MDG programs in the ESCAP and ADB region can be found at www.mdgasiapacific.org.

4. Purchasing power parity is a measure of relative purchasing power made by converting a currency's market exchange rate to a standardized weighted dollar rate.

5. Asian Development Bank, *Governance: Sound Development Management* (Manila: ADB Policy Paper, 1995).

6. As quoted in "In an Unusual Move, Red Cross Criticizes Myanmar," *International Herald Tribune*, 29 June 2007.

7. "Joint Press Statement, the Special ASEAN Foreign Ministers' Meeting on Indochinese Refugees," 13 January 1979, accessed at www.aseansec.org/3707.htm.

8. Data on U.S. refugee programs and financing can be accessed at the State Department's Bureau of Population, Refugees, and Migration, at www.state.gov/g/prm/refadm.

9. "Myanmar Refugees Leaving Thailand for Third Countries Passes 20,000 Mark–UN," *UN News Service*, 12 December 2007.

10. Report of the special representative of the secretary-general for human rights in Cambodia, Peter Leupracht, "The Human Rights Situation in Cambodia," 19 December 2003, Human Rights Council document E/CN.4/2004/105, p. 17.

11. "US Downplays Montagnards Threat," *BBC News/World/Asia-Pacific*, 9 February 2007; "Rights Experts Doubt US Official's Confidence that Vietnam's Montagnards Not Harassed," *Voice of America News*, 2 February 2007.

12. The declaration, signed at the twelfth ASEAN Summit, 13 January 2007, can be accessed at www.aseansec.org/19264.htm.

13. For a full discussion of migrant labor in Malaysia see Vijayakumari Kanapathy, "Migrant Workers in Malaysia: An Overview," country paper for the Workshop on an East Asia Cooperative Framework for Migrant Labour, 6–7 December 2006, at www.isis.org.my/files/pubs/papers/VK_MIGRATION-NEAT_6Dec06.pdf.

14. "Indonesian Migrant Workers Face Abuse in Malaysia," *Antara News*, 20 December 2006.

15. As quoted by Hazlin Hassan, "Yudhoyono's Mission in Malaysia: Justice for Indonesian Workers," *The Straits Times*, 12 January 2008.

16. "Thai Security Agencies to Meet to Prevent Illegal Workers Entry," Thai News Agency, as reported by Bernama, 12 April 2008.

17. Ann Marie Kimball, "When the Flu Comes: Political and Economic Risks of Pandemic Disease in Asia," in Ashley J. Tellis and Michael Wills, eds., *Trade, Interdependence, and Security* (Seattle: National Bureau of Asian Research, 2006), 365.

18. ADB, "Assessing the Impact and Cost of SARS in Developing Asia," in *ASEAN Development Outlook 2003 Update* (Manila: ADB, 2003), 75.

19. ASEAN Secretariat, "ASEAN is SARS Free: The First Region in the World to Work on a Region-wide Response to SARS," accessed at www.aseansec.org/pis_sars.htm.

20. "UN Says Indonesia is Losing Battle to Fight Avian Flu Epidemic," *VOA News*, 19 March 2008.

21. These statistics are drawn from the WHO's "Regional Influenza Pandemic Preparedness Plan (2006–2008)," accessed at www.searo.who.int/LinkFiles/Avian_Flue_SEA-CD-148_A4.pdf.

22. Regional and country statistics on HIV/AIDS can be found on links at websites of the Joint United Nations Program on AIDS, www.unaids.org, and the Southeast Asia regional office of WHO, www.searo.who.org.

23. Peter Piot in a report to the ASEAN heads of government at the ASEAN Second Special Session on HIV and AIDS at the twelfth ASEAN Summit, January 2007.

24. For the patient versus patent issues in Thailand, see Simon Montlake and Elizabeth H. Williams, "Thailand's IP Gamble: Potion or Poison," *Far Eastern Economic Review* 170, no. 6 (2007): 39–45.

25. As reported by the Associated Press and carried in the *International Herald Tribune* 20 June 2007 and other news outlets.

26. The bureau can be accessed at www.state.gov/g/drl with links to its various activities, including the annual human and religious rights reports.

27. Amnesty International can be accessed at www.amnesty.org and Human Rights Watch at www.hrw.org.

28. The "Vienna Declaration and Programme of Action" can be accessed at www.unhchr.ch/huridocda/huridoca.nsf/(Symbol)/A.CONF.157.23.EN.

29. The ASEAN charter can be accessed at www.aseansec.org/21069.pdf.

30. "Statement of the President on Myanmar, ASEAN Leaders Informal Working Dinners," 19 November 2007, accessed at www.news.ops.gov.ph/archives2007/nov20.htm.

31. Thitinan Pongsudhirak, "ASEAN's Bang Ends in a Whimper: Regional Alliance Loses International Credibility as Charter Fails to Deliver on Promises," *Bangkok Post*, 28 November 2007.

32. "Continuation of the National Emergency with Respect to Burma: Message from the President of the United States," House of Representatives, 16 May 2002, House Document No. 107-211.

33. Paragraph 25 of the "Press Statement by the Chairperson of the 9th ASEAN Summit and the 7th ASEAN + 3 Summit," 7 October 2003, accessed at www.aseansec.org/15259.htm.

34. UN News Service, "Myanmar's Human Rights Situation Has Regressed—UN expert," accessed at www.un.org/apps/news/story.asp?NewsID=8867&Cr=Myanmar&Cr1=.

35. UNGA, "Situation of Human Rights in Myanmar," A/RES/61/232, accessed at www.un.org/Depts/dhl/resguide/r61.htm.

36. UNHRC, "Situation of Human Rights in Myanmar," accessed at www2.ohchr.org/english/bodies/hrcouncil/docs/specialsession/A.HRC.RES.S.5-1.pdf.

37. "Myanmar Rejects UN Envoy's Bid for 3-way Talks," *The Straits Times*, 7 November 2007.

38. "Statement by the President of the Security Council," S/PRST/2007/37, 11 October 2007, accessed at www.un.org/docs/sc/unsc_pres_statements07.htm.

39. "Ban Ki Moon of UN Warns Myanmar," *International Herald Tribune*, 10 December 2007.

40. "Secretary-General Convenes Meeting of 'Group of Friends' on Myanmar," UN News Service, 19 December 2007. The fourteen countries are Australia, China, France,

India, Indonesia, Japan, Portugal, Norway, Russia, Singapore, Thailand, United Kingdom, United States, and Vietnam.

41. Security Council, "Security Council Press Statement on Myanmar," SC/9228, 16 January 2008, accessed at www.un.org/News/Press/docs/2008/sc9228.doc.htm.

42. Asian Human Rights Commission, "Cambodia: Ten Years after UNTAC, Not an Inch of Progress in Cambodia's Rule of Law," 4 February 2003.

43. The reports of the special representative can be found at www.ohchr.org/EN/Countries/AsiaRegion/Pages/KHIndex.aspx.

44. "ASEAN Joint Statement on the Situation in the Philippines," 23 February 1986, accessed at www.aseansec.org/4997.htm.

45. Office of the Press Secretary, Republic of the Philippines, "General Order No. 5," 24 February 2006, accessed at www.news.ops.gov.ph/go_no5.htm.

46. Deputy Assistant Secretary of State Eric John, "Extrajudicial Killings in the Philippines: Strategies to End the Violence," testimony before the Subcommittee on East Asian and Pacific Affairs of the Senate Committee on Foreign Relations, accessed at www.senate.gov/~foreign/testimony/2007/JohnTestimony070314.pdf.

47. Ian Martin, *Self-Determination in East Timor: The United Nations, the Ballot, and International Intervention* (Boulder, Colo: Lynne Rienner, 2001), 124.

48. The peacekeeping force structure is summarized in Michael G. Smith, *Peacekeeping in East Timor: The Path to Independence* (Boulder, Colo: Lynne Rienner, 2003), 173–78.

49. "Remarks by Vice President Al Gore, APEC Business Summit, Kuala Lumpur, 16 November 1998," accessed at www.state.gov/regional/ea/apec/wwwhgore.htm.

50. Accessed at www.whitehouse.gov/news/releases/2002/05/20020514-8.html.

51. "Remarks by the President and Prime Minister Mahathir of Malaysia in Photo Opportunity," accessed at www.whitehouse.gov/news/releases/2002/05/20020514-8.html.

52. Ambassador Thierry Rommel, as cited in "M'sia is a virtual one-party state," *The Straits Times*, 14 November 2007.

53. White House, Office of the Press Secretary, "President Bush Welcomes President Nguyen Minh Triet of Vietnam to the White House," press release, 22 June 2007, accessed at www.whitehouse.gov/news/releases/2007/06/20070622-2.html.

54. The full CAVR report titled "Chega" (in Portuguese, "no more") can be read at the CAVR website www.cavr-timorleste.org as well as other websites including that of the East Timor Action Network (ETAN). CAVR is the abbreviation of the Portuguese name of the commission: Comissão de Acolhimento, Verdade e Reconciliação de Timor-Leste.

55. "Report of the International Commission of Inquiry on East Timor," accessed at www.unhchr.ch/Huridocda/Huridoca.nsf/TestFrame/251360e57c80b674802568770052c47a?Opendocument. The commissioners were from Costa Rica, Nigeria, India, Papua New Guinea, and Germany.

56. The commission members were distinguished independent jurists from India, Japan, and Fiji. The full report can be accessed at daccessdds.un.org/doc/UNDOC/GEN/N05/426/17/pdf/N0542617.pdf?OpenElement.

57. The Commission on Truth and Friendship's terms of reference and activities can be accessed on the CTF's website, www.ctf-ri-tl.org.

58. "Indonesia–Timor Leste truth commission seeks consensus," *The Jakarta Post,* 26 March 2008.

59. Megan Hirst, *Too Much Friendship, Too Little Truth: Monitoring Report on the Commission on Truth and Friendship of Indonesia and Timor-Leste* (New York: International Center of Transnational Justice, 2008), accessed at www.ictj.org/images/content/7/7/772.pdf.

Suggestions for Further Reading

Anthony McGrew and Nanak Poku, eds., *Globalization, Development, and Human Security* (Malden, Mass.: Polity, 2007); Terrence Chong, ed., *Globalization and its Counter-Forces in Southeast Asia* (Singapore: Institute of Southeast Asian Studies, 2008); Jonathan Rigg, *Southeast Asia: The Human Landscape of Modernization and Development* (London: Routledge, 2002); Aris Ananta and Evi Nurvidya Arifin, eds., *International Migration in Southeast Asia* (Singapore: Institute of Southeast Asian Studies, 2004); V. O. Sutter, *The Indochinese Refugee Dilemma* (Baton Rouge: Louisiana State University Press, 1990); Ann Marie Kimball, *Risky Trade: Infectious Disease in the Era of Global Trade* (Burlington, Vt.: Ashgate, 2006); Philip J. Eldridge, *The Politics of Human Rights in Southeast Asia* (London: Routledge, 2001); Daniel A. Bell, *East Meets West: Human Rights and Democracy in East Asia* (Princeton, N.J.: Princeton University Press, 2007); David I. Steinberg, *Turmoil in Burma: Contested Legitimacies in Myanmar* (Norwalk, Conn.: Eastbridge, 2006); Joseph Nevins, *A Not So Distant Horror: Mass Violence in East Timor* (Ithaca, N.Y.: Cornell University Press, 2008); Ben Kiernan, *The Pol Pot Regime: Race, Power, and Genocide in Cambodia under the Khmer Rouge, 1975–1979,* 2nd ed. (New Haven, Conn.: Yale University Press, 2000): Tim Fawthrop and Helen Jarvis, *Getting Away with Genocide: Elusive Justice and the Khmer Rouge Trials* (Sydney, Australia: UNSW Press, 2004).

9

Environmental Issues in International Relations in Southeast Asia

T HE PURSUIT OF RAPID ECONOMIC GROWTH has been carried out in Southeast Asia out with little regard for environmental degradation and resource sustainability. It has also had social and cultural costs for populations affected by the exploitative ravaging of their lands and the wastes of industrialization. More than a decade ago, James Rush documented in *The Last Tree* the destruction of human habitat in Southeast Asia by economic growth policies without environmental safeguards.[1] The choices made by national governments in Southeast Asia in the name of economic development have led to accelerating patterns of misuse and inefficient use of forest, land, and water resources, with little attention to sustainability. The cumulative impact of what Rush termed "acts of violence" against the environment has consequences not just for local environments but for regional and global environmental interests as well.

Environmental issues have become part of the nontraditional international relations agenda in Southeast Asia. Environmental insecurity is the term used to describe the patterns of unsustainable development and resource depletion intrinsic to economic growth strategies in Southeast Asia.[2] At one level, the issues pit the interests of the developed West in environmental conservation and protection against Southeast Asian efforts to maximize the utilization of their natural resource endowments. Environmental concerns are a relative latecomer to the West's interactions with Southeast Asia. The postindustrial shift in the West's developmental paradigm from rapid development to sustainable, clean development has not altered Southeast Asia's drive to catch up economically with the developed West. The new Western-spurred environmental agenda is sometimes interpreted as a jealous effort to thwart progress.

At the regional level, environmental problems impact bilateral and multi-lateral relations. It is not just a question of the spillover effect of polluted environments or upstream-downstream problems. Thailand's depletion of its own resource base and its growing industrial needs have led to aggressive efforts to exploit legally and illegally the forest, mineral, and maritime resources of its neighbors. Thailand, in fact, is a kind of "worst case" example of environmental mismanagement, where all too often at the end of the policy process economic security was sought at the cost of environmental insecurity for itself and its neighbors.[3] This is one of the reasons why Thai subregional cooperation frameworks are viewed warily (chapter 4). The Thai fishery fleet, for example, regularly encroaches on Myanmar's and Indonesia's Exclusive Economic Zones (EEZ) and territorial waters. Arrests, seizures, and violence are not uncommon as Myanmar and Indonesia defend their fisheries from Thai predations. Western Cambodia is becoming an environmental wasteland. Roads from Thailand drive into Myanmar's forests.

While the definition of environmental impacts is scientific, policy choices and disagreements with respect to those impacts are political. It has been asserted that "no other issue in the [Southeast Asia] region's domestic, inter-regional, and international affairs" has so swiftly assumed prominence "as the emergence of an increasingly politicized ecological awareness."[4] The policy question is how to reconcile the demand for development with responsible environmental practices. In the words of the executive director of Greenpeace, "Southeast Asia has emerged as a key arena in the battle to save the planet."[5]

The Environmental Policy Setting

Like human rights, safeguarding the environment is no longer viewed as a matter of just sovereign jurisdiction. The normative framework in which international environmental concerns are embedded is epitomized in the twenty-seven principles enunciated in the "Rio Declaration on Environment and Development" adopted by the 1992 United Nations Conference on Environment and Development—better known as the Earth Summit.[6] While accepting the traditional rule that states have the sovereign right to exploit their own resources, the "Rio Declaration" quickly added that states also have the responsibility to ensure that their activities do not cause damage to the environments beyond their borders. It detailed the kinds of policies, structures, and agencies states need to have in place to prevent environmental degradation caused by economic development. (See box 9.1.)

BOX 9.1
Rio Principles 2–4

Principle 2
States have, in accordance with the Charter of the United Nations and the principles of international law, the sovereign right to exploit their own resources pursuant to their own environmental and developmental policies, and the responsibility to ensure that activities within their jurisdiction or control do not cause damage to the environment of other States or areas beyond the limits of national jurisdiction.

Principle 3
The right to development must be fulfilled so as to equitably meet developmental and environmental needs of present and future generations.

Principle 4
In order to achieve sustainable development, environmental protection shall contribute an integral part of the development process and cannot be considered in isolation from it.

The Rio process was not without controversy. Malaysia's Prime Minister Mahathir was an articulate critic of an agenda that he and other spokespersons of the developing world found loaded against the economic and social needs of their countries. Mahathir and others argued that the appeal to environmentalism harbored a desire to prevent the Third World from industrializing and becoming global competitors. If the developed West truly wanted countries like Malaysia to forgo the exploitation of their resources to their fullest productive potential, then, according to Mahathir, the West should pay for environmental safeguards. According to him, the poor should not bear burdens imposed by the rich.

While no longer couched in a deliberately provocative manner, the sentiment that the West should pay its fair share for environmental safeguards in Southeast Asia is still prevalent. For example, Indonesia has vigorously championed a proposal known as Reduced Emissions from Deforestation and Degradation (REDD) that would transfer from a global fund millions of dollars to rainforest countries as carbon credits to underwrite the prevention of deforestation and promotion of reforestation.[7] The Indonesian initiative was adopted by a forum of tropical rainforest countries, the F-11, in September 2007 in anticipation of the December UN Bali conference on climate change.[8] At Bali, the REDD was adopted in principle, with a 2012 target for implementation.

At Rio, an action program called Agenda 21 was promulgated to achieve the Earth Summit's goals. Five years later in 1997, a special session of the UN General Assembly was held to evaluate progress. The review was based on national reports. All of the reporting Southeast Asian states claimed bureaucratic progress in meeting the standard of environmentally responsible development policies and practices. The policy commitment, however, is uncertain. The bureaucratic existence of governmental structures with environmental oversight should not obscure the fact that the legislative and legal frameworks as well as enforcement mechanisms are weak and in many cases are embedded in a pattern of corruption that fosters environmental depredation.

The United Nations' signature structure for environmental concerns is the UN Environment Program (UNEP). In addition to being an information clearinghouse, the UNEP provides technical support for programmatic implementation. The UNEP Regional Office for Asia and the Pacific is in Bangkok. Its regional priorities are land and coastal degradation, deforestation, atmospheric pollution, biodiversity loss, urbanization, and freshwater availability. In 2002, at Rio + 10, the UN General Assembly authorized the Johannesburg World Summit on Sustainable Development (WSSD). The purpose was to evaluate progress since Rio and especially to energize international and national efforts to implement the Rio principles and Agenda 21. In the regional preparatory work for the WSSD, the Asian Development Bank (ADB), UN Economic and Social Commission for Asia and the Pacific (ESCAP), and UNEP prepared analyses showing that the environment of the Asia-Pacific region had seriously degraded in the decade between Rio and Johannesburg. The developed Western nations, using their economic leverage, try to persuade and pressure Southeast Asian states to cease destructive environmental practices. They routinely attach environmental requirements as conditions for trade, economic assistance, and project funding. In the U.S. Department of State, international environment and conservation matters are dealt with in the Bureau of Oceans and International Environmental and Scientific Affairs (OES) headed by a deputy assistant secretary of state for the environment. To address transboundary environmental issues, OES has established regional environmental hubs. The Southeast Asia-Pacific Hub is located in the U.S. embassy in Thailand. It focuses on sustainable management of forests, water, and biodiversity resources. Similar bureaucratic structures are in place in other developed states.

In determining international environmental policy, Western policymakers and parliaments are not only informed by their own scientific experts but, politically perhaps even more important, by an assertive and powerful global NGO community that seeks to influence environmental policy and actions. Many of the long-established groups have status and credibility with their official environmental counterparts. The developed countries are the major equity holders in the World Bank and the ADB. Both banks now make environmental assessment and risk a major part of their approval process for project funding. The linking of environmental issues to trade and finance is decried by Southeast Asian economic nationalists as a form of discriminatory protectionism and the efforts to influence domestic policy are viewed as a new kind of imperialism.

In Southeast Asia, the INGOs provide support and assistance to linked regional and national domestic environmental NGOs. In Thailand, the Philippines, Indonesia, and Malaysia, where the political settings have allowed civil society development, NGO stakeholders have limited input into environmental decision making. Financial and technical support is given to domestic Southeast Asian NGOs through the official assistance programs of the United States, EU member countries, Australia, New Zealand, and even Japanese official development agencies. In Southeast Asia, the environmental NGOs often have databases, technical skills, and field experience superior to that of their government counterparts. Governments can draw on NGO expertise, but in many cases they find themselves at odds with NGO protests and activism.

The ASEAN Framework

Environmental issues first appeared on ASEAN's bureaucratic agenda in 1977, a decade after the organization's founding. Assisted by the UNEP, an ASEAN Expert Group on the Environment, working under the ASEAN Committee on Science and Technology (COST) developed a five-year ASEAN Subregional Environment Program (ASEP). Four years later, in 1981, the first ASEAN ministerial meeting on the environment (AMME) took place in Manila. At the Manila meeting the ministers responsible for the environment endorsed the first of the continuing series of declarations, resolutions, and statements committing ASEAN to environmental sustainability. In their "Manila Declaration on the ASEAN Environment" the ministers expressed their awareness that the ASEAN nations faced common environmental problems and the need "to ensure the protection of the ASEAN environment and the sustainability of its natural resources so that it can sustain the highest possible quality of life for the people of the ASEAN countries."[9]

The AMME meets formally every three years with informal sessions in the intervening years. At the tenth AMME in November 2006, the ministers issued the "Cebu Resolution on Sustainable Development," reconfirming their commitment to address environmental issues through national, regional, and global cooperation.[10] They also launched the third *ASEAN State of the*

Environment Report, a comprehensive assessment of ASEAN's environmental record and aspirations.[11] Routine oversight of the machinery of ASEAN environmental concerns is delegated to the ASEAN Senior Officials on the Environment (ASOEN). Four ASEAN working groups report to the ASOEN: Nature Conservation and Biodiversity; Coastal and Maritime Environments; Environmentally Sustainable Cities; and Water Resources Management. This bureaucratic structure has produced twelve strategies and fifty-five programs, but few quantifiable results other than the meetings that produced them.

The original three five-year ASEPs were succeeded in 1992 by a five-year "Strategic Plan of Action on the Environment" (SPAE), 1993–1998, and again for 1999–2004. At the 2003 AMME in Yangon, the ministers affirmed that the WSSD and Johannesburg Plan of Implementation provided an effective framework for international and regional cooperation. They commended the bureaucratic and scientific architects of the second SPAE for being responsive to the environmental concerns noted in the 1997 "ASEAN Vision 2020" and the "Hanoi Plan of Action" to implement it (chapter 4).

As noted in chapter 4, at the 2003 Bali ASEAN Summit, future ASEAN regional activities were placed in the context of building the ASEAN communities. The AMME efforts are now placed within the framework of the prospective ASEAN Socio-Cultural Community. The first task was to fashion the environmental provisions for the 2004 Vientiane Action Programme (VAP) for community building. Although the AMME instructed the ASOEN to formulate concrete and realistic strategies, the actual measures in the VAP were framed in the typical ASEAN-speak of promoting cooperation and enhancing coordination.[12] Nevertheless, the AMME's 2006 Cebu Resolution expressed the ministers' "satisfaction on the progress of implementation of environmental programs and measures and related activities in the VAP."

On paper, in declarations and resolutions, and in rhetoric, ASEAN's agenda is environmentally correct, conforming in principle to the globally recognized benchmarks of Agenda 21 and the WSSD. Yet, ASEAN has not been able to make operational environmental programs that have instrumentally led to meaningful progress toward meeting the environmental challenges of development. This is because in this functional area of intergovernmental cooperation, as in the other areas of ASEAN activity, ASEAN is not institutionally capable of implementing its strategies or action plans. The achievement of ASEAN's goals depends on the commitment, the political will, and the capabilities of the individual national governments. No matter how well-intentioned or scientifically valid planning at the ASEAN level might be, at the implementing state level, political decisions are made in the context of balancing near-term economic gain against long-run environmental costs. This is often embedded in a nexus of government and capital in which too often corruption is at play.

The full scope of state and NGO concerns for environmental issues and interests that have become part of the international relations of Southeast Asia touches on nearly every activity that involves patterns of industrialization and the utilization of natural resources endowments and their human impacts. The litany of ecological devastation includes disappearing forests, mining tailings, contaminated water, disappearing coastal mangrove zones, toxic waste dumping, polluted air, and the list goes on. In this chapter, only a few of the more internationally prominent issue areas can be treated to illustrate this nontraditional aspect of international relations in Southeast Asia.

Deforestation

The environmental issue in Southeast Asia that has the greatest global impact is the loss of forest cover, with its implications in terms of climate change and loss of biodiversity. Global deforestation is the cause of 20 percent of greenhouse gas emission through burning, deforested soil, and smoldering peat. Southeast Asia's contribution to this can be gauged by the fact that although only 5 percent of the world's forests are in Southeast Asia, 25 percent of global deforestation is taking place there. It is not surprising, therefore, to learn that Indonesia is the world's third-largest emitter of greenhouse gases. Deforestation has been described as "the fundamental problem of environmental degradation facing Southeast Asia today."[13] Forests disappear because of logging, the spread of settled agricultural cultivation, including plantation agriculture and the rush for biofuels, and fire in the perpetuation of traditional swidden shifting cultivation or as a quick way to clear. It is intensive logging that has attracted the greatest international concern. The introduction of tracked vehicles and chainsaws, replacing oxen and axes, has accelerated the clear-cutting of millions of acres of Southeast Asia's tropical forests. Clad and Siy remark that "no topic evokes more outrage nor prompts more resentment than the loss of Southeast Asia's tropical hardwoods."[14] For those who live in the areas that are being clear-cut, and who often are the poorest of the population, the denuded land presents new dangers of flood and mudslide.

Global and Regional Responses

Deforestation has been an important element in global conferences and actions with respect to the environment and sustainable development. At the Rio Earth Summit, the assembled governments adopted a "Statement on Principles for the Sustainable Management of Forests."[15] Purporting to represent a global consensus on the conservation, management, and sustainable development of the world's forests, it was explicitly stated that the statement was legally non-binding. In 1983, a binding International Tropical Timber Agreement (ITTA) was negotiated that entered into force in1985. It brought together timber-producing countries, chief among them Brazil, Indonesia, and Malaysia, and the consuming nations led by the United States, Japan, and the European Union. The ITTA provided a treaty basis for consultation and cooperation on issues relative to the management of the international timber economy, including trade and management of the forests on a sustainable basis.

The International Tropical Timber Organization (ITTO), headquartered in Tokyo, was established to facilitate the achievement of the treaty's goals, which give equal weight to trade and conservation. The choice of Tokyo, rather than a Southeast Asian timber producer, was political and tied to Japan's willingness to be a major financial underwriter of the organization's programs.

A successor agreement to the 1983 ITTA was negotiated in 1994 and came into force in 1997. It was succeeded by a new ITTA in 2006. The long-term objective is to have all tropical timber entering international trade come from sustainably managed sources. In Southeast Asia, this goal has been endorsed by the ASEAN Ministers of Agriculture and Forestry. The international agreements do not cover the growing domestic consumption of timber in timber-producing nations.

In 2000, a United Nations Forum on Forests was established as a subsidiary body to the UN Economic and Social Committee. Its objective was to promote the management, conservation, and sustainable development of forests and to strengthen long-term commitment to that end. The major consumer states in the West have sought to limit the trade in illegally felled tropical hardwoods. The United States claims that its Initiative against Illegal Logging, launched in 2003, is the most comprehensive strategy undertaken by any nation to combat illegal logging, including the sale and export of illegally harvested timber.[16]

ASEAN summits and the ASEAN ministers of agriculture and forestry (AMAF) meetings regularly address the problem of deforestation and the illegal logging trade. The forestry officials have become part of a wider regional framework that was established at a 2001 East Asian Ministerial Conference on Forest Law Enforcement and Governance (FLEG). FLEG task forces were set up to coordinate relevant agency cooperation. A second FLEG ministerial meeting was scheduled for the Philippines in 2008. In 2007, the AMAF began the process of developing an ASEAN FLEG collective mechanism to combat illegal logging and its associated trade.[17] On the demand side, no country in Asia has laws prohibiting the import of timber or wood products that were illegally sourced in the country of origin. Even if it did, how would it be policed?

The Southeast Asian Toll

Even as the national governments try to manage their forests in a sustainable manner through licenses, quotas, and forest preserves, illegal logging and cross-border illegal trading continues apace. The greatest demand is from China, which over ten years has transformed the world's raw wood trade. China has the second-largest wood manufacturing sector in the world and is the largest trader in tropical hardwoods. Half of the tropical logs traded globally go to China. China banned domestic logging in 1998, and has avariciously turned to Southeast Asia for supply—legal or otherwise. Myanmar's forests, like other components of Myanmar's resource base, have become adjuncts to China's rise. It is estimated that over a million tons a year of illegally logged Myanmar timber is delivered to China.[18] Former timber exporters Vietnam and Malaysia have emerged as major markets for illegal timber imports from their ASEAN partners.

Fragile ecosystems in Southeast Asia already have been destroyed. Thailand, the Philippines, and Vietnam have essentially lost their productive forests. The Philippines' forest cover is below 20 percent. Between 2000 and 2005, Vietnam lost 51 percent of its remaining primary forest, much of which had been destroyed in the Second Indochina War through the use of chemical defoliants. In order to meet domestic demand, Thailand has to import wood from Myanmar, Laos, and Cambodia. The last thing that logging operators in those countries are concerned about is environmental damage and sustainability. Rampant logging to satisfy Asian markets has stripped Cambodia of more than half of its forest cover since 1970. In 1999, the London-based NGO Global Witness, with international donor funding, was named "independent monitor" of the Cambodian government's forestry programs. In January 2003, Prime Minister Hun Sen terminated its work, angry over Global Witness reports of corruption and intimidation. It is estimated that from 2000 to 2005, Cambodia lost nearly 30 percent of its primary tropical forests. According to Global Witness, the illegal logging "is part of a massive asset-stripping for the benefit of a small kleptocratic elite" that included Prime Minister Hun Sen's family.[19]

Laos, caught between timber-starved Thailand and Vietnam, is seeing its forests illegally felled to supply its neighbors. The Lao PDR officially prohibits the export of logs, but as the British NGO Environmental Investigation Agency (EIA) and the Indonesian-based NGO Telapak documented in 2007, hundreds of thousands of cubic meters of logs are being delivered to Thailand and Vietnam annually.[20] Vietnam has become the world's fourth-largest exporter of wood products, but half of its raw wood supply is illegally cut, with Laos being the major source. The Laos case is a model of the illegal logging industry. Bribery is paid to officials for logging concessions from which logs are diverted from a domestic value-added wood industry to the illegal cross-border trade.

The government-licensed allowances for cutting are massively exceeded. Local officials and the military are involved. Theoretically protected forest preserves are invaded while the forest rangers look the other way, bribed, physically threatened, or killed. When the hundreds of logging trucks reach the border, customs and immigration agents are paid off. As Lao forests follow in the wake of Cambodia, Thailand, and Vietnam—with Myanmar's forest endowment under heavy Chinese pressure—the largest remaining tropical forests in Southeast Asia are in East Malaysia's Sabah and Sarawak states and Indonesia's Kalimantan and Papuan provinces.

Although the export of logs is banned in Malaysia, its booming building and construction industry has an insatiable thirst for wood. With peninsular Malaysia planted over in palm oil, new plantations are being cleared in Sabah and Sarawak. Forest loss in East Malaysia is proceeding steadily. Logging in Sarawak became a high-visibility international human rights issue in the 1980s and 1990s when international rights groups adopted the cause of the Penan tribesmen in their conflict with Malaysian logging interests.[21] The Penan are an indigenous tribal group whose traditional forest habitats were being logged over. Penan customary rights were overridden by Malaysian facilitation of clear-cut logging. Foreign and domestic defenders of the Penan were no match for the Malaysian government-backed logging industry juggernaut. The plight of the Penan has been echoed in all of the remote margins of developing Southeast Asia—Myanmar's border regions and Indonesia's Papua are cases in point—where the rights of indigenous minorities are trumped by the imperative of resource exploitation.

Government-controlled cutting in East Malaysia's forests has not satisfied Malaysian domestic demand or Malaysian brokers for illegal export to China and Vietnam. Indonesia's porous borders with the East Malaysia states are regularly violated by illegal loggers. According to the Indonesian environmental watchdog WALHI, more than ten million cubic meters of timber is illegally shipped to Malaysia yearly. Indonesia has protested to the Malaysian government, but to little avail. Malaysian officials are loathe to admit Malaysian logging companies are complicit in the trade since many of the larger ones are politically connected. At a 2007 G-8 meeting on illegal logging, an EU representative charged that a number of Malaysian businessmen were involved in illegal logging in Kalimantan and Papua for export to China. The Malaysian representative categorically denied it.[22] Stewarded by the World Wildlife Fund (WWF), a trilateral "Heart of Borneo" scheme involving Brunei, Malaysia, and Indonesia was launched in 2006 to conserve 85,000 square miles (220,000 sq km) of transboundary tropical forests. The problem will be, as it is in national conservation and preservation areas, how to keep the would-be trespassers at bay.

According to the NGO Forest Watch Indonesia, Indonesia, with the largest tropical forests in the world outside of Brazil, is losing more than 14,000 square miles (36,400 sq km) a year of forests, nearly the size of Switzerland. This is the largest rate of deforestation in the world and, if continued, the result would the loss of productive forests within two decades. Indonesia has already lost 72 percent of its forest cover. Illegal logging is uncontrolled, with as much as 80 percent of Indonesian log exports being illegal and with the cost to Indonesia placed at $3.2 billion a year. A number of factors contribute to the rate of forest loss. First, there is an unabated domestic and foreign demand for the wood. Logging concessions continue to be given. The military and the police are in the logging business. The decentralization of enforcement and corruption leave forests open to plunder. One analysis argues that decentralization of Indonesia's timber regime has led to increased logging, both legal and illegal, without consideration of social and environmental consequences.[23] Although the Indonesian government consistently promises reform, the best available NGO data demonstrates that even if policy reforms were to be successful, Indonesia will still follow the path of Thailand, the Philippines, and the other countries of Southeast Asia where the tipping point has been passed, and the lungs of Southeast Asia will cease breathing.[24]

The "Haze"

The "haze" is the ASEAN euphemism for airborne smoke pollution caused by uncontrolled forest fires. The principal source of the haze is in Indonesia's Kalimantan (Borneo) provinces and Sumatra. The haze is the single most important transboundary environmental issue in Southeast Asia. Smoky air generated by forest fires and peat-bed fires is a regular occurrence. In 1997, it was an economic and human disaster. Smoke from Indonesian fires blanketed nearly two million square miles (five million sq km) for seven months, covering Singapore, parts of Malaysia, Thailand, the Philippines, Australia, and of course, the country of origin, Indonesia. Public health was endangered. The Malaysian government, alarmed by angry public reaction, even stopped issuing routine air quality announcements. Economic loss from business and tourism was estimated at more than $9 billion. The severity and extent of the air quality crisis was unprecedented.[25] The haze has become an annual occurrence, irritating not only the eyes and lungs of Southeast Asia's publics, but relations between Indonesia and the downwind suffering states. In 2000, more than five hundred fires raged out of control. In 2002, fires resulted in moderate to thick haze. In 2006, the region saw the worst haze since 1997, and it was forecast to be even greater in

2008. Indonesia is not the only source of transboundary haze pollution. There have been fires in Myanmar and along the Thai–Cambodian border, but the frequency of occurrence and extent of the Indonesian fires, together with its location and prevailing winds, make Indonesia the primary source of airborne environmental assaults on its neighbors.

The causes of the fires are both natural and manmade. Some fires are caused by lightning strikes, but human agency is the major cause. Illegal loggers use fire to cover their tracks. Fire is the fastest and cheapest way of converting forest to other uses. Once fires start, Indonesia does not have the human, technical, and logistical capabilities to fight them in the remote areas where they burn. Nature in the form of monsoon rain eventually quenches the fires, but hot spots smolder under the carpets of decaying vegetation. The problem of causation, leaving aside lightning, is part of the wider problem of forest management in Indonesia. Indonesian state capability to protect its forests from the human agents of forest fires is limited by weak central authority, decentralization of enforcement, and corruption. While Indonesian rhetorical commitment to root out the plunderers of its forests is politically correct, that is little solace for its ASEAN neighbors in the face of the realities of poor governance at national, provincial, and local levels in Indonesia.

ASEAN has organized itself bureaucratically, if not operationally, to try to help deal with the haze problem. The haze has had a prominent place at the environment ministers' meetings. In 1995 the ministers endorsed an "ASEAN Cooperation Plan on Transboundary Pollution." The ASOEN leads an ASEAN Regional Haze Action Program that is administered by the ASEAN Haze Technical Task Force. The action plan has three components: prevention, monitoring, and mitigation. Implicit in the ASEAN approach is an assumption that Indonesia will improve its domestic capabilities in the three areas. In 1999, the ASEAN ministers announced their consensus on a region-wide zero burn policy—but without enforcement measures. One analyst of ASEAN's response to the haze problem concluded that efforts at the regional level while leading to a "proliferation of meetings and plans have produced little of consequence."[26]

The ASEAN ministers struggled to frame a legal basis for their collaborative efforts to solve the haze problem. Finally, in June 2002, an "ASEAN Agreement on Transboundary Haze Pollution" was signed.[27] The agreement has provisions on monitoring, assessment, prevention, technical and scientific cooperation, mechanisms for coordination, lines of communication, and simplified customs and immigration procedures for disaster relief. It called for the establishment of an ASEAN Coordinating Centre for Transboundary Haze Pollution Control. It came into force in November 2003 with its sixth ratification, not including Indonesia, and was hailed by UNEP as a potential model for tackling transboundary issues worldwide.

Indonesia's failure to ratify the haze pact made suspect elsewhere in ASEAN any sense of Indonesian urgency in responding to the regional concerns. In 2006, as the haze blanket over the region rivaled 1997, the affected countries demanded that Indonesia ratify the pact before they would offer assistance, but the exigencies of the impact on their own populations and their economic losses forced them to address the problem collectively. In October 2006, President Yudhoyono offered an apology for the haze and promised ratification of the haze agreement. Brunei, Indonesia, Malaysia, Singapore, and Thailand then agreed to a series of joint measures aimed at fire prevention and enhancing fire-fighting capabilities. A key innovation was a proposal to allow Indonesia's partners to work directly at the district level in Kalimantan and Sumatra. The first memorandum of understanding was negotiated in 2008 between Malaysia and Indonesia to allow Malaysian participation in haze mitigation in Riau Province. At the November 2006 AMME, the environment ministers established a transboundary haze pollution subregional ministerial steering committee from the five most affected countries and initiated a voluntary "haze fund" of $500,000.

Subregional ministerial cooperation and the fund got off to a rocky start. Indonesia was defensive and sensitive. When Singapore Prime Minister Lee Hsien Loong brought up the haze issue at the UN General Assembly, an angry Yudhoyono refused to shake his hand. It is perhaps because of Indonesian embarrassment that the 2006 haze was not mentioned at the 2006 ASEAN Summit (actually held in January 2007). Indonesian nationalists have adopted the position that the ASEAN Agreement on Transboundary Haze Pollution was unfair since it singled out the haze (and by inference Indonesia) and did not mention toxic waste disposal in Indonesia, Singapore's sand mining, Malaysia's refusal to curb illegal logging by Malaysian companies, Thai poaching in Indonesian fisheries, and other alleged depredations on Indonesia's environment committed by its ASEAN neighbors. These issues sharpened as the Indonesian parliament finally began discussing ratification of the ASEAN haze accord. In March 2008, parliament unanimously rejected ratification of the "ASEAN Transboundary Haze Pollution Agreement," illustrating again that, even in the ASEAN setting, it is individual state behavior—not the ASEAN way—that is ultimately determinative.

The Maritime Zones

With the exception of landlocked Laos, all of the Southeast Asian states have maritime zones that, with the exception of Singapore, include territorial waters, EEZs, and continental shelves. Myanmar is bordered by the Andaman Sea. The other shores of Southeast Asia are washed by the gulfs, straits, and expanse of the South China Sea, a semi-enclosed sea with 90 percent of its circumference rimmed by land. The jurisdictional shape of the South China Sea is like a doughnut, with open sea being the doughnut hole. Even that hole might close if future sovereignty in the disputed Spratly Islands archipelago creates even more extensive jurisdictional claims (chapter 5).

More than 2,500 species of fish and invertebrates are found in the sea, constituting 14 percent of global marine resources. The fisheries, a major source of protein in Southeast Asian diets, are being depleted by uncontrolled overfishing. Poaching in another country's EEZ is common as flagged, falsely flagged, and unflagged vessels venture farther from their national waters in search of catch. Coral reefs are being destroyed by illegal blasting. On the margins of the sea, spreading urbanization and industrialization have produced a flood of toxic effluent runoff. In the tidal zones, the coastal mangrove forests whose rich biodiversity is important for the marine food chain are being converted to fish and prawn farms at a rapid rate. Thailand has lost more than half of its mangrove forests since 1975; Indonesia, 70 percent; the Philippines, 75 percent. The figures are similar elsewhere in Southeast Asia. Oil sludge and ballast discharge foul the water's surface. The South China Sea has been described as "a sink for regional environmental pollution."[28]

In his introduction to the most comprehensive analysis of the environmental ills of the South China Sea and adjacent waters, the director of UNEP's South China Sea project wrote: "Countries bordering the South China Sea have exploited the available resources far beyond their capacities and that without some intervention now they will be destroyed forever."[29] UNEP's programs, directed through its Bangkok-based Coordinating Body for the East Asian Seas (COBSEA), are focused on three key issues: habitat degradation, overfishing, and land-based pollution. In the absence of any regional convention on the South China Sea, it promotes national compliance with existing environmental treaties and, in COBSEA's own words, "is based on member countries' good will." There are no ASEAN agreements mandating regional coordination or integrated programs in any of these areas of concern.

Outside of the ASEAN framework, the Indonesia-led South China Sea workshop process (discussed in chapter 5) identified resource management, environment, and ecology as functional areas in which China and the other claimant states to South China Sea jurisdictions could cooperate. While there has been some measure of scientific and technical exchange and inquiry, there are no operational programmatic results. If future joint development schemes are worked out between China and the Southeast Asian claimants, new environmental threats will further burden the South China Sea's already stressed environment. China's abysmal environmental record in resource exploitation gives no reason to expect that its activities in the South China Sea will be ecologically sensitive.

Potential environmental damage from offshore development is not limited to the marine zone. Oil and gas have to be brought ashore and then delivered by pipeline to consumers.

Thailand's need to fuel its electrical generating plants has brought it into collision with environmental NGOs and local populations. In the 1990s, a highly controversial pipeline was constructed by the Petroleum Authority of Thailand to bring gas from Myanmar's Yadana and Yetagun offshore fields in the Gulf of Martaban to the Electrical Generating Authority of Thailand's (EGAT) plants. The construction provoked strong protest from human rights and environmentalist NGOs. It was alleged that Myanmar's military conscripted ethnic minority labor for the project and that villagers were forcibly displaced. The path of the pipeline and the roads to build it cut through protected forests. The Yadana and Yetagun experience was repeated in Thailand's southern Songkhla province, where a pipeline from the Thai–Malaysian joint development gas field in the Gulf of Thailand lands at a gas separation plant from which a pipeline carries the gas to Malaysia. Although the original contracts were signed in 1998, environmental protest and angry local popular demonstrations stalled the project for two years before the first gas was delivered in 2005. There were allegations by NGOs that Thailand was pressured by Malaysia to override negative environmental impact studies. In a July 2002 bilateral meeting between Prime Minister Mahathir and Prime Minister Thaksin, the latter called on Malaysia to be patient with the delay caused by opponents, but pledged that the project would go ahead.

Even grander pipeline projects are on the drawing boards. China will lay a pipeline to bring gas ashore and to China from the concession Myanmar granted it in 2007 in the coveted Shwe gas fields off the Arakan coast—beating out India and South Korea in the process. More grandiose is the prospect of a Chinese oil pipeline from Myanmar's Sittwe port to Kunming in Yunnan. It would run 500 miles (800 km) to the border, then another 400 miles (650 km) to a refinery. This would allow oil from the Middle East and Africa destined for China to bypass the Malacca Strait. Malaysia approved in 2007 the construction of a transpeninsular oil pipeline across the north of the country from Kedah to Kelantan, bypassing the straits. The $7.5 billion scheme is targeted for a 2014 completion. It could carry up to 20 percent of the oil that now passes through the Malacca Strait. A similar proposed transisthmus pipeline in South Thailand, which at 60 miles (100 km) would be considerably shorter than the 185 mile (300 km) Malaysian project, is in limbo, in part because of the insecurity of the region. It is doubtful that environmental "goodwill" will account for much in the realization of perceived economic and strategic imperatives of national interest.

Rivers, Dams, and Ecosystems

One of the most intensely debated issues in the dialogue between development and the environment is the adverse environmental, social, and economic impacts of large or mega-dams. The most environmentally disruptive form of energy generation is hydroelectric. The damming of free-flowing rivers has been an important element in economic development strategies in Southeast Asia. Large multipurpose dams are utilized for hydroelectric power generation and water impoundment for irrigation and flood control. Governments have been eager to tap this natural resource and harness it to present and future energy requirements. International funding agencies such as the World Bank and the ADB have historically promoted large dam building in Southeast Asia. Institutions and corporations in donor nations have also enthusiastically supported dam building and vied for contracts.

It has been only in recent years that the cost-benefit analysis of dam building and river development has been calculated in other than financial terms. The damming of a river has enormous impact on its ecosystem and the life of the people who depend on it for their livelihood. The natural flood cycle along a dammed river is interrupted. Behind the dam, forests give way to reservoirs. Biodiversity is negatively affected. Villagers are displaced. Fisheries are disrupted and decline. The changed volume of flow downstream leads to new patterns of erosion and river-carried nutrients. The balance of nature that took thousands of years to emerge is altered. The decision to build a dam is not just economic, it is political. It is the national decision makers' task to balance the potential benefits of a dam against the immediate and longer environmental and social costs of the dam. Unfortunately, those most affected by the negative impacts of the dam are often the politically weakest in the domestic political system.

In 1996, stung by criticism, the World Bank, the most important single funding source for large dams, began an internal study of fifty dams it had funded. Its report and subsequent consultations and conferences led to the establishment in May 1998 of the independent World Commission on Dams (WCD) to address the controversial issues associated with large dams. The WCD embarked on a systematic global-wide review of the experiences and lessons of large dam building in terms of benefits, costs, and impacts. The WCD's report was issued in November 2000.[30] The empirical basis was a comparative survey of 125 representative large dams around the world—12 in Southeast Asia—and eight detailed case studies.[31] The WCD's report provides new criteria for the evaluation, building, operation, and decommissioning of dams. The follow-up was coordinated in UNEP's Dams and Development Project. The WCD's criteria are recommendations, not mandates, and have largely been ignored by states committed to rapid economic development at any cost. The WCD report has been seized upon by umbrella INGOs like the International Rivers Network (IRN) and Rivers Watch East and Southeast Asia (RWESEA) to bolster their campaigns against environmental and human rights-destructive damming. The environmentalists' call—unheard by national authorities—is for a moratorium on large dam construction until the recommendations of the WCD are implemented and reparations paid to dam-affected communities.

The WCD's Southeast Asia case study was Thailand's Pak Mun dam, which sits three miles upstream from the Mun River's confluence with the Mekong River. It was built by EGAT as a run-of-the-river hydropower electrical generating plant. From its conception in the early 1980s to its completion in 1994 and its operations today, it was been a source of controversy and protest on site, in Bangkok, at Thai embassies overseas, and at the World Bank's headquarters in Washington. The WCD's conclusion about the Pak Mun dam was that if all of the benefits and costs had been adequately assessed, the project as it stands would not have been built. EGAT and the Thai government rejected the report.

In the 1990s, Malaysia's Bakun dam project was another poster-child of anti–large dam protesters. The dam, on the Balui River in a remote area of Sarawak's rainforest, as originally conceived would have been one of Southeast Asia's largest infrastructure projects. The dam's energy production was to be delivered to peninsular Malaysia by undersea cable. The project will flood 800 square miles (1,300 sq km) of tropical forest and displace ten thousand indigenous people under a policy of relocation before compensation. Prime Minister Mahathir scornfully denounced the protesters as tools of Western vested interests. At the 1996 symbolic rock-blasting ceremony inaugurating construction at Bakun, Mahathir told the audience that "Malaysia wants to develop and I say to the so-called environmentalists: Mind your own business."[32] Like so many other Southeast Asian mega-infrastructure projects, the Bakun dam, originally planned to go on line in 2003, was put on hold as a result of the financial Crash of '97. Site preparation continued. The proposed reservoir area was logged over and thousands of inhabitants removed to resettlement areas. In 2001, the government revived the dam project minus the plan for an undersea cable to the peninsula. To its domestic and foreign NGO critics, the Bakun dam is a an economic boondoggle destined to be a prestige "white elephant" without the benefits that would outweigh its human, social, and environmental costs. As the dam neared completion in 2007, plans were announced for an aluminum smelter linking a company connected to Sarawak's chief minister and the mining giant Rio Tinto.

Damming the Mekong River

Along its more than 3,000 mile (4,800 km) course, once it drops from the Tibetan plateau and through the gorges of Yunnan, the Mekong River with its tributaries is the life's blood of the Mekong Basin's sixty million inhabitants. Its fisheries are a major source of protein. In its navigable stretches, it is a commercial and market artery. Its flood-borne deposits of nutrient-rich silt and irrigation water are critical to the region's agriculture. Life along the river is geared to its annual cycle of high and low water. In Cambodia the Mekong flood reverses the flow of the Tonle Sap, filling the "Great Lake," Cambodia's rice and fish basket. In Vietnam, it is the river's flow through its multiple mouths into the South China Sea that keeps back salt water intrusion into the delta's rice fields. The 800,000 square mile (207 million sq km) drainage basin is larger than France or Texas. Even though the river borders and flows through six sovereign states, geophysically it is a hydrological unit. All water management projects, whether for flood control, irrigation, or hydroelectric generation, require alterations in the flow of the river through diversion, canalization, or damming. Any change in the river's rate and volume of flow affects the balance of the ecosystem and pattern of life along the Mekong.

That pattern is challenged today, as political leaderships of the riparian states seek to harness the river's potential as an agent of modernization, industrialization, and social change. In chapter 4, the competitive overlapping Mekong basin development programs were outlined. Theoretically, the Mekong River Commission provides a framework for harmonizing the different national interests in river development as well as technical project assessments. It, like the World Bank and ADB, has historically promoted hydropower.

Over the past decade more than a hundred large dams have been in various stages of construction or planning to manage the river system in ways that effect changes in its natural course. This has produced conflicts of interest in two politically sensitive issue areas: the different needs of upstream and downstream countries and the social and environmental costs of development. Any activity by upstream countries that changes the flow or pollutes the water can have disastrous consequences for the ecology of downstream countries. Both Cambodia and Vietnam have already complained of adverse effects in their downstream stretches of the river from upstream activities. Upstream–downstream issues are central to the international politics of the development of the Mekong basin. The problem pits China's view of its national interests against the interests of the downstream states of continental Southeast Asia. The question is whether a regional framework for coordination and planning can emerge for the exploitation and utilization of transboundary rivers that will reconcile the conflicting economic and political interests as well as satisfy the demands for environmental and social safeguards.

China's Upstream Threat

China has embarked on an ambitious dam building program in Yunnan Province that already is negatively impacting the downstream Southeast Asian states. Its plans call for eight dams. Two have been completed. The Manwan dam was completed in 1996 and the Dachaoshan in 2003. Both dams were built without assessment of upstream or downstream environmental or social impacts. China, a nonmember, is not bound by the consultative commitments of the Mekong River Commission. The third dam, the Xiaowan, is the highest planned and will be second only to the Three Gorges dam on the Yangtze. It will be completed in 2012.

The effects of the dams and their construction on the river's volume and quality are already being felt in northern Thailand and Laos. They block the flow of nutrient-laden sediment that is vital for agriculture and degrade the fisheries. There is also concern that as southwest China industrializes, China's notorious disregard of the environment will allow unchecked industrial waste discharge to destroy water quality. China has scorned the WCD process and its UNEP follow-ups on large dams as not applicable to China's economic growth needs and an unwarranted intrusion into China's internal affairs. The environmental consequence of China's unilateralism for the lives and livelihood of the people who live along the Mekong is a matter of great concern. The introduction to one study is headed "China's Lancang Dams Endanger Millions both Upstream and Down Stream."[33]

Most of the electricity generated by the dams will be transmitted to China's power-short east coast population and economic growth centers. Continued development will involve ever greater energy demands. China has made it absolutely clear that it will not allow industrialization to slow down to appease Western environmentalists or downstream concerns in Southeast Asia. When the full complex of dams is completed, perhaps in a quarter of a century, China's hydraulic mastery of its reaches of the river means its decisions on opening and closure of sluices and gates can give it control over the water level of the river to its Vietnam delta outlets to the sea. This is a feared outcome in Phnom Penh and Hanoi.

It is not just dam building on the Lancang/Mekong that troubles the downstream inhabitants. China is widening and deepening the river by blasting rapids and dredging so that even in the dry season five-hundred-ton vessels can commercially navigate from Yunnan to river ports in northern Thailand and Laos. Ultimately, up to one hundred rapids are set for demolition. Environment officials in Laos, Thailand, and Cambodia have repeatedly warned of the damage to the Mekong ecosystem that is being caused by the navigation project. Upstream migration of fish species for spawning will be impeded as well as downstream changes in water flow as the elimination of the rapids causes stronger currents and greater riverbank erosion. There have also been negative economic consequences for Thai and Lao small businesses as Chinese goods and agricultural products flood the local markets. The river projects fit into a plan for an integrated transportation system—roads, rail, and river—linking continental Southeast Asia to southwest China (chapter 4). The fear is that the upper reach of the Southeast Asian stretch of the Mekong is becoming part of a greater-Yunnan economy.

It is hoped in Southeast Asia that by engaging China in a web of multilateral programs for Mekong River development, China's unilateralism might be tamed to greater consultation and cooperation on upstream–downstream matters. Even if China were to accept in principle a policy premise of interdependence, there is no legal or treaty basis to hold China to a riparian consensus. Individual countries have the sovereign right to carry out national projects unilaterally without the approval of other riparian states—despite the "Rio Declaration." China's actions on the Mekong are being viewed by some as a test of its "peaceful rise" based on mutually beneficial cooperative endeavors rather than challenges or threats. However, its behavior to date shows that it seeks to maximize opportunities. Describing China's role on the river as "trickle-down hegemony," one analyst has concluded that "China has by and large pursued its own interests without regard for how these actions will affect its downstream neighbors."[34]

The Laos "Battery" of Southeast Asia

With its numerous Mekong tributaries, Laos is envisioned as a future hydroelectric "battery" at the center of a Southeast Asian power grid supplying power to energy-thirsty China, Thailand, and Vietnam. According to the LPDR's July 2007 updated power development plan, ten dams were in operation, four under construction, another ten had planned operation dates between 2010 and 2015, thirty-eight had memoranda of understanding with investors and sponsors, and fourteen were under study.[35] It is argued by proponents of hydropower development in Laos that the export of hydroelectricity will be for the foreseeable future the main economic resource available to the government for the achievement of its economic goals. Six of the proposed dams are Mekong mainstream dams. This has brought angry protests from Cambodia and Vietnam.

Dam building in Laos has come under the same environmental and social scrutiny as dam building elsewhere in Southeast Asia. Just as the Bakun and Pak Mun dams became iconic symbols of anti–large dam activity, the Nam Theun II dam was the focus in Laos. Impounding the Theun River, the Mekong's fourth largest tributary, it will be the largest dam built in Laos. It sits on what was once the heavily forested Nakai Plateau. The lake behind it will inundate more than 170 square miles (440 sq km) and more than a thousand households will be displaced. Originally proposed in the early 1990s, heavy opposition from environmentalists caused the World Bank to delay a loan decision. The economic crisis intervened, but the plan is back on track. In July 2003, the Thai cabinet approved an EGAT twenty-five-year purchasing power agreement that gave the green light to the Lao government and the developing consortium to go ahead. The dam may provide $150 million a year in revenue to Laos. Construction began in 2004 and it is expected that full commercial operation will be on line in 2009. At the end of 2003, the World Bank still had withheld its participation. The dam's development consortium had requested a political risk guarantee from the Bank and the government had requested a loan to buy a 10 percent equity stake in the project. In a WCD framework, however, the Bank, at the end of 2003, was still unsatisfied with the analysis of the environmental and social costs and benefits of the project. In March 2006, over the strident objections of the dam's environmentalist opponents, the World Bank, satisfied with the social and environmental mitigation measures, agreed to subsidize the project.

Cambodian–Chinese Partnership

Not to be left out of the rush to harness the rivers, Cambodia also wants to be a battery for Southeast Asia. In the ADB-driven Mekong Power Grid Plan, Cambodia is viewed as an eventual power exporter. Six of a possible fourteen projects are under development, all by Chinese companies. China's single largest investment in Cambodia is a dam being built on the Kamchay River in Kampot. The area to be flooded is in a national park. A second dam being built at Stung Atay will flood a protected forest. With China providing $600 million to fund construction, there is not the kind of transparency that would give assurances that the social and environmental impacts of the dam building will be mitigated. One possible Mekong mainstream dam is being studied.

The Salween River Basin

The Salween River, known in China as the Nu Jiang, rising on the Tibetan Plateau, runs nearly 1,750 miles (2,800 km). It is the region's longest free-flowing river. Its course takes it through China's Yunnan Province, Thailand, and Myanmar, emptying into the Andaman Sea's Gulf of Martaban. The Salween basin covers more than 200,000 square miles (518,000 sq km). The river forms more than 70 miles (112 km) of the Thai–Myanmar border, on the Thai side much of it national park and wildlife refuge. The Southeast Asian part of the basin is the homeland of ethnic minorities: Karen, Karenni, Kayah, and Shan, who depend upon it for their livelihood of rice farming and fishing. New large dam projects are on the drawing board and the Nu/Salween, like the Lancang/Mekong, has become a focus of environmental concern in Southeast Asia.[36]

In 1989, Myanmar and Thailand established a working group to promote and coordinate the development of hydropower projects in the Salween Basin. The Crash of '97 (chapter 7) put large infrastructure planning on the back-burner, but with Thai economic recovery and Myanmar's desperate search for cash and economic partnerships, both sides are pushing plans for damming the Salween. A 2005 memorandum of understanding between Yangon and Bangkok was for five dams. The first to be started was at Hutgyi, located in the Karen state, opposite Thailand's Mae Hong San province. This is to be a joint development of EGAT and China's Sinohydro state corporation. Activity at the dam site came to a dramatic halt in September 2007 after it was shelled by Karen insurgents. EGAT was forced to abandon the site until greater security could be put in place.

Critics of Myanmar–Thai dam building argue that the Thais are ignoring, or even manipulating, Myanmar's oppression of the border region's ethnic minorities. The environmental impact will be felt largely by Myanmar's ethnic minorities. Many of the tens of thousands of ethnic minorities displaced by dam building will likely end up joining other Myanmar refugees in Thai camps (chapter 8).

While Thailand and Myanmar jointly plan for the Salween, north of them, China has its own plans for exploiting the Nu Jiang. Like China's Lancang projects, its plans for the Nu Jiang have not involved environmental consultation with downstream riparians. China has on the drawing boards a twenty-year plan for thirteen hydropower dams on the river, more than the Lancang projects. There has been no expectation, given past history, that China will follow the cost-benefit guidelines urged by the WCD or cooperate in a transboundary framework for environmental and social impact assessments. The first dam, at Liuku near the Sino-Myanmar border, was scheduled to begin construction in 2004. Thai Prime Minister Thaksin stated, "China, which is a big country, will be careful not to be accused of taking advantage of smaller countries."[37] Thaksin's relative insouciance may be connected to Thailand's own dam building plans for the Salween.

In an unprecedented move, in April 2004 Chinese Prime Minister Wen Jia-bao, noting the high level of environmental concerns, put the Liuku project on hold and called for a full review of the Nu River hydro projects. Although no official statements have been made, work on the site recommenced in 2008.

When ASEAN looked to the twenty-first century in its 1997 "Vision 2020," it envisioned a "clean and green" Southeast Asia with fully implemented mechanisms ensuring the protection of the region's environment, the sustainability of its natural resources, and a high quality of life for its populations. The record to date of aggressive pursuit of these goals in terms of actions and enforcement has not been particularly impressive at either the regional or national level. One analyst has concluded that ASEAN has been unable to respond effectively to regional environmental challenges for normative and material reasons.[38] As in other areas of ASEAN undertakings, environmental cooperation has been constrained by the ASEAN way. ASEAN has no authority to intervene to safeguard the environment or to hold nations like Indonesia legally accountable for environmental damage and pollution. Nationally, the primary obstacle has been the domestic policy dominance of economic interests that have benefited from environmental laxness where regulative structures and law are violated with impunity.

Notes

1. James Rush, *The Last Tree: Reclaiming the Environment in Tropical Asia* (New York: The Asia Society, 1991).

2. Lorraine Elliott, "Regional Environmental Security: Pursuing a Non-Traditional Approach," in Andrew T. H. Tan and J. D. Boutin, eds., *Non-Traditional Security Issues in Southeast Asia* (Singapore: Institute of Defence and Strategic Studies, 2001), 438–47; R. T. Maddock, "Environmental Security in East Asia," *Contemporary Southeast Asia* 17, no. 1 (1995): 20–37.

3. The Thai "worst case" model is discussed in Donald E. Weatherbee, "Environment, Development, and Security in Southeast Asia," in Sheldon W. Simon, ed., *The Many Faces of Asian Security* (Lanham, Md.: Rowman & Littlefield, 2001), 145–47.

4. James Clad and Aurora Medina Siy, "The Emergence of Ecological Issues in Southeast Asia," in David Wurfel and Bruce Burton, eds., *Southeast Asia in the New World Order: The Political Economy of a Dynamic Region* (New York: St. Martin's, 1996), 52.

5. Thilo Bode, as cited in a Greenpeace press release on the opening of Green-peace's Southeast Asian headquarters in Bangkok, 17 November 2000.

6. The "Rio Declaration" can be accessed at www.unep.org/Documents/Default .asp?DocumentID=78&ArticleID=1163.

7. "Indonesia Calls for the Rich to Pay Poorer Countries to Keep Forests," *The Standard*, 1 February 2007.

8. The 24 September 2007 joint statement by the tropical rain forest countries' leaders can be accessed at www.unfcccbali.org/unfccc/images/stories/joint_state-ment.pdf. In addition to Indonesia, the countries were Brazil, Cameroon, Colombia, Congo, Costa Rica, Democratic Republic of Congo, Gabon, Malaysia, Papua New Guinea, and Peru.

9. The "Manila Declaration" and succeeding ASEAN declarations and resolutions on the environment can be accessed through links at www.aseansec.org/8919.htm.

10. The Cebu resolution can be accessed at www.aseansec.org/18915.htm.

11. ASEAN Secretariat, *Third ASEAN State of the Environment Report* (Jakarta: ASEAN, 2006). The first report was published in 1997, the second in 2000. In addition there is a 2002 *ASEAN Report to the World Summit on Sustainable Development* (www.aseansec.org/viewpdf.asp?file=pdf/WSSD.pdf).

12. The "Vientiane Action Programme" can be accessed at www.aseansec.org/VAP-10th%20ASEAN%20Summit.pdf.

13. Mark A. McDowell, "Development and the Environment in Southeast Asia," *Pacific Affairs* 62, no. 3 (Fall 1989): 310.

14. Clad and Siy, "The Emergence of Ecological Issues," in Wurfel and Burton, eds., *Southeast Asia in the New World Order* (New York: St. Martin's, 1996), 54.

15. UN General Assembly document A/CONF.151/26 (Vol. III).

16. "President's Initiative against Illegal Logging," accessed at www.usaid.gov/about_usaid/presidential_initiative/logging.html.

17. "ASEAN Statement on Strengthening Forest Law Enforcement and Governance (FLEG)," Bangkok 1 November 2007, accessed at www.aseansec.org/21032.htm.

18. "China Accused over Burma Forests," *BBC News*, 18 October 2005.

19. "Group Says Illegal Logging Benefits Ruling Class in Cambodia," *International Herald Tribune*, 1 June 2007.

20. "Illegal Logging Hits Laos Forests," *The Nation*, 1 April 2004; "Illegal Logs from Laos Fuel Mekong Region's Furniture Industry," *The Straits Times*, 22 March 2008.

21. For the Penan, see Wade Davis, Ian McKenzie, and Shane Kennedy, *Nomads of the Dawn: The Penan of the Borneo Rainforest* (Bristol, U.K: Pomegranate, 1995).

22. "EU, US Report Malaysian Businessmen in Illegal Logging in Indonesia," *The Jakarta Post*, 6 June 2007.

23. Ida Aju Pradnya Resosudarmo, "Shifting Power to the Periphery: The Impact of Decentralization on Forests and Forests People," in Edward Aspinall and Greg Feally, eds., *Local Power and Politics in Indonesia: Decentralization & Democracy* (Singapore: Institute of Southeast Asian Studies, 2003), 230–45.

24. Emily Matthews, Restu Achmaliadi, and Charles Victor Barber, eds., *The State of the Forest: Indonesia* (Washington, D.C.: World Resources Institute, 2002).

25. David Glover and Timothy Jessup, eds., *Indonesia's Fire and Haze: The Cost of Catastrophe* (Singapore: Institute of Southeast Asian Studies, 1999).

26. James Cotton, "The 'Haze' over Southeast Asia: Challenging the ASEAN Mode of Regional Engagement," *Pacific Affairs* 72, no. 3 (Fall 1999): 351.

27. The agreement can be accessed at www.aseansec.org/6086.htm.

28. David Steinberg, "Environmental Pollution around the South China Sea: Developing a Regional Response," *Contemporary Southeast Asia* 21, no. 1 (1999): 142.

29. L. Talaue-McManus, "Transboundary Diagnostic Analysis for the South China Sea," East Asian Seas Regional Coordinating Unit, Technical Report No. 14, 2000, accessed at www.cobsea.org/documents/Transboundary_Diagnostic_Analysis.pdf.

30. World Commission on Dams, *Dams and Development: A New Framework for Decision Making* (London: Earthscan, 2000). It is also available as a PDF file at www.dams.org/docs/report/wcdreport.pdf.

31. The Southeast Asian dams were, in Indonesia, the Seguling; in Malaysia, the Muda and Semeyih; in the Philippines, the Magat and Pantabangan; in Thailand, the Bhumibol, Lam Pao, Pak Mun, and Sirindhorn; and in Vietnam, the Nui Coc and Ea Yu dams. The Pak Mun dam was selected as one of the case studies.

32. "Mahathir Slams Critics of Dam Project," *The Straits Times*, 17 March 1996.

33. Kaori Ohsawa et al., *Lancang-Mekong: A River of Controversy* (November 2003), accessed at www.rwesa.org/lancang.

34. Alex Liebman, "Trickle-down Hegemony? China's 'Peaceful Rise' and Dam Building on the Mekong," *Contemporary Southeast Asia* 27, no. 2 (2005): 281.

35. "Power Development Plan in Laos," 17 August 2007, accessed at www.power-ingprogress.org/energy_sector/pdf_files/Electric_Power_Plants_in_Laos_as_of_August_2007.pdf.

36. In addition to the International Rivers Network and Rivers Watch East and Southeast Asia, the Salween Watch (www.salweenwatch.org) provides coverage of environmental issues in the development plans for the Salween basin.

37. As quoted in "Salween River Dams: PM: China Sure to Be Considerate," *Bangkok Post*, 19 December 2003.

38. Lorraine Elliott, "ASEAN and Environmental Cooperation: Norms, Interests, and Identity," *The Pacific Review* 16, no. 1 (2003): 29–52.

Suggestions for Further Reading

Paul G. Harris, ed., *Confronting Environmental Change in East and Southeast Asia: Ecopolitics, Foreign Policy, and Sustainable Development* (Tokyo: United Nations University Press, 2005); Andrew Tan, ed., *Southeast Asia: Threats in the Security Environment* (Singapore: Marshall Cavendish, 2006); Philip Hirsch and Carol Warren, eds., *The Politics of Environment in Southeast Asia: Resources and Resistance* (London: Routledge, 1998); Andrea Straube, *Institutions, Livelihood and the Environment: Change and Response in Mainland*

Southeast Asia (Copenhagen: NIAS press, 2001); Peter Dauveregne, *Shadows in the Forests: Japan and the Politics of Timber in Southeast Asia* (Cambridge, Mass.: MIT Press, 1997); James David Fahn, *A Land on Fire: Environmental Consequences of the Southeast Asian Boom* (Boulder, Colo.: Westview, 2003); Milton Osborne, *The Mekong: Turbulent Past, Uncertain Future* (New York: Atlantic Monthly, 2000); Edward A. Gargan, *The River's Tale: A Year on the Mekong* (New York: Alfred A. Knopf, 2002). The ASEAN/ADB assessment of regionalism and the "haze" is presented in S. Tahir Quadri, ed., *Fire, Smoke, and Haze: The ASEAN Response Strategy* (Manila: Asian Development Bank, 2001). It also can be read as a PDF file at www.aseansec.org/viewpdf.asp?file= /pdf/fsh.pdf.

10

Conclusion: Nation-States, ASEAN, and Autonomy

THE SUBSTANCE OF INTERNATIONAL RELATIONS in Southeast Asia consists of transactions based on a complex of broad and deep interests pursued by state and nonstate actors in a dynamic interaction. Policymakers and academics tend to focus on security in the usual sense of defense of sovereignty, territory, and populations as a singularly important interest that realists would argue is fundamental. Other vital interests are pursued as well: political, economic, social, and cultural. A traditional balance of power analytical framework with its fixation on security gives only a partial glimpse of the interest agendas that inform international relations in Southeast Asia. The chapters in this book have attempted to show broadly the scope of interests at play, both traditional and nontraditional, and the policies that have been chosen to further them. The starting point for this study of international relations in Southeast Asia has been the state as the primary actor. While acknowledging the intellectual richness of international relations theory, by focusing on the state actor and national interests, one almost perforce arrives at a realist perspective.

The State as Actor

For policy purposes, the controlling interest agendas are set by national authorities and are embedded in unique domestic historical, economic, political, cultural, and psychological settings. At times, of course, national authority may be reacting to policies serving the agendas of other states or nonstate actors;

nevertheless, state behavior in Southeast Asia, as elsewhere, is firmly tied to perceptions of national interest. A more comprehensive analysis of international relations in Southeast Asia than that presented here would have to identify the important domestic determinants of a state's international behavior. Jörn Dosch, for example, has looked at international politics in Southeast Asia in a two-level game framework linking the national and international contexts of decision making.[1] That is what gives country case studies in works like Clark Neher's comparative significance.[2]

A realist perception is amplified by the fact that outcome for policy depends on the state's capability to influence decisions and actions by other states. That capability is a manifestation of power. The foreign policy tools that are utilized in Southeast Asia are those of traditional statecraft, from diplomacy and suasion through coercion. The tools have been applied unilaterally, bilaterally, or multilaterally through ASEAN. An important theme of the book is that ASEAN is only a piece of the pattern of international relations in Southeast Asia. We do not pretend to have looked at all of the pieces but certainly have demonstrated that the process of international relations in Southeast Asia is not unique to the region because of ASEAN. Despite the protestations of ASEAN cultural reductionists, Southeast Asia is not analytically sui generis. It is a regional setting for an international relations regime that is a part of a global international order.

As state actors, the Southeast Asian states continue to assert vigorously their claim to sovereignty. Despite ASEAN, or perhaps obscured by ASEANophiles, the Westphalian model is still dominant in Southeast Asia. In the ASEAN context, the claim to sovereignty, as we have repeatedly seen, is affirmatively formulated as the principle of noninterference. We have underlined the fact that adherence to this principle sets sensitive political limits to the effectiveness of ASEAN's cooperative arrangements. In Southeast Asia there is no central supranational authority with regulative or enforcement capabilities above the state actors. In the regional Southeast Asian international setting, as in the global nation-state system, it is the state's choice of policy tools as related to the vitality of its interests that will determine the levels of conflict, competition, and cooperation in its relations with other states.

The greatest part of intraregional political relations relates to the traditional issues of sovereignty, protection of citizens, territoriality, immigration, and other important and sometimes mundane cross-border issues. For example, when Malaysian Foreign Minister Rais Yatim met his Indonesian counterpart Hassan Wirajuda in Jakarta in May 2008, the agenda was illegal logging, migrant workers, visa problems, the contest in the Sulawesi Sea, and emotive cultural and image problems that have stirred anti-Malaysian feelings in Indonesia that are reciprocated by anti-Indonesian feeling in Malaysia. Many of these kinds of bilateral issues—the daily grist for Southeast Asian foreign policy mills—have been discussed in the preceding chapters. When nationalist passions are aroused, the task of peaceful resolution becomes more difficult. After more than half a century, contention over the Preah Vihear temple precincts can still inflame Thai–Cambodian relations. We have also seen in the earlier discussions that in some cases the threat of the use of force is in the background. We have also seen the unwillingness of the states to raise the issues to the regional level where theoretically ASEAN mechanisms for peaceful resolution of disputes are in place. The management of competitive interests will become more difficult in the future in areas where energy and resources security are at stake. This is already the case in the South China Sea and Mekong Basin (chapters 5 and 8).

The working out of relations between and among nations in Southeast Asia, while based on real capabilities, takes place against a normative background of principles and law. Regional norms and principles have not replaced national interests as the independent variables in the decision making of Southeast Asian national elites. They are among the items that have to be factored into policy cost–benefit analyses. The normative framework in Southeast Asia has its origin in international law and the principles of the charter of the United Nations. These have been augmented and enhanced in the regional setting by formal reference to the Bandung Principles, the TAC, and other expressions of regional norms and injunctive rules of conduct alluded to in the text. International law provides no guide to international practice in Southeast Asia; all of the participants in the South China Sea jurisdictional tangle claim UNCLOS as justification. To this list, we can add the affirmations of the ASEAN way. On closer inspection, the ASEAN way itself, stripped of cultural romanticism, is at its heart a reformulation of traditional rules of the diplomatic game: respect for sovereignty, noninterference, and the search for consensus. As we have seen, however, law and norms cannot trump national interest unless there are measures of censure and enforcement. The deterrent to norm breaking in the Southeast Asian regional international system is, as it is in the global system, reciprocity and retaliation.

Where Does ASEAN Fit In?

ASEAN is an intergovernmental platform to promote interstate cooperation in areas of state activity where there is a high degree of complementarities of member states' interests. Unlike constructivist theory, which looks to identity, or liberal institutionalism, with its focus on integration, the approach adopted in these pages reflects, it is believed, how Southeast Asian practitioners of international relations understand their own relationship to ASEAN. They look to real outcomes promoting national interests. There is no regional interest derived independently of or transcending national interest. An ASEAN interest is an expression of a policy consensus reflecting the national interests of the members. Nor is there a regional capability that exists separately from the national capabilities of the ASEAN member states. We have pointed out regional transboundary problems that require transnational solutions. Problems like the "haze," the ecology of the Mekong Basin, and the health of the South China Sea, for example, all fit into that category. However, it is not until national actors recognize that it is in their national interest to attack the problems that action will follow. The originally Indonesian concept of regional resilience is understood only in terms of a notional additive process of national resilience, not something that springs from a pooling of resources in a unitary ASEAN.

In their relations within ASEAN, the member states prioritize their interests just as they do in their other international environments. From this vantage, ASEAN can be understood as an agent of state actors, not as an actor itself. But what happens if a member state feels confined or constrained by the demand for ASEAN solidarity? We have noted some occasions when an ASEAN member has strayed from the reservation at critical times. In the Third Indochina War (chapter 3) both Indonesia and Thailand broke the ASEAN consensus to make unilateral overtures to the Democratic Republic of Vietnam. The other members had little choice but to follow on or possibly rupture their strategic alliance. Today, for ASEAN's long-run future, the growing political gulf between the CLMV countries and the more democratic states poses a threat to ASEAN solidarity. Since ASEAN's expansion more than a decade ago, the CLMV countries have been a brake on ASEAN's evolution from a loose association toward a rules-based international organization.

The vetoes wielded by the CLMV countries through the ASEAN way on a liberal ASEAN charter proved exceedingly disappointing for proponents of a forward-looking document. The huge gap between the draft proposals and the final document left embarrassed leaders in Thailand, the Philippines, and Indonesia trying to explain it away to their own civil society constituencies. The letdown became greater as the world saw the savage way the Myanmar junta treated its people and accused ASEAN of aiding and abetting. In a startling commentary that warned of the consequences of the corrosive impact of the CLMV countries on ASEAN solidarity, Jusuf Wanandi, one of Indonesia's and Southeast Asia's most senior foreign policy analysts, wrote that "Indonesia has become too dependent on ASEAN as the instrument of foreign policy," and if ASEAN cannot move beyond its lowest common denominator it is likely that Indonesia will seek to become more independent from ASEAN.[3] The existence of ASEAN does not prevent Indonesia or any other state from pursuing its national interests using whatever capabilities and tools are at its disposal. As Wanandi rightly pointed out, ASEAN was only an instrument of Indonesian foreign policy. If the instrument does not do the job of securing national interest, other instruments can be utilized. The state is in command. Indonesia's attitude toward ASEAN's political qualities is critical. Although Wanandi did not say it, other Indonesians have: ASEAN needs Indonesia more than Indonesia needs ASEAN. A former editor of the *Far Eastern Economic Review* put it more diplomatically. "Without Indonesia's presence and responsible leadership, Southeast Asia's chemistry is thrown out of balance and it becomes a region diminished in the eyes of the world."[4] It already has become a region diminished in the eyes of the world. The question is how long will Indonesia and other members of ASEAN 6 value solidarity over the norms and rules they purport to uphold?

ASEAN has been important in providing a structured forum in which the member states can collectively engage their extraregional interlocutors. The discussion in the book emphasizes this aspect of ASEAN. From this vantage, ASEAN can be seen as a diplomatic caucus or concert in which the complementary interests of the member states can gain a politically amplified hearing by dialogue partners. In ASEAN + 1, ASEAN + 3, and ASEAN + 10 settings, the grouping has been able to elicit commitments and pledges that might not be as forthcoming on just a bilateral state-to-state basis. But the commitments and pledges are fulfilled in bilateral arrangements. ASEAN's function as a diplomatic alliance has been given form through a rhetorical unity that has tended to obscure the fact that there has been no real pooling of the members states' capabilities in instrumentally effective ways. The limits to any influence that such an ASEAN diplomatic caucus might have are clearly indicated by its role in ARF. Despite its proclaimed leadership of ARF, ASEAN has in fact been a relatively ineffective follower, unable to give institutional shape or real policy relevance to the grouping.

The effectual inutility of ASEAN when confronted by challenge was again demonstrated in spring 2008. In the face of the human disaster in Myanmar caused by the cyclone and the refusal of the junta to allow the international community to come to the aid of its stricken population, ASEAN essentially stood aside. There was no ASEAN-coordinated or concerted regional response. There was agreement within ASEAN, however, that the West should not use the junta's stalling on relief efforts to further pressure the junta on democracy. A second example was the nonresponse by ASEAN to the threat to food security in the region as rice stocks tightened and prices escalated. As ASEAN's rice importers, particularly the Philippines, scrambled for supply, rice exporters like Vietnam defended local supply and prices by halting exports. Even as the ADB announced emergency loans to consumer countries as

rice exporters pushed prices up, Thailand, the largest exporter, floated the idea
of a Thailand, Cambodia, Myanmar, and Vietnam exporter cartel.

The Westphalian underpinning of ASEAN in its practical application limits
the institutional developmental capacities of ASEAN. It has been pointed out
that all of the major undertakings of ASEAN have carried the caveat of the
ASEAN way. This has been why, as so often remarked upon in the chapters
above, so many of ASEAN's initiatives, often announced with rhetorical flour-
ishes, have had little success programmatically. In efforts to try to escape from
the trap of consensual unanimity, ASEAN has sporadically experimented with
"ASEAN minus" mechanisms—a kind of ASEAN-lite—but this too requires
consensus. The achievements attributed to ASEAN on closer inspection often
turn out to be a kind of shorthand aggregation of outcomes of national actions. This does not mean that the existence of ASEAN is not an important element in international relations in Southeast Asia. With differing degrees of
commitment and enthusiasm, the organizational preservation of ASEAN has
become part of the regional states' national interests. For them to see ASEAN
as an end in itself helps explain the lengths to which member states will go to
accommodate or ignore egregiously cruel member-state behavior; the contemporary case in point being Myanmar. ASEAN has become symbolic; what
was described in the introductory chapter as a "virtual" or "imagined" expression of a yet to be achieved level of an integral regionalism. Why this should
be so valued seems related more to ASEAN's past than its future.

The ASEAN Communities

What does the record set so far by ASEAN suggest in terms of the ASEAN
Community project? The notion of community is bandied about with great
imprecision in discussions of Southeast Asia and ASEAN. It has only been
since the 2003 ASEAN Bali Summit, however, that the idea of future community has been officially adopted by the ASEAN heads of governments. Chapter 4 and subsequent chapters note the call for an ASEAN Economic Community (AEC), ASEAN Security Community (ASC), and ASEAN Socio-
Cultural Community (ASCC): the three "pillars" of an ASEAN Community to
be realized by 2015. The question is, what policy content will be given to these
communities that distinguishes them from an association, grouping, caucus,
alliance, or other multilateral formal or informal but temporally persistent
linking of sovereign states in pursuit of a common purpose?

It is commonly understood that an international community has some institutionalized integral structure that defines the community independently
from the state membership. That is, it has a suprastate organizational format.

This is certainly not to be the case with the ASEAN communities, which, like every other ASEAN endeavor, will have the ASEAN way's insistence on sovereignty and noninterference as a founding platform. Second, a successful community presumes a degree of convergence of national characteristics. It can be suggested, however, that in Southeast Asia there are significant divergences that mark even greater differences among the ASEAN states than was the case at ASEAN's inception nearly four decades ago. We have especially remarked on three: sharpening of cultural divisions, absence of a unified strategic orientation, and levels of economic growth and performance. A third attribute of community, first mentioned in chapter 1, is its value base. If anything, ASEAN's expansion has widened the value gap in ASEAN, not narrowed it. Nor is there any evidence that ASEAN-ization through constructive engagement leads to value change, Myanmar and Laos being but two examples.

In examining the actual proposals for ASEAN's community building and the kinds of programs that have been identified, it would appear that this is another effort to reinvent from the top a process that does not have at the bottom a truly integrative thrust. As such, looking back, it may well become one more blurred blueprint. It also reflects a realization that ASEAN as it stands in a changed global political and economic environment is not as relevant to its member states' national interests as it once was.

The proposed AEC is a case in point. As chapter 7 shows, basically the AEC accelerates and collapses already existing programs. All of the issues that impeded greater integration through the PTA, AFTA, AFAS, and so on, still exist, however. At a number of points in the text, allusion has been made to an economically tiered ASEAN. As was suggested in chapter 7, the rewards of the AEC will tend to widen the gap between the ASEAN haves and have-nots. The less-developed AEC members risk becoming market appendages of their stronger partners unless there is a fundamental reshaping of their domestic political economies. It cannot be expected that ASEAN's leading economies will wait for the laggards to catch up so that an integrated ASEAN economy can be achieved.

The economic relevance of the AEC is being overtaken by the growing number of bilateral and multilateral extraregional arrangements. The centripetal force of intra-ASEAN economic integration is exceeded by the centrifugal pull of integration into the extraregional and globalized economies. These extra-ASEAN arrangements suggest that the upper-tier, most productive ASEAN countries are outgrowing ASEAN as the center of their economic focus. As ASEAN countries become ever more functionally and legally integrated in wider regional and global structures, the AEC becomes economically less important.

The AEC is politically important since it is the only ASEAN community that has any structural substance. The ASEAN Security Community is best defined by what it is not rather than what it is. It is not a defense arrangement. It does not have a peacekeeping role. It does not have a common foreign policy. Although claiming to enshrine democracy and human rights, because of the ASEAN way, it cannot guarantee them. We could argue from a constructivist perspective and view the ASC as a state of mind. The action plan for the ASEAN Socio-Cultural Community laid out four elements of the community. These are building a community of caring societies, promoting environmental sustainability, managing the social impact of economic integration, and strengthening regional identity. All of these categories have been the subject of numerous ASEAN declarations, initiatives, work plans, workshops, studies, and the other consultative devices common to organizations with ideal agendas but little real capacity for action. The building of the ASCC does not require political sacrifice or involve traditional security concerns. The human security problems to be addressed are amenable to measures of functional cooperation. The ASCC is one project in which the major actors could be civil society groups and NGOs. ASEAN as a grouping, however, has historically distanced itself from the peoples it claims to be acting for. ASEAN's preference for the Myanmar junta rather than the Burmese people is an indicator of ASEAN's group-think priorities.

There is every reason to expect that the future ASEAN community will institutionally, procedurally, and normatively be very much like the existing ASEAN; an association of sovereign states that have sacrificed no sovereignty for the collective good. If this is the case, it would seem unlikely that it will add measurably new capabilities to the member states as they interact with each other and, especially in the struggle for autonomy, with extraregional states with far greater capabilities.

The Nontraditional Agenda

It cannot be demonstrated that ASEAN has enhanced the capabilities of its member states to deal effectively with the issues on the nontraditional international relations agenda. Chapters 8 and 9 examined a number of the regional manifestations of economic, social, and political problems that are part of the global dialogue. In looking at issue areas of human security, human rights, democracy, and the environment, it does not appear that their cogency and prominence have been fully internalized at the collective ASEAN level or the national levels by elites whose goals are political stability for rapid economic growth. These are issues pressed on Southeast Asia by Europe, North

America, and, to a lesser extent, Japan. One of the points emphasized in the discussions of these issues is that it is in this area of international relations that the activities of NGOs are the most relevant. Southeast Asian domestic NGOs have found support for their challenges to the status quo from their international counterparts, who in turn mobilize popular and political support in the West. In many instances, however, these activities are resented by leaders in Southeast Asia as nonsovereign interference in domestic affairs.

Democracy and human rights are the most politicized items on the nontraditional agenda. There is a perceptual gulf between Southeast Asia and the liberal West. The labeling of Myanmar as Southeast Asia's pariah state has been almost a leitmotif throughout the book. The intransigence of the junta has isolated it from the West even as ASEAN has embraced it, even if by some members reluctantly. Public advocacy for human rights raises the question— and not just for Myanmar—of what the best foreign policy approach to encourage change might be: confrontation, constructive engagement, or behind-the-scenes quiet diplomacy. The experience in Southeast Asia suggests that where successes have been achieved, no matter how modest, effective human rights advocacy requires activity in all three policy approaches. There is no question but that pressure on rights violators is necessary. In the immediate and intermediate time frame, domestic NGOs and INGOs keep the issues alive and credible threats of sanctions back up diplomacy. Constructive engagement, on the other hand, is designed to promote structural and attitudinal change in the rights violator's society. It assumes the growth over time of a civil society as a product of economic growth, expanded communications, and education. This is little solace to groups and individuals currently denied basic freedoms.

The question of human rights in the international relations of Southeast Asia is not one of absolute versus relative or East versus West. It is where and with what priority specific rights issues fit into the national interests of the state actors in their complex networks of bi- and multilateral interactions. For China, there is little problem in identifying its interest in Southeast Asian human rights issues. To support Southeast Asian resistance to U.S. and EU pressure on human rights violations is to defend its own poor human rights record. China, however, unlike Myanmar or other Southeast Asian rights violators, has such enormous economic importance to the West that it is relatively immune from sanctions and can ignore the rhetoric.

It is much more complicated for the United States. All of the interests involved must be considered in a decision-making milieu where the voices of Congress and advocacy NGOs have weight. The results sometimes seem puzzling to hard-core realists who see U.S. assaults on the rights record of allies and friends as counterproductive in terms of the U.S.–Southeast Asia–China triangle. To political liberals, however, it is necessary as evidence, even if imperfect and inconsistent, of the commitment of the United States to the global cause of human rights.

Myanmar will continue to be an obstacle in U.S.–ASEAN political relations as long as the junta remains in power in Yangon and no significant progress is made in transferring political power in the country to a democratically elected government. Even though ASEAN may claim that constitutional government is being returned to Myanmar, the United States will not accept the outcome of a referendum at gunpoint or military-managed election of a parliament as legitimate. China, of course, has no such objections. While Washington remained fixed on the Myanmar question in ASEAN, Beijing's diplomacy has focused on the economic and political coincidence of its national interests with ASEAN's agenda.

One of the questions raised in chapter 1 is whether democratization and regime change would change the dynamics of international relations in Southeast Asia. The hopes that the third wave of democratization would lead to the building of civil societies in Southeast Asia in which there would be greater congruence of interests between the West and ASEAN in the nontraditional international agenda have waned. What little democratic space has been won is under constant assault from poor governance, corruption, ethnic violence, and religious sectarianism. ASEAN, despite its expressions of democratic norms and commitment to human rights, has not furthered democratization in Southeast Asia. The ASEAN way has no place for democracy. In fact the ASEAN way has made ASEAN a conservative illiberal defender of authoritarianism and human rights violators.[5] As argued in chapter 4, there is no reason to expect that the new ASEAN charter will change that. Myanmar was ASEAN's litmus test and it has failed. In some ASEAN quarters there may be concerns about a possible spillover effect if Aung San Suu Kyi and the NLD were to emerge triumphant over the junta. This would revitalize democratic activism and NGOs region-wide. ASEAN is an intergovernmental grouping. Its constituents are sovereign states, not the people. There is no space for the vox populi in ASEAN's table of organization. There is little space for the vox populi in most ASEAN states.

The environmental issues discussed in chapter 9 have a different political quality from those of democracy and human rights. The rights issue is ideologically defended by violators in a framework of cultural relativity and domestic jurisdiction. The victims are trapped behind national frontiers. There are no frontiers for air and water pollution or for downstream degradation because of upstream development. In order for transboundary environmental problems to be solved, however, they have to be attacked at their sources, which are to be found in sovereign states. To find solutions will require much more than simply technical advances or greater financial contributions. Like the other areas of international cooperation in Southeast Asia, the political will and capabilities of national leadership will be decisive.

For ASEAN's leaderships, China's economic growth could pose formidable environmental challenges. While Southeast Asia in its framework agreement with China on economic cooperation, and even the ASEAN–China FTA, envisages complementary industrialization, there is a possible alternative future. In chapter 9, we have already seen the environmental impact of competition for utilization of hydro resources in China's Mekong River schemes. China's seemingly open-ended demand for natural resources to fuel its growth may force ASEAN, not up the international division of labor, but down, to primary product exporting to keep China moving. Future exploitation of Southeast Asia's forest, mineral, and marine resources as a junior partner to China will place new pressures on the sustainability of an already badly degraded Southeast Asian natural environment.

Transformations in the Regional International Environment

During the first decades of their independence, the primary definition of Southeast Asian states' place in the international system was by their ties to the Cold War great power actors. The states adapted to the internal and external challenges in different ways: alliance, nonalignment, and confrontation (chapter 3). The creation of ASEAN and its first quarter of a century history was part of that adaptation in the context of collective political security as the global great power competition became regionalized in the Third Indochina War (chapter 4). The last decade of the twentieth century—interrupted by the Crash of '97—was a period in which ASEAN embraced all of the Southeast Asian states in a common but competitive search for markets and foreign direct investment (chapter 7).

The fact that at the opening of the new millennium, Southeast Asia's security environment was no longer dominated by great power competitive maneuvering or revolutionary movements did not mean there was not intra–Southeast Asian political strife and conflict (chapter 5). With the disappearance of the shadow of Cold War politics, old antagonisms—territorial, ethnic, and religious—got new priorities. This was most internationally visible in the problem of East Timor, discussed at several points in the text. The situation in East Timor exposed the fragility of ASEAN's function as a regulator of regional stability. The same requirements of the ASEAN way that politically required ignoring the crisis in East Timor seem to be at work with respect to Myanmar and Southeast Asia's other trouble spots.

The terrorist attacks on the United States on 9/11 gave new impetus to U.S. security interests in Southeast Asia in the war on terror (chapter 6). The dark forebodings that the problem of terrorism would dominate international relations in Southeast Asia after the United States pushed it to the top of its regional security agenda did not come to pass. Counterterrorist measures and cooperation have reduced whatever real threat terrorist groups presented to Southeast Asian governments. The real impact on the international environment in Southeast Asia was the changed view of Southeast Asian publics and leaders toward the United States. Although there was an ASEAN consensus on counterterrorism, there was not similar consensus on strategic orientation toward the United States. The American conflation of the war on terror with the invasion of Iraq was hugely unpopular in Southeast Asia. Indonesian and Malaysian policymakers had to tread lightly in their relations with the United States given their Muslim majority populations. The fact that the Philippines, Singapore, and Thailand stood shoulder-to-shoulder with the United States with boots on the ground in Iraq accentuated a possible new political divide in ASEAN cohesion. The geostrategic continental–maritime division of Southeast Asia was identified in chapter 1. The communist–noncommunist division of the Cold War was traced in chapter 3. The economic divide between the ASEAN 6 and the CLMV countries has been noted in several chapters along with the different shades of democracy and authoritarianism. To the war on terror and strategic orientations to the United States, we can add religion to the political division of ASEAN. The cleavage of religion in ASEAN has implications for both the proposed ASEAN Security Community as well as any ASEAN collective stance with respect to a regional political balance with the United States and China.

American concentration on the war on terror has led to an exaggerated concern that this interest has overridden or displaced its other interests in Southeast Asia. The perception of a one-dimensional U.S. policy agenda is put in the context of the rise of China as an economic, political, and possible future military presence in the region. China's rise is equated with a U.S. decline. China is viewed as a challenger to American great power predominance in Southeast Asia since the defeat of Japan in 1945. Leaving aside the fact that there is no empirical basis for the jeremiad that the United States is losing a zero-sum power game with China for influence in Southeast Asia, the changing *relative* relationship poses strategic questions for all three involved—the United States, Southeast Asia, and China. Is U.S. great power dominance a necessary condition for the defense and promotion of U.S. national interests in Southeast Asia? Can Chinese aspirations and interests accommodate a U.S. stake in Southeast Asia's future? If the answer to the first question is "yes," and to the second, "no," then the future political environment of the region will be marked by tension and insecurities.

The third question is what can the Southeast Asian states do themselves to help the Americans and Chinese shape their answers? In the worst case scenario—again without an empirical base, but hand-wringing—they will be sucked into the vortex of China's rise as part of a China-centric satellite system. This would be a modern version of the historical traditional Confucian suzerain–vassal relationship. This conclusion or other variants of Chinese paramountcy is highly deterministic. It leaves out of consideration the fact that it is not just the United States with interests in Southeast Asia. It is not a two-player game. Japan and the EU are as heavily engaged economically in the region as is the United States, and India is aspiring. It is highly unlikely that Singapore, Malaysia, Thailand, the Philippines, Indonesia, and even Vietnam would forgo their major markets and sources of FDI for a closed regional structure centered on China.

The vision of inevitable Chinese hegemony excludes the fact that the Southeast Asian states themselves are projecting a strategic environment that is nonthreatening to either China or the United States. The book has noted the effort to place their bilateral relationships with extraregional actors in a regional political context. The hope is that growing region-wide interdependencies with both the United States and China will help mediate their regional great power bilateral relations through a common interest in a stable region in which they can pursue their interests in a win-win fashion. The region's economic and political stability depends on predictable peaceful relations between China and the United States. The most often mentioned risk is war in the Taiwan Straits. As we have seen, the Southeast Asian states even in their ARF leadership role have little or no real input into great power relationships.

Rather than ASEAN integrating their economies, let alone their political preference, in a web with China at its hub, the Southeast Asian states through ASEAN are the hub of their own network. The spokes run out to Japan, China, the United States, the EU, and India, and others as exemplified in ASEAN + 1 relations, and RTAs, as well as bilateral ties of varying scope and intensity. In terms of China's rise, this has sometimes been described as hedging or balancing. More accurately, it is a strategy of maximizing opportunities.

The Subordinate Regional State System

A subordinate Southeast Asian regional international system was defined in chapter 1 as one in which the policy autonomy of the regional states was constrained by controlling political and economic forces originating in the dominant global state system, itself driven by the interests of the great powers. Nothing in this study of international relations in Southeast Asia suggests that after more than six decades of independence the basic structure of the subordinate system has fundamentally changed. What has changed are the kinds of adaptive demands being made on the Southeast Asian states. The political demands are no longer those of Cold War bipolarity. American political hegemony, mislabeled a balance of power, is giving way to an emerging real balance. China has replaced the USSR as a countervailing great power in Southeast Asia.

As the dynamics of international relations in Southeast Asia shift from political security to economic security, the regional balance of power has become more complex. It is not just a tug-of-war between China and the United States for influence in Southeast Asia. At different points in the text we have indicated that the China–Japan relationship and the China–India relationship are also very important for the interests of the Southeast Asian states. Both India and Japan have close ties to the United States, ideologically underpinned by shared democratic values. While the EU is also important, it does not have the proximate presence that the other significant actors have. The ASEAN states are attempting to manage their place in this complex balance by generating as many interdependencies as possible. It is through interdependency that the region seeks greater policy autonomy.

In the early decades of independence, the fact of economic subordination was captured in the terms neoimperialism or dependency, both suggestive of the asymmetry of the market relationship between the developed and newly independent, less developed, world. Globalization, economically institutionalized in the WTO, brings new kinds of snares seeking to limit states' autonomy. Protest or invective, whether in the streets or meetings of NAM, will not change the fact that to have a part in the global economy, the countries of Southeast Asia must play by the rules of a game that many leaders in Southeast Asia see stacked against them. Part of the globalization process has been social and cultural. The penetration of the nontraditional agendas, vigorously pursued by legions of advocacy groups and NGOs as well as Western governments, has challenged leaderships from within their own citizenries.

As the pages above have shown, in many respects Southeast Asia's political and economic futures still depend on the quality of their relationships with the extraregional great powers and, because of their links to them, the quality of the relationships among the great powers themselves. The ability of the Southeast Asian states to manage these relations collectively through ASEAN is, as we have seen, very limited. The membership configuration and function of ASEAN itself as a regional voice is not immutable. As ASEAN states struggle to make real the ambitions of the ASEAN charter, they may end up with a real ASEAN minus one with Myanmar suspended, expelled, or simply quitting. Also, the continental–maritime divide in ASEAN may sharpen as China's economic encroachments in the least developed ASEAN states, the CLM countries, and the gradual sinicizing of Yunnan border regions of the northern tier reorient them from the more globalized maritime states, with Thailand in the balance. Finally, the possibility that separatism could fracture ASEAN unity cannot be ruled out (chapter 5).

Has ASEAN become an indispensable center of the subordinate regional international subsystem? The failures of ASEAN in terms of its pretensions of functional cooperation and integration have been amply documented. Its success has been as an interface between the subordinate system and the international system, giving an outward coherency to the disparate collection of states that make it up. ASEAN has forced the great powers to address Southeast Asia as a region in addition to their bilateral relations. This has added a sense of political stability, which in turn has enhanced the economic climate. As long as the member states find that their national interests are furthered through ASEAN, they will support it. However, if a state chafes under the rules of lowest denominator consensus, support may wane. The emergence of Indonesia and Vietnam as potential northern and southern poles in a local Southeast Asian balance may give new political form to ASEAN. ASEAN is not indispensable but it is a valuable tool in the management of the balance of power in which Southeast Asia is embedded.

Notes

1. Jörn Dosch, *The Changing Dynamics of Southeast Asian Politics* (Boulder, Colo.: Lynne Rienner, 2007).

2. Clark D. Neher, *Southeast Asia in the New International Era*, 4th ed. (Boulder, Colo.: Westview, 2002).

3. Jusuf Wanandi, "Insight: RI's Foreign Policy and the Meaning of ASEAN," *The Jakarta Post*, 6 May 2008.

4. "Michael Vatikiotis, "Susilo, Regional Affairs and Lessons from Sukarno," *The Jakarta Post*, 3 November 2004.

5. Erick Kuhonta, "Walking a Tight Rope: Democracy Versus Sovereignty in ASEAN's Illiberal Peace," *The Pacific Review* 19, no. 3 (2006): 337–58.

Index

About the Author

Donald E. Weatherbee is the Donald S. Russell Distinguished Professor Emeritus at the University of South Carolina, where he specialized in the politics and international relations of Southeast Asia. A graduate of Bates College, he holds an M.A. and Ph.D. from the Johns Hopkins School of Advanced International Studies. In addition to the University of South Carolina, Weatherbee has served on the faculty of the United States Army War College and has held teaching and research appointments at universities and institutes in Indonesia, Malaysia, Singapore, Thailand, Germany, the Netherlands, and England. He has an extensive list of publications on Southeast Asian international relations. His most recent book is *Historical Dictionary of United States–Southeast Asia Relations* (2008). Other recent publications include "Strategic Dimensions of Economic Interdependence in Southeast Asia," in *Strategic Asia 2006–2007*; "Southeast Asia in 2006: Déjà vu All Over Again" in *Southeast Asian Affairs 2007*; "Political Change in Southeast Asia: Challenges for U.S. Strategy" in *Strategic Asia 2007–2008*; and "ASEAN's Identity Crisis " in *Legacy of Engagement in Southeast Asia* (2008). His professional recognition includes the U.S. Army's Distinguished Civilian Service Medal for his contribution to strategic planning for post–Vietnam War Southeast Asian international relations.